"We are fools for Christ's sake"

——THE APOSTLE PAUL IN HIS FIRST
LETTER TO THE CORINTHIANS

Books by Louis Cochran

The

FOOL

of

GOD

A NOVEL BASED UPON THE LIFE OF

ALEXANDER CAMPBELL

By Louis Cochran

Wipf & Stock
PUBLISHERS
Eugene, Oregon

Wipf and Stock Publishers
199 W 8th Ave, Suite 3
Eugene, OR 97401

The Fool of God
A novel based upon the life of Alexander Campbell
By Cochran, Louis
Copyright©1958 College Press
ISBN: 1-59244-079-7
Publication date 10/18/2002
Previously published by Duell, Sloan and Pearce, 1958

Author's Note

The life of Alexander Campbell is told here as a work of fiction, but in its essentials this is a factual book. Every event actually occurred, or had its basis in solid fact; each person lived, and played his role much as is related here.

The story does not presume to be a study of Campbell's religious thinking, or an account of the movement to re-establish Christian unity by the elimination of human creeds and the restoration of New Testament Christianity. It is, rather, the portrait of a man whose heart embraced all Christians as brothers; whose mind was open to all truth; whose eyes had seen the vision of the coming of one church.

Contents

BOOK I

From These Roots

Chapter 1

ALEXANDER MADE HIS WAY TOWARD THE CABIN ON THE FOREDECK WITH wide, irregular steps, as though unable to make up his mind whether to walk or run. Already the mainsails were unfurled and the *Hibernia* was beginning to quiver and lean into the wind. He reached his mother's cabin and knocked loudly on the door as the topsails opened to the breeze and the ship began to roll gently in the Lough.

It was Saturday afternoon, October 1, 1808, and the family had been aboard since the preceding Wednesday. The *Hibernia* had first weighed anchor on Thursday morning at Londonderry, only to put down again in the Lough Foyle when the wind became adverse. Now, at last, they were about to sail for the future which was America, and where Thomas Campbell had been for more than a year.

Within the doorway stood sixteen-year-old Dorothea, as alive with enthusiasm as he, but restrained, thoughtful, as though in the absence of their father she shared with her older brother some of the responsibility for the family. Nancy, three years younger, more like the restless Thomas than any of his other children, perched on the edge of their bunk, her arms about nine-year-old Jane whose face beneath her long yellow hair was still faintly pitted from the smallpox that had afflicted her three months before. Six-year-old Thomas stood beside them with Archibald, aged four, as if poised for a race, while their mother, Jane, sat at the end of the little cabin on the hand-hewn log chair with two-year-old Alicia on her lap.

Mrs. Campbell's brown eyes lighted at the sight of this tall young

3

man, so much like her in his personal appearance. She spoke in a voice that was full and resonant. "Well, son?"

He closed the door carefully behind him to shut out the noises of the deck and the rushing waters.

"We're off!" He clapped his hands and held out his arms as Alicia struggled from her mother's lap and scampered toward him over the swaying floor. He scooped her in his arms and stood, slightly stooped, his bare head with its brown hair almost touching the ceiling that crowded upon them like a box lid. "Everybody join hands! We'll go out on deck now and wave good-by to the Auld Sod."

"The children did that Wednesday," Mrs. Campbell reminded him. "And you know what a time we had gathering up the boys again. Wouldn't it be better just to wait here until all the bustle is over?"

"But that was a false start!" Alexander said. "The wind is right this time. The captain has ordered all the cannon fired. The boys shouldn't miss it. They'll rattle every window in Londonderry!"

"You're the anxious one!" Mrs. Campbell smiled, as elated as any of her children that the interminable delays seemed at an end. "Well, come along, boys!" She caught Tommie and Archie firmly by the wrists. "There'll be no little Campbells running wild on deck this day. You, Nancy and Jane, go ahead with your brother and the baby. Dorry and I will follow. God willing, we'll be seeing your father soon."

As she spoke there was a roar to larboard, and the ship quivered violently. Instinctively they clutched at the sides of the bunks.

"That was the larboard watch! Now for the starboard," said Alexander. "Hold fast now!"

They waited, tight with expectation, as the floor beneath their feet steadied to a tremor and the ship rolled gently until a hoarse command was heard through the swaying, half-open door, guttural and unintelligible against the wind.

This time the roar of the cannon, and the rolling of the deck, came at them from the other side of the little room. The walls shook and the wire-cradled lantern in the center of the cabin hastened its violent swaying on the ceiling hook.

4

"Well done!" Alexander called to his mother. "Now let's go on deck and view the ruins!"

He pushed outside, carrying Alicia. Dorothea and the girls followed with their mother and the two squirming, excited little boys.

All appeared confusion on the main deck below. The noise of the cannon, straining against their mounts; heavy black smoke drifting before them in a thick, dark cloud as though to guide them out to sea; the catcalls of the sailors, scurrying frantically about the rigging; the cries and the hoarse cheers of the passengers—all merged into an uneven, rumbling roar that rose and fell with the swaying of the ship.

Alexander squinted at the silver-plated watch given him by Father Thomas when he had sailed on the *Brutus* from this same port for Philadelphia seventeen months before. He leaned toward his mother.

"It's two-ten, almost six bells," he announced solemnly. "The *Hibernia* is a stout ship, faster than the *Brutus*. We'll make it to New York in thirty days."

His mother smiled. "Slow or fast, my son, may God will us a safe journey," she said. "Give me the baby now. It's time for her nap."

Alexander unclasped the tiny hands about his neck. "Nothing disturbs you, does it, Mother?" He spoke admiringly. "I wonder if Father Thomas knows how much everything depends on you."

With the words, his thoughts went again to that mild-mannered, inflexible little man who had so confidently sailed away in April of the year before. Whether they would transplant their roots to the New World would be as the Lord willed, Thomas Campbell had said. Nevertheless, it had come as something of a shock when he had written from a place called Washington, Pennsylvania, early in January 1808, directing that they sell all they had and join him there. God's will, he said, had become manifest.

From the beginning he had been among friends, he wrote them. The Anti-Burgher Synod of the Seceder Presbyterian Church of North America was in assembly in Philadelphia when he arrived, and had received him as a respected and honored preacher of the Word from the Presbytery of Market Hill and the church at Ahorey, Ireland. With confidence in the guidance of the Lord, he had accepted an assignment by the Synod as a traveling itinerant to the scattered Seceder Presbyterians of western Pennsylvania. This territory included the town of Washington where they would live, and where some of their former neighbors from Rich Hill had already settled: James Foster and his young wife; the Thomas Hodgens; the Thomas Achesons; the James Hanens; old friends together again in a wonderful new world, freed forever from the incessant theological bickering of the old.

Alexander had often pondered the inscrutable ways of Providence as he sold their possessions at Rich Hill and prepared for their departure. And although there had been sadness in the farewells, and in the knowledge that in all probability none of them would ever look again upon the green hills of Ireland, he had never doubted that the Lord had made known His will, and that whatever lay ahead, it was for each of them His holy design.

Mrs. Campbell smiled as though aware of his thoughts. "You've been the man of the family for over a year now, son. You've done well. Your father will be proud of you."

"You're the sturdy one, Mother!" He looked around for Thomas and Archibald. "I'll round up the little Yahoos for you." He caught the boys and with one under each arm went into the cabin. He deposited them firmly on separate bunks.

"Sailors must get their rest," he said sternly. "One watch above, one below. I'll go on deck and you boys can take the dogwatch."

"I want my puppy dog!" wailed Archibald in sudden memory.

"I'll walk the deck with you, Alex," said Dorothea from the doorway. "I want to see what's going on."

"You're interested in those handsome sailors," said Alexander. "That's your trouble."

"Now, Alexander," cautioned Mrs. Campbell. "You mustn't tease your sister."

"It's her Irish youth," he said gravely. "But I'll walk her to the mizzenmast and back. Provided she promises to read some good book afterward. She needs to cultivate her mind."

"You can read it to me," said Dorothea. "Nancy and Jane, you come along, too." She looked to her mother for approval.

6

Mrs. Campbell smiled. As if they had not all been on deck enough for the three days the ship had been becalmed. "You can be gone thirty minutes," she said. "Then we'll get ready for supper."

"I want my doggie!" said Archibald.

"It's 'mess' on board ship, Mother," admonished Alexander. "The third mess. Come along, girls."

As they walked he studied the sailors, now busily securing the cannon to their mounts under the vigilant, sometimes obscene scrutiny of Mr. Ryan, the chief mate. They appeared hearty and willing enough, though none too familiar with their duties. Should Barbary pirates attempt to board the ship, the crew of only twelve men, including the cook's mate and the cabin boy, would be little protection.

"A sailor's wife is not the life for you, Dorry," he said gravely. "Too many are lost at sea. Besides, you ought to look over the American Indians first. You're only sixteen. You won't be a real old maid for two years yet."

"I want a sailorman!" Jane spoke with surprising vigor for a little girl just recovered from the smallpox. "I want a sailorman doll!"

Alexander guffawed, his laugh rising with the voices of his sisters above the creaking of the rigging and the whistling of the wind as the sails stood firm against the breeze.

"You shall have one," he promised. "You can make it yourself. Look closely so you will know how to cut the cloth." He motioned toward the sailors, now climbing with more haste than agility into the rigging. "But here's the one for you, the big fellow coming up now."

He motioned toward a tall, muscular, redheaded sailor who had begun taking soundings near the foremast. With his low-crowned, well-varnished black tarpaulin hat on the back of his shock of reddish hair, its long black ribbon stringing over his left eye; the black silk handkerchief around his neck, worn by all sailors in memory of the death of Lord Nelson at Trafalgar; the loose checkered shirt; the blue duck trousers, tight as a hatband around the waist and falling long and full and loose about the feet; and his bronzed and

7

toughened hands always half-open as though about to grasp a rope, he presented a picaresque contrast to the somber dress of the passengers.

"They call him the 'Redheaded Dutchman,' " said Alexander. "The mate says he's the best sailor aboard."

"I'll make a sailorman doll," said Jane, "just like that one!" She pointed to the Dutchman. "Is he going to run out on those ropes like the other sailors?"

Alexander laughed. "Those ropes," he said, "are the riggings used to unfurl the sails so we can get the full benefit of the wind, and to furl them tight again when there's a storm."

"What is the wind, Alexander?" asked Nancy solemnly. "Is it the breath of God?"

"Yes," said Alexander soberly. "The breath of God."

They halted before the railing of the steep steps that led down to the main deck. Despite orders of Captain Jumer, many of the passengers were below, milling about, admiring the cannon, casting appraising glances at the masts, trying to engage the sailors in nautical talk—tiny particles of human life on a limitless ocean.

Alexander hallooed to a tall, youngish man walking forward amidships, only the checkered shirt and round blue cap perched squarely on top of his head and his unconscious air of authority setting him apart from the passengers. He knew his business, this Chief Mate Ryan, a sailor who already inspired confidence and respect.

Mr. Ryan looked up and then paused in quick recognition of the little group. "Ah, and 'tis the Campbell clan for sure," he said gravely. He climbed the steps to the poop deck. "All ready now to catch some of Mother Carey's chickens." He nodded at Alexander and for a moment let his hand rest lightly on Jane's head. "You will all be well acquainted with this ship before we reach port, Mr. Campbell."

"No doubt," said Alexander. "We're more than glad to be away; and with a full head of sail, too. At this rate we should soon be rounding Malin Head."

The mate grinned. "Aye, you prophesy generously for a Scotsman. But bide your faith, Mr. Campbell." He hurried forward.

Alexander stared after him, puzzled. There was meaning behind

8

those words. He looked aloft. The skies were still clear with only a few clouds hovering far to the west like dark sentinels. It was a good start. The wind was light but they were now well out in the Lough Foyle, and were running with the tide.

"I like Mr. Ryan," said Jane. "He might make a good match for Dorry, except that he's a little old for her."

"See what you started!" Dorothea said. "You shouldn't joke about sacred things like marriage before the wee ones."

Alexander playfully tousled the head of his younger sister. "You're right, Jane. He's much too old."

Mealtime found the Campbells part of a straggling procession of passengers along the main deck headed for the mess cabin.

Captain Jumer was already seated at the center of the horseshoe-shaped table when they arrived. Alexander knew that the tone of every ship was set by its master. If he were a religious man, grace would be said before meals, and public worship conducted on Sunday. But by this time it was known to all the passengers that Captain Jumer was not a religious-appearing man. He had come on board under the influence of strong Irish whiskey, and while he seemed a good sailor and pleasant enough, it was already clear there would be no public grace before meals on board the *Hibernia*. Whether there would be public Sunday worship would be determined the next day.

Tin cups and plates and a combination fork and spoon marked the seating places along the backless benches about the table. Swinging by chains from the ceiling above the table were iron pots filled with hot stew, to be ladled into the plates by the steward. Salted beef and pork, with potatoes and dried beans, Alexander knew, would be their main food for the trip, with plenty of hardtack, biscuit, and water which, as time passed, would be seasoned with vinegar to disguise its taste. But at the start of every voyage there was always fresh meat and vegetables, and pork and chicken would frequently be served from the crates of live pigs and poultry snugged under the cannon on the main deck. If the voyage took only six weeks, the passengers might expect fresh meat at least twice a week for a month. The vegetables would be gone in a few days.

9

When they came again on deck and headed for their cabin, Alexander saw the sails were hanging listless from the shrouds; only the topgallant sails puffed faintly before the breeze. The ship rocked gently; the sluggish lapping of the waves against the sides, the blue waters shimmering in the dusk, and the steady outline of the shore indicating that, almost in the center of the Lough Foyle, they were becalmed.

A half-hour later and Alexander had concluded the brief evening worship in their cabin and the children had again gathered about to listen to their mother's promised stories of the wonders of early Ireland, and of that faraway land of France from which her own Huguenot grandparents had escaped during the Great Persecution. The younger children never tired of stories of that flight from death for conscience' sake, and of that first meeting of Jane Corneigle with the young teacher, Thomas Campbell.

They had heard many times, these jewels the Lord had given her, all these stories of the past, but with each telling they were as interested as before. If she garnished them now and then, or softened them, it was, she felt, no more than her parents and her grandparents had done before her. Some of them were of dreadful, heroic, fearful days, and young hearts should not be burdened too early with the knowledge that pain and tortuous death were still inflicted by men upon other men in the conviction they were instruments of the will of their common God. Perhaps even in America there were self-styled God-filled men, unshakable in the conviction that they alone had the truth, and all the truth, and that it was God's will they should persecute all those who would reach God by another way. The thought erased the smile on her lips, and as she unconsciously stared at her eldest son, as if seeking a cue for her opening words, there came a faint jarring, clanging sound, muffled by the bowels of the ship.

"They're dropping the anchor." Alexander nodded. "It's the usual thing when the wind fails, to keep from drifting. We shall sleep easily tonight."

"Drifting?" She attempted to speak lightly but there was an uneasiness in her voice. "Perhaps it's to keep us from running away, like Jonah."

"Oh, we know about Jonah and the whale," said Jane. "Tell us how you and Papa got married!"

The gleeful concurrence of the others was led by the high-pitched laughter of Alexander, and she felt again reassured. She was a good wife, and where her husband felt called to go, it was her duty and her wish to follow. But she was not easy in her heart about this removal to the wild new country of America. She was a worrier, she told herself, overly responsive to the mood of the moment.

"First I'll tell you the story of the boy Jesus in the Temple," she began. "And then I'll tell you of the first time I saw your father in the town of Ballymena, oh, years and years ago. Now, the little boy Jesus when he was about the age of our Nancy—"

When Alexander returned the next morning from the cook's galley with his pail of hot water for shaving, it was already daylight. The wind was rising from the southeast and the *Hibernia* was on the wing again, her sails spread. The anchor had been lifted while they slept, and they would soon head into the great Atlantic. He felt his blood race at the thought, and suiting his action to his mood, ran up the steps of the half deck toward the tiny cubicle he shared with Thomas and Archibald, adjoining the larger cabin of his mother and the girls. Soon breakfast would be ready, and then he would conduct their first Sunday-morning family worship at sea. He stood for a moment and looked shoreward, the outline of land dim in the morning mist. For the first time he felt a tinge of home-sickness, a depthless, tantalizing regret. Perhaps he would never again see his uncle Archibald and his cousins, or the school for boys at Newry where he had taught, or attend the worship service at Ahorey or Rich Hill. He thought of his uncle James, a big-bearded silent man who, unlike his brothers, was given but little to religious disputations. Uncle James had emigrated years ago to Canada and after a few letters had never been heard of again.

Suddenly, with a twinge of conscience, he thought of his own lack of plans for the future. Lawyer, doctor, merchant, chief; teacher, soldier, farmer, priest? Father Thomas' wish, he knew, was that he follow in his footsteps and become a preacher. But the thought made him uncomfortable. The world had enough religious leaders. And enough of religious controversy. He felt no urge to emulate the stern John Calvin or John Knox, or even the less forbidding John Wesley. His prime interest would not be in the field of religion. He wanted action, achievement, eminence, authority. His face alive with health and the visions of youth, he knocked on his mother's cabin and, as the door opened, called loudly:

"Seven bells, seven bells,
Cat's in the well!
Up and about, sleepyheads! First mess in fifteen minutes!"

Back in their cabin, the bunks straightened, the room swept, the family grouped in their accustomed positions for the morning worship, with Mrs. Campbell at one end of the room in the pegged-down chair with Alicia on her lap, and Alexander standing just within the little door, the porthole opened for the breeze. For a moment he smiled at them, his Bible open in his hand, his feet wide apart, braced against the pitch of the ship as it raced, with all sails spread, down the coast of their native Ireland. In his tight brown woolen suit, loomed by his aunts at Newry as a farewell gift, his gray woolen shirt open at the neck, and his thick brown hair stirred lightly by the breeze, he made a pleasing picture of young manhood standing tiptoe, his mother thought, on the threshold of life, his deep-set blue eyes shining with the vision of far-off places, a capacity for leadership within him for good or evil. Her thoughts flew to that humble, restless man of God waiting for them, and the foreboding which had never quite left her since those uneasy days of waiting at Londonderry ebbed away, and she bent her head, a smile about her full, firm lips. Her children were with her, safe and well; Thomas was waiting for them in the new world; and her eldest son was leading the family in prayer.

As usual she gave the benediction as the service concluded, her prayer simple, the resonance of her faith like a comforting arm about her flock.

At the final syllable of the "Amen," Alexander raised his head and answered the unspoken inquiry in his mother's face.

"I asked Mr. Ryan about it," he said. "Captain Jumer will permit no public worship."

Mrs. Campbell's face clouded. "Then we shall invite all who will to join us, Alexander. That is what your father would do."

A jerk, a quivering, as though the plowing forward of the ship had been abruptly halted, and Alexander opened the door and looked out. The breeze was still strong in the southeast, but the sails were half-furled, the sailors in the rigging struggling with canvas still alive with wind.

"We're anchoring again, just offshore! I can see a town!"

"Not again!" said Mrs. Campbell. "We have prayed for this wind!"

"I don't think we're in trouble," said Alexander. "Perhaps more provisions. I'll find out."

He ran to the main deck where the chief mate stood shouting orders to the sailors aloft.

"Captain's orders!" the mate told him brusquely. "Last chance for passengers to buy whiskey. At Innishowen!" He pointed with a short stubby finger at the cluster of buildings rising from the shore line a quarter mile beyond. "We've hove to till morning!" He turned and began to bawl instructions to a young sailor clinging to the topgallant mast.

Alexander made no reply; a slow anger, a sense of outrage rising in him. After the days of waiting and two false starts, were they casting anchor on a fine Sabbath day with the wind steady in the halyards in order to buy whiskey? As a Scots-Irishman, Alexander knew the worth, and the evil, of spirituous liquors, and while nothing was ever said of it in the family, and most of the men he knew with the exception of his father took their daily dram as regularly as their salt, he had seen too much of the sodden dreariness generated by the pubs to relish a long voyage with a bibulous captain and a cargo of roistering passengers. But already the longboat and the larboard

13

quarter boat were being lowered over the sides, filled to the brim with boisterous men.

Suddenly he was conscious that the Catholic priest aboard stood near him, speaking to the mate.

" 'Tis a fair, steady wind for the *Hibernia*, Mr. Ryan," the priest said. "We should spread her wings and give her the muslin. There must be plenty of whiskey in the steward's pantry for what sickness we must endure."

"Aye, Father O'Flathery," said Mr. Ryan shortly. "But not enough. Some of the passengers may be sick a long time." He wheeled about as though to end the conversation. "Captain's orders, sir."

Although Alexander had not talked with the priest, he liked what he had seen of him; big-boned and ruddy-faced, his rugged features lively with humor and sturdiness of spirit. His own grandfather, Archibald Campbell, had been a stanch Catholic before becoming an equally stanch member of the Church of England "to worship God," as he had said, "according to Act of Parliament." He smiled at the recollection, and turned to make his way to the cabin. "An omen for the voyage," he said to the priest. "We'll have a lively time of it."

"An omen, indade!" said the priest. "I like it not. Instead of worship on this holy day we halt our voyage with this fair wind to buy whiskey so that passengers and crew may souse themselves. And, indade, trouble enough will I have with my own flock. I shall speak to Captain Jumer about it."

"Agreed," said Alexander soberly. "I'll go with you, Father."

"A good Irishman, and a good son of the Holy Mother, I take it." The priest looked at him sharply. "You shall join us at Mass. We have many of the Faith aboard."

"Campbell is the name," Alexander corrected gently. "Originally from the west of Scotland but for over four generations now born in County Down or Antrim in auld Ireland. And a member of the Old Light Anti-Burgher Seceder Branch of the Church of Scotland; a Covenanter Presbyterian, you might call me. But incorrectly," he added hastily.

14

He smiled a little stiffly at the amused gleam in the gray eyes of the older man.

"Ah, a strayed sheep!" said Father O'Flathery. "But remember the parable of the prodigal, my son. There is always hope. Let us go to the captain."

But Captain Jumer was in no mood for amicable discussion. He listened, a round-faced, barrel-shaped man with small eyes and big hairy hands, standing beside the Dutchman at the helm.

"Some of my passengers want their whiskey, enough to last the voyage, and so do I," he said. "Innishowen is our last port of call. Tomorrow we pass Malin Head, and our next port is New York. It will be a long voyage."

The priest spoke sternly. "I like my grog as well as any man, sir. As a son of Auld Eire I was weaned on Irish whiskey. But there is a time for all things, Captain. Because of the weather we have twice cast anchor since we left Londonderry on Wednesday. Now the Blessed Virgin sends us a favoring wind on this holy day and you scorn her by casting anchor to store whiskey for those who should be counting their beads."

"Whiskey is good medicine for a long voyage," said Captain Jumer gruffly. "We sail at daybreak."

" 'Tis an ill omen." The priest crossed himself. "I shall pray for you, Captain Jumer."

The captain stared at him, a sullen amusement in his face. "Say your prayers privately, mind you!" he said. "There will be no public religious service of any kind on this ship while I'm master!"

"I am a Presbyterian, a communicant of the Seceder Branch of the Church of Scotland," Alexander spoke up. "There must be a number of us aboard. We believe we should have public ship's worship every Sunday for all the crew and passengers. Why should this not be permitted?"

"Any public worship by one faith would be an offense to the others." The captain spoke firmly. "Not to mention the infidels and the atheists. And I shall have peace aboard this ship if I have to clap you both in irons." He grinned as though in sudden good humor at the thought and took the helm from the Dutchman, a gruff sober-

15

ness now in his voice. "I like my bottle, and occasionally I swear a bit," he said. "I'm stubborn and headstrong, and I flog my men when they need it. I 'ave a weakness for a pretty lass. But I am no atheist. I simply have nothing to do with the quarrels of men claiming they alone are the children of the Almighty, and damning those who disagree to hell. We are all the children of God; the earth is His footstool; the ocean and all that's in it showeth His handiwork. That's my religion! That's the reason there are no public religious meetings for men to quarrel about on my ship!" He stared toward the faint cluster of rooftops on the shore. "There is peace in those pubs," he said. "Peace for troubled souls. And I shall need many drinks tonight, Father. I talk too much."

The priest crossed himself, mumbling a prayer. "You talk well, my son. But the peace of the bottle is stupor. I shall pray for you."

Alexander nodded, conscious that this Catholic priest was wise in ways in which he was ignorant; and that he liked and respected him. Suddenly he was conscious, too, of an upsurge of respect for the captain, staring stonily ahead as though he wished no more of them, his face set in heavy lines. And with it again came the thought of his father, Thomas Campbell, waiting for them in America, and of his own impatience with the warring sects of Christendom.

For a few moments he stood with the priest; then, together, they turned and walked in silence, each lost in his own thoughts.

"I'm glad we talked with him," Alexander said abruptly. "There is much truth in what he said."

"Yes," said the priest. "There is hope for him. And there is hope for you, my lad. The Blessed Virgin is always ready to welcome her wayward children back into the fold."

Alexander smiled and impulsively offered his hand. "I like you, Father," he said, "but I abhor your church. Man needs no intermediary between him and God."

The priest clasped his hand firmly. "I like you, too, my errant son," he said. "But you are a heretic. I abhor heretics!"

16

Chapter 2

ALTHOUGH THE NIGHT'S PEACE WAS BROKEN INTERMITTENTLY BY boats returning to the *Hibernia,* each filled with its quota of roisterers, toward morning quiet descended upon the little ship; the only sounds the breathing of the wind through the rigging and the measured step of the watch.

At daybreak a wind arose and again the anchor was lifted. All that day the ship sailed, close-hauled against a rising headwind. Only four of the crew, Alexander learned, had ever been to sea before, with the big Dutchman the only experienced and capable sailor among them. But they would be good sailors, all of them, the mate said, before the *Hibernia* returned again to drop anchor in Londonderry. Slowly and clumsily, under the mate's orders, they close-reefed the topsails and trysail as the wind increased; furled the courses and jib, set the foretopmast staysail and held the ship to her course, with only the weather braces hauled in a little to ease her.

Because of the heavy winds and the plunging of the ship, the women and children were ordered confined to their cabins. Their food was brought to them in covered vessels by the male members of their families, with what assistance the overworked steward and cabin boy could give them.

Alexander was making his way forward for the second time the next day, his tarpaulin coat flapping in the wind, one hand clutching the covered pail containing the mess of hot scouse made of biscuit pounded fine, salt beef cut into small pieces and boiled with potatoes seasoned with pepper, and in the other a large pot of tea, which would be breakfast for the family, when he saw through a rift in the clouds a dim shore line to the northeast. When they

17

had rounded Malin Head during the night, they had passed the most northern point of Ireland, and this rugged, misty shore must be Scotland, the home of his father's people; those rocky bays and inlets the graveyard of many sailors.

Quickly delivering the food, he went back on deck, crowding against the railing with other male passengers. There was no rain but the wind was as fierce as ever, and the cragged outlines of the coast had aroused misgivings among them all. As they watched, the *Hibernia* slipped unexpectedly and quickly into a bay that jutted out like a crooked elbow from the shore. For the fourth time they dropped anchor. But where?

It was soon plain enough that neither Captain Jumer nor the mate knew their position. Toward midmorning a boat from the shore pulled alongside and four men, representing themselves as pilots, climbed aboard. Those close about the captain's quarters heard muffled sounds of rapid talk, broken occasionally by the bull voice of Captain Jumer. And then the pilots emerged, their faces grim, followed by the captain. As the men clambered into their boat, the captain glared about at the passengers for a moment and then bellowed for attention.

"We are in no danger!" he announced. "Every good Scot aboard should know we are in the Lochin Daal, off the Hebrides Islands. That land"—he pointed with a stubby finger—"is the Island of Islay, and up the coast a bit is the town of Bowmore where some say we should anchor." He paused derisively. "But I say we have cast anchor enough. We are safe here, and we'll remain where we are. We'll proceed on our voyage as soon as the good Lord gives us a favorable wind, for which let us pray." His eyes lighted on Alexander and his features tightened into a hard grin. "I trust you will join us in our prayers, Mr. Campbell."

Alexander's face flushed, conscious of the mockery in the hoarse voice. And then from the rear of the group against the halyards came the deep voice of the Catholic priest.

"We shall all pray," he said solemnly. "We shall pray to the Holy Virgin for good weather and a safe voyage for all of us, saint and heretic alike. We shall all pray!"

18

For a moment there was silence against the roaring of the wind, and then the captain turned abruptly and re-entered his cabin. When Alexander went to thank the priest, he was gone.

All day and night the ship rocked at anchor in the Lochin Daal. Wednesday came, and Thursday, and there was no change. Almost it seemed as if the elements had conspired to keep them locked all winter off that rocky, forbidding coast. The harsh, short days, crowded with heavy clouds, hovered over them like black omens; the sails close-reefed, the flying spray making icy sodden those venturing on deck, the passengers growing morose and irritable. Only the sick were served meals in their cabins now, but heavily burlapped against the cold and wet, the Campbells welcomed the excursions on deck, and the affability, tinged with uneasy uncertainty, of the mess hall. But not even the confident bantering of the captain could dispel the growing belief of the passengers that he should have accepted the assistance of the coast pilots and anchored in the safer harbor of Bowmore; nor the uneasiness caused by his occasionally alcoholic breath. Whiskey brought peace to troubled souls, he had said. But Alexander agreed with the sober-faced Catholic priest, when they chanced to meet again on the third day, that troubled times and stormy weather called for clear heads and steady hands which no brand of alcohol could induce.

Alexander brought up from the hold an armful of his father's books and stacked them beside his bunk. The one luxury Thomas Campbell had permitted himself was books. As a lifelong student of theology, his library consisted mainly of works by such writers as Eusebius and Calmet on church history; Fisher's *Marrow of Modern Divinity*, and Thomas Boston's *Fourfold State of Man*. Alexander scanned the titles. John Bunyan's *Pilgrim's Progress* and his fervent spiritual autobiography, *Grace Abounding to the Chief of Sinners*, were there, as were Milton's *Paradise Lost* and *Paradise Regained*, and John Locke's *Letters Concerning Toleration*, and *Human Understanding*. Dante's *Divine Comedy* and Shakespeare's tragedies were each in one large, closely printed volume. And Robert Burns, so recently dead, was represented in a copy of the Edinburgh edition of his *Poems, Chiefly in the Scottish Dialect*, a gift to Alex-

19

ander from his uncle Archibald two years before, who had told him half-jokingly that too much reading of theology and philosophy and too little knowledge of human foibles would make him a dull lad indeed. Another favorite poet with Alexander was the supernaturalistic and melancholy James Macpherson whose *Temora*, a translation of the legendary Gaelic poet, Ossian, had aroused such recent controversy among scholars. There were no novels in Thomas Campbell's library, the reading of which he considered a waste of time, if not a downright sin. The logical and independent mind of the son frequently differed with the more utilitarian, salvation-centered mind of the father, but in this judgment they were agreed, and since his filial sense was heightened by his father's absence, Alexander passed over the *Temora*, which tempted him, and picked up Boston's *Fourfold State*.

It was the latest addition to his father's library, purchased only a few weeks before his departure for America. Thoughtfully Alexander turned the pages. Thomas Boston had been among the first seceders from the strict Presbyterian doctrinaire and practices of the National Church of Scotland, and Alexander had promised his father he would be well read in Boston's interpretations before they met again.

He went into his mother's cabin, stretched out on the long wooden bench against the outer wall, tucked a cushion under his head, and began to read. It was the fourth day of waiting, and his mother and the children were visiting among some of the other passengers in an adjoining cabin. After a turgid hour of reading, Boston's *Fourfold State of Man* proved dull and unreal and he was relieved when Dorothea unceremoniously came in and interrupted him.

"This awful waiting has gotten on my nerves," she told him. "Anyway, you promised to read to me." She glanced at the book in his hand.

"I said you should read, yourself." His tone was light but his eyes were serious as he noted the lines of strain about her young face. "But never mind, I'll read to you." He made room for her on the bench. "Now, take Boston's idea of a fourfold state, for instance. Boston examines the four primary states of man. He tells us first

20

what man was like in the state of Innocence; second, what he was after the Fall; third, what he is under the Gospel of Grace; and fourth, what shall be his Eternal State. And then—"

Dorothea snugged a pillow at her back and folded her hands in her lap, her face half-turned toward her brother as though unwilling to miss a word. And gradually, as she listened, the steady tone, the regular beat of the long, sonorous words, the assurance of strength in the rugged outlines of her brother's face through the half-gloom, caused her fears to ebb away slowly, and she closed her eyes.

"I'm listening," she told her brother. "I hear every word you say."

Alexander read on, conscious that the spoken words were more of a sedative than a stimulant to them both; equally conscious that they both needed recuperation and strength for whatever lay ahead. In a few minutes his sister was sound asleep.

Placing the book opened upon his chest, he stretched out his long legs and let his mind wander over the events, the meanderings, the false starts, the trials of the ten days since they had lifted anchor at Londonderry; ten days of unwanted calms and adverse winds; and now anchored uncertainly in an exposed, rocky bay. Waiting.

He thought of his mother, full of serenity and hope but no longer confident and assured; a strain and a perplexity and a fear upon her which she could never quite conceal. He stirred restlessly; the book slipped to the floor; his head tilted forward, and he drowsed, fitfully, all unnoting that the wind, veering toward the south, was blowing directly into the bay and rising to the intensity of a gale.

It was almost midnight, hours after the family had uneasily retired for the night, that the *Hibernia* struck the sunken rock. A tearing, crashing shock, as though the ship were being suddenly ripped apart, a shattering of timbers; a violent keeling over of the vessel, the force of the wind and waves throwing her almost upon her beam end; and a torrential rushing of water into the hold as if the bottom had been knocked out of her. And then shrieks and moans and cries of sudden terror as the passengers picked themselves up and rushed frantically for the decks.

One moment Alexander was sound asleep in his bunk; the next he was rolling on the floor. Scrambling to his feet, he slipped into his clothes and a moment later, with Archibald clutched under one arm and holding Thomas by the hand, he forced open the door to his mother's cabin.

Silently, with no lost motions, the girls were dressing themselves. His mother, still in her brown woolen nightgown and stocking cap, stood braced against the slanting floor, methodically wrapping the half-awakened Alicia in a blanket. The whale-oil lamp, still alight, swung slantwise from the ceiling; the door to the upper deck, un-latched with the violence of the crash, opened and shut full width on its iron hinges with each pitch and toss of the ship.

For a crowded second Alexander surveyed the scene, and then he spoke directly to the boys, his voice confident and reassuring above the din of the storm.

"We're real sailormen now," he told them. "Looks like we've struck something. Put your pants and coats on over your night-gowns. Like this!" Holding them firmly, he began to suit the ac-tion to the words. "Now, hold hands and keep quiet, and Brother Alex will go on deck and see what's happened."

Mrs. Campbell spoke for the first time. "Hurry back, son," she said quietly. She held the squirming Alicia in one hand and with the other unloosened her throat band and stepped out of her nightgown, revealing herself as fully clothed. A half-smile played about the corners of her mouth as Alexander stared. "Yes, hurry back. Some-thing really unexpected might happen!"

Alexander nodded, a warmth flooding his heart for this brave Gallic-Irish woman who never lost her wits, nor her gift for any emergency.

"You're a canny one, Mother," he said. His sudden grin warmed them all. Bracing himself against the wall, he edged through the door.

The scene was hopeless confusion. Half-clad men and women ran about the slanting decks, clinging to whatever came to hand. Others huddled on the upper deck near the cabins, primitive fear

22

of the elements in their eyes. Some were cursing, a wild, incoherent babbling of words; others sobbed in terror. Only a few appeared in full possession of themselves. But one of these few was Captain Jumer.

Whatever else might be said of their captain, Alexander thought, he was a man unafraid. Like a fat little bull defying the elements, he spraddled the quarterdeck, bellowing orders. Beside him the big Dutchman fought the helm, pitting his strength and skill against the forces that held it fast. As Alexander struggled toward them, now flat against the cabin wall, now half-sprawled on the deck, the waves breaking over him with every step, the captain megaphoned his hands and shouted again—a shout that crashed through the lashing of the waves and the fear and confusion like the blows of a muffled sledge hammer.

"Ahoy!" he yelled. "All hands! Cut away the masts!"

As Alexander watched, enthralled by the spectacle of possible violent death, Mr. Ryan ran from the direction of the cook's galley with a broadax. At a word from the captain, the Dutchman left the motionless helm and, taking the ax, began to hack furiously at the base of the mainmast. The mate came quickly to the quarter-deck.

"She's fast on a rock, sir," he reported. "If we can get the masts down, she'll right herself."

"Get more axes," said the captain. "Cut the damned masts down!"

"The only ax aboard is the carpenter's, sir. We're using that now. When we dragged anchor and struck the rock, the deck axes jarred loose. They're gone!"

"Fool!" For a moment the captain seemed beside himself. "That's your fault, Mr. Ryan. Get those masts down! Clear the decks and get them down!"

Without a word the mate turned and ran past Alexander toward a cluster of passengers grouped about the close-reefed mastheads.

"We can use your prayers now, Mr. Campbell." The captain spoke as though he had known Alexander was there all the time. "We've got to get those damned masts down so we can right our-

23

selves on this rock or we'll all drown!" He glared at Alexander accusingly as a shaft of lightning for one blinding second made the scene bright as noonday. "We need all the help we can get!"

Alexander was suddenly filled with hot anger at the insolence of the man, but he did not reply, and after a tense moment, soaked to the skin and gasping for breath against the wind and rain, he began to fight his way back to the cabin. They were in desperate straits. Should the ship slide from the rock on which it was poised like a bug on a pin, the voyage would end before it had begun. The anger within him grew into frustration—a helplessness that made him cling weakly to the railing of the deck, his thoughts on the little family which was his charge and his responsibility. Unconsciously, his lips formed the opening words of the Forty-sixth Psalm he had known since his earliest days:

God is our refuge and strength, a very present help in trouble.
Therefore we will not fear, though the earth be removed, and though the mountains be carried into the midst of the sea.

Above the beating of the waves, the carpenter's ax rang clearly; cutting, penetrating strokes, powered deep by man's urge for self-preservation, while half-a-dozen passengers hacked vigorously with broadswords against the stays.

Two hours later the masts had been swept away and the *Hibernia*, partially righting herself upon the hidden rock that had crushed her bottom, was settling more firmly upon it as her hold filled with water. With whatever belongings they could gather, the passengers had gathered on deck, waiting, hoping, praying, cursing. Fortunately one of the ship's longboats was still intact, and the deck cannon securely moored. There was nothing now to be done except endure the night. At least they were still within sight of shore.

Alexander secured a place against the wall of the poop deck for his mother and the children where they waited for whatever the next rushing wave might bring. Gradually silence fell upon the passengers, broken by the occasional whimpering of a child, or the half-hysterical gasp of a woman. The waves still broke over them, shaking the ship from bow to stern, sweeping the decks, and threatening destruction. But the *Hibernia* held tenaciously, if precariously, to her perch on the rock, her broken sides clinging to it like tentacles; riding steadier and more firmly in the saddle as the hold filled with water. The captain ordered the cannon fired at minute intervals and although they sounded like the hollow puffing of toy balloons amid the noise of the wind and water, they gave hope that help would come; the gale and the night could not last forever.

For a long time Alexander stood with his back against the wall of the poop deck, the center of the family group, holding Alicia, shielding her from the flying spray. His mother's arms were about Jane and Archibald, while Thomas sat between his two older sisters, his efforts at bravery dissolving into troubled sleep. Even Nancy's eyes grew blurred, and Dorothea, though as wide awake as he and as conscious of their danger, watched the scene with quiet resignation. For the most part there was little movement and less talk among the passengers. Cold and sodden, they huddled together against the storm, each one reduced to his elements. And as they waited the past became like a dream, the present their only future; and the very young and the stupid, and the completely exhausted, began fitfully to sleep.

But there was no sleep for Alexander. He stood for two hours and then gave his place against the poop deck to a young mother and her child, and seated himself on the stump of the broken foremast, his head hunched between his shoulders, his hands braced against his knees for steadiness. He sat wide-eyed and tense, swaying with the buffeting of the ship, oblivious of the cold and the darkness and the water trickling down his back and his chest, clamping his clothes with chilling sogginess against his body. The loss of his family would crush Thomas Campbell; he would rack his soul for the sin he would believe had brought such grief upon him. He would be bereft of God.

But somehow Alexander knew his father would never be bereft of God. Where he walked God walked also; his humble and self-sacrificing life had long before been given into His keeping. Beside his father's consecration, and the trusting faith of his mother, he saw himself as a vain and strutting fellow; a pompous and self-righteous Pharisee. Their hold on God stood out now more than

25

ever as the one secure anchor against the mocking vanities of what he had thought great, and from his heart there arose unbidden the resolve that whatever happened from that night onward, he would follow their example. This life which was not his life, since he had not willed it, would be given in some manner to the service of God who gave it. In Jesus' name. Amen.

He was not conscious that he had uttered a prayer, but the uncertainties and the tensions and the fears which had ridden him intermittently since their first day out from Londonderry suddenly left him, and he felt a sense of liberation, of freedom; a confidence and an assurance in him he had never known before. He was bound, and yet he was free. Whatever vocation he followed, he was God's man now. Slowly he stood erect, conscious that he was physically weary to the bone, but with a new proudness in the stance of his body, a humbleness as though rising from a dedication.

With fresh eyes he looked about at the passengers, huddled together like rain-soaked sheep waiting the slaughter. Mr. Ryan was a tower of confidence, moving constantly about, keeping the sailors busy lashing ships' lanterns to the wall of the poop deck to give some relief from the blackness of the night; directing the placement of stools and benches for the comfort of the women; supervising the separation of luggage into family groups.

Near the center of the upper deck Alexander saw the Catholic priest, his black cassock flying in the wind; stooping now and then to hear a rambling confession; absolving a soul from sin according to the rites of his church; preparing his flock for the fate which seemed upon them all. As he watched he felt a new admiration and a deeper respect for the man. The priest walked in the truth as he knew it, and brought hope and comfort to those who believed with him. He was a good and holy man, and his life was a blessing.

Back with the family, Alexander took the sleeping Alicia from his mother and snugged a place for himself between his two brothers, a pride in him that for all their cold and misery this family did not cry or whimper. At the first shafts of daylight the captain came down from his perch on the quarterdeck.

"Pick me a crew, Mr. Ryan, and lower the longboat!" he shouted. "We'll get help from the shore, come hell or heaven. And for each man a bottle of the devil's holy water. It's a cold journey!"

Mr. Ryan promptly took command. He called out four members of the crew, beginning with the big Dutchman. "We'll need the help of you other men when it's time to get the women and children ashore." His eyes roved over the passengers. "Father O'Flathery can come along. No others."

The priest waved his square, rain-soaked hat jubilantly, and as he pushed his way toward the longboat, Alexander caught him warmly by the hand.

"God keep you, Father O'Flathery," he said. "He needs you."

"He has a plan for you, too, I dinna doubt." The priest grinned. "Even heretics have their purpose for the Lord."

A few minutes more and the longboat was clear of the ship. With the captain at the tiller and the priest in the stern, and the sailors lustily pulling at the oars, it slid into the trough of a giant wave and was lost to view.

An hour later and the wind had shifted landward. In the growing daylight the passengers could make out the dim shore. The longboat had reached it, and attempts were being made to launch rescue boats, but the heavy waves pounding the shore capsized the crafts. Then they saw the group on shore hurl small casks into the bay which they would immediately pull back by ropes attached to them, repeating the performance again and again. The meaning of the maneuver was soon clear, and Mr. Ryan brought two empty casks from the half-flooded cook's galley and with stout marlines tied to them, tossed them into the bay where they bobbed rapidly to shore. There they were seized and the ropes tied to the longboat which was soon pulled alongside the *Hibernia* by Mr. Ryan and the crew.

Alexander, as excited as the others, kissed his mother triumphantly on the cheek. "We'll all soon be ashore, Mother," he said. "Women and children first. I'll come along as soon as I can."

"I'm no children," Thomas announced hoarsely. "I'll wait with you, Brother Alex. I'll help you row the boat."

"You're a little man for sure," Alexander confirmed proudly. "And so is Archibald. I'm proud of you. And the girls, too. You are little angels!"

"I'll be an angel later," said Nancy. "Right now I want something to eat. I'm hungry!"

It was with a tightening in his throat that Alexander assisted his charges into the second boat and watched until it got safely to the shore. Then he turned to salvage such of their property as he could. Their trunks and boxes he found floating between decks, and the cask in which was packed all the rest of his father's books that he had not brought to his cabin. The books, he felt, must be saved at any cost. Finding no means to hoist the cask onto the deck, he seized the carpenter's ax and, breaking it open, began throwing the books upon the deck, intending to take along as many as he could carry. Working frantically, oblivious that he was almost the last on board, he was startled to hear Mr. Ryan call to him from the upper deck, a lilt in his voice as though at the release of a great burden.

"Ahoy there, Mr. Campbell!" he called. " 'Tis the last boat for Scotland! Or will you be staying longer?"

Alexander looked up from the waist-deep water, a desperation in him. "They're my father's books!" he said. "Books! I can't leave them!"

"We'll come back for them. Unless you're a mind to stand guard for a week." The mate laughed, and in sheer exuberance began suddenly to chant:

> "Oh, the crew have gone and the rats have, too,
> Leave her, Johnny, leave her;
> And it's time, my boy, that we leave, too;
> It's time for us to leave her!"

He waved his arm upward and Alexander clambered after him. A man could ask too much of God. He felt suddenly ashamed.

He found the family safe, their clothing almost dry, standing together a short distance from the shore where they could watch the movement of the rescue boats. As he kissed them one by one, the sense of dedication and blessing he had felt when seated upon the broken mast the night before came upon him again. They had

28

come a far way since they had left Rich Hill; farther than any of them could know.

Then quietly, soothingly, came the calm voice of their mother, healing the pitfalls and the fears of the night with the triumphant thanksgiving of the Psalmist:

"Bless the Lord, O my soul, and all that is within me, bless his holy name.

Alexander, my son, will you lead us in our prayer?"

Chapter 3

EXACTLY ONE MONTH AFTER THE *Hibernia* HAD BROKEN HER BOTTOM against the sunken rock in the Lochin Daal off the Island of Islay, a little man in a worn black coat stared impassively at a sprawling new signature on the register of the University of Glasgow.

"November 8, 1808, Alexander Campbell." He read slowly, rolling the words under his tongue. He picked up the quill pen that Alexander had used and wrote rapidly in the blank space under the name: *"Filius Natus Maximus Viri Reverendi Thomae Pastoris in parochia de Ahorey in comitatu Armagh."*

He looked up. "Twenty-five years ago I matriculated the father. And now, the son. An auld habit of the University, and a good one. But I dinna ken ye will do as well." He shook his head doubtfully. "Your father was a vurry gude mon; and ye are entering the sessions late."

Alexander nodded gravely, aware of the welcome in the eyes of the old registrar; conscious of the Scotch wariness that caused him to speak cautiously. "I shall do my best, sir," he said. "Father has a good mind, an excellent perception. I am not confident I can equal his record as a student."

"Aye." He nodded. "A gude mind, though, as I remember, a bit on the argufying side for a divinity and medical student; never one to lack for a word."

"Aye," Alexander agreed. "A ready man."

The old man relented, a slow smile softening his weathered face. "No more than his son, let us hope." He extended his hand. "Mac-Allister, Enoch. Registrar here these forty years. Ye have met your professors?" He paused doubtfully.

"Yes," said Alexander. "Reverend Ewing introduced me. Professors John Young and George Jardine remembered Father." His face glowed in recollection. "They were very kind."

"Ah! Reverend Greville Ewing!" The old man shook his head. "An Independent. No longer with the Kirk of Scotland. Young man, ye seek bold pastures." His tone hardened. "Ye will begin classes today. First class is this afternoon at two o'clock. Professor Ure in Experimental Philosophy." He rummaged briefly among the papers on the table. "Ah, yes. The third lecture of the session, this one on the 'Microscope.' Modern science, marvelous! Professor Ure's next lecture, let me see, will be on 'Electricity,' which the American Benjamin Franklin claims to have discovered; and his fifth lecture will be on 'Light.' Ye understand, of course, that ye'll be examined on all lectures missed?"

"I will do my best, sir." Alexander held the notebook which he had purchased at the stationer's the day before so that the registrar might see it under his spectacles. "Professor Ure has already given me assignments."

The old registrar nodded. "Thomas Campbell would like that. He was a studious young man, vurry thorough and methodical. A gude Presbyterian." He raised his finger. "Ye know the rules, the customs, here?"

Alexander nodded doubtfully, and the old registrar continued, a twist of a smile about his dry lips, his Scotch burr firming to formal speech.

"You are now a Young Gentleman of Glasgow. You have enrolled in the Humanities; a student of Greek, Logic, Natural Science, and Moral Philosophy. You are a Togati, a gown student. The scarlet

30

cloak, your academical robe, must be worn at all celebrations, laureations, and official events. Since you will be living with your family in the city and not within the college quadrangle, there will be no restrictions as to rising and retiring, and no visits from the hebdomadar, whose duty it is to thrash students who are caught dozing in bed at five o'clock in the morning, or retired to it by nine o'clock at night. But even though you reside in town, such offenses against morals as carding, dicing, and play-acting are strictly forbidden. Any *lapsus* will be punished."

A bell sounded. "The hurry bell. You have five minutes to get to your class. Off with you! And God's prayers!" The old man extended a bony hand across the narrow table that ran like a money-changer's counter the width of the narrow room—a room lighted only by four high-ribbed windows opening into an inner court. As Alexander shook it, the carrot-topped, long-legged assistant, leafing through filing papers in the row of wooden cabinets against the wall, looked up and clucked gravely, as if conscious for the first time of his presence—a wiry, youngish man who might have been forty or fifty, a solemnity about him as though acutely conscious life ended but in the grave.

Alexander hastened down the fore-hall stairway into the inner court, and back again into a long, rectangular building which he knew was the College. Professor Ure's lectures were held in a square, loftlike room on the second floor.

As he walked, his footsteps lost in the muffled tread of students making their way along the stone corridors, he felt a familiarity about it all; an invisible warmth as though at a long-deferred homecoming; a feeling that somehow he had seen it all before. As, of course, he reflected, he had. He had been three years old when Thomas Campbell, in 1791, completed his studies at the theological school maintained by the Anti-Burgher branch of the Seceder Church of Scotland at Whitburn, midway between Edinburgh and Glasgow, after graduating with honors from the College of Glasgow. And it had been through reminiscent stories told during the long winter evenings of his childhood in County Antrim that this sense of renascence was on him, of re-entry into scenes long familiar.

31

Since its establishment by the Bull of Pope Nicholas V in 1451, the University had changed and grown until it was now the citadel of Presbyterianism, the center and the pride of the Golden Age of Scotland. Its students numbered almost two thousand; shaken and energized by the stimuli of the French Revolution, stirring with new ideas which could change the world.

He fell into step with other students as they neared the massive wide-hinged doors of the classroom, and looked curiously at the censor standing in sober gravity beside it, the student appointed each week by the professor to assist in the preservation of decorum. Soberly he went forward and took his seat with the others.

Night had fallen across the city before Alexander started for the three-room flat on Broad Street, Hutchinsontown, where the family had been snugly enough anchored the past three days. As his father had often said, Glasgow was still little more than one long, meandering street. The Cathedral stood at its northern boundary, stanch, proud, enduring, and the gentle Clyde was still its southern. Between the two wandered High Street, pausing as it crossed the Trongate and the Gallowgate near the river and climbing furiously by Rottenrow and Drygate as it approached the Cathedral. But High Street was Glasgow, and on High Street stood the University, the fairest sight between the Cathedral and the Market Cross.

As he hurried homeward he lived again, like the kaleidoscopic shuttering of a dream, that last frantic flight from the sinking ship, the joyous reunion of the family, and the friendliness of the islanders. There had been no fatalities, and in his mind's eye he could see Captain Jumer as he had stalked among them with a paternal oversight only mildly reinforced by the bottle, exhorting them to file their claim for the refund of their passage money. And Mr. Ryan, a kind of boyish satisfaction in him, as though he had feared the worst and was vastly pleased it had not happened. Father O'Flathery had been as friendly as ever, but tired; an abruptness, an asperity about him as if he had almost reached the limit of his endurance. Alexander had liked the hearty, outspoken Catholic priest, and now he would never see him again.

He stumbled over a pig that had taken asylum for the night in a

32

muddy hollow before the Pug-o'-my-Eye Tavern just outside the college quadrangle on High Street at the Trongate, but recovering his balance, walked rapidly on. Supper would be waiting, a good Scotch supper of broth maybe, and salt beef or boiled fowl—a feast fit for any of the Campbells of Argleshire.

Prompt refund of the passage money by the owners of the ship had induced some of the passengers to embark again for the New World, but not the Campbells. A winter voyage could well be the end for some of the younger children, and Mrs. Campbell could see no good purpose in chancing it. They would spend the winter in Glasgow, and Alexander would be a student at the University.

During the two weeks they had remained at Bowmore, salvaging and repairing their goods, Alexander had become acquainted with the school principal, George Fulton, who also kept the Sunday school, and it was George Fulton who, learning of their plans, had given him a letter of introduction to the great Independent preacher of Glasgow, Dr. Greville Ewing.

From Bowmore the distance to Glasgow was one hundred and thirty miles by Port Askeg and Greenock. By the time he got the family as far as Greenock, Alexander found the money allotted for the trip was running low. He made arrangements for them to proceed on to Glasgow by flyboat and himself walked the remaining twenty-three miles to the city. He spent the night at the Boar's Head on High Street, and early the next morning called at the home of the Reverend Greville Ewing. Graciously, the distinguished preacher helped him find furnished lodgings for the family.

And now, three days later, a registered student at the great University on the river Clyde, he impatiently hastened over the damp cobblestones of the city, shuttering itself against the winter's night.

As he pushed open the door of their lodgings, Dorothea's face framed just within the doorway against the firelight beamed at him, the tantalizing odor of an Irish stew filling him with a sudden ravenous hunger.

"I'm that hungry I could eat a wolf!" He pinched her chin and, as the door closed behind him, hung his mackinaw and cap on a peg against the wall.

33

"You mean like a wolf!" Dorothea corrected him. "That's your usual appetite! But now that you're a 'Gentleman of Glasgow' you must assume the manners of your betters!"

On rare impulse he kissed his mother lightly on the cheek as she turned toward him from the boiling pot. "There's no lack of appetite where Mother is the cook," he reminded her. "Where are the children?" He let his eyes sweep the bare furnishings of the all-purpose room—a room where the family would cook and eat and where he would study and later sleep with Tommie on the two wooden benches which, when lashed together, furnished a comfortable enough bed before the hearth.

"They're in the bedroom listening to Nancy's Irish fairy tales," his mother said. "She's good at keeping the little ones while we cook."

"Irish tales in Scotland?" mocked Alexander. "I shall tell them of Robert the Bruce, the one mon who fought the British, aye, that he did, to a standstill, and made himself the king of all Scotland at Bannockburn!"

Supper was over now and the earthen bowls had been scraped clean. They sat about the steady blaze of the hearth, their faces aglow as Alexander told of his day.

"It has been a good beginning," his mother agreed. "Your father will be proud when he hears of it."

"That is all very well," said Dorothea. "Father is an honor graduate of the University, and now you are a student here. But what of me and Nancy and Jane? We are barely taught to read and write. Perhaps we would like to attend a university, too!"

Her brother nodded. "One of these days, perhaps. But not now. Do you know what the University thinks of women? Here, let me read you. I copied it today from the bulletin in the registrar's office while I was waiting." He took a paper from his coat pocket.

" 'Women are vain, frivolous, and gifted with an exceeding great gift of words,' " he read soberly. " 'And by their blandishments are apt at time to distract the mind's eye even of grave professors, wherefore the latter are strictly counseled not to marry; but in the event of their being compelled by ontoward Force of Circumstances to choose between two evils, they are prohibited, on pain of removal from their chairs, from bringing their better halves within the College walls.' Now, what do you think of that?"

"One of these days I shall have a college of my very own for females," said Jane. "And I won't let any boys attend at all! That will show them!"

" 'Never put out your arm farther than you can draw it back,' " cautioned their mother. She gazed fondly at her indignant young daughter. "That's a good old Scotch proverb, Jane, and you will do well to hearken to it the more as you grow older."

" 'Make a spune or spoil a horn,' " quoted Alexander. "With that iron will of hers, little Jane will either do great things or make a great failure. And I dinna doubt that our little sister will do just as she says. She will be right, too. I canna see that women are any more dull than their male folk, come take them as a lot."

"Females can at least go to the Cathedral, I suppose," said Dorothea. "That's where I want to go next Sabbath. It's to the glory of all Scotland!"

"If the spirit of John Knox should hear you!" chided Alexander. "We should hear the Reverend Greville Ewing this Sabbath. He helped me find these lodgings and introduced me to my professors; we owe him at least the courtesy of our first hearing." He stood up and turned his back to the fire, his hands deep in his pockets. "I learned many things this day."

"Saint Patrick be praised!" said Dorothea, her eyes laughing. "Name us one!"

" 'That should fair put my beard in a blaze'—another Scotch saying with meaning clear enough. But I shall tell you. There are thirteen colleges at the University. Do you want to know them all?" He stared at Dorothea in assumed reproach. "There is the College of Divinity, which of course is the most important. Then, the College of Oriental Languages, Church History, Natural Philosophy, Moral Philosophy, Logic, Greek, Mathematics, Civil Law, Medicine, Anatomy, Practical Astronomy, and Humanity. I am a student in the College of Humanity; a Togati, a gown student, I would have

35

you know. On special occasions, such as the laureation, the town sacraments, funerals, or visits of His Majesty the King, which heaven forbid, I shall have to wear a scarlet cloak. Doesn't that sound important?"

"How about the fees, son?" asked his mother quietly.

"The bursarius classified me as a *secundar*. Had I been the son of a noble, or laird, I would have been a *primar;* or if of low estate, an *inferior*. The fees are charged according to the ability to pay, provided, the rules say, that 'always none of the regents exact anything at all for the schollage from those of the poorer sorts who can maintain themselves only with straits and difficulty.' So my fees are eight pounds, seven shillings, and sixpence, which includes the fees to the regents. If I choose to live at the University, I could secure board, lodging, and instruction, all for ten pounds, and be inspected by the regents at five in the morning and nine at night; and subject to rebukes, fines, imprisonment in the church steeple, or such bodily chastisement as they might deem it well to mete out to me."

"Perhaps they might hang you from the church steeple," said Dorothea hopefully.

"Since it's Scotch proverbs we're using so freely, 'let that flea stick in the wa'.' Which means there is a time to let bygones be bygones," their mother explained. "Go on with your story, Alexander. And I might add that even though we shall be spending the winter in Scotland, we need not forsake the English tongue altogether."

"Nor the Irish," said Nancy. "Mother is French and Father is Scotch, and we were all born in Ireland." She turned to Alexander. "Now, what does that make us, Professor?"

> "Breathes there a man with soul so dead,
> Who never to himself hath said,
> This is my own, my native land—

That's from a poem by Walter Scott, a Scotsman, aye, whose works seem vurry popular here noo. That's my answer," he said. "I first heard it from Professor Jardine when Reverend Ewing introduced us the other day. He said Father was a good Scot, and told me this

36

was 'my own, my native land.' He was welcoming me home, he said. Back to Scotland."

Tommie looked up from his knees-to-chin position before the hearth with its red-hot peat coals. "I'm a Scotsman, a burr Scot like Father!" he insisted stoutly.

"All right then," said Alexander. "All together now!" He began to beat time with his hands, his exuberance spreading to them all.

> "Great Argyle he goes before,
>   He makes his cannon and guns to roar,
>   Wi' sound of trumpet, pipe, and drum;
>   The Campbells are comin', Oho, Oho!

The last stanza," he announced. "Now—"

Even their mother, joggling Alicia in her woolen nightgown on her knee, joined in, her clear soprano leading the children in the triumphant lay:

> "The Campbells are comin', Oho, Oho!
>   The Campbells are comin', Oho, Oho!
>   The Campbells are comin' to bonnie Lochleven,
>   The Campbells are comin', Oho, Oho!"

A heavy pounding on the door, unheard until the last note died away, caused them to stare at one another in bewilderment.

As Alexander swung wide the thick pine door, a tall figure of a man walked in, muffled under his heavy mackinaw, his ears and chin buried in the folds of the woolen shawl wound round and round his neck. For a moment he surveyed the suddenly silenced group and then swept off his hat and bowed deeply, first to Mrs. Campbell and then to the group, his rosy angular face exploding into a grin that spread from ear to ear.

"The Reverend Dr. Greville Ewing!" Alexander greeted him. "Welcome, sir!"

"So the Campbells are here, oho, oho! The Campbells are here, oho! Well maught it be Rob Roy himself for all the noise! But rejoicing is ever godly in the sight of the Lord, I dinna doubt." He paused as though dimly aware of their surprise at his appearance, and handing Alexander his hat and shawl permitted him to help him

37

off with his coat. "And he knows of Bobbie Burns, too. God rest his soul."

"Aye, sir," Alexander said. He hung the hat and coat carefully on a peg against the wall, and offered the guest a chair. But the noted preacher stood, spreading his hands before the hearth.

"My apologies for this unexpected visit," he said, turning to Mrs. Campbell. "But I was only a few minutes away on Gallowsgate at prayer with a sick parishioner and could not resist the temptation to visit your lodgings. I feel responsible, you know, as I suggested them. I fear they may be too crowded for so many bairns."

"We are most grateful," said Mrs. Campbell. "Without your kindness we might have been undone."

"It is I who am grateful for the chance, madam, to do a wee good turn. I kenna what may be the result of your biding here this winter. Aye, it is God's will."

"We feel that it is so," said Mrs. Campbell.

"Let us imagine"—he turned to Alexander with an air of mock severity—"that these are your lodgings at the College and I am the regent whose duty it is to inspect them. And I do not find your nose in your books, sir. Now, with your permission, a look around." Without more ado he strolled to the doorway of the adjoining room and looked about with an appraising eye. "As crowded as a ship's fo'c'sle with such a jolly crew. You must have larger quarters. I shall see to it."

"But we are very comfortable here," said Mrs. Campbell. "God has been good and you are more than kind, sir."

"The Lord is good to all who do His will," said Dr. Ewing. He came back and stood before the fire. "Another reason for my visit, in addition to my duties as a self-appointed hebdomadar, is to invite you to worship with us at the Tabernacle, come Sabbath. They call us 'Independents,' but you will find us congenial." He turned to Alexander. "If you would know more of us, sir, join us on Friday evening at my home at eight o'clock. James Alexander Haldane and John Campbell will be there, and Alexander Carson of Tubbermore. There are mighty deeds being wrought in Scotland, my son, and these are some of the men responsible. It will interest you as a student to hear their views."

Alexander flushed, flattered by the invitation. "I shall be there gladly," he said.

Dr. Ewing bowed again to Mrs. Campbell. "Now I shall leave you, madam, with your bairns, and my apologies."

" 'The Campbells are comin',' " said the irrepressible Tommy. "You come again, too, sir. Maybe then we can have mutton for supper." He looked at his mother inquiringly. "Oho! Oho!"

For a few minutes they talked while Alexander handed Dr. Ewing his belongings, and even little Alicia scrambled from her mother's lap to give him a hug. Truly they had fallen among friends.

As the family settled into a routine, Alexander found his days beginning at four o'clock. At six he attended his first class in French; and from eight to ten o'clock his Latin classes. Returning home, he breakfasted on porridge and hard bread, washed down by a cup of hot tea, and studied in the bedroom or went to the University library with its boasted twenty thousand volumes, until his more advanced course in Greek under Professor Young began at two o'clock, followed by lectures in Logic and Belles Lettres under Professor Jardine, with several extra lectures a week in Experimental Philosophy accompanied by experiments in Natural Science under Professor Ure.

Originally situated on Rottenrow but since 1460 removed to the broad expanses of High Street, the University had been little scathed by the Protestant Reformation. The main buildings of the College now formed an inner and an outer court, or quadrangle, the range of buildings that separated the two courts crowned by a tall, square tower. Beyond the inner court were the college gardens, luxuriant with fruit trees and potted herbs and stiff hedges where the masters and the selected students were allowed to walk, while behind the gardens the Molendinar flowed placidly on its way to join the river Clyde.

The Cathedral Church of Glasgow, nearby, was equally the pride

39

of all Scotland and even more impressive in its symbolic majesty. It was the only metropolitan church in the country, so Dr. Ewing had told Alexander during their tour of it the preceding Monday, excepting the Cathedral of Kirkwall in the Orkneys, that had escaped serious damage during the Reformation; the townspeople gathering to do battle when the overardent followers of John Knox came to Glasgow to "destroy Popish knickknacks and purge the High Kirk." Nor was it love of popery which had moved the people, he explained, but rather a devotion to their ancient Cathedral itself and all it had meant to them as the house of God. So they had compromised with the marauding zealots. The idolatrous statues of the saints were taken from their nooks and broken into pieces by scriptural warrant, and flung into the Molendinar, leaving the old minster church standing as proudly as before.

"If the same common sense had been used with every Popish kirk in Scotland, the Reformation would have been just as thorough," said Dr. Ewing, "and the cause of Christ would have been better served."

It was Friday night. Uncertain of his direction under the dim light of the whale-oil street lamps, Alexander stopped at the curb of a cobblestone crossing to get his bearings. For all the lowering clouds and the high, biting wind, the streets were dotted with passers-by: men shrouded to their ears in heavy plaid woolen coats and shawls, headed homeward, or to the hilarity of a tavern, with here and there a family group huddling together, or a woman hurrying silently through the evening from the fish markets.

He knew he stood on the Trongate, within a few yards of the famous Market Cross, the center of the business life of the city. Colonnades extended along the street floors of the buildings on both sides of the streets that formed the cross, and under the shadow of the pillars supporting the piazzas were the shops, entered by half-doors, now shuttered but over which the merchants leaned in the daytime waiting for customers, chattering with their neighbors. There were silks and calicoes inside, and tobacco, and earthen and glass and ironware, and dried fish and yarn and candles and bro-

40

cades. Glasgow was a bustling city now, already beginning to over-flow the borders of Lanarkshire into Renfrewshire and Dumbarton-shire—an important seaport with shipyards and increasing wealth, and with an unchanging poverty in its growing slum area, mollified in the civic consciousness by the great public park with its one hundred and eight acres, its fine trees and plants, and its more than three miles of graveled walks.

Glasgow was a big city—already in the imagination of some of its merchants a destined rival of London four hundred miles to the south; aware of its new importance as an industrial center and the site of a university whose rise to world fame was nonetheless definite because its pathway had been uncertain. The unbending penalizing orthodoxy of the National Church of Scotland, following the days of John Knox, had been relaxed and there had arisen an independent searching attitude of mind that had now won for every Scotsman the right to think what he pleased and act as his conscience decreed, provided he did no other man mortal harm. New religious sects were springing up over the land, each with its own interpretation of the Scriptures, and each of them hostile to the other. But men were seeking the truth, whatever that might be and wherever it might lead. They were studying the Word of God for themselves. And that was good.

Under the light of the broad-wicked lamp, Alexander looked at his silver-plated watch, and grinned with satisfaction. He had his bearings now. And he would be on time.

Ten minutes later he raised the iron knocker on the door of Number Four, Carlton Place, an uneasy quickening in him that within those walls, among these independent thinkers, might be the seeds of a reckoning he did not anticipate. "Young man, ye seek bold pastures," the registrar had said.

And why not? He, Alexander Campbell, *filius natus maximus viri Reverendi Thomae Pastoris*, was a student, a seeker after truth, a Young Gentleman of Glasgow. He was entitled to bold pastures.

He lifted the knocker as high as it would go and let it fall, once, twice, against the metal plating of the door.

41

Chapter 4

A MOMENT LATER THE DOOR WAS HELD WIDE BY DR. GREVILLE EWING, the sound of voices within dwindling to a murmur.

"I thought it was you, my boy." He clasped Alexander by the hand and drew him into the warming shelter of the room. "Only a north-country Scots Irishman of the Campbell clan could make a clarion call out of a door knocker. Come on in!"

Alexander grinned sheepishly and surrendered his mackinaw and cap. "I was having a wee struggle with myself," he said. "But I won."

The preacher clapped him good-humoredly on the back. "You have been listening overmuch to a Scotch Covenanter," he guessed shrewdly. "But we would do ye no harm. My associates and I"—he indicated the group of men about the hearth—"have many friends at the University but, theologically speaking, they dinna believe there that we are up to muckle good. Mr. Campbell, some of my fellow heretics! My friend, James Alexander Haldane, pastor of our Independent Church at Edinburgh." He indicated a lean, smiling man with wide-set blue eyes. "Mr. Haldane has just returned from another preaching mission to the north country. He's the younger brother of the equally famous Robert Haldane. And here is John Campbell, our celebrated ironmonger of Edinburgh who has established more Sabbath schools in Scotland than the devil himself can count; and Dr. Alexander Carson, my college classmate, now minister of the Independent Church at Tubbermore in auld Ireland. He not only left our Scotch National Church but will nae sprinkle the newborn bairns into salvation any more. He must immerse them, though he is no Baptist."

At the remark, Dr. Carson, a dark-browed giant of a man, lifted his hand, palm outward, in solemn protest. "Na, Greville," he corrected, "since they are nae cursed by original sin, as I once believed, I canna baptize them. The bairns should be at least of the age of ten years."

"Before he believes they are accountable for their sins," explained Mr. Ewing. "This stout gentleman is William Stevens who forsook the thespian paths for the pulpit, and is now a teacher in our Edinburgh Seminary. And ah, last but not least, my friend and coadjutor, Dr. Judson Wardlaw."

He turned to the group. "Alexander Campbell," he explained, "is a Young Gentleman of the University, following in the footsteps of his father, the Reverend Thomas Campbell of Ahorey and Rich Hill. A good, stout Anti-Burgher Seceder Presbyterian. But of an inquiring mind," he added.

The inner door opened and a round, rosy face peered at them inquiringly.

"I thought I heard a lad's voice!" Mrs. Ewing walked with short, rolling steps into the center of the room, a rotund, smiling woman in a voluminous skirt of hodden gray and a worsted shawl, bearing a tray of steaming mugs of hogmanay tea and a platter of soda scones and crumpets. "Fair fa'! Young men are always weelcome here!" She set the tray on a low hassock before the fire and stood, one hand on her broad hip, the other wagging a finger at Alexander. "That is, if they can make themselves comfortable amidst so muckle talk of creeds and confessions and baptisms and such notions as not even Saint Paul himself would vouch for."

"There now, gudewife," said Dr. Ewing. "The young lad may think you dinna have the proper respect for the domines. He knows the great apostle said, 'Wives be in subjection unto your own husbands as unto the Lord.' "

"Never mind the man!" The deep voice of Mr. Haldane boomed for the first time. "Paul also said, 'Let the husband render unto the wife due benevolence'; and it was Solomon himself who told us that 'A virtuous woman is a crown unto her husband.' No one knows that imperishable truth better than the friends of Greville Ewing. We salute the gudewife!"

43

"There is a time to work and a time to pray," intoned John Campbell. "There is also a time which comes too seldom to feast upon Mistress Ewing's baking!" He helped himself generously from the platter of breads, and took a mug, while the others, close-knit by friendship and the common passion which was dearer to them than their lives, joined in the laughter.

For several minutes the banter continued and Alexander noticed with surprise that Mrs. Ewing had no hesitancy in expressing her own opinion. Nothing she said, however, was in direct contradiction to her husband, and within a few minutes she withdrew.

"Mr. Haldane had just remarked," Dr. Ewing turned to Alexander, "that those of us here tonight are but a few of a growing number who feel the teachings of Christ have been clouded with doctrinal creeds."

"You would be independent of them?" Alexander asked.

"Exactly," said Mr. Haldane. "Man-made creeds of any nature, whether they be pronunciamentos of the Pope at Rome, the Augsburg Confession of the great Martin Luther, the Thirty-nine Articles, or the Westminster Confession of Faith of our own John Knox, serve no purpose except to bind men to the opinions of other men."

"In brief," interjected John Campbell, "it is our faith and our love and our works which mark us as Christians; not mere compliance with church ordinances and symbols of worship. We are not permitted to preach this, however, and remain in the House of the Presbyterians, so we are called 'Independents.' "

For a moment the conversation stopped as a murmur of assent ran about the bright little room. The men sipped their tea thoughtfully and crunched the hot scones, Alexander acutely aware he was in the presence of men who had been names to conjure with in his father's household. He looked about with an ease of manner he was far from feeling.

Except for the blazing fire in the big coal grate, with its overhanging brick mantle and protruding sandbox that served as both a spit box and a catchall for popping fire coals, and the well-worn buckram-bound books against the opposite wall, the room would

44

have appeared cheerless. There was no furniture except the chairs on which they sat, and a square pine table in the corner adjacent to the hallan with its neatly stacked notepaper, ink, sandbox, and goose-quill pen; a comfortable, masculine room, Alexander thought, the maroon-colored curtains against the narrow-ribbed front windows lending a subdued color in the candlelight.

He was fortunate, he thought, to be in such a company, men who for conscience' sake had broken bonds of orthodoxy as rigid and as uncompromising as those of the Church of Rome. But he was puzzled. The multiplication of creeds, the splintering of the Lord's church by doctrines, could not be cured by the creation of still other religious bodies, no matter by what name they called themselves. Every effort at such reform had only shattered it further. Even the Presbyterianism of Calvin and Knox, established as the National Church of Scotland in 1690, had split in 1733 into an Associate, or Seceder, Church; the Seceders themselves dividing fourteen years later over the burgess' oath, which bound those who took it to adhere to the established church, and again in 1795 over the power of civil magistrates in religious matters. And now, here were the Independents.

Troubled by his reflections and encouraged by the friendliness about him, he spoke directly to James Haldane.

"You do not remember me, sir, but I heard you preach at Rich Hill. I accompanied my father, who has always been tolerant of the views of others. Your preaching greatly interested Father, but I must confess he remained unshaken."

"Aye, I remember him," said Mr. Haldane. "He was the gentle Seceder pastor with the open mind at Ahorey who would sometimes come to hear me. I remember," he smiled gently, "among ourselves we called him 'Nicodemus' because he came by night."

"He dared much to come at all," interposed Mr. Carson. "It is heresy to tolerate any belief other than that of your own church. Tolerance, in the view of every orthodox Presbyterian, Episcopal, or Roman Catholic, is the work of the devil; his masterpiece and chief weapon, the one sure way to destroy all religion. I cannot understand why the Synod did not censure him."

45

"He was questioned by the elders," admitted Alexander. "Father is not in sympathy with the division among Christians. He believes we are all one body in Christ. But instead of creating another division, as he thought you were doing, he works to heal them. He even offered a resolution to the General Assembly here in Glasgow only three years ago to bring about union between the Burghers and the Anti-Burghers in the Seceder Church."

"I recall the occasion," said Dr. Wardlaw. "I attended the General Assembly as a visitor and heard your father. But, sir, while in my opinion he outargued them, they outvoted him."

James Haldane turned directly to Alexander, his deep, cragged blue eyes searching him. "There are many who say we seek to found a new sect. That is not so. But we must somehow escape the obscurantisms, the tyranny, and the dogmatic decrees of the professional prelates, whether they be of the Roman papacy, the English Episcopacy, or the Scottish Presbytery, if we are to present the real Christ of the Scriptures."

"You would say that the Episcopacy and the Presbytery are unscriptural and unchristian?" asked Alexander.

"Unscriptural, yes; unchristian, no," said Mr. Haldane. "Their creeds, the dogmas, are unscriptural; there is no authority for them in the teachings of Jesus, nor were they tolerated by the early church. They are barriers between the penitent sinner and God."

"There seems sound reason for them today," said Alexander. "Our judges are lifelong students of the law; our physicians must convince us they know more of medicine than we. Why should the minister of the kirk not interpret the Scriptures to the people?"

"The boy is a true Scot." Greville Ewing took a long sup of tea and, rising, placed the mug on the mantel. "He wants the proof of the pudding. It is simply this, my boy. Those fields are secular and appeal to men's minds alone. We, in religion, appeal not only to the mind but to the heart and spirit. No minister, however highly trained, can know the soul of a man; only God can enter there. The Bible reveals the mind of God, and it should be the right of every man to read it and to interpret it for himself, living by the truth as it is revealed to him. We repudiate the authority claimed by the presby-teries, the synods, the bishops, and the popes to do that for us."

"It seems to me, sir," Alexander spoke slowly, anxious not to give offense, "carried to its ultimate conclusion, that would be anarchy! We must have authority."

"That we do have, the authority of the Scriptures!" said Alexander Carson. "There can be no better authority than the words of Jesus and His Apostles. That is all we need."

"Then you agree with John Locke," said Alexander. "As I recall it, Locke said in his first *Letter on Toleration* that nothing in worship or discipline can be necessary to Christian communion but what Christ or the Apostles have commanded."

"Another young Daniel come to judgment!" said Dr. Ewing, his words a volley of approval. "But when did you read Locke, my lad? He is stiff medicine for the orthodox."

"He is not considered so in the Campbell home, sir. Father gave me Locke's *Essay Concerning Human Understanding* when I was seventeen, and the *Letters on Toleration* a little later. We regard him as a great Christian philosopher. But John Locke believed in an established church, not in independent congregations."

"Locke did believe in an established church," admitted Carson, "but one characterized by the broadest possible toleration. And toleration has never been a principle of any established church, and never can be. For instance, I practice adult immersion as the only scriptural baptism while my friend Greville accepts sprinkling as a sufficient symbol and even baptizes infants who, I believe, are born without sin and are not subject to that ordinance. Yet we accept each other not only as Christians, but equally as ministers of the gospel. No established church would tolerate such differences within its own organization."

"For the benefit of our young friend, let me explain the paradox," said James Haldane gently. "It proves that men can differ in their interpretations of the Scriptures and yet commune with one another as Christians. But that is not easy. Our tendency to confuse matters of opinion with those of faith has divided Christendom into armed

47

camps that fight each other with more earnestness than they do the devil himself. Conditions are so bad here in Scotland that metal tokens are now issued by the different sects, admitting only selected members to participation in the Lord's Supper. Yet who are we to judge the hearts of men? It is sacrilege!"

For an hour longer the talk continued, now bantering, now in deep seriousness, before Alexander took his leave, an exhilaration about him at being admitted to such a gathering, and yet with a tinge of guilt—a doubt lest by participating in the heretical discussion he had found himself too loosely moored to his own convictions.

Greville Ewing was as good as his word about the lodgings. Two weeks later the Campbells moved to an upper-floor furnished flat located by him at Youngsland, in Hutchinsontown, where they had a combination kitchen-dining and living room, with a separate bedroom for their mother and Alicia, a connecting two-bunk cubicle for Tommie and Archibald, an adjacent room for the older girls, and a bedroom-study for Alexander. Entered only by a flight of narrow inside turnpike stairs, the upper flat was considered less subject to molestation by night prowlers. The neighborhood was quiet and respectable, with a school for girls only two blocks away, kept by the Reverend Titus McElroy, a retired Seceder minister. Considering their circumstances, the family felt they could not have been better situated, and the interest of the Independent preacher in their welfare did not lessen his influence among them.

In order to increase the family income, Alexander began to solicit pupils for private tutoring, and before Christmas he had turned his study into a schoolroom for classes in beginners' Latin and English grammar and reading, and in writing and arithmetic, which he conducted in the afternoons between his own classes at the University. Judson Wardlaw, assistant to Dr. Ewing, was the first to send his two young sons, and before the holidays began, the classes were as large as he could manage.

And the concern of Greville Ewing did not lessen, now that the family was well settled. Instead, he seemed to take an increasing interest, particularly in the tall, ungainly, yet dignified young man with the big hands and spreading feet, and the twinkle like a spark of light in the recesses of his deep blue eyes. Alexander was often invited to the home on Carlton Place, sometimes alone and sometimes with the family, or with other students. At one of these gatherings he met the celebrated Robert Haldane. The knowledge that this man was spending his entire fortune in the furtherance of religion; that he had purchased the old Circus building on Jamaica Street and had converted it into a tabernacle for Dr. Ewing; and that both he and his younger brother James had surrendered lucrative careers in order to preach the gospel, profoundly impressed him. "Sell all that ye have and come, follow me," Christ had said. No man could do more than that.

So it was natural that on Sunday evenings, after attending the Seceder services in the morning, Alexander went more and more frequently to the big tabernacle on Jamaica Street, with its pulpit in the center of the building, to hear the eloquent Dr. Ewing. The experience fostered the independence of his own mind and as often as he could he attended services of other denominations, weighing their claims, studying their beliefs, analyzing their organization. Gradually, as the winter days passed, the rigid bonds of his thinking began to loosen, and the fenced-in ordinances of his Old Light Anti-Burgher Seceder Branch of the Church of Scotland began to appear narrow, almost irreconcilable with the teachings of Jesus. But always a twinge of guilt remained with him. As if to appease his conscience he went regularly every Sunday morning to the square-topped brick Seceder Church on West Market Street, and listened patiently to Pastor Benjamin Montre. Father Thomas would fear he was losing his faith. He would not approve.

Christmas, 1808, a day of holy remembrance, made tedious and overlong by three hours' attendance under the singsong preaching of Pastor Montre, and the two cold meals which the sanctity of the day permitted. As the family of a pastor of the Seceder Church, and in thankfulness of Divine Grace in saving them from the storm, strict austerity was observed by the Campbells. No meals were

49

cooked for two days before the day of the Nativity. It was a day of solemn observance, undefiled by popish celebration or Episcopal festivity in accordance with the injunction of the Seceder Church, and made more meaningful by receipt of their first letter from Father Thomas, a psalm of thanksgiving and wholehearted approval of their plans. Nevertheless, after the family worship at the close of the day, there were gifts of hand-knitted mittens and shawls, and new, bright plaids and earmuffs, and long woolen underwear, and bannocks and a huge Yorkshire pudding for the evening meal which lost none of its flavor by being placed in a warming pan and set before the blazing hearth for a full hour before suppertime.

Truly the ways of the Lord are good, and His blessings are many to those who love Him.

The second week in May brought the annual observance of the sacred solemnity of the Lord's Supper by the Seceder Church. From early childhood, Alexander had known its significance, the most holy ordinance of the church. As the occasion approached, the officiating elders of the Seceder Church visited and catechized all members in the parish, ascertaining their worthiness to partake of the sacred emblems. Since the Campbells were members of the Seceder Church of Ireland instead of Scotland, they were examined separately by the sessions and duly certified. Each was given a leaden token, attesting to his worthiness.

As a family they attended the two services on Thursday and Friday held in the churchyard of Pastor Montre's church, the three services on Saturday, and the daylong Communion service beginning at nine o'clock on Sunday morning. The devout, as well as the sinners, Alexander noted, were put into a fearful dilemma. They were warned that if they partook of the emblems unworthily they "would be made seven times more of the devil than before," yet they were also told it was a sin to withdraw. "Dare ye bide away," warned Pastor Montre in his Action Sermon, "and give that affront to His Supper and frustrate the grace of God, ye take His wrath upon thee from this holy place!"

As he wandered about the crowded churchyard on the final day,

Alexander was both repelled and attracted by the scene. The farmers in their clean, coarse homespun blouses and breeches, their wives in hodden gray skirts and white aprons, and shawls of scarlet and green with white-ribbed caps drawn close about their ears; the townspeople in their richer apparel; the young lairds, some of them wearing laced three-cornered hats and gay-colored, gilt-braided coats and jackboots escorting their ladies in bright silks and plaids, all blended into a scene which made the churchyard like a "parterre of flowers."

Some of the communicants, he observed, came with fear, not certain that they were Christ's; others came in joy, "having found an interest in Him." Others retired to secluded spots, seeking "light at the throne" until they felt worthy to partake, while still others wandered into the church or out on to the street, pouring out their emotions in moans and tears.

The emblems of unleaven bread, cut into thin slivers on heavy pewter plates, and port wine in pewter goblets covered with napkins of white Irish linen were served to the communicants in solemn succession by the elders and deacons from nine long tables placed upon trestles in the churchyard. Alexander seated his mother and the children at a table and then stepped back and stood against the wall of the church, observing the scene, wrestling with his conscience. Pastor Montre, standing erect in his bob wig and long gray coat and high cravat, speaking in a monotonous clerical singsong that rose in curious melodious cadence in the still spring air, admonished each table by turn before the bread and wine were passed. His talks were interspersed with psalm tunes, broken by alternate reading and singing of each line which rose plaintive and sweet from the chorus of communicants; and the prayers by different pastors, full of earnest pleas, came forth in a stillness broken only by sudden sighs and exclamations.

Long after his mother and the family had partaken, with only Alicia not participating because of her infancy, and Alexander had carted them home in the coach he had hired for the occasion, he waited, his doubts still unresolved, hopeful that at the last he could with conscience join them in the Holy Communion. But it was a communion to which other men had been excluded. Restlessly, he fingered in his pocket the sliver of lead in the shape of a cross, the token that set him apart as one of the worthy.

He went back to the churchyard and watched the clergymen "fencing" the tables, barring from them "all unclean and unworthy persons." At last, in the dusk of the evening, the issue could be evaded no longer. He seated himself at a table, the last to be served by the elders, and listened with waning hope as Pastor Montre addressed it, his flat, sepulchral tones enumerating with elaborate detail the many sins that would render even the most faithful unfit to take part in the sealing ordinance. And then, as the emblems reached him, he slowly and deliberately, a finality about him, his body strained as though with much effort, placed the token on the plate and passed the bread and wine untouched to his neighbor.

There was no outward emotion attached to his action, no display of bombast or renunciation, and whoever may have noticed it, paid him no attention. But in the instant when the leaden token rang dully upon the pewter plate before him, in that instant Alexander Campbell in his heart renounced any allegiance to the Seceder Church of Scotland, or any other ecclesiastical body by whatever name that proclaimed itself the only doorway to the throne of God.

The University examinations came and went, and the sessions drew to a close at the end of May. Alexander's private school also came to a close as the families of most of his pupils, he learned, would spend the summer away from Glasgow. As there was no immediate prospect of obtaining suitable passage to America, he was glad to accept the invitation of Dr. Wardlaw to continue his tutoring at Helensburgh, where the Wardlaws, the Monteiths, the Burns, and the Buchanans would summer. So the second Monday in June found him quartered at the White Horse Inn in the seaside resort, a watering place in Dumbartonshire, opposite Greenock on the north shore of the Clyde, as tutor not only to some of the boys he had taught in the winter but to a group of sons and daughters of local people.

The sudden release from the taxing confinement of his studies and the responsibility for the family cast its spell. He was young, and the girls he tutored in the Lives of the English Poets, Latin Versification and Composition, and walked with in the shady groves and on the beaches, were high-spirited and of his own age. It became an indulgent, an idyllic time for him, a dreamlike march of days. Sometimes he felt a fleeting sense of guilt, as though he had wandered into forbidden gardens, and he would return to the gray-walled emptiness of his room and furiously scribble in his commonplace book overly pious reflections which for the most part were promptly destroyed. And always, at such times, he would lay his pen aside and stare motionless at the vacant walls for a long time before going to bed. Once, after a brief, impulsive embrace in the shadows that rang bells in him for hours, he found himself leafing through his Bible to The Song of Solomon:

For, lo, the winter is past, the rain is over and gone; the flowers appear on the earth; the time of the singing of birds is come, and the voice of the turtle is heard in our land.

He closed the book quickly and went to bed. Love and marriage were not yet for him. His blood might race at the sudden pressure of a soft hand, or the brushing of a fresh young body in its bright silk bodice and ruffled skirt, but he would harden his heart. Although his charges were as beautiful as Tirzah and as comely as Jerusalem, they could also be to him as "terrible as an army with banners."

Desperately, as though he felt himself sinking into a sea of spices, he began to renew his inquiries for passage to America.

Five weeks and two days after his arrival at Helensburgh, he learned that a ship, the *Latonia*, Captain Benjamin McCray master, was scheduled to sail from Greenock for New York in late July. With relief but also with regret, he began to make preparations to leave.

It required about two weeks in Glasgow before he succeeded in making final arrangements for the voyage. The *Latonia* was primarily a merchantman, he discovered, somewhat smaller than the *Hibernia*, with a cargo of woolen goods and linens and seventeen passengers. Although they had every prospect of a safe and a reasonably comfortable voyage, the family took leave of their new friends, and especially the Ewings, with a reluctance that faith and prayer could not completely overcome. On the last day of July they went to Greenock on the flyboat. After two days of final preparations, the *Latonia* weighed anchor on the third day of August 1809.

No sooner were they on the Atlantic than Alexander was confined to his bunk by a seasickness that for three days emptied him of all will to live. When he recovered sufficiently to appear on deck, he learned that the ship had sprung a leak. With only eight seamen on board, besides the mate, the cook, and the cabin boy, the sailors openly feared they would be unable to manage the vessel. But the captain refused to turn back, and ordered the pumps to work. The following day the ship ran into a heavy gale and all male passengers were assigned to assist the sailors at the pumps. Then came a week of calm; and on Tuesday of the third week another gale that cost the *Latonia* her foretopmast. Two harrowing days passed before it could be replaced. Headwinds, calms, the sudden death of a child followed, and then another storm on Sunday, August 27, again took away the foretopmast, with the maintopmast barely escaping the same fate. Soon after the quarter railing was broken off by a heavy sea; then the bowsprit cracked halfway through at its thickest part, the tiller rope gave way, and for a time the ship was unmanageable. The passengers grouped on deck, awaiting the ship's momentary destruction, when the wind veered to the northwest and the storm ceased. The sea still ran heavy, however, and it was not until September 4 that the wind again became fair.

It was on Saturday, September 23, that a kingfisher circled the *Latonia* in a vain attempt to gain a foothold on its rigging and then flew away. The following Tuesday the dim outlines of Sandy Hook could be discerned, and the next day, for the first time in fifty-three days, the passengers obtained a distinct view of land. Taking a pilot off Sandy Hook, they passed through the Narrows and on Friday, September 29, 1809, Alexander gazed with awe and wonder and thanksgiving at the skyline of the city of New York which ringed the harbor like a friendly, encircling hand.

BOOK II

First the Blade

Chapter 5

THEY WERE ELEVEN DAYS FROM NEW YORK NOW, AND ALMOST A DAY'S
wagon journey from Philadelphia, and as he walked beside the horses
Alexander no longer tried to match the long, regular paces of the
wagoner, their feet raising little shuffling whorls of dust on the
road behind them. He was tired, his eyes rimmed with dust, his face
powdered with tiny particles that choked his nostrils and coated his
throat with a fine, feathery burr.

They were walking more slowly now, the two horses settling
into the harness, straining forward into a long, steady pull of the
covered wagon against a steep incline that shut out the view of the
countryside ahead. Soon they would be entering the mountain
country; then would come the rolling hills and valleys, and somewhere, days beyond, was Father Thomas, waiting for them in the
town of Washington, Pennsylvania.

Alexander's eyes grew somber as he thought of his father. The
older man did not know his son no longer counted himself a member of the Seceder Church, or of any of its divisions. Even Mrs.
Campbell had not been told. There would be time enough to tell
them all about it; time enough for many things in this land of freedom and opportunity. Perhaps he could find a school to teach, or
start one; maybe he could work on a farm, and someday even own
one. And if he should decide to preach the Word of God, it would
be as a man free of all restrictions after the manner of Greville Ewing
and the Haldane brothers, and Alexander Carson.

They were almost at the top of the hill now, and the deep-chested field horses stopped, their legs slightly atremble, their sides lathered with sweat. Alexander rubbed the white streak in the forehead of the one nearer him.

"Good animals you have here, Mr. Hunter," he said. "But thirsty if I know my horses. They've come many a furlong today."

John Hunter, a lean, bearded man who might have been thirty or sixty, stepped from beside the horses, a broad grin on his face.

"They've been over this road plenty of times," he said. "They know what's ahead. They're just taking a breather before the last pull up the hill. Give a horse his head and he'll do the smart thing every time. That's better'n a lot of folks I could name, as won't."

"Not meaning anything personal?" Alexander grinned.

"Not meaning nothing personal," repeated Hunter. "Now, you keep your eyes open and your wits about you, and you'll be seeing something mighty purty purty soon."

He clucked to the horses and they moved ahead. And it was a sight worth waiting for, Alexander agreed a half-hour later as he stood with the teamster and gazed into the valley below.

Directly ahead a two-story tavern, sheltered along its side by a row of stables and sheds, cast a deep purple shadow against a small clearing, while on all sides of it stretched an unbroken forest tinged in the autumn sunlight with gold and scarlet and green. There were comparatively few trees in his native Ireland, or in the Glasgow region, and for a moment Alexander stared in wonder.

"That's the William Penn Tavern," said Hunter. "One of the best on the road. Man who runs it says he's a distant kin of old William Penn himself. We've done nigh thirty miles today, and I calculate that's fair enough for the first day out, especially considering we'll be going into rugged country tomorrow. Your ma and the young 'uns will like it here."

A sudden clamor under the canvas cover of the wagon and Hunter and Alexander climbed without a word onto the driver's seat, the horses jogging faster now, anticipating the comfort of clean straw and fresh hay, the wagon bed under them vibrating as though

58

in a pleasurable excitement. Tommie braced his feet wide apart behind his elder brother's back and encouraged the horses with whoops and yells in which Archibald and Alicia lustily joined.

" 'Tis a lively bunch ye have here, ma'am." Mr. Hunter turned and directed his comment directly to Mrs. Campbell, sitting on a stool in the wagon bed. "But don't ye worry none. They'll all be plumb tuckered out long afore we cross them mountains." He waved his whip in the general direction of the mist-covered range in the distance, and then cracked it merrily above the horses.

Mrs. Campbell smiled wearily in reply, and in a few minutes they circled past the stables and barns and came to a full, slow stop before the broad open door of the William Penn.

The wide-porched building was built of blue limestone, with white window frames and green Venetian shutters; the stables and sheds and outbuildings beside it circled a great wooden trough supplied by an everlasting spring. Although it was still early twilight, the forty-foot porch that extended across the front was already clustered with guests: men, women, and children, travelers all, cleaned and refreshed and taking their ease in the high-backed, cane-bottomed rockers. Others stood about in knots of bantering talk. In the yard a group of men was playing quoits, ringed by eager watchers, while other men were grooming their horses before turning them loose to romp within the log-notched enclosure behind the stables.

Two Negro boys came running to help the new arrivals as the guests turned to eye them with friendly curiosity; men and women in homespun for the most part, a few in silks, but an earthy elegance about even the most rustic of them, a sturdiness that was almost a swagger, it seemed to Alexander as he unconsciously contrasted their attitude with the defiance, or obeisance, so much the manner of those in the old country.

"First come are best served," cautioned Hunter. "You folks better 'tend to your rooms while I look after the horses. I'll scrub up and see you in the common room after supper."

Mr. William Penn VI, a rotund, redheaded, perpetually flushed middle-aged man with a loose-fitting calfskin coat and leather leggings, and with a cartridge belt slanted across his hips, welcomed them himself and took them to two upstairs bedrooms which, with the introduction of cots, would furnish them comfortable shelter for the night.

"You're the lucky ones," he assured them. "The Richmond–Philadelphia coach is due and we'll be making up pallets in the common room after that." He bowed as low as his waistline would permit, a gallantry in him. "Any lady and her bairns from auld Ireland are welcome here. Or from bonny Scotland either," he added hastily. "Even a bloody Britisher can have a pallet if he takes his nose from the air and pays for it in advance. That's the William Penn way. Cash on the barrelhead, and brotherly love for all."

With a smile Alexander handed over his purse of coin. "I had some quid changed in New York," he said. "Here, take what is due you. I am not yet used to American money."

The landlord snapped open the purse and gazed affectionately at its contents. "Good George Washington money," he said. "Not a Continental in the lot. You were lucky there. Congress will redeem it, so they tell me, but we nearly went broke before the bloody British would take their licking and go home." He extracted two huge shining dollars and handed back the purse. " 'Tis enough to charge a bonny lady and her bairns, fresh from the auld country," he said. "Supper is at the ring of the bell, and breakfast at six in the morning. Mine house is thine!"

He bowed again with a flourish and with the Negro porter left the room, his footsteps loud on the rough planked stairway.

"He is no Irishman." Alexander turned to his mother. "Or a Dutchman either. That mon is a canny Highland Scot if I ever saw one. He will not risk his rental for the night."

" 'There's na gude in speaking ill of the laird in his ain bounds,' " quoted his mother. "You were the foolish Irish one, handing him a closed pocket of money."

"He charged us less than if I had asked him the price," Alexander said shrewdly. "Come along, boys. If you scrub up real fast, maybe we can take a look around before the bell rings."

60

Supper was over now, a lingering, tempting, ample meal, and even Tommie and Archibald were torpid with appeasement when at last the family rose from the long bench beside the table and trooped into the common room. The room ran the length of the building and was almost full, the round pine tables crowded about with men and a few women playing cards and checkers and drinking beer from great pewter and earthenware mugs; the air thick with the smoke of strong tobacco; the wooden shutters open to permit relief from the heat of the iron stove against the wall with its pot of simmering, vaporizing water. Some of the latecomers would sleep on pallets already being placed in parallel rows on the dining-room floor; others would sit and drink, and exchange tall stories, and discuss the Embargo Act and the policies of President Madison and the younger generation of statesmen such as Henry Clay and John C. Calhoun who were rising to take the place in American politics of the aging Revolutionary fathers, and finally stagger to bed more drunk than sober, to rise with the first streak of morning light and resume their journeys.

The scene was new and strange and fascinating to the Campbells, an air of bustling energy and individuality and independence and hope so different from the rigid, formalized life they had known. This was America, the land of equal justice and unlimited opportunity to every man. As they sat and watched, they talked little, absorbing the feel of the place, even Tommie and Archibald subsiding finally into drowsy silence which in the torpor of the room and the drone of voices passed into sleep.

At a nod from his mother, Alexander picked up the boys and carried them squirming to their room while she followed with the girls. Then to quiet them after he had tumbled them into bed and heard their prayers, he blew out the candle and stretched full length upon the pallet beside them, the moonlight filtering through the shuttered windows as though to place upon each of them its silver band of welcome. He was used to late hours and early rising, and a straining glance at his silver-plated watch told him it was not yet nine o'clock. He stirred restlessly, and crossed his legs, and stared at the rough beamed ceiling, the noises of the common room coming to him in a subdued drone through the closed door; covering again in his thoughts the travels of the day. America was a land of trees —uncounted forests of them, stretching interminably into the distance. And every man in America was like a tree, standing straight and tall before the Lord as a free man should. He stared at Tommie and Archibald in the rope bed, sound asleep now, their faces above the patchwork quilt flushed, like rosy beacons of the future. Soon their memories of Rich Hill and Glasgow and even of the storm at sea would grow dim, and their native land become a fading picture. They would be like the trees of the forest about them, proud and independent; their roots deep in the soil of this new world which would be their home.

Noiselessly he arose and after a moment stood outside the bedroom door of his mother and the girls. But no sound came from within. Like the boys, they were asleep now, or perhaps staring at the ceiling, too tired to sleep, too restless. He hesitated, his hand reaching for the iron knob. But he wouldn't disturb them. They needed their sleep.

The common room was thinning now. Only a few stalwarts sat at the round tables in the center of the room with their pewter mugs before them, bent over their cards. Even the bar at the front end of the big room was empty except for a solitary bearded woodsman who sprawled lingeringly, his hand gripped about a half-empty mug. William Penn sat on his high stool in the corner near the door, his brows puckered drowsily. He aroused as Alexander passed him and lifted a hand in greeting.

"A nightcap, my son?" he queried hopefully. "A stiff dram of good Irish whiskey to conjure sleep and make you ready for tomorrow's travel? The bar is open for half an hour yet."

Alexander smiled at him. "I have faults aplenty but I don't drink. I've seen enough of it in the old country."

"A teetotaler!" Penn scoffed at him, his hands on his knees as if to brace himself against the shock. "An Irishman fresh from the auld sod who dasn't want his wee drap? I can't believe it! You a preacher?"

"Perhaps," said Alexander. He turned toward the door. "I'm going for a walk."

62

"Most preachers here can take their dram with any man. And can hold it too. Well, go along with you. But remember"—he shook a stubby forefinger in warning—"breakfast is at six o'clock. Heed what old Ben Franklin said: 'Early to bed and early to rise, will make a man healthy, wealthy, and wise.' "

Alexander stopped, his hand on the door, his slow grin twisting his face in a pleasant grimace. "Benjamin Franklin was a great man," he said. "As great as even William Penn the First. They make me proud that I'm going to live in Pennsylvania."

The wide-planked porch was darkened now except for a single four-sided candled lamp swinging from the center of the ceiling, the chairs backed decorously against the wall. For a moment Alexander stood on the stone steps, half-expecting his host to follow him with some parting repartee. He could hear the water bubbling gently in the horse trough by the stables to his right as he made his way softly across the yard toward the row of pines, tall sentinels of the forest, that stretched on all sides of the cluster of buildings like a dark, rustling sea. For a moment he thought of waking John Hunter, asleep over the stables. But none of this would be new to Hunter. He saw it often and would be tired and grumpy, wondering why he had been awakened.

For ye shall go out with joy, and ye shall be led forth with peace: the mountains and the hills shall break forth before you into singing, and all the trees of the fields shall clap their hands.

The words of Isaiah came to him as clearly as though they had been spoken in his ear. "Ye shall go out with joy." He plunged ahead, his footsteps against the soft, cracking pine needles reverberating in the stillness. He reached the woods and walked slowly, feeling his way, carefully to keep in mind his sense of direction, an awe in him. He had never before felt such a communion with nature; man was his prime concern, he had always thought. But then, he had never been in a forest before.

There was no sound now beyond the rustling of the trees and the occasional fall of a ripened pine cone. If animals were about, they kept their distance, suspicious of him. In the filtered moonlight he

63

could make out logs, strewn about as though by an impetuous hand among the trees; trees of oak, hickory, beech, their scarlet and orange leaves faintly discernible against the darker background of the pines. He thrust his hands in his pockets and stood, looking up, the leaves spreading like a canopy dotted with peepholes through which the light of the moon filtered. After a moment he seated himself on a stump, hugging his knees to his chest, and the years fell away and he was a boy again in Rich Hill.

He thought of Molly, the cow the family had owned, and almost laughed aloud. Father Thomas had ordered him to translate from the French the story of Telemachus. But it was dull stuff then, and when the time to recite had come, Father Thomas had found him fast asleep in a corner of the farm, the book he had placed beside him wrecked, and the story of Telemachus stored in the cud of the family cow. Almost he seemed to smart again in recollection as the memory of this final thrashing fell upon him.

"That cow has more French in her stomach," Father Thomas had said, as he wielded the birch, "than you have in your head! No son of mine can sleep away the day while others work!"

And work he did on the farm thereafter without the urge or use of books, until he began to feel the need of them and Father Thomas, delighted, reinstated him as a scholar. A wise and just man was Father Thomas.

And then the hunger for books had crowded upon him, never appeased once his mind had awakened to their riches—the days at Rich Hill; his duties as his father's assistant in the day school; Uncle Archibald's school at Newry where he taught; the countless hours of reading, guided by his father; the memorizing of whole chapters in the Bible; the wonderful months at Glasgow. And now he sat alone at night on a vine-covered stump in a Pennsylvania forest.

He had been surprised at New York. Somehow he had expected it to have wide, uncluttered spaces with men wearing boots and beaver caps and hunting knives, and even feathered Indians stalking about. New York was like Glasgow, with more than one hundred thousand people packed into its narrow, winding streets on its little island. But the buildings, unlike Glasgow, were newly built, of brick with slated or shingled roofs, and many of the streets were lined with trees. Only a week ago he had walked the length of Bloomingdale Road, from the Battery to the Bowery Road, marveling at it all—the poplar trees that lined it; the Customs House; Trinity Church; the white-marbled City Hall, the most elegant building in the city that fronted that tiny triangular piece of ground called The Park, where people sat and talked and made their plans and were proud of their city, and made no secret of their pride; the Fly Market, the pride of Manhattan, where beef, mutton, and veal sold for nine cents a pound and enough for all. The two-room lodging the family had secured on Chatham Street had been comfortable, and he recalled how the family had walked from it to the brick Seceder Church off Greenwich Street where they had sat in passive admiration that first Sunday in America under the flaying eloquence of Dr. John M. Mason. Then had come the three-day journey to Philadelphia by wagon, as no coach could hold all their luggage.

Philadelphia had seemed even larger than New York but there was about it a more comfortable sense of space with its broader streets, lined with trees and brick houses with white steps and names that suggested the deep forest: Mulberry, Sassafras, Chestnut, Walnut, Locust, Spruce. And High, or Market, Street as they were beginning to call it, at least one hundred feet broad, running the length of the city, so different from the High Street he knew in Glasgow. The dome-topped Water Works in Center Square, its drinking water conducted through wooden pipes from the Schuylkill River a mile away, had placed fountains in every street. William Penn, he had been told, had planned for a park by the Delaware River but that spot had become Front Street, thickly covered with wharves, warehouses, and shops. The Market Place on High Street had goods at prices even lower than in New York; and every organized faction of the Lord's people was represented in the churches, with the Presbyterians outnumbering even the founding Quakers.

It had been a busy, happy weekend they had spent in this City of Brotherly Love, and after he had chanced upon John Hunter and

65

hired him for the following Monday, they had made the most of it, and what they could not see for lack of time, Hunter had told them. The imposing State House and the adjoining Court House and Philosophical Hall intrigued him. Its Philosophical Society had been founded, Hunter said, by Benjamin Franklin himself in 1769, and already had several learned published works to its credit. Alexander liked Philadelphia. Somehow it was more like the America he had expected than New York.

The darkness settled more thickly about him as the moon went under a cloud; something moved in the pine needles before him, then slithered away into the darkness, its long coils making a stealthy, sinister sound. He stretched to his full height, a sudden strain about him as he flexed his arms, suddenly aware that he was cramped and chilled. There was evil in the world, too. As firmly as he believed in an all-loving God, he believed in a force of evil which some called the devil. He turned and began to retrace his steps back to the tavern.

Again they were in the open country, the road hard-packed, the rising sun bathing the earth in a resplendent light. It had been difficult getting up this morning; even the lively chatter of his young brothers had not awakened him until the voice of his mother, tinged with an unaccustomed excitement, had aroused him in time to follow the family downstairs to a breakfast of ham and hominy, with side dishes of hard-boiled eggs and fresh honey, and mugs of steaming black coffee that Landlord Penn had said had been imported from Brazil and which he reserved for special guests. The landlord had been warm and jovial, and Alexander thanked him for leaving the front double doors unlatched and a candle lighted for him inside the doorway the night before.

"This is Pennsylvania," William Penn VI had reminded him. "We country people never lock our doors over here. And I left a candle for you because no Dubliner could find his way home from the pubs, or the woods either, without a street lamp to guide him. I had pity on you."

Alexander grinned, while his brothers tugged impatiently at his coat. "I've never seen Dublin, but I was out too late," he admitted.

"Your forest cast a spell on me. I like it here. One day I'll be coming back."

The landlord slapped him good-humoredly on the back. "Naturally. And then maybe you'll be a two-fisted drinking man like a good Scots-Irish-American woodsman should be, and you'll patronize my bar. You'll change afore you know it, my young friend. Time works fast in this country."

Alexander laughed. He liked the jovial William Penn. He liked his tavern, the best they had seen. And he could well agree that time could work its changes quickly in this new land.

They were all in the wagon, settling down for the long day that stretched ahead, Alexander beside John Hunter. For a time they drove in silence, the countryside becoming more rugged, the patches of cleared land with their solitary log farmhouses few and far between. Indians still roamed this region and sometimes warred against the whites, Hunter had said; panthers and bears and wolves lurked in the woods, and even daytime travel could be full of danger on these narrow, rutted, hard-packed roads. Alexander glanced back to see his mother, seated on the pallet in the rear of the wagon, talking softly, her arms about Alicia and Jane, while Dorothea and Nancy across from her listened. He did not see the boys but they were there, listening drowsily, or in a last tenuous sleep before planning their mischief for the day.

Soon they began to enter the more rugged country of central Pennsylvania, the road sometimes hardly more than a trail against the side of a mountain, at other times descending through forest so dense it seemed a heavy veil had been drawn over the face of the sun. At such times the spirits of the party dampened, and unconsciously they huddled together. Never in all their lives had they seen so many trees, crowded untold thousands of them, stretching into the interminable distance. The forests in Ireland and Scotland had been slaughtered for man's need long before their time, and the motley patches of woods that still existed were like distant sickly relatives of these magnificent forests, stretching their long branches across the narrow road as though in sheltering protection. Prodded by their eager interest, Hunter pointed out the yellow maples, the scarlet oaks, the broad-leafed laurel, the mountain ash, and in the less thickly timbered regions the dwarfed black oak and the tall hemlock.

Each day's journey was as different as the moods of the sea. Sometimes at the top of a mountain ridge they could see parallel ridges stretching endlessly toward the southwest; descending into the valley they would come upon cultivated farms with wheat and a hard-kerneled stalk grain that John Hunter called Indian corn, already gathered into long barns never far from the house; occasionally they saw a gathering of houses into a village, with a blacksmith shop and a general store and sometimes a post office. Sometimes they met other wagons; and twice they met with the elliptical-shaped wheeled stagecoaches drawn by teams of four horses, which John Hunter said were coming into fashion, the luggage strapped onto a rack in the rear, the whole thing suspended on thoroughbraces, or heavy leather springs, which lifted the body off the axles and cushioned the heavier jolts of the road, the passengers sitting with cramped legs and feet facing each other in the narrow seats. Such a contraption might be for style but not for her, said Mrs. Campbell. Their wagon bed at least was broad, with room for stretching out for sleep if one did not mind the bumps and jolts. The vehicles paused, and the passengers got out and stretched their legs, and there was friendly inquiry and conversation until the drivers cracked their long whips, and the parties went again their separate ways with much waving and many good-bys, as if they were long-parted friends.

The inns were located in the valleys, scattered along the road at intervals of ten and twenty miles, by streams or bubbling springs, all of them built on the same general design, Alexander learned, with the sleeping quarters upstairs and the stables and sheds sheltering the tavern on one side; some of them of log construction, others of blue limestone of which there seemed an abundance, and which contrasted pleasantly with the white mortar between the blocks and the white window frames and green shutters. Twice it rained, heavy downpours of water that turned the road into mud and sent them all under the canvas of the wagon.

Another day or two and they would cross Chestnut Ridge, Hunter told them, the most western of the mountain ranges, and would begin their descent into the great plain of the Mississippi River stretching hundreds of miles into the west. And then the crossing of the Monongahela River, and they would be in Washington County.

They were ascending Chestnut Ridge on the tenth day, the family all walking with the exception of Jane and Alicia to lighten the load and for warmth against the chill of the October morning.

Suddenly the muffled clatter of galloping hoofs was heard, coming toward them. A posse of some kind, thought Alexander, or some state dignitary honored by an escort of horsemen. He had been walking ahead and he looked back. The others had heard it, too. Hunter had stopped the wagon, waving the family to one side, waiting until the horsemen should draw abreast. The road stretched ahead almost level for a hundred yards, and then rose steeply; the last hard pull before the summit.

As the horsemen appeared over the ridge, Tommie and Archibald ran to Alexander and he guided them to one side. There were two riders. They pulled up sharply at sight of the straggling company, and sat staring for a moment. There was no word spoken as the smaller of the two men dismounted with an awkward, stumbling movement and stood motionless, his fur cap slipping from his head, his thin brown hair ruffled in the breeze.

Unbelieving, a shining tenseness upon her, Mrs. Campbell started to push forward and then drew back. Slowly she extended her arms, her voice choked.

The other rider dismounted and gave the horses loose rein at the roadside, and as John Hunter stood solicitously by his team, Alexander ran to take Jane and Alicia from the wagon while Thomas Campbell went forward with short, stumbling steps to greet his family.

"My little bairns!" he called to them. "My little Irish towheads!"

Chapter 6

ALEXANDER GREETED HIS FATHER LAST. FOR A MOMENT THEY STARED silently at each other, their hands locked tight.

"My son!" said Father Thomas. And with the words he pronounced a blessing of respect and gratitude and affection.

It was John Hunter who broke the spell by climbing back onto his wagon seat and cracking his long whip in reminder that it was almost noon and there were still many miles to go. The children got into the wagon beside their parents while Alexander took the saddle vacated by Father Thomas and rode with his father's companion, John McElroy, toward the summit of the ridge.

McElroy, he found, talked readily, proud of his friendship with the Scots-Irish preacher and quick to extend it to his son. He was a farmer near Washington, a backsliding Methodist, he said, who had first heard Thomas Campbell preach a year before and had been his friend ever since. And when Thomas had told him he planned to ride eastward to meet his family, McElroy had offered to accompany him. They had left Washington two days before and with two days' steady driving could be there again.

They reached the summit and unconsciously reined in the horses and gazed about. The road behind them was hardly more than a cleared trail through the scraggly underbrush; toward the west it descended gradually with serpentine turns and twists into a thickening forest, the land leveling out into a broad plateau, with here and there spots of cleared ground.

"I feel like Moses on Mt. Sinai," Alexander said, his feet unconsciously tightening in his stirrups. "It looks like the Promised Land."

"It's like this for hundreds of miles." McElroy stretched his hands toward the west. "It's the upper part of the Mississippi and Ohio River valleys, the richest land on earth, and most of it unsettled. I fought against the British at Brandywine and Monmouth for this land, and was under arms at White Plains when Cornwallis surrendered to General Washington at Yorktown. I was young-grown and maybe harum-scarum, but I knew what I was fighting for. It *is* the Promised Land!"

It was late afternoon, and Alexander was riding with his father now, ahead of the wagon, their course now past a field of long, dry-leafed stalks swaying rigidly in the gentle October breeze. Cornstalks —Father Thomas designated them with a wave of his hand; Indian maize, already plucked for the harvest, a staple food, both palatable and nourishing, and with tobacco the American Indian's gift to the human race. They crossed a brook that had meandered along the side of the roadway and then cut across it as though impatient of restraint, and entered a scattered forest of oak and ash and black walnut trees. A mile beyond was the Frontier Tavern where they would spend the night.

As they topped a rise in the road, Father Thomas reined in and looked back over the twisting road, the slow-moving wagon far behind them. He motioned Alexander to pull up beside him and then started forward again in a slow walk, their mounts side by side.

"You wanted to talk with me, son?" His face crinkled into an understanding smile. "Something you couldn't put into a letter?"

Alexander's face colored. He had written of his friendship with Greville Ewing and his admiration for the Haldane brothers and Alexander Carson and the others. His father had read between the lines.

He nodded, groping for words. "I've—well, I've changed my religious views," he said finally. He turned in the saddle and faced his father. "You should know that I no longer consider myself a member of the church."

Father Thomas stared at him, a blankness in his face. His hands trembled as he reined in his horse and together they sat, oblivious of their surroundings, staring at each other as though in sudden shock.

"You mean—you have renounced God?"

Alexander reached out and in an unconscious gesture of supplication placed his broad hand on the bridle arm of the little man beside him. "No, Father Thomas, I hope I am a better Christian than I have ever been." His hand tightened as though to force the other into belief. "But I no longer can accept the Anti-Burgher Seceder Branch of the Presbyterian Church as the only church of Jesus Christ, and only the members of that sect as my Christian brothers. I declined the last Communion for that reason." He withdrew his hand and slapped the end of his reins lightly against the neck of his mount to draw away, unwilling longer to bear the pain and doubt and struggling hope in his father's face.

"You have become a member of the National Church perhaps? Or an Independent?"

"No, sir. I have rejected all church parties, all man-made creeds. Christ alone is my creed! All Christians are my brothers!" He paused, and when he spoke again a despair was in his voice. "I'm sorry, Father. I was afraid you wouldn't understand."

Father Thomas let the reins fall and clasped his hands together before him. He blinked rapidly to clear away the moisture in his eyes. In the distance came the rumble of the wagon, still hidden from view by the winding road, the chatter of laughing voices now distinctly heard.

" 'Eye hath not seen, nor ear heard, neither has it entered into the heart of man the things that God hath prepared for them that love Him.' " The older man spoke in benediction, his voice hoarse with emotion. "The older I grow, son, the more I realize the truth of that divine statement. I have never been so happy!"

Alexander looked his astonishment and Father Thomas smiled, glancing back at the wagon drawing close behind them. "I'll tell you why tonight." He spoke hoarsely, a joy in his face, and spurred his horse forward.

The Frontier Tavern was no different from other taverns they had visited except that it was built entirely of logs with a thatched roof, and the floor of the common room was of white sand gathered, so the landlord said, fresh each week from nearby sand hills. The food was generous, and the other guests, leather-jacketed, bearded men for the most part, were mindful of their own business but quick enough to show friendliness. Supper was a merry occasion, the family grouped about a rough-hewn table in a corner of the big room, and then they trooped to the upper-floor bedroom where Father Thomas conducted family worship, gladly attended by both Hunter and McElroy, a deep rejoicing in them all at the ultimate goodness of God.

After the younger children had been bundled into bed in an adjoining room, and Hunter and McElroy had stomped their way downstairs, Father Thomas sat down beside his wife at the end of the room in the only two chairs the room afforded, a twin-candled lamp on a low table between them. The three older girls sat on the broad plank bed that extended from the wall, with Alexander standing just within the closed doorway, his arms folded across his chest.

Dorothea looked about at her brother, and as their glances met, her deep brown eyes, so like her father's, lighted with a sudden roguishness. "Do give us the news about Hannah Acheson, Father. Alexander has been worried she would up and marry before we got here."

Alexander grinned, his naturally high color deepening. "And if you have any young men in Washington between the ages of, say, twenty and sixty, tell us about them. Our Dorry, you know, isn't getting any younger!"

Mrs. Campbell shook her head, disapproving, while Father Thomas nodded at his children in fatherly pride. After a separation of nearly three years he was again in the heart of his family, and he beamed with the joy of it. He took out the gold snuffbox that had descended to him from his soldier Romanist-Episcopal father, Archibald, and ceremoniously took a pinch of snuff, and then he spoke, a half-repressed smile crinkling the corners of his lips.

73

"We can sympathize with Alexander's concern," he said in mock solemnity. "Hannah is a fine girl. She behaved like a dutiful daughter coming over with me on the *Brutus*, high-spirited but well-disposed. I became quite fond of her. I understand from her father that she is well attended with beaux, and it may be that your brother is too late."

"You can see what I have been put against these two years." Mrs. Campbell smiled at her husband. "Your bairns missed the firm hand of their father more than you realize. Will your itinerary permit you to be at home fairly often, Mr. Campbell?"

Father Thomas wet his lips, as though measuring his words. "I have no itinerary, wife. I am no longer a minister of the Presbyterian Church."

A silence greeted his words, as though some unseen force had suddenly sucked the breath from their bodies.

"God never deserts His own in time of trouble." Mrs. Campbell spoke at last, quietly. "He will not desert us now. What happened, Mr. Campbell?"

Alexander sat down heavily on the end of the bed beside his sisters, tense. He leaned forward, his hands clenched, staring at his father, who glanced at him and nodded, as if reading his thoughts.

"Yes, son, it happened to me, too," he said. He turned to include the others. "My itinerary called for me to visit certain scattered members of the flock in the Alleghenies near Pittsburgh," he began slowly. "With a young Reverend William Wilson I was to conduct a sacramental celebration of the Lord's Supper. I found in the flock of Anti-Burghers some other Presbyterians who had not had the opportunity for some time of partaking of the Holy Sacrament. I invited them as Christians to join us. That was my crime, my children." His voice stopped, a fading away of the syllables, a slow smile softening the sternness in his face.

" 'By their fruits ye shall know them,' " quoted the practical Jane. "There must have been a spy in camp, Father."

Father Thomas joined in the laughter, a pent-up release from strain, and then his face sobered again. "Not exactly a spy. But while Brother Wilson offered no objection at the time, he felt it his duty to file a libel against me at the next meeting of the Chartiers Presbytery, charging me with violation of the rules of the church."

Alexander leaned back against the rough pine wall, a surge of admiration for his father welling within him. While he had felt courageous in quietly rejecting the leaden token because he could not sanction the exclusion of other Christians from the Communion, this little man, alone and without support except his own conscience, had deliberately offered Communion to those excluded because of theological opinion. He had taken positive action to remedy the wrong to which his son had only passively objected at Glasgow. He spoke almost gruffly to hide his emotion.

"And then what happened? Did the Presbytery censure you?"

"It did. I appealed to the Synod, but while it set aside the formal verdict of the Presbytery because of irregularities in the proceedings, a committee appointed to rule upon the charge upheld the censure. And then, may the Lord forgive me, like Peter, I weakened." He paused and looked about at the faces of his family as if pleading for understanding. "I had no wish to leave the church," he went on. "I merely wanted to be free to love and minister to all Christians, all children of God. So I submitted to the censure although I filed a declaration that I did so as an act of deference to the judgment of the court and to show I had no refractory spirit. I had hoped that this submission would placate those who opposed me. But it did not. Religious intolerance is a dreadful thing; I do believe that if some of those who opposed me had had their will, nothing but the law of the land would have kept my head on my shoulders."

"What happened?" Alexander pressed, his voice hoarse.

"The Presbytery did not give me any preaching assignments; I was accused by some of heresy and infidelity; I was constantly watched. And so, at the next assembly of the Synod in Philadelphia last September, I resigned from the Associate Synod of North America. Like Peter, I recovered my courage and renewed my faith. I am now simply a Christian."

Alexander swallowed and ran his hand across his face, the wonder growing in him at the ways of God. Separated by thousands of miles of land and sea, with no communication on the subject, he and his

75

father had reached the same turning point in their religious views.

"To think of you being all alone in this wild country with all that trouble!" Dorothea's voice enveloped them like a warm cloak. "If we had known, we could at least have prayed for you!"

"Why, you're a martyr, Father!" said Jane gleefully. "Just like Stephen and the Apostles!"

Suddenly the room was a babel of voices, filled with relief and love and admiration. For a few moments Father Thomas sat awkwardly as the warmth of their affection swept over him, and then began to fidget nervously for his snuffbox.

"I am still a preacher, my dear ones. I will always be a teacher and a preacher of the Word," he said. "But at last I have found the creed that is above all creeds, and abolishes all creeds, the only rule that any Christian need follow to be a true disciple of Jesus Christ."

"What is that, Father?" Alexander asked quickly.

" 'Where the Scriptures speak, we speak; where the Scriptures are silent, we are silent.' No Christian can ask for clearer guidance than that. The silence of the Bible is to be respected as much as its revelations, and the opinions of men upon matters it does not make clear must never be forced upon others."

"What do you do then with the Westminster Confession, the Nicene Creed, the Augsburg Confession of Martin Luther, and the other creeds? Do you repudiate them?"

"I read them, my son, as the opinion of men. They are not divine revelations, and their multiplicity tends to divide Christians into warring, sectarian camps and hinders the spread of the Gospel. In their essence, man-made creeds are the greatest triumph of the devil!"

"Father Thomas, have you started an independent church," asked Dorothea. "Like Dr. Ewing in Glasgow?"

Father Thomas arose and walked the length of the room and back. "There are some who claim I am trying to start a new church party," he said quietly. "As though I would create another division in the body of our Lord if I could! The church of Christ upon this earth is essentially, intentionally, and constitutionally one. That is what our Saviour taught and that is what I preach. No, I have started no church."

"How do you expect to spread this idea, then?" asked Alexander.

"We have formed a society—a society of Christian believers. Some of them belong to the denominations, a few are members of no sect. We have banded together not to advocate a separation from the church but to bring about a rebirth within the church."

"That's a wonderful idea!" Dorothea exclaimed. "You have great faith, Father!"

"Father is a man of faith," said Nancy loyally. "And the Bible says faith can do anything."

Father Thomas smiled his gratitude and turned to his wife, her needle clicking furiously against her china darning ball. "You have been through more than any good wife should have to bear, and now to ask this of you," he said tenderly. "But I could do no other, wife. The Lord led me."

"I am sure of it, Mr. Campbell," she said. "I have never doubted the care of the Lord to those who trust Him."

"What do you call your organization?" Alexander asked.

"The Christian Association," Father Thomas replied.

"You found others, then, who agreed with you?"

"I found to my surprise that after I left the Presbytery I preached to larger groups than before! I preached in groves, in the homes of friends, wherever a group would gather to hear me. Last July some of us met at the home of Abraham Alters, a non-churchman, and agreed to adopt the rule: 'Where the Scriptures speak, we speak; and where the Scriptures are silent, we are silent.' We agreed to work with other Christians, acting on the principle voiced years ago by Rupertus Meldenius: 'In essentials unity; in non-essentials liberty; in all things, charity.' Now we are meeting most of the time in a log building we put up at the crossroads of the Washington–Middletown pikes."

Alexander drew a long breath. "I am struck with the similarity of your views with the Haldanes and Dr. Ewing and Alexander Carson," he said thoughtfully.

"Yes," replied Father Thomas. "But where they are still seeking the formula, as I gathered from your letters, we have found it. At the request of the Association I have written it down. We call it 'The Declaration and Address.' It's being printed now."

He stood up and placed his arm affectionately about his wife's shoulders. "Is anyone else as tired as I am?" He smiled at the group and then said quietly, "Let us say our prayers and go to bed."

One by one they knelt, a silence upon them all, and then Father Thomas began to pray—a dedicated man leading his family humbly and thankfully and in hope into the presence of his Lord.

Chapter 7

THE NEXT TWO DAYS WERE A HAPPY, BUSY TIME, ALL TRACES OF SHY-ness gone now from the children. As easily and naturally as though they had never been separated Father Thomas resumed his position as the head of the family and source of authority. And there were no further discussions of religion. Instead, Father Thomas, aided heartily by John McElroy and Hunter, regaled them with stories of the country, of which they could never hear enough.

In the early afternoon of the second day they ferried across the Monongahela River at Williamsport, and found themselves in Washington County. By nightfall they were at the home of Reverend Samuel Ralston, a Presbyterian minister who had retained his close friendship with Father Thomas despite their theological differences, where they spent the night, nourished in body and spirit by the warm hospitality which the frontier reserved for its own. And the next afternoon, Monday, October 28, the thirteenth day of their journey from Philadelphia, they passed the last rolling hill that ringed the valley of the Chartiers and drove into the frontier village which was to be their home.

Washington, Pennsylvania, in 1809 was a borough of a thousand people, situated on rising ground near the sources of Chartiers, Ten-Mile, and Buffalo creeks. It was a rapidly growing town, the seat of Washington County, and an important trading center, its cultural atmosphere fostered by three-year-old Washington College, already boasting fifty students, and with a Seceder Presbyterian Church, a Nationalist, or Union, Presbyterian Church, and an Anglican Church to call the righteous to worship. It even had a weekly newspaper, the Washington *Reporter*, established the year before. The meetinghouse of the Christian Association was seven miles away at the Washington–Middletown crossroads.

It was a comfortable, energetic-looking place, Alexander thought as they drove down straggling Market Street. Eight general merchandise stores dotted the street, their square roofs extending in the front over brick-paved entrances. Wooden benches for customers with no immediate urge to trade flanked the doorways. They passed tree-shaded Washington Tavern opposite the square brick two-story courthouse with a cupola like a church tower topped by an arrow weather vane on a metal globe. In front of the courthouse a ten-foot watering trough fed by a gurgling spring invited refreshment for man and beast. Behind a sprawling blacksmith shop they could see the back of box-shaped Washington College fronting Chartiers Street.

People turned to stare as their canvas-covered wagon rumbled by, and then waved in welcome as they recognized the bouncing figure of the little Scots-Presbyterian preacher on his spotted gray mare riding close alongside. Only Mrs. Campbell, seated between her smiling eldest son and the calmly appraising John Hunter, seemed for the moment removed from the scene, her eyes suddenly misty, her brown bonnet falling loosely behind her dark hair. These rough log buildings in this raw, unsettled country were a long way from the centuries-old stone houses of Rich Hill or Ahorey or Glasgow. But it was home now. And the past, like the records of the prophet of Israel, was a closed book. She turned to her son as they passed the watering trough where two saddlebagged horsemen turned to stare at them solemnly, to find his eyes upon her, a soberness in his face as though he had been caught unawares. He placed his hand over hers and patted it gently.

"You'll like it, Mother," he told her. "It will be worth all the trouble and more, once you get used to it." He pressed her hand, and to cover his emotion, turned and waved impulsively at a slight, youngish bearded man leaning against the front of a low log building bearing the sign, the Washington *Reporter*.

At some of the intersecting lanes crude signs had been erected— Spruce Alley, Chestnut Street, Cherry Alley—and when they came to a roadway, hardly more than a path, reading "Strawberry Alley," Father Thomas and McElroy turned and led the way down the rutted road toward a square two-storied log house where Chartiers Street dissolved into a field. Even in the gathering darkness it seemed a friendly place, two giant oaks ranged in front like friendly sentinels, their gnarled limbs extending toward them in welcome.

Father Thomas had ridden ahead to open the house, and as the wagon bumped into the yard, the light of an oil lamp streamed from the doorway and sparks began spiraling from the center chimney.

"The preacher aims to make you feel welcome, ma'am," Hunter said, pulling back lightly on the reins.

"That I will," said Mrs. Campbell warmly. "This is a wonderful place." As though the words were a cue, Tommie and Archibald began to pummel each other in sheer exuberance, and as Alexander leaned backward in his seat to separate them, the wagon rolled to the front of the house and stopped with a jolt before the open door.

An hour later both John Hunter and McElroy had gone on their way, Hunter to the Washington Tavern which he declared was one of the best in the state and where he expected to take on freight and passengers for his return journey, and John McElroy to his own farm at Mount Pleasant, an hour's easy jog away. For the first time in almost three years the family was again together in a home of its own.

Situated on the edge of a five-acre wooded field, the house was the largest they had ever had. Built of pine logs, two great square windows, now shuttered, flanked a broad, thick door. Inside, a narrow hallway ran the length of the house, separating the sitting room and kitchen from a downstairs bedroom, and at the far end a rough open stairway led to four bedrooms on the upper floor. At the rear of the house a wagon shed and two-stall barn, a woodhouse packed with cut fire logs, a smokehouse for curing and storing meat, and a branch-covered privy, completed the outbuildings.

"It's a place I rented from Thomas Acheson," Father Thomas explained the next morning as the family finished breakfast in the kitchen. "But if we like it, we can buy it. We'll own a little piece of the United States of America."

Before nightfall their boxes had been unpacked and Mrs. Campbell and the girls began preparation of flax and wool for the wheel and loom. Father Thomas philosophically began the construction of quilting frames while Alexander with his muzzle-loading rifle, and Tommie tagging at his heels, went into the woods for game. Hours later Alexander returned with a brace of rabbits and some quail. As the days passed, they would acquire barnyard fowls, and a sow or two, and carpenter and farming tools, and before they knew it they would be settled in their new home.

"It is a good beginning," said Father Thomas that night. "With the coming of spring, and a crop of oats and corn of our own in the ground, the Campbells will be as self-sufficient as any family in Washington County."

But it was not necessary to wait until next spring to enjoy the feeling of well-being. Within a few days James Foster drove up in a deep-bottomed wagon with a gift of a Berkshire sow already heavy with litter; Thomas Hodgens came with his wife Lucy and his daughter Martha, the wife of Foster, bringing a crate of young hens and pullets and a single crowing rooster in their wagon bed. And then came George Archer with a bushel of Irish potatoes, and William Gilchrist and James Hanan and Abraham Altars, each with a goat to furnish fresh milk for the younger Campbells, and Thomas

Acheson with a wagonload of shucked corn for the cow and a stone crock of peach preserves for the family. The Achesons had been among their oldest and warmest friends in Rich Hill. Thomas Acheson, a widower, had emigrated to America three years before with his two sons, leaving his young daughter Hannah with relatives, eventually to make the journey in Father Thomas' care when her father remarried in the new country. He was one of the most substantial landowners in the area, and by special appointment of the governor himself a brigadier general of the Pennsylvania State Militia.

"The womenfolks have been putting up fruit for a month," he told them proudly. "They're winding up now. That's the reason they couldn't come along. But Hannah said to tell you the preserves are her own specialty." He turned to Alexander in shrewd appraisement. "You'll learn more about women after you marry, son, than your good mother and sisters can ever teach you. They're none the same, but not one of them can stand a man about the house at times like that, more luck to us."

Alexander joined in the general laughter, a sudden wariness upon him. He started to speak when the older man abruptly continued.

"And they're all for telling me the Campbells must come over Sunday after worship for dinner and a good Sabbath visitation, and communion among the saints. We'll not take no for an answer," he said firmly. He turned to Mrs. Campbell. "Fresh from bonny Scotland, ye'll give your tongue a rest from this new way of speaking, and if we canna talk about the blessed auld country on the Sabbath day, at least we can hear a sermon on that church unity your gude mon is trying to bring about, since I ken fair well we'll nae keep him off the subject."

The next few days brought more visitors, new friends to the family, old friends to Father Thomas as time was held in this western land: Jonas McClellan, Thomas Sharp, David Bryant and his son Joseph, Jacob Donaldson, Major John Templeton, who had earned his title in the Revolution and was a prosperous landowner, and the Reverend Aaron Riddle of Washington who invited the family

82

to worship the following Sunday at the Union Presbyterian Church.

To the surprise of the family, Father Thomas promptly accepted the invitation. "We are still considered Presbyterians," he explained to them later. "Reverend Riddle is a good friend and an earnest Christian after the manner of John Knox. It would be a pleasure for us to worship together the first Sunday under his preaching. Besides," he added, an unexpected twinkle in his eyes, "the Achesons are members of the Union Presbyterian Church, and we'll be visiting them after worship."

On Friday, Alexander went with his father to the office of the Washington *Reporter.* The proofs of the "Declaration and Address" would not be ready until the following week, the young editor, William Sample, said, unless he and his printer worked on the Lord's day which, as Reverend Campbell would understand, he could never do. They stood for a while, watching the editor help his printer set up Sample's lead editorial on President Madison and the British Orders in Council. Suddenly Sample looked up, indicating a three-inch stick of type.

"I'm putting the story of the arrival of the Campbell family right on the front page with the advertisements. You're news, sir." He turned to Father Thomas. "Anyone who can arouse the religious controversy you have is news!"

"It's the Gospel that's news," amended Father Thomas. "The Gospel is welcome news. That's the meaning of the word."

Sample turned to Alexander. "Could you create as much interest as your father?" He looked at him quizzically.

"What do you mean?" Alexander asked.

"I hear you come from the University of Glasgow. Why not give me an essay on, say, the comparison of that university with our colleges here. We have two colleges in our county already. Your father here knows President Matthew Brown, I imagine, the president of Washington College."

"I do indeed." Father Thomas smiled. "He is also pastor of the Seceder Presbyterian Church. I once occupied his pulpit here—but not recently."

"Jefferson College is another Presbyterian school at Canonsburg, seven miles up the road. Comparisons from the viewpoint of a student from the old country would create interest, I'd say."

"And I fear needless controversy," said Father Thomas, shaking his head. "We have enough dissension among the people now."

Alexander nodded doubtfully. "Father may be right," he said to Sample, "but I feel printer's ink on my hands just the same. Someday, maybe, I'll write something for your paper, Mr. Sample. Who knows?"

Had it not been for the air of newness about the Union Presbyterian Church, and the strange faces in the pews, Alexander could not have distinguished the worship service conducted by the Reverend Riddle from that of any other National Presbyterian Church back in Rich Hill or Ahorey.

There was no change in the ritual. The solemn procession of the worshipers as they filed past the pulpit, the men and boys going to the right, the women, girls, and infants to the left; the subdued occasional murmuring before the entrance of the minister with his long frock coat buttoned to his throat, Bible in hand; his dramatic gesture as he dropped to one knee beside the pulpit and closed his eyes, the congregation sitting with heads bowed, only their hushed breathing like the slow lapping of the waves breaking the stillness as he wrestled for long minutes in silent prayer. And then, with a sudden lifting of his hands, the preacher arose, and the people struggled to their feet in the crowded benches; the psalm, sung by the congregation, and then a prayer, a long prayer closing as if in afterthought with a petition that the righteous head of a newly arrived family would soon be restored into the path of truth.

A faint stir, a shifting of feet beside him in the pew, and Alexander resisted the urge to smile. Father Thomas had been prayed for before by other ministers, complimentary prayers, calling forth God's blessings upon him, but he was not used to prayers that pinned him to the wall as an erring sinner.

For an hour and a half the sermon ran on, a discourse filled with denunciations upon the wicked and warnings of the wrath of God.

There was no word of love, Alexander reflected, nor of the mercies of a forgiving Jesus. He sat stolidly while the congregation alternately stiffened and relaxed under the simmering heat of the stove in the center of the room and the pressure of the close-packed bodies. With the benediction, the people began filing past the preacher, his face now benign and kind and full of compassion for his flock. And as Alexander edged out of the pew he saw Hannah Acheson.

She was whispering to her stepmother, a stout, plain, intelligent-looking woman with kindly brown eyes. He looked at the girl he had played with as a child in Rich Hill. She was prettier than he had remembered her. He looked at her daring off-the-face blue bonnet with its wispy feathered crown, her tight bodice, her voluminous, flowing blue silk skirt held off the floor by one small lace-mittened hand. She turned, and he caught her glance, and bowed gravely across the wooden barriers, and then turned to speak to Thomas Acheson who had been seated behind him.

Together, with Father Thomas going ahead, the two men edged forward with the other worshipers and walked slowly past the pulpit and through the men's doorway into the open air.

"Alexander, I hardly recognized you!" Hannah had come up behind him. "You've changed in the last two years!" She spoke as though she did not disapprove the change, her gray-green eyes dancing. "Welcome to the United States!"

Alexander pumped her hand solemnly. He tried to speak, but the words stuck in his throat.

"You might let go of my hand," she said. "After all, in front of all these people!"

"Alexander has become a flirt," Dorothea said at her brother's elbow. "You should have seen him with the girls in Glasgow, Hannah."

"Such talk!" said Mrs. Campbell. "And right outside the church, too!"

"Well, Hannah is like another sister, aren't you, Hannah? She ought to know about Alexander."

For a moment the two girls exchanged glances, measuring each other, each on guard. And then Hannah broke into a peal of laughter. "Alexander Campbell a flirt? Oh, no! Come now, Mr. Casanova Campbell!" She slipped her hand into the crook of his arm. "You're to ride in the phaeton with me. Papa and Mama will follow with your family in your wagon. As a sister I'll give you a lecture on the dangers of trifling with a woman's heart."

Father Thomas placed his hand on the shoulder of the high-spirited girl, his eyes twinkling under his bushy brows. " 'She openeth her mouth with wisdom,' " he quoted. "I think such a lecture would do Alexander a lot of good, Hannah. He probably needs it."

It was almost nightfall when they returned home, a damp chill and lowering clouds, the forerunners of early snow, replacing the crispness of the day. It had been a pleasant enough afternoon, with hardly a mention of the sermon of the morning. After the heavy, cold dinner of sliced beef and pickled beets and thick slices of oat bread, washed down with rich buttermilk, others had come. John and Fanny McElroy, and James Foster and David Bryant and his son Joseph; and the Reverend Daniel Mordecai Anderson of the National Presbyterian Church on Upper Buffalo Creek, and finally William Sample and the Hodgens. They had sat around the open hearth in the large, square sitting room and Father Thomas had discoursed to them on God's redeeming love, and had prayed with them —a long prayer for the unity of God's people. Then there had been an exhilarating walk through the apple orchard, now bare and empty against the sky, with Alexander and Hannah pairing off as naturally as did Dorothea and Joseph Bryant.

As they walked, Alexander found himself defending the ministry as a profession for a young man against Hannah's frank criticism of it.

"But there are enough preachers!" she had cried. "Surely you are not going to add to them? What we need in this country are statesmen, leaders in developing this land, great businessmen!"

He had refused to commit himself, smiling away her barbed comments. But long after the evening chores had been completed, and the family worship was over and the rest of the family had gone to bed, he sat before the fire in the sitting room, staring vacantly

86

into the flickering embers. There was wisdom in the words of Hannah Acheson. Not everyone that saith, "Lord, Lord," or prophesied or cast out devils, would enter into the Kingdom of Heaven, but "he that doeth the will of my Father which is in heaven." He had never actually decided on the ministry; there were other ways to serve the Lord. In this new land of opportunity, who knows what he might do?

Chapter 8

A LIGHT SNOW FELL DURING THE NIGHT AND, ALTHOUGH THE WOODSHED was filled with thick, sawed logs, Alexander went out with Tommie as a willing helper to gather needed kindling before breakfast. Afterward would come other chores, with the afternoon given to the schooling of the children in reading, writing, grammar, Latin, and the Scriptures.

They were almost through the meal of boiled eggs and fried salt pork, and golden honey on hot scones, supplemented by hot tea and goat's milk, when Father Thomas rapped on the table for silence. He stared for a moment at the open kitchen hearth with its black kettle steaming on the long crane, and then at his four daughters seated along one side of the long table, with Alexander between his two brothers across from them.

"While you and Tommie were out in the woods," he said, turning to Alexander, "Mr. Sample brought over the proof sheets of the 'Declaration and Address.' Wife and the girls and I have been examining them. Now I'd like your opinion. I'll excuse you from conducting school this afternoon so you can look them over."

It was almost five o'clock and getting dark before Alexander, seated at the table in the upstairs bedroom which Father Thomas had set aside as a study, had finished the last of the fifty-six closely printed sheets. Normally a fast reader, he had found himself lingering over the pages, flavoring the meaning of the formalized Addisonian sentences; measuring their pronouncements against his own thinking. And as he read and pondered and read again, the conviction grew that this simple, unassuming Presbyterian clergyman who was his father had come upon a vision—a vision born as much of the Holy Spirit as had been that of Martin Luther when he rose from his knees upon the scarred stairway in Rome. This document, the "Declaration and Address of the Christian Association of Washington," as written by Thomas Campbell in a little attic room in the home of Nathan Welch, was no ordinary document. It was a Magna Charta, a religious declaration of independence.

And yet, he thought, the futility of it. How did this obscure little man in this remote part of the world hope to effect a revolution among the great, entrenched organized sects? How could he dream of success when so many reformers had failed? He thought of Robert and James Alexander Haldane, of Greville Ewing and Alexander Carson in distant Scotland—powerful, eloquent, famous men. Yet their teachings were little more than a disruptive influence; their followers already known as a separate sect.

He picked up the proofs and ruffled the pages. The three pages of the first part, the "Declaration," set forth the reasons, purpose, and form of the organization of the Christian Association. The next part, the "Address," covered eighteen pages, listing thirteen principles as the means for the unification of all branches of the Christian religion. The Appendix answered actual and anticipated criticism.

He closed his eyes for a moment and put his elbows on the table, resting his chin in his open palms, a sympathy akin to pity in his heart for this father who dared so greatly and against such odds. There were only strife and division in Zion, and a call for Christian unity would be interpreted only as the birth cry of another sect. He shuffled the pages again, reluctant to admit that he could not share the grandeur of the dream. Aimlessly now, probing his mind for answers he did not find, scanning the pages briefly, he came again to the thirteen propositions.

Proposition 1. That the Church of Christ upon earth is essentially, intentionally, and constitutionally one; consisting of all those in every place that profess their faith in Christ and obedience to Him in all things according to the Scriptures. . . .

For a moment Alexander stared at the words. All obedient believers in Christ were Christian brothers to Father Thomas as they were to him. But that was revolutionary doctrine; it was anathema to the clergy; heresy which no established church would accept in America any more than in Scotland. But it was the truth, a truth that could break down all barriers between churches once it was accepted. He read on, as though fearful the words would fade before his eyes:

Proposition 2. That, although the Church of Christ upon earth must necessarily exist in particular and distinct societies, locally separate from one another, yet there ought to be no schisms, no uncharitable divisions among them. They ought to receive one another as Jesus Christ hath also received them, to the glory of God. And for this purpose they ought all to walk by the same rule; to mind and speak the same things, and to be perfectly joined together on the same mind and in the same judgment.

Proposition 3. That, in order to do this, nothing ought to be inculcated of them as terms of communion but what is expressly taught and enjoined upon them in the Word of God. Nor ought anything to be admitted as of Divine obligation in their church constitution and management but what is expressly enjoined by the authority of our Lord Jesus Christ and His apostles upon the New Testament Church, either in express terms or by approved precedent.

Alexander pulled up his chair and, picking up a sheaf of blank paper and a quill pen, began to write. He was still writing a half-hour later when Father Thomas came up the stairway unnoticed and walked into the room, a restrained eagerness about him.

"It's late for reading such fine print, my son," he said almost shyly. "Why don't you put it aside and finish it tomorrow? There will be plenty of time to give me your opinion."

Alexander leaned back, locking his hands behind his head. "I've read it twice, Father." He spoke warmly, an intensity in his voice. "You've had a great vision. But there are a number of points I'd like to talk over with you tonight. I've been briefing your propositions, the thirteen principles which will affect the—the—" He hesi-

89

tated for a moment. "The Restoration or Reformation, or whatever you call it, of Christian unity. I find four of the principles stress the necessity for unity and with them all can agree. But the others seek to explain how this unity can be brought about." He pushed back his chair and stood up. "That will be your difficulty, Father Thomas. The churches cling to their established positions. They are rigid, intolerant of other views, as you know. They will never compromise. They will fight you to the death."

"We can discuss them after supper," said Father Thomas. "But the answer is so clear that even he who runs may read. It's all summed up in two simple words: obedience and freedom. Implicit obedience to the Divine commands as set forth in the Scriptures, and freedom of opinion where there are no commands. Doesn't the document make that plain enough?"

"But there are so many things on which Christians don't agree," Alexander protested. "So many different interpretations."

"Then let us disagree," said Father Thomas patiently. "But as Christians, maintaining unbroken our fellowship. You doubt, my son, because you carry the shadow of the old country with you," he went on gently. "But this is a new country, an expanding country. The United States is a pioneer among nations, basing its government upon the liberty and freedom of the individual. That means freedom in religious matters, too. And union. As the separate states retain their rights as sovereign states while acknowledging the authority of the central government, so, too, can our religious parties retain their separate distinctions of opinion while acknowledging the supreme authority of Jesus Christ. Regardless of differences, we are all equal as citizens of the Kingdom of God." He paused for a moment, as though savoring the thought, and then ran his hand over his face. "There are bigots here also, as I know only too well. But the minds of the people are open. And I tell you, my son, if the spirit of unity among Christians ever develops, as it must, that spirit will be born and grow first in these United States of America."

Dorothea's voice called to them from the foot of the stairs. Supper was ready. Affectionately, almost tenderly, Alexander rested

90

his hand on his father's shoulder and together they started down the stairs.

After the evening worship in the sitting room, the family gathered in a close-knit unit before the hearth, the "Declaration and Address" uppermost in the minds of all of them. It was, Alexander thought as he looked about, a historic event. They had often discussed together the meaning of the Scriptures and the religious happenings of the day, but there was nothing in the family history to duplicate the significance of this new situation. Did Father Thomas have a vision of the future which his family here, tonight, could help set in motion? He cleared his throat, holding between his hands the loose pages of the proofs, his sheaf of notes on top, his eyes on his father seated in a cane-bottomed chair directly across from him.

Nancy seated herself beside him on the high-backed bench and laid her hand for a moment on his knee. He grinned at her nervously. They were all here except the boys and Alicia, now in bed asleep: eleven-year-old Jane with her feet tucked under her before the hearth, her homespun skirt spread decorously over her knees; Dorothea on the low stool beside her mother who rocked gently in the hickory platform rocker, her hands filled with darning.

His mother looked over at him and smiled. "What do you make of it, son?"

Alexander stared at the proof sheets thoughtfully. "The heart of the 'Declaration and Address,' as I see it, the essential theme, is that if human innovations and creeds were eliminated, the followers of Jesus Christ could then unite upon the basis of the New Testament alone."

Jane spoke impulsively. "That must mean we won't have to study the Catechism any more. I never did understand it anyway, Father. I'm glad you're getting rid of it."

Mrs. Campbell paused in her darning to wave a warning finger. "You are not to interrupt, Jane," she said.

"The child's confusion is natural," said Father Thomas. "That is the reason I stopped examining children on the Catechism before

I left Ireland. Too many of them confuse it with the Scriptures, or the Confession of Faith."

"The Westminster Confession of Faith is the true creed," said Nancy, preening herself on her knowledge. "It was written by John Knox and adopted at Edinburgh in 1647. It is accepted by all good Christians and Presbyterians. Isn't it, Father?"

Her father removed his silver-rimmed glasses and polished them vigorously on his coat sleeve. "Daughter, you have put your finger upon one of the excellent reasons why we cannot accept any human doctrine or creed as a term of communion among Christians. There is no true creed except as recorded in the teachings of Christ."

"Does that mean everything we've been taught except that which came directly from the Bible is all wrong?" asked Dorothea.

In the silence that followed, broken only by the crackling of the pine logs on the hearth, all eyes were turned upon the little man sitting hunched forward in his straight-backed chair, his spectacles now pushed over his forehead, his eyes closed as though seeking for words to resolve for his children this dilemma of his own making.

"No." He spoke slowly, choosing his words carefully. "Human creeds are useful in developing the reasoning powers of the Christian. But they are filled, of necessity, with human error; they differ with each sect; they change from time to time as conditions change."

He paused, as if unwilling to influence his children beyond their reasoning, conscious that to a degree he was repudiating his own teachings. While Mrs. Campbell rocked, her eyes fixed upon her flying needle, he spoke again, quietly, and one by one their voices joined him, rising together in a crescendo of faith in the magnificent affirmation they had known since their earliest days:

"I believe in God the Father Almighty, maker of heaven and earth, and in Jesus Christ, his only Son our Lord; who was conceived by the Holy Ghost, born of the Virgin Mary, suffered under Pontius Pilate, was crucified, dead and buried; he descended into Hell; the third day he rose from the dead; he ascended into Heaven, and sitteth on the right hand of God the Father Almighty; from thence he shall come to judge the quick and the dead. I believe in the Holy

Ghost, the holy catholic church; the communion of the saints; the forgiveness of sins; the resurrection of the body, and the life everlasting."

As they finished there was a moment of silence and then Dorothea turned to her father, her face strained. "If we don't have creeds like other churches do, wouldn't that mean that the Christian Association would be a separate church?" she asked.

Father Thomas got up and went over to Alexander and took from him some of the proofs. "No, daughter, the 'Declaration' definitely settles that question." He began to read:

" 'That this society by no means considers itself a church, nor does it assume to itself the powers peculiar to such a society; nor do the members as such consider themselves as standing connected in that relation.'

"What could be plainer than that?" he asked, looking up at the group. "And again it says:

" 'That this society, formed for the sole purpose of promoting simple evangelical Christianity . . . shall support such ministers of whatever church who are of similar persuasion.'

"And further on it provides:

" 'That this society meet at least twice a year, viz., on the first Thursday of May and of November . . .'

"Can you, my children, imagine any church which meets only twice a year? Oh, no! The Christian Association is a voluntary society of individuals dedicated to working only within the established churches, changing them, yes, but only to the extent of restoring to them the original unity, peace, and purity of the early New Testament church. Who can object to that?"

Alexander arose and placed a small log from the woodbox on the now-smoldering embers. He ran his fingers thoughtfully through his thick brown hair. "There's your answer, Dorry," he said. "It will satisfy everybody but the preachers and the infidels, and maybe the Synod."

"You're right," Dorothea said. "I'm not surprised they consider it a revolution, a rebellion against the established order." She turned

93

to her mother. "Father may yet be hanged as a heretic, Mother dear, if he isn't careful!"

"I suppose I am something of a heretic." Father Thomas laughed ruefully. "Certainly if being censured could have hanged me, I would have been dead long ago."

Jane squirmed over on her stomach, her face to the fire. "It must be exciting to see a hanging," she said. "I'd like to see one."

"It is long past bedtime." Mrs. Campbell spoke firmly. "And I'm not at all sure such talk at night is good for young minds. Jane is already talking out of her head." She looked at her daughter sternly and turned to her husband. "They should be in bed, Mr. Campbell."

Jane pushed herself to a sitting position, a mock contrition in her brown eyes. "Oh, Mother, you know I was only joking. I'm quite sure I wouldn't want to see a hanging, even if it was Father."

"There! There!" said Father Thomas. "Another word and you'll march right up to bed."

"What makes you think, Father"—Alexander spoke slowly, hesitantly, as if reluctant to express his doubts—"that the effort of the Christian Association to establish unity in the religious world can succeed? Every such movement in the past, even the one being led by the Haldanes and Greville Ewing and Alexander Carson in Scotland today, results only in the establishment of another schism. What is the difference?"

Father Thomas fumbled in his coat pockets and took out his gold snuffbox, no larger than a thimble. He looked suddenly old, Alexander thought, weary with much explaining.

"One great difference," he replied after a moment, "is that which is inherent in the repeated efforts of men to attain any goal of magnitude. The goal may seem ever receding but history reveals that each attempt actually brings it closer to attainment." He paused and stared into the fire as the little group sat silent, considering his words. "But the great difference, the basic difference, is this: Other reforms failed because they advocated changes only in the present man-made system. We, on the other hand, seek no such changes. We work only to restore the original church. We do not seek to add to or take away or change in any way the original inspired, apostle-directed church. Thus we can never be considered just another sect unless the original church can be so considered."

Alexander nodded, as if almost against his will, his imagination captured by the boldness of the dream. As though by the slow unrolling of a parchment scroll, the implications and significance of his father's vision stood sharply revealed. He coughed to hide his emotion and stooped and picked up his notes.

"I see now what you mean in Proposition Twelve," he said. "You state there"—he paused, looking over his notes and then went on—"that the established churches need do only three things to become again like the first church: Receive any professing and obedient Christian into membership; preach only those doctrines revealed in the Word of God; follow only the observance of the Divine Ordinances as they are stipulated in the New Testament, without the addition of any human opinion. In other words"—he looked at his father closely, and nodded in solemn agreement—"Christianity as it came from Christ is a perfect system, incapable of being improved. And if the churches will only follow it, leaving out encumbering human opinion, unity among Christians will follow as surely as the day follows night."

For a moment there was silence, and then Father Thomas got slowly to his feet.

"That is it, son." He spoke almost in a whisper. "That is it!"

Chapter 9

FOR MINUTES NOW THEY HAD DRIVEN IN SILENCE; THE SLUMBERING quiet of the early morning of Thursday, November 2, 1809, broken only by the hoofbeats of Old Zeke and the roll of the wagon wheels against the frozen roadway. Alexander glanced at Dorothea bundled between him and their father, wondering how deeply interested she really was in this first meeting of the Christian Association. Dorry was eighteen now, he reflected, already a young woman; her best marriageable years were slipping by. Perhaps the hope that young men might also be at the meeting this morning partially accounted for her request to accompany them. It was a business meeting, Father Thomas had warned her, and although he would make a short talk, it was not a preaching service, and no place on a winter's day for young people who would best be at their books.

They rounded a bend in the road and suddenly at the crossroads a log building came into view, thick black smoke pouring from its snub-nosed chimney.

"It's like a fort!" said Dorothea. "It doesn't look like a meeting-house at all!"

And it did look like a fort, Alexander agreed, a deep-rooted massive strength about its square frame resting upon barked posts anchored firmly in the ground; the gray fieldstone chimney barely topping the sloping roof. Even the door and the two windows flanking it were of split logs, the bark still on them; a sturdy, primitive strength about the whole structure matching the spirit of the men who had built it.

He pulled up beside the half-dozen tarpaulin-topped wagons before the building. The air inside was still chilly, the damp pine logs, fired by dry leaves and pine cones, spluttering in the open fireplace at the rear, flaring now and then into shooting flames, harbingers of the steady heat to come.

It was not until he had followed his father and sister past the box-like rostrum beside the door that Alexander saw Hannah. She was seated with her stepmother almost at the end of a narrow, backless bench near the rear, a piquancy about her erect, scarlet-cloaked figure in striking contrast to the sober garb of those about her.

"Mr. Acheson is treasurer of the Association," Mrs. Acheson explained as they greeted him. "And Hannah simply insisted that she and I come along with him. She became devoted to your father, too, Alexander, during their trip over on the *Brutus*. She thinks he is wonderful."

96

"Father more than reciprocates," Alexander said. "He thinks as much of Hannah as any of his own children." He felt Hannah's fingers move within the embrace of his hand, the pink of her cheeks deepening under his gaze.

"Thank you kindly, sir," she said, her eyes downcast. And then she looked up at him, laughing. "You can't imagine all the Scripture I memorized on the voyage over." She withdrew her hand and gathered her skirts to make room for him beside her at the end of the bench. " 'Favor is deceitful and beauty is vain: but a woman that feareth the Lord, she shall be praised.' Do you remember that verse in the last chapter of Proverbs? I do believe that's your father's favorite. He was always quoting it to me."

"I can well imagine," he said. He remained standing, his cap and mackinaw tucked under his arm, suddenly conscious that Dorothea was standing alone before the hearth.

"Oh, there's lots more than that," said Hannah. "I had to memorize whole chapters. But I liked best that very last verse in Proverbs: 'Give her of the fruit of her hands; and let her own works praise her in the gates.' That means that women will have their rights some-day and the men had better beware."

"You're talking now like Dorry." He beckoned to his sister. "You modern women will be wanting to own property next, and even make speeches in church. Why, Dorry even believes in colleges for women!"

Hannah turned to Dorothea, a faint impatience, as swiftly gone, in her quick, appraising glance.

"Sit here, Dorothea," said Mrs. Acheson. She patted a place beside her. "Why didn't your mother come?"

While Dorothea and Mrs. Acheson talked, Alexander seated himself. Hannah had been a provocative, fanciful girl when they were growing up together back in Ireland, with her prattling talk of lords and barons and ladies in waiting, enamored by the folderol of the royal courts. Someday, she had confided often enough, she was going to marry a nobleman. He grinned at the recollection and relaxed comfortably, letting his eyes rove about the tight little building.

"They're still coming in." He spoke as though the others did not know. "It will be a good meeting. This is an eventful occasion."

He looked at Hannah for corroboration, but she did not reply, and for a moment they sat in silence, a subdued babble of voices about them. He saw his father and Thomas Acheson detach themselves from a group at the front of the room and move to take seats on the small rostrum. As they mounted the platform, a sober, unconscious dignity upon them both, the angular figure of David Bryant pushed open the door, followed by his son Joseph, a fresh-faced towering young man with sandy hair and a big grin that lightened the seriousness of his dark eyes. For a moment they stood facing the audience and then stalked back and took the vacant space across the aisle from Dorothea.

"It's just like being in church," whispered Hannah. "Except they let the men and women sit together. But the last to come should have to take the sinner's seat right under the nose of the preacher. That would kill Joseph Bryant, though. He's the shy one!"

"He doesn't look shy to me," said Alexander. "He looks like the big landowner type: no foolishness about him."

"His father owns a good farm. And Joseph is lots of fun. But he has no real ambition. That's all he wants to be, just a farmer. I like men with push and go, men who want to do big things."

"I'm a farmer," said Alexander. "There's nothing I like better than working on a farm. One of these days I'm going to own one of the best!"

"Of course you will!" As though by accident her hand touched his, and then fled into the recesses of her muff. "But you're going to do lots more than that, Alexander. Why, in this country you could be a statesman like President Madison, or Thomas Jefferson, and maybe even governor if you half tried."

"Why not be president?" he asked mockingly. "If I listened to personal ambitions, Hannah, I would try to make my mark in literature, be the editor of a publication like the *Spectator;* maybe own a newspaper or two. And of course a big farm. But I'll probably be a preacher, a minister like Father Thomas."

"You couldn't be president because you're not a native-born

citizen," she told him, "but you might be governor or go to Congress. Or be a big businessman and landowner, and own a lot of newspapers. And in Virginia you can own slaves. There are plenty of preachers, Alexander, and you could never be as good as your father, anyway. You are not as good a man." She spoke as though the words were a compliment, and despite himself he felt a glow of response.

He resisted the sudden urge to touch her. "That I know," he said soberly. "But I could do the best I can."

"Foolish!" She laid her hand upon his for a moment, and then quickly withdrew it. "You could do anything you wanted to do, Alexander. You are no ordinary man. I've known that ever since we were children."

He flushed and glanced at Mrs. Acheson and Dorothea, wondering if they had overheard. But Mrs. Acheson was chattering volubly while Dorothea sat listening, their eyes upon the scene before them.

The meetinghouse was filled now, every seat taken, with a group standing in the rear, a soggy warmth in the air that caused some of them already to stir restlessly in their heavy clothing. The wooden shutters on either wall were pushed wide open, with only those nearest seemingly conscious of the outside chill; there was an attitude of expectancy about them all which surprised him. No small children were present, he noticed, and the men twice outnumbered the women—at least a hundred persons packed together on hard wooden benches in a little crossroads log building like ninepins in a row, plotting to reform the world.

He looked about, trying to piece together the identity of those about him. What were they starting, this little group gathered on a winter's day at the edge of the American wilderness, these few simple, earnest, God-fearing Pennsylvania farmers and their families, immigrants, most of them, who would set the world upside down with a goose quill pen and a bottle of homemade ink?

He had shaken hands with James Foster, John McElroy, Thomas Hodgens, and a few new acquaintances: Abraham Altars, Andrew Munro, postmaster and bookseller at Canonsburg, William Sample, John Welch, William Gilchrist, George Archer, and others whose names he could not recall. Some were curiosity seekers; others would drift away after the novelty had worn off and the hard work had begun; among them not a man of substance and influence beyond his community except Thomas Acheson, and not a single minister except his own father.

As he looked about, Father Thomas came to the front of the rostrum and lifted his hands, and at the gesture the shuffling of feet, the coughs, the low-voiced murmurings passed into silence, and the audience stood to its feet for prayer.

Three hours later and the first official semi-annual meeting of the Christian Association of Washington was history, as Hannah said half-mockingly when they stepped into the aisle together. It was good history, Alexander had replied, a history that could record a new era. Then others came between them and she was walking with her stepmother. He stood for a moment, following her with his eyes, and suddenly Dorothea prodded him sharply in the back.

"Careful, brother," she said softly. "She may not be good for you."

He made no reply, but his color deepened, and, grasping his sister by the hand, began to make his way toward the door.

For some time after they were back in the wagon and headed homeward they talked of the meeting. The Association had voted to send a copy of the "Declaration and Address" to every preacher of every sect in Washington County, and Father Thomas was convinced that soon many of them would join the Association and preach the Restoration Plea, as he called it, in their pulpits. From this bastion of Presbyterianism the Plea would then spread to all sections of the country, and thence to the world.

The Association was off to a good start in a business way, too. A standing committee of twenty-one had been chosen to conduct the business affairs, with Father Thomas as executive secretary and Thomas Acheson as treasurer. The interest shown by questions from the floor; the sacrificial contributions; the prayerful consecration of the men and women; the resolution that Father Thomas should preach for them each Sunday at the Crossroads, until the established churches recognized the Plea and incorporated it in their teaching;

all these were signs that the Lord was giving His blessing to the movement.

It was not until they had stopped before their doorway and Father Thomas had stepped from the wagon that Alexander turned to his sister. He gave her his hand to assist her as she stepped onto the wheel hub and to the ground.

"I saw you after meeting flirting with Joseph Bryant, Dorry," he said. "Careful yourself, young lady. He's the shy type, you know."

"Maybe that's what Hannah thinks," she guessed shrewdly. "He's not so shy when he knows what he wants. There's going to be a party at his house next Friday, and he wants to escort me."

"A party?"

"Well, his father called it a husking frolic for the men and a quilting for the women, with supper and singing and games afterward. It sounds like fun." She turned to start for the house and then looked back. "You might ask to escort Hannah; I'm sure she'd let you."

Early the next morning Alexander walked into town. It was the day the post rider picked up the mail, and he wanted to post a letter Father Thomas had written his brother Archibald at Newry, Ireland. He was passing the office of the *Reporter* when a voice hailed him, and he turned to see Editor Sample beckoning from the doorway.

"Come on in," he said warmly. "Saw you from the window and want to talk to you. That was quite a meeting at Crossroads yesterday. I'm going to run an item about it for the benefit of posterity."

They went inside, and the editor closed the door and motioned toward the high, barrel-shaped iron stove glowering in the sandbox in the center of the room.

"Sit down, Mr. Campbell." He pushed forward a chair. "Did you bring the proofs?"

"Father is reading them for the last time," Alexander said. He seated himself and spread his hands before the warming heat, his eyes roving the big room, the long cases of type, the two Washington hand presses, the rolls of white paper along the walls, the waist-high partition marking off the space in the corner from where Sample at his desk could keep an eye on the door and his printer, hunched now over the type cases, and on the teen-age Negro boy who grinned at them over his broom at the rear. There was a fascination about a print shop, Alexander thought—a permanent power and influence to the printed word which no spoken effort could equal.

"You thought the meeting yesterday was significant?" he asked.

The editor shrugged. "Revolutions begin with a few dedicated souls," he said. "Who am I to say? But what I wanted to see you about were those articles you promised me. I've been operating this paper for a year now and I want to stir up some excitement."

Alexander shook his head, smiling. "I'm not a fiction writer."

"No fiction!" Sample said promptly. "Something along the line of the London *Spectator:* a little satire, a little humor, a lot of truth. With your Glasgow University background, you can see us barbarians here in our naked state. I can't pay you anything, but I'll promise you the best printing job on that document of your father's you can get this side of Philadelphia."

Alexander felt tempted. "I've hardly muddied my boots in America yet," he said. "How could I be qualified to write about it?"

"That's just the point," insisted Sample. "You're new; your observations would be fresh, unwarped by your emotions. That's why I want them."

"Let me think about it for a while," Alexander said, standing up.

The door was pushed open and an immense whiskered man walked in, his beaver hat and long bearskin coat filling the doorway.

"The mountain has come to Mohammed!" His booming voice had a happy undertone. He removed his hat with a flourish, revealing thick black hair.

In the introductions Alexander learned he was a lawyer, Marcellus Mountain from Pittsburgh, arrived to attend the November session of the Circuit Court. He had heard Thomas Campbell preach, he told Alexander, pumping his hand. And he had learned from his client, General Acheson, that he had been one of the best classical schoolmasters in the old country.

"And he told me also," said Lawyer Mountain, "that his son is a pretty fair instructor himself, something this country needs badly." He looked at Alexander shrewdly, his eyes twinkling. "Welcome, sir, to the United States, and especially to western Pennsylvania. We can use you!"

Alexander felt a sense of well-being as he later walked up the cinder sidewalk to the post office in the front of Hugh Wylie's store, north of the courthouse. The Reverend Aaron Riddle, just entering the courthouse yard, turned and waited for him, a kindly appraisement in his long face. He offered his hand.

"It was a fair sight to have the Campbell clan at church last Sabbath," he said. "I could have you there Sabbath after Sabbath and never bat an eye." He laughed, and Alexander noted the thoughtful wrinkles about the dark, steady eyes, the stern creases of duty about the full mouth.

"And we could see you at the meeting of the Christian Association with pleasure," Alexander assured him. "You belong with us, Dr. Riddle."

"Your father has talked with me about it. He is a good man, a sturdy domine, rooted in the faith, and a powerful servant of the Lord if he would put by his heresy of ministering unto unbelievers and the foolishness of church unity and return where he belongs, sir, to preaching the Gospel according to John Knox."

The voice was unexpectedly stern, the smile gone from the long face, and Alexander looked his surprise, glimpsing the opposition his father must have faced from the clergy.

For a moment a stilted silence fell upon them and then Reverend Riddle spoke again, his face softened.

"I don't mean to be harsh," he said, "but there are enough divisions in the church of God without an able teacher like your father causing another one." He stopped abruptly, as though he had said too much, and turned toward the courthouse door.

"That is just the point, sir," Alexander said. "The movement is to unite the church, not to divide it. We all agree that the church of Christ on earth is, as Father says, 'essentially, intentionally, and constitutionally one.' To restore that unity is all Father and the Christian Association advocate. How can there be a disagreement about that?"

The preacher looked at him steadily. "Those are unsound words," he said. "The one true faith is as set forth in the Westminster Confession of Faith and interpreted by the Synod of North America. All else is heresy. I am sorry for you, my lad." He placed his hand kindly on Alexander's arm. "A young man so full of promise, and already a heretic."

"I have been called that before," said Alexander. "A Catholic priest, a sincere Christian according to his lights, gave me that title some time ago. And although I disagree with him on many things, I would welcome him into the Association as a Christian brother."

The preacher stared at him. "Young man, I'm shocked! Surely that is not your father's teaching?"

"Simply my own reasoning and conscience," said Alexander. "I cannot deny the name of Christian to any who follow His teachings. Neither would I have them deny that name to me. As Father said in his 'Declaration and Address,' 'Nothing ought to be enjoined upon Christians as articles of faith, or required of them as terms of communion, except what is expressly taught in the Word of God. Neither should anything be required of them as a matter of faith and duty for which a Thus saith the Lord cannot be produced either in express terms or by approved precedent.' That is all Father asks of the Catholic or Presbyterian or any other religious party. It is as simple as that."

"My son," said Dr. Riddle kindly, "those words are misleading. If you really believe them, you should become a Baptist."

"A Baptist? Why?"

"You were baptized a member of the Presbyterian faith?"

"Yes, sir. Baptized as an infant by my own father according to the rites of the Westminster Confession."

"According to your own words then, a moment ago, you should not have been. That is why I say they are misleading, for if you follow them you must reject infant baptism."

At the bafflement in Alexander's face the preacher placed his hand on his shoulder, a fatherly kindness in his manner.

"It is the privilege of youth to play with strange notions, my son. When you pass on to sound doctrine, there will be a place for you back home with the Presbyterians. We need you."

"You mean," insisted Alexander, "there is nowhere in the Bible a divine command or precedent for infant baptism?"

"Can you think of one? No. There are none." As though he forgave him his follies and still held to hope, the preacher slapped him paternally upon the shoulder and walked rapidly up the path and went into the courthouse.

Alexander stood looking after the tall, angular figure, his mackinaw snugged about him, his forehead wrinkled in troubled thought. And then slowly, almost chilled, he went on to the post office to mail the letter to Uncle Archibald in Newry.

It was after evening worship before Alexander found the opportunity to speak to Father Thomas alone. He had gone about his school duties and barnyard chores with an abstraction unusual with him. Even the quick run with his younger brothers through the apple orchard, and the news that Joseph Bryant had driven by with a setting of geese and an invitation for Alexander, Dorry, and Nancy to attend the husking frolic and quilting at his home the next Friday, failed to dislodge from his mind the inquiry the Presbyterian preacher had planted. But when he went to Father Thomas in his study, he found the older man inclined to treat the problem as of small importance.

"Let it slip for the present," he said. "The great problem is how to unite the churches, not how further to divide them on such details. Baptism is, after all, merely a symbol."

"But, Father," insisted Alexander, "the Association bases its whole plea on following only Divine commands. 'Where the Scriptures speak, we speak; and where the Scriptures are silent, we are silent,'" he quoted. "And I find there is nothing in the Bible to indicate infant baptism was ever practiced or authorized. If we follow the rule, doesn't that mean the end of infant baptism?"

His father sighed. "Andrew Munro asked the same question at one of our early organized meetings," he said. "There was considerable discussion about it. If the authority be not found in the Scriptures, we can have nothing to do with it. But for those who are already members of the church and participants of the Lord's

Supper, I can see no propriety in their unchurching themselves because of it. They would merely be going out of the church for the sake of coming in again." He paused, and from his seat behind the littered table smiled at his tall son standing so solemnly before him. He pushed his glasses over his forehead and folded his arms. "Let us not make mountains out of molehills." He gestured as though dismissing the subject, and then abruptly spoke again. "Do you plan to go to the Bryant frolic next Friday? I told Joseph he could escort Dorothea and Nancy. I'll keep school for you if you want to go." He paused, a twinkle in his dark eyes. "You might see Hannah Acheson there. They are fine people, the Achesons. But it's hard to know that girl. I'm not sure I could ever understand her."

Alexander took out his watch and studied it soberly for a moment. He grinned at his father. "Yes, I'll probably go," he said. "It might furnish material for an article for Editor Sample."

A half-hour later he sat at the kitchen table and by the light of a single candle wrote a note to "Andrew Munro, bookseller, Canonsburg, Pennsylvania," asking him to list every book he had, or could secure, in favor of infant baptism. The next time he had an argument with the Reverend Aaron Riddle he would be prepared. And then, in sudden decision, he wrote a note to Hannah Acheson requesting the honor of her company at the Bryant husking and quilting party on the following Friday, A.D. November 10, 1809.

Chapter 10

THE BRYANT FROLIC WAS IN FULL SWING WHEN ALEXANDER AND Hannah arrived in the Achesons' buggy early the next Friday afternoon. He had left Old Zeke munching contentedly on corn and oats in the Acheson barn. Although there was no comparison between the wagon he had to offer and the fine buggy of General Acheson, the resentment in him, that he had agreed so readily to its use at Hannah's suggestion, had not entirely worn away when they completed the five-mile drive and stopped at last before the sprawling log house which was the Bryant home.

Hannah promptly joined the dozen girls already at work over the big quilting frames set up about the sitting room, and Alexander was guided by Joseph to the adjacent barn, almost as big as the house itself, where the men were at work. Corn, gathered in the fall and thrown into the barn loft, was being shucked, some saved for the stock, the rest shelled for the gristmills on Buffalo Creek. A dozen pair of hands made it quick work, and before the short afternoon sun had sunk in long shadows over the fields the shucked corn was neatly corded and stacked in the loft, and the shelled grain poured into iron-hooped oaken bins ready for the mills.

There was no heat in the barn, and twice during the afternoon some of the girls appeared with great pails of hot tea and coffee. And finally Hannah and Gracie Bryant came out to call them to supper, and Andrew Chapman and George Gilchrist promptly circled the girls about their waists, and arm in arm began a gay promenade about the barn, while Joseph Bryant sang to the accompaniment of stomping feet:

> "Old Brother Silas, how merry was he,
> The night he sat under the juniper tree;
> The juniper tree, hi oh, hi oh, hi oh;
> The juniper tree, hi oh!"

Seated spraddle-legged against the wall, with a bushel basket of shelled corn between his knees, his resentment forgotten, Alexander clapped his hands with the others, but Hannah did not glance at him, and when the girls left he arose with a grin and went with the others to the well house to clean up and brush his clothes.

The fifty-foot sitting-bedroom of the Bryant house had been decorated with gay informality. On the wall bed was displayed the patchwork quilting the girls had made. Cane-bottomed chairs lined the opposite wall, and at one end of the long room a table formed of planks on wooden horses and covered with a green checkered cotton cloth held steaming platters of baked pork chops and spareribs, thick slices of hickory-cured ham, and hand-sized patties of fresh sausage sprinkled with pepper and spices. Fried chicken and bowls of sweet milk gravy, thick and creamy, with flagons of buttermilk cooled in the stone cellar, candied sweet potatoes, cucumber pickles, and pots of hot coffee and tea with huge baskets of biscuits, and berry pies and a four-tiered cake, completed the feast which would vanish into crumbs and picked bones before the games and riddles and the songs had actually begun. In the center of the table, giving it elegance, as Sarah Hanan said, was an earthen bowl packed with brown pine cones and scented pine sprays. Holly branches and strings of corn and red peppers ran along the table and festooned the astral lamps and clusters of bayberry candles on the walls, adding an astringent, pleasant odor that offset to a degree the heat from the walnut logs blazing in the stone hearth. Piles of big yellow pumpkins gleamed at them from every corner and covered the mantel shelf, while suspended in the center of the room by a string of red peppers from the hand-hewn rafters hung a tuft of mistletoe.

As Alexander halted at the door, he felt a surge of rising affection for these sturdy people who could so readily turn work into play, and could offer and accept such hospitality as ample compensation for a hard day's work. He had never seen anything like it in the old country: the exuberance of spirit, the abundance of food, the festive air with which even the daily chores could be garlanded. There was almost an air of excitement, an exhilaration, about the whole country, he reflected—a joy in living rather than a mere stout endurance of life by the grace of God.

A short but fervent grace by David Bryant standing at one end of the table, and the girls began filling the china plates for their escorts. The evening's festivities had begun.

As though there had been no restraint between them, Hannah presented Alexander with his plate, her eyes sparkling, her cheeks rosy with excitement and the fresh corn meal she had rubbed on them. Dorothea, he noted, was with Joseph Bryant across the room and Nancy seated beside the lanky Andrew Chapman who seemed awkward and shy compared with his exuberance in the barn a few minutes before.

Alexander and Hannah found seats against the wall, her plate held precariously in one hand while she maneuvered a chicken drumstick with the other.

"You're a self-willed little redhead," he said, shaking a pickle at her. "You need a strong hand to manage you."

She took a bite of the drumstick, her eyes laughing at him. "When did you decide that, m'lord?"

"While you were sashaying about in the barn." He started to say more when the door suddenly swung open and four young men entered.

The Bryants went to greet them, and Hannah turned to him, answering the inquiry in his eyes.

"You know Larkin Munro, the son of the Canonsburg bookseller, and Henderson Blake who works in his father's store in Washington. And that gentleman"—she indicated the tallest one—"is Dr. Wilson of West Liberty, and the other one, Lawyer David Barkeley of Pittsburgh. A friend of mine," she added as the young lawyer, catching sight of her, waved his hat. "He's here attending court with Lawyer Mountain."

David Bryant's voice filled the room. "Drones who come too late to work have to sing for their supper," he called out. "Now, what is it going to be? Here, you!" He motioned young Barkeley and his companions into the center of the room. "Sing, if you loafers want to eat with us working folks!"

A laughing, whispered conference among the four arrivals, and young Lawyer Barkeley stepped a pace forward.

"This one is about a girl who almost got her man," he announced solemnly. "It's a Virginia mountain song I just learned:

> "A maid all alone in the poorhouse did dwell
> With a father and mother, three sisters as well;
> She lived all alone, and all was serene,
> Her hair was red and her age was nineteen."

"Poor thing!" chanted his three companions in shrill falsetto chorus behind him.

> "And not far away her lover did dwell,
> With a humpbacked rooster, bowlegged as well;

109

Says he, Will you fly by the light of yon star,
For I am the I of the you that I are!"

Again the chorus in solemn unison, "Poor thing!"

Barkeley's baritone voice sank to its deepest pitch, a mock sadness
on his face. He spread his hands despairingly.

"The father then told the lover to bolt,
He got his horse pistol he'd raised from a colt;
Said the villain to his true, I'll bid you adieu;
And he went to the chimney and flew up the flue!"

"Poor t-h-i-n-g!"

The last word rolled out in deep sonorousness by the four of them
brought loud clapping and cries of approval, and as the young men
went into an adjoining room to leave their coats, Hannah leaned
toward Alexander, her voice lowered to a whisper behind her hand.

"Mr. Barkeley thinks he wants to marry me," she said.

"Then you knew he was coming," he said accusingly. "You
probably invited him yourself."

"It's a very nice party, isn't it?" She smiled at him enigmatically,
and without waiting for his response arose to place their half-empty
plates upon the table.

And it *was* a good party, he admitted long before the evening
was over—the games for choosing and changing partners; the chant-
ing, marching songs: "Coffee Grows on White Oak Trees," "Skip
to My Lou," "Under a Juniper Tree," all sung to the accompaniment of Joseph Byrant's fiddle, engendered a rollicking, carefree
atmosphere. During the playing of "The Jolly Miller," the group
formed concentric circles, with the girls in the inner circle facing
the men, and Alexander found himself keeping step and singing at
the top of his voice with all the others:

"Happy is the miller boy, stands by his mill;
Everywhere the mill turns, turns to his will;
One hand in the hopper and the other in the sack,
Every time the mill turns, turns right back.

Happy is the miller boy, stands by his mill;
Every time the mill turns, turns to his will;
One hand in the hopper and the other in the sack,
Ladies step forward and the men step back."

In the shifting circles as the song ended, David Barkeley stopped directly opposite Hannah and directly under the mistletoe. To the delighted squeals of the girls, he kissed her promptly on her open lips. Alexander missed a step before guiding his own partner away.

It was almost ten o'clock before the party ended.

"I'm proud of you, Alexander," Hannah said as they edged their way with the others to say their farewell to their hosts. "You didn't embarrass a single girl. You were the perfect gentleman!"

He stared at her, quick to note the implied disdain, but bundled to her ears in her cloak and hood, she smiled at him, and when she tucked her hand demurely inside the crook of his elbow, his resentment vanished.

It was a cloudless night, the road carpeted with a light freshening of snow. For a time they rode in silence, the heavy bearskin rug tucked about their knees, the regular hoofbeats of the horse ringing rhythmically in the cold air. Soon now, with the hard-packed snow and the steady cold, sleighs would be about and bells would begin to jingle.

It was Hannah who spoke first, her voice low. "I forgot to tell you something coming over," she said. "It's about you. It could be important." She paused, as though expecting him to encourage her.

"About me?"

"Yes." She turned to him as she spoke, and although he looked straight ahead he could feel her soft, quick breath. "Yes," she repeated. "Lawyer Mountain has been talking to Papa about you."

"Lawyer Mountain?"

"He said he met you at the *Reporter* office the other day. He said he liked you."

Alexander slowed the horse. "I don't understand," he said. "Why on earth should Mr. Mountain be interested in me?"

"He said he was looking for a young man for principal of a boys' academy at Pittsburgh. He's the chairman of the trustees. And I —we—Papa, that is, recommended you."

Alexander laughed. "I'm most grateful. Now, if Mr. Mountain makes me an offer, I'll know whom to thank."

"He practically told me he would offer you the position." She edged closer, as though for warmth against the cold. "And it would be a handsome offer, Alexander. It could be the beginning of great things for you. You could even study law in his office."

"You little schemer!" Suddenly his arm was about her. He tilted her head back against his shoulder, as though he was going to kiss her. But he did not kiss her, and after a moment as suddenly released her, a confusion upon him, and riveted his attention on the road unwinding before them.

"Mr. Mountain is still in town." She spoke almost petulantly. "At the Washington Tavern. Why don't you see him about it?"

"I'll think about it," he said stiffly. "And I'm grateful, Hannah. You're right: it would be a great opportunity."

"I would love to live in Pittsburgh. Mr. Mountain says it already has nearly five thousand people and is certain to be one of the big cities of the world. I'm sure I would like it there. Mr. Barkeley told me again tonight—" She stopped with a sudden intake of breath and drew away from him, as though she had said too much.

"He told you he would love to have you live in Pittsburgh, too," he finished for her. "Well, what sort of answer did you give him?"

Although he stared straight ahead, bracing himself, he knew that she was studying him, a half-smile on her lips, her breath a little quick.

"I told him," she spoke slowly, "that—there was something about Washington County I liked, too. He's going back to Pittsburgh to-morrow. He's giving me time to think it over."

They were almost home now, passing the snow-topped railing fence before the Acheson farm, the wind-stripped fence posts dark sentinels under the moonlight.

She stirred, her voice soft, almost pleading. "You could be a great man, Alexander, a big lawyer, or you could hold a big public office. That way you would be a servant of the people, if you want to call it that. And you could own land and become wealthy. Oh, I would be so proud of you."

Quietly he drew up before the Acheson home and jumped to the ground and unlatched the gate. He would see her to the door and then put the buggy away and get Old Zeke and the wagon. The moon was high, casting short shadows. It was a world of dreams.

"Mebbe," he said hoarsely. "Let's think about it, Hannah. I'm confused somehow!"

Noiselessly he let himself into his father's house and closed the door, standing for a moment pressed against it. The others were asleep, his sisters long back from the party. He should go to bed. He crept upstairs and then in sudden compulsion turned into his father's study. He took a light from the embers in the fireplace and lighted the stump of a candle on the table. He sorted out several sheets of paper from the woven basket, dipped the long pen into the pot of ink, and began to write.

"Miss Hannah Acheson: My very dear and lovely friend." He wrote rapidly, almost feverishly, running his hands through the heavy mop of his hair, a strain upon him as though he would hurry his words by the intensity of his effort. He would ask her to marry him. He lived over again in the words he wrote their days as children in Ireland, his awakening to her as a woman. One page, two, three pages of foolscap scattered before him on the table. And then, as suddenly as it had begun, the urgency ceased.

"You could be a great man, Alexander," she had told him. "A big lawyer, a statesman, a businessman. There are plenty of preachers."

The ink dripped upon the unlined sheets. His head in his hands, he stared as though fascinated at the blots on the paper, his eyes hot, an ache across the arc of his forehead, his thought centered on a little band of disciples on a Palestinian hill.

"And another also said, 'Lord, I will follow thee, but first let me go bid them farewell which are at home at my house.' And Jesus said unto him, 'No man, having put his hand to the plough and looking back, is fit for the Kingdom of God.'"

Slowly, as though he were very tired, he crumpled the papers before him into a twisted wad and threw them into the hearth. For a moment the pages seemed to struggle against the smoldering fire before a flame shot up, lighting the room. He watched until it died

113

down, and then dropped upon his knee beside his chair as the candle flickered its last and the room guttered into darkness.

Hannah met him in her doorway the next afternoon, an air of expectancy about her. He had never seen her in a pinafore before, and the ruffles of white cambric over her red bodice, with her dark red hair drawn tightly back from her tiny ears and caught in a bun low on her neck, made her seem absurdly domestic. While he stood, suddenly awkward, twirling his hat in his hands, she turned and led the way into the parlor, and closed the door behind him.

"What happened?" she asked, her eyes shining. "I've been watching for you all day. I knew you'd come. You've seen Mr. Mountain, haven't you?"

He stood just within the room and tried to smile but felt the effort die on his face.

"Yes, Mr. Mountain came to see me this morning. I felt you should know about it right away since you, I mean your father, tried so hard to help me."

"What did he offer you?"

"One thousand dollars a year, beginning in January. I would be principal of the Academy in Pittsburgh. There were other inducements, too. He mentioned the opportunities in law." He smiled faintly. "It was a good offer, Hannah. Most men would have jumped at it. I may be a fool."

She stared. "Alexander, you didn't refuse it?"

He nodded. "Yes, I refused it." The words came with an effort.

A spot of red appeared in the center of her forehead, spreading slowly over her face, a blankness about her.

"I told him—I said I had a prior commitment." He stared down at his feet, and then looked up, meeting her gaze squarely. "I told him I expected to spend my life working for the unity of Christians. I can't explain it, but I feel God has called me to that work. Father Thomas has opened the way with his plan for the Restoration of the early church, and the Christian Association is only the beginning."

"You mean this is final? There's no taking it back?"

"There's no taking it back, Hannah," he repeated. "I'm too weak to step aside even once."

She turned and went to the window and stood motionless, staring out through the open lattice of the shutters.

"You don't understand, do you, Hannah?" Slowly he turned to leave, a heaviness in him.

"I might have made a great man of you." Her voice was almost toneless, without emotion, as though he were already in the past. "And you refused. You threw everything away." She turned to face him, rigidly erect, her eyes cold. "Good-by, Alexander. I feel sorry for you. But I wish you well with your—your preaching or whatever it is you'll do."

He bowed, his face flushed, but now as self-possessed as she; an aloofness, a finality about them both from which there could be no appeal.

She led the way from the room and stood just outside the front door on the high porch, folding her arms about her as though for warmth as he went down the steps and mounted Zeke.

"I'm sorry, Hannah." He wheeled about and faced her, a distance between them that he knew would never be bridged again. "I'm grateful for everything you've done. But I must do what I consider my duty as a"—he hesitated, and then smiled, a broad smile, a grin, somehow, of triumph—"as a man of God, I suppose you'd call it."

She stared at him, her hands clenched into tiny balls under her crossed arms.

"You mean a fool of God, Mr. Campbell. A fool!" She turned and without a backward glance went into the house.

Chapter 11

Alexander waited until the next morning to tell his father of his rejection of the offer of Lawyer Mountain, and of his decision.

"The Lord gave you a vision when you wrote the 'Declaration and Address,'" he said finally as they sat together in the upstairs study. "I'm not as convinced as you that the established sects will accept it, but I'm going to spend my life promoting it."

Father Thomas shuffled the papers on the table, a solemn joy on his face. "And I feared you had little faith in my plan," he said gently.

"I have faith in God," Alexander said. He went on, recounting frankly his doubts and fears. "I suppose it will mean that I'll go into the ministry, but I dislike the thought of it somehow, of being paid, that is, for such work. So many of the salaried preachers seem to me to be obstacles to Christian unity, entrenched, like vested interests. Paul was no paid hireling. And look at the Haldane brothers in Glasgow. If they can do it, with the help of God I should be able to!"

"But the Apostle Paul followed a trade," Father Thomas said. "He was a tentmaker. And the Haldane brothers are wealthy. The circumstances are not the same. A preacher must eat and wear clothes, and support his family like other men. Upon such a principle, my dear son, I fear you will wear many a ragged coat."

Alexander smiled. "You think I sound foolish, don't you?" He told briefly of his break with Hannah. "She said I was a fool, a

116

'fool of God' she called me, for going into the ministry at all!"

"Dear child!" Father Thomas shook his head. "There is no higher compliment. We are indeed fools for Christ's sake, as Paul said so many years ago. The world will call you that many times, and not realize the honor it does you. My hope for you, my son, is that as you grow older you may also be able to say with Paul: 'I am become a fool in glorying; for in nothing am I behind the very chiefest apostles, though I be nothing!' "

He pushed his glasses back on his forehead, a light in his face like a benediction.

"Now that you have chosen to follow, as Paul said, 'the foolishness of preaching to save them that believe,' let me give you some advice, my dear son. Make the Divine Book the subject of intensive study. Learn to read it in the original languages. Later I'll arrange for you to speak here and there among the brethren, according to their patience and your growth in power." He relaxed in his chair, a glimmer of a smile about his lips, studying his son, and then in swift decision continued earnestly: "James Foster and Abraham Altars want me to direct a personal course of study for them in the Scriptures. James has been a close student of the Bible for years but Abraham will need more elementary guidance. Since I will be out visiting among the churches much of the time, I want you to assume the teaching of Abraham while I am away. Perhaps you can combine his instruction with that of the children. Draw up a schedule of study for yourself and a teaching schedule, and let me see them tonight."

After the family had retired Father Thomas took the three loosely scrawled pages Alexander handed him and shook his head. "Somehow I failed to teach you penmanship." Shunting his glasses to his forehead, he handed the pages back to Alexander and relaxed in his chair, a twinkle in his eyes. "You decipher it."

Alexander laughed in apology. "It does look a little like Greek script, doesn't it? But remember how partial you are to the classical languages, Father. I am a product of the old school." He cleared his throat a little self-consciously and, moving nearer the three candles on the table, began to read:

117

"Arrangements for Studies for AC during Winter of 1809–1810. One hour to read Greek—from 8 to 9 in the morning. One hour to read Latin—from 11 to 12 in the morning. One half-hour to read Hebrew—between 12 and 1 p.m. Commit ten verses of Scripture to memory each day. And read the same in the original languages, with Henry and Scott's notes and practical observations. For this exercise we shall allow two hours. These exercises, being intended for every day, will not be dispensed with. Other reading and studies as occasion may serve. These studies in all require four and a half hours. Church history and divers other studies are intended to constitute the principal part of my other literary efforts."

He paused, waiting for his father to speak, but the older man only nodded, and motioned for him to continue.

"As you suggested, I combined the instruction of Abraham Altars as much as possible with that of the children, but since he is to be the principal student, I've headed it 'Regulations for Abraham Altars':

"1st. Read to me in the morning from 7 to 8 in Scott's Family Bible. Say one lesson every day in Greek grammar. One lesson also in Latin and one in rhetoric. Two days of the week to recite in English grammar and parse. To prepare a theme each week, which is to be corrected and to be written clear and fair in a book.

"Abraham and the children, from 10 to 11, will read a Scripture lesson.

"These attentions will occupy three hours of my time each day.

"Dorry, Nancy, and Jane say English grammar and parse with Abraham Altars—the Mondays appointed for this purpose. Thomas is to prepare a lesson every day in Latin grammar. One hour for writing and half an hour to hear any particular lesson from D., N., and J.

"The whole time spent thus will be nine hours.

"I am not trying to make a classical scholar out of Abraham," Alexander spoke in reply to his father's half-amused, half-quizzical expression. "But he appears very much in earnest."

"As schedules, they listen very well. Since your translation, let

118

me see if I can decipher them." Father Thomas extended his hand, his eyes twinkling. "With your other duties, this should certainly keep you out of mischief."

The days crowded into weeks and months. The books on baptism Alexander had ordered from Andrew Munro at Canonsburg arrived, but, as Father Thomas had intimated, they proved of little value. Neither did his own search of the Scriptures furnish enlightenment. Each member of the family had been baptized as an infant by sprinkling, and at the worst, he conceded, no one could say they had been harmed. If there was no authority in the Scriptures for the practice, neither was it condemned, and whatever its origin, he told himself, it was justified by use through the centuries. He tried to dismiss the subject from his mind.

Christmas came and went. Abraham Altars discontinued his studies in March to resume his farming, and with the coming of the spring thaws in April, Father Thomas made arrangements for Alexander to make his first public talk at the home of Jacob Donaldson. Other talks followed, and occasional encounters with William Sample kept him reminded of his half-promise to write for the Washington *Reporter*. After attending several social gatherings of young people with his sisters, he submitted to Sample three essays on the weaknesses and foibles of the younger generation, patterned after the style of the London *Spectator*.

At one of the gatherings he met Hannah Acheson, but their encounter was brief, their greeting polite and cool. She was a pretty girl, he thought, looking askance at her across the room, attractive in her ambitious, self-willed way, but she was not for him, and he felt no regret at his decision. His studies of the winter had not only increased his knowledge of God's word but had strengthened his conviction that on it, and on it alone, the foundations of the church should rest.

He wrote the essays for the *Reporter* in the form of letters to the editor from a young woman named Clarinda, and surprised even himself at the ease with which he could fall into biting, penetrating sarcasm.

The Washington *Reporter* was the only newspaper in the county and Alexander's essays immediately set its readers talking. Some felt the articles insulting; others voiced approval; but all agreed they were brilliantly written. Who is Clarinda? became the question on the streets and about the firesides.

"Only a man, and a woman hater at that, would write such letters!" Dorothea indignantly announced to the family the night after the second piece appeared. "Saying that women are geese and have no brains! No woman would say that. And listen to this: 'You will observe that when someone breaks the silence at our community parties there arises a general chatter among the rest, as when one goose of a flock chatters all the rest begin, and by and by you'll have them all chattering at once. When I am a spectator at one of these gabbing matches, the Turkish maxim comes to mind, namely: "Women have no souls," and although this sentiment shocks me and causes me to search my own breast, yet frequently I must confess if I were to judge from the frivolity of the conversation and the levity of the sentiment at these parties, I must conclude that female minds are not capacious.'" She fixed her eyes upon Alexander seated across from her at the supper table, and, despite himself, he grinned self-consciously.

Dorothea had no suspicion, he felt, that he was the author of the essays, but he had little doubt that his parents knew. He looked at his father, and caught an amused gleam in his eye.

"Now, Dorothea," said Mrs. Campbell, "it's all in fun, and there is a bit of truth in what this Clarinda says, whoever she is."

"If it's true, the younger generation is not what it was when we were young." Father Thomas looked the length of the table at his wife for corroboration. "The young people in our day would spend their time discussing the state of their souls."

"Somehow," said Mrs. Campbell, "I have a different recollection."

"I suspect Clarinda is an old maid," Nancy said. "She's disappointed in love."

Father Thomas laughed outright. "That well may be," he said. He turned to Alexander. "I have an errand for you, my son. On my last circuit I promised to lend some books to my friend John Brown on

Buffalo Creek. He wants them by tomorrow. I will hear the children's lessons in the morning if you will leave early and deliver them."

Alexander pushed back his end of the bench from the table and arose. "I'll be glad to go," he said. He grinned broadly. "It may be a healthier climate for me there than around here."

Alexander had never been in the Virginia Panhandle before, and as he rode away the next morning at daybreak, the winding roads, the heavy underbrush of dogwood and myrtle drenched with fragrant blossoms still heavy with mountain dew, the solemnity of the tall pines and the beauty of the fields from the crest of the gentle, rolling hills, made the twenty-mile journey seem shorter than it was. At a fork in the road he turned from the Washington Pike, as his father had directed him, and at the beginning of a rolling knoll saw a two-storied white frame house, its windows of real glass glistening in the sun. This must be the home of John Brown, the stanch Presbyterian Father Thomas liked so much, who owned the surrounding farm and the gristmill on the creek just below. It was not yet ten o'clock. He would make the acquaintance of Mr. Brown, deliver the books, and be home again by midafternoon.

As he reined his horse to a halt at the turnstile before the house, a Negro boy ran to meet him. Alexander had seen slaves in New York and a few freed ones in Philadelphia, but there were none at all in Washington, and for a minute he stared at the boy in curiosity. In his gray homespun shirt and pants he looked as happy and well cared for as most of the white boys he knew in Washington. But he was a slave, and slavery in this land of freedom and independence was a paradox he could not understand. He took the books from the saddlebags and, grinning at the boy, tossed him the reins, climbed over the stile, and walked rapidly up the wide coal-ash walk that led to the house.

A pull at the wooden knocker and the door swung open to reveal a fat black-faced woman, her woolly hair, tied with bits of bright-colored string, standing out from her head like the miniature snakes of Medusa, he thought, her hands deep in her checkered apron, her wide grin tightening into mild disapproval as her bright black eyes rested on the books under his arm.

"Massa Brown, he is in de field." She spoke in a rolling, guttural voice. "And de missus and Miss Jane is gone to town. But I'll tell de young missus you is here. Is you a book peddler or a preacher?"

Alexander laughed. "I'm neither. But I'm going to be a preacher. These books are for Mr. Brown."

The woman peered at him and then swung the door wide. "You doan look lak no preacher to me," she said suspiciously.

Rapid footsteps sounded from the stairway and a moment later he looked into a pair of saucy brown eyes that stifled the words rising in his throat. The girl was tall, with a flowered calico skirt billowing about her ankles. Her white muslin bodice was cut low, revealing erect white shoulders, and about her neck a velvet band was caught at the throat with a tiny cameo pin. She smiled easily in welcome.

Alexander bowed stiffly. "My father sent Mr. Brown some books. I'm Alexander Campbell."

"I'm Margaret Brown," she said simply.

For a moment they stood, staring at each other, and then she stepped aside. "Do come in, Mr. Campbell. And please forgive Holly. She likes both peddlers and preachers, but she doesn't care for books. That's because I'm making her learn to read."

For a moment Alexander stood silent, a quick suspicion in him. He remembered now that John Brown had a daughter and a step-daughter, but Father Thomas had called them young girls. Cautiously he stepped across the threshold.

"Place an extra plate for dinner, Holly," Margaret said as she led the way across the hall into the sitting room. "And ring the yard bell for Papa. Run now; these books are not for you."

"Please don't trouble," Alexander said. "I'll just leave the books here and start back. I have some teaching to do myself this afternoon—my younger brothers and sisters."

"Unheard of!" she said gaily. "Of course you must stay!" She seated herself on a sofa against the window and looked up at him, indicating a place for him beside her. "May I see the books?"

He placed the books on the sofa beside her, his eyes sweeping the big square room. The hand-hewn rafters and walls were of black walnut, polished to a dull luster, and around the ceiling ran a hand-carved cornice; the center of the quarter-sawed oak floor was covered with a great oval rag rug reflecting the rich red and green of the curtains draped back from the windows. A four-foot fireplace occupied the center of the east wall, overhung by a broad mantle; and in the northwest corner a narrow stairway, leading to the upper floor, was partially enclosed. A hatrack stood by the stairway, and bookcases lined the walls on either side of the door, while opposite the door stood an escritoire, with a quill pen standing erect in a jar of sand. A round table occupied the center of the room, and pulled up to it were four fiddleback chairs, the seats covered with heavy green homespun, while two comfortable mahogany-framed rockers, covered with the same cloth, were on either side of the fireplace. The room had a lived-in feeling of friendly intimacy that he liked.

"Papa made most of this furniture himself," she said in answer to his unspoken admiration. "He likes to work with wood." She picked up the books. "But he also likes to read, and when Papa gets his hands on these, there'll be no getting them away from him. So now is my chance to see what you've brought him."

Alexander placed his hat on the hatrack and glanced furtively in its tiny mirror, smoothing his hair before he sat down beside her.

"This small one," he said, "is Booth's *Essay on the Kingdom of Christ*. And these three"—he held them in his hand—"are *Owens on the Holy Spirit*, all twelve hundred pages of them."

"Any writer who takes twelve hundred pages to explain his subject is a bit confused, don't you think?" she said. "It required only the four Gospels to give us all the teachings of Jesus, and some of that is repetition. I think I'll start with the little one and let Papa struggle with Mr. Owens." She patted the books and set them aside on the sofa. "Besides, Mr. Campbell, I've only a woman's mind. And I've a confession to make. I like to read fiction." Her eyes laughed at him. "Do you ever read fiction, Mr. Campbell?"

"Novel reading is a waste of time; worse than that, it dissipates and weakens the mind." He attempted to speak sternly, but the attempt failed, and he laughed. "What have you been reading, Miss Brown?"

"*Pilgrim's Progress* by John Bunyan," she said primly. "If it weren't fiction, I'd suggest you read it, Mr. Campbell. I haven't felt it to be a waste of time at all."

Alexander looked askance at her. The girl was laughing at him. "*Pilgrim's Progress* is not a novel," he said shortly. "It's a great Christian allegory—a story of every man's progress from destruction to salvation."

"I didn't say it was a novel," she said sweetly. "I've never even seen a novel. Papa won't allow them in the house. But I don't believe they'd dissipate my mind nearly so much as some other reading I've done lately."

"What's that? Maybe Augustine's *Confessions* this time?"

"Well, they are confessions of a sort. The Clarinda letters in the Washington *Reporter*. Have you seen them?" Without waiting for Alexander to reply she went on. "Of all the awful, silly things! I certainly don't recommend them, so if you haven't seen them—"

"I have seen them," he said slowly. "And I don't think they are silly at all. It seems to me they are a serious commentary on the times. I would say that the writer, Clarinda, is a very intelligent young woman," he went on steadily. "No doubt the exposure of these follies will do much good."

She laughed as though at a merry joke. "You surely don't think that Clarinda is a woman, do you, Mr. Campbell? Some man is writing those letters; most probably a confirmed old bachelor who has soured on the world. To say women have no souls! What could be more like a man—a bitter old man, or maybe a young man disappointed in love!"

Alexander crossed his legs warily. "Clarinda did not say women have no souls; that was a Turkish maxim she was quoting."

"Well, anyway," she said, and stopped and looked at him curiously. "You must have read them pretty carefully, Mr. Campbell."

He flushed and said nothing, and after a moment she went on. "And a woman would have written about the follies of the men. Goodness knows they have plenty of them!"

"You are a most unusual young lady, Miss Brown." Alexander grinned at her, a warm admiration shining from his eyes. "I wouldn't be surprised if you weren't Clarinda yourself."

For a moment she looked at him in astonishment, and then they laughed together, a warming bond between them. If Father Thomas had laid a trap for him, he had done it well, Alexander thought as he arose to meet Margaret's father.

It was midafternoon when Alexander rode away from the Brown home, a lightness of spirit upon him he had not felt for weeks. He liked John Brown, a genial, kindly man, quick of mind and ready of speech. Dinner had been served in the grape arbor beside the house, the three of them seated about a small round table laden with turnip greens and okra, slices of ham, hot biscuits, and tall glasses of cool buttermilk. Mr. Brown had been pleased with the books, and Alexander found himself promising to bring over others within the week. They had talked of the early days in the land, and Margaret told of the capture of her stepmother by Indians only twenty years before; and Brown talked of his youth in Maryland and the long years of the War for Independence. At the last, Alexander found himself telling of his own boyhood on the farm in County Antrim, and of his dedication to the establishment of Christian unity. And although John Brown frankly stated that for him the millennium would come when the various breeds of Presbyterians could be made to recognize even each other as Christians, much less other denominations, and indicated no intention of joining such a movement, he spoke of it with admiration. And the Clarinda letters were not mentioned again by any of them.

Father Thomas returned in midweek without completing his circuit, sick with a stomach complaint and discouraged by the lack of response he had received to his Plea. A copy of the "Declaration and Address" had been posted to every preacher in Washington

County, and to many others in surrounding areas, but the document had been ignored. No voices were raised in protest and none in approval.

"I'll complete your schedule for you," Alexander had offered cheerfully. The Parkingsons and the Askews, where his father was scheduled to meet with groups, lived in the vicinity of Charlestown, Virginia, on the Ohio River eight miles below the village of Buffalo. The road led directly past the Brown home. "I can take Mr. Brown those other books I promised him at the same time," he added, as if in afterthought.

Four days later he rode again down the shadowed Buffalo road and reined in at the now-familiar turnstile of the Brown home. It was late afternoon. Another Clarinda letter had been published, this time on the foibles of men, as Margaret Brown had suggested. It would be interesting to observe her reaction.

Mrs. Brown met him at the door—a diminutive woman with an intelligent, forthright air about her; she was joined shortly by Margaret and by Jane Glass, her daughter by a previous marriage. Alexander laid the books on the round table in the sitting room, and for several minutes they sat in formal, almost stilted conversation. When he arose to leave, Mrs. Brown halted him with a wave of her hand.

"It's getting late and Mr. Brown would not hear of your leaving before he saw you. He's horse trading in the back pasture or I'd call him. So you must spend the night."

Alexander demurred, half-heartedly. A night's lodging in the home of a friend was a common courtesy for a traveler on these hill roads, he had learned, and after a few moments he resumed his seat. His father would think he was staying with the Askews in Charlestown.

"I don't read much." Mrs. Brown picked up the books on the table. "But Mr. Brown and the girls are always at it. I guess that proves that not all women are geese, like Margaret says you think."

"Like I think?" Alexander's eyes widened in injured surprise.

"I feel Miss Margaret must be quoting that person Clarinda, who is writing for the *Reporter*." He turned to Margaret. "I suppose you noticed that Clarinda gave her opinion of men this week?"

Margaret's eyes twinkled. "I was more impressed by the fact that Clarinda got around to it right after our discussion, Mr. Campbell. It was rather a coincidence."

Alexander felt his face grow warm, and unconsciously he grinned. Margaret Brown was a subtle, intelligent young woman. She might be an uncomfortable person to be around.

Heavy footsteps sounded on the porch and John Brown bustled through the doorway followed by a thin-faced, red-haired smiling man in clerical black. Brother Obadiah Jenkins, he explained, was a traveling evangelist then circulating with the Redstone Baptist Association, caught at nightfall just outside the Brown home while returning from a meeting at Charlestown.

"Besides being nighttime," Brother Jenkins explained to Alexander, "it kind of looked like Presbyterian weather—a little sprinkle here, a light patter there, and so I ran for cover. I'm a good Baptist and I ain't a-feared of water, but I don't aim to be pitty-pattered into salvation."

John Brown slapped him on the back. "Brother Obadiah is an all-or-nothing Baptist preacher," he explained. "You go-all-under and get-wet-all-over or you're not baptized, and if you're not baptized, you don't go to heaven. And he's got Scripture for it, too. But I guess maybe they'll let a few of us Presbyterians slip in through the pearly gates whenever there's a good dry spell on."

"Not unless you've been baptized," said Brother Obadiah firmly. "I'm sorry, brother, but you can't put on Christ and go to heaven unless you've been baptized, and that means you got to be a Baptist. That's what the Bible says, if it says a word of truth."

Alexander smiled. He had never talked freely with a Baptist preacher. Most of the people in Washington were Presbyterians, or Lutherans, or of no fixed belief at all. He thought of Dr. Aaron Riddle and his remark that the Campbells should be Baptists, and his smile broadened. He could never be a Baptist. They were too literal

127

and adamant in their belief, and too much given to excessive emotionalism. But they were devout, earnest people and close students of the Bible.

Supper was almost over and they had finished the big helpings of peach cobbler swimming in rich cream and were sipping the soothing, unfermented blackberry cordial when Brother Obadiah Jenkins launched into tales of his meetings with the Baptist churches at Little Redstone, Turkey Foot, Ten-Mile, and Pidgeon Creek, mentioning the numbers who had fallen slain before the Lord under his preaching at these points.

"Sin and damnation! Those two words sum up the history of the world." He stared at Alexander seated opposite. "My brother, that's the trouble with mankind. Hell is filled with good people who refused to believe that our Saviour meant exactly what He said."

"I knew Brother Obadiah would get to that sooner or later," John Brown said, letting his grin rove the table in triumph. "He believes that hell is chock full of Presbyterians."

"I didn't say that, Brother Brown." Brother Obadiah shook his head in mild protest. "No man can limit the mercy of God. But there's no critter under the sun except a mule that can be as stubborn as a Presbyterian. If he won't be baptized in spite of the command of our Saviour, how can he expect mercy? That's the trouble."

"We Presbyterians," said Alexander, "most of us, were baptized when we were infants. How can you say we won't be saved?"

Brother Jenkins stared at him, an earnest, ironic expression on his face. "That was Brother Brown's statement, not mine," he said. "Nothing is impossible with God. Even the thief on the Cross was saved. But that was an exception, a direct act of mercy of Christ himself. The trouble with you Presbyterians and lots of others is that you defy the direct command of the Saviour. You believe, but that ain't enough. You must be baptized, too!"

"I've been baptized." Alexander spoke more sharply than he intended, his own uncertainty heightened by the older man's assurance. "I was baptized at the age of three months."

"That's infant baptism," said Brother Jenkins. "And that's wrong. Besides, you were probably sprinkled, and that's not baptism at all.

Jesus said, 'He that believeth and is baptized shall be saved.' We must have believers' baptism. A baby can't believe. Infant baptism, whether by sprinkling or pouring, or even by immersion, is no more baptism in the meaning of the Scripture than pouring water on a duck's back. The fact about it, brother, is that you just ain't never been baptized, and nothing you can say can get around that simple gospel truth!"

"Baptism is a mere symbol," Alexander persisted, "a ritual, an expression of compliance with the will of the Saviour. The method of baptism is not essential."

Brother Jenkins pushed his empty plate aside and leaned his elbow on the table, his face flushed now, shaking his long, bony forefinger at Alexander in warning emphasis. "Brother, you couldn't be more wrong! Paul said, 'Know ye not that so many of us as were baptized into Jesus Christ were baptized into his death? Therefore, we are buried with him by baptism into death; that like as Christ was raised up from the dead by the glory of the Father, even so we also should walk in newness of life.' You can't say a man is buried in water if only a few drops are sprinkled on him. You've got to be a believer, and you've got to be immersed. That's the only scriptural baptism!" He leaned back, a sternness in his lean face. "Since you're already a believer, I can baptize you tonight in Buffalo Creek if you're ready. But you won't be sprinkled. Not if Obadiah Jenkins does the baptizing. You'll be a believing Baptist when you come up out of the water, and you'll be wet all over!"

John Brown slapped his open palm on the table before him. "Brother Obadiah, you'll make a Baptist out of me yet!"

Mrs. Brown addressed them all impartially, a touch of patient resignation in her manner. "Why don't we transfer the discussion to the sitting room? We'll all be more comfortable there and it won't be so far to the creek!"

Amid general laughter John Brown arose and pushed his chair under the table. "I want to hear you preachers on Philip and the eunuch. I want you to explain how Philip baptized the eunuch in the desert if he didn't do it by sprinkling. Did he use a mirage?"

As Alexander went with the group into the sitting room he

thought of the Haldane brothers and Greville Ewing and Alexander Carson in faraway Glasgow. They believed in immersion, too. Suddenly he wished fervently that Brother Obadiah Jenkins had gone elsewhere to spend the night.

The three women took places on the sofa and Brother Obadiah settled himself in one of the rockers while John Brown sat in a straight-backed chair by the big table. Alexander glanced at Margaret and she smiled, a half-shy, half-mischievous intimacy in her eyes. As he was about to seat himself in one of the straight-backed chairs beside her father, she suddenly spoke.

"Tell us about Philip and the eunuch, Mr. Campbell. How did that baptism take place?"

Alexander straightened his shoulders and thrust his hands into his coat pockets. "With pleasure, Miss Brown." He bowed in mock gravity, and then he sobered. "The eighth chapter of the Acts of the Apostles tells us that Philip preached to the eunuch as they traveled together in the desert, and that the eunuch believed on Christ and wanted to be a Christian. We also know that as they traveled they came 'unto a certain water,' an oasis probably, and that the eunuch was baptized. He may have been immersed, or he may have been merely sprinkled by Philip. The method is unimportant. What is important is that he believed. What if they had not come to the water? Would we say the eunuch would have been lost because he could not have been immersed in water? What is it we seek? Salvation in water, or salvation in the Lord Jesus?"

John Brown slapped his knee in approval. "Young man, a good point! A good lick for the Presbyterians!"

"You are wrong, brother!" The evangelist spoke in a stentorian tone, his face set sternly. "We cannot evade the direct commandments and example of Jesus. The eunuch and Philip went 'down into the water' and when Philip had baptized him, the Scriptures tell us they 'came up out of the water' and the eunuch went on his way rejoicing. Do you mean to tell me that they went down into the water just so Philip could sprinkle a little water on the eunuch's head? Oh, no!" He shook his head vigorously. "The eunuch had to believe and he had to be immersed. And since infants can't believe

130

and aren't immersed, just sprinkled, at the best that kind of baptizing ain't anything but a waste of time and water!" He paused, staring about solemnly, a sudden pity in his voice. "I'm sorry, folks, but according to the Scriptures you Presbyterians just ain't been baptized! That's the Gospel!"

"Nonsense!" Alexander spoke indignantly, his face flushed. "You're talking nonsense, Mr. Jenkins!"

Brother Jenkins rose to his full six feet, his long forefinger pointed at the younger man accusingly. "Brother, according to the Scriptures you've never been baptized, and without baptism there is no salvation. You're a lost soul!"

In the silence that followed Alexander seated himself, a strained smile on his face. Whatever might be said of him, Brother Obadiah Jenkins was a sincere preacher, a conviction upon him like an ancient prophet thundering more in sorrow than in anger the doom of the Lord upon the sinful.

"I think we should all have a cup of tea." Mrs. Brown's voice came to them as though from a distance. With a tight smile on her face, she went hurriedly into the kitchen with Jane.

Margaret arose as though to follow them. "I was two months old when I was baptized by sprinkling." She looked from Alexander to Brother Jenkins and back again. "You have me worried. Would I be considered a lost soul?"

"I can make a Baptist and a good Christian out of you first thing in the morning, Miss Margaret." Brother Jenkins spoke with feeling. "Buffalo Creek right back of your house is as good a place to baptize a sinner as the river Jordan."

Margaret turned to Alexander as though for advice. "What would you say to that, Mr. Campbell?"

Alexander met her gaze squarely. "I'm quite sure you have nothing to worry about, Miss Margaret." He spoke gently. "The method of baptism can be of little importance as long as the heart is right. I'm confident that you are a Christian."

"Thank you, Alexander." She looked at him in gratitude, using his first name unconsciously. "I hope you have occasion to lend Papa another book soon so you can come back to see us again."

She turned toward the door. "I don't care for any tea, so I'll say good night." She smiled at them all, and, kissing her father lightly on the cheek, again smiled at Alexander and left the room.

Chapter 12

ALEXANDER SAT TENSELY ERECT ON THE BENCH AT THE FRONT OF the rough, unshaded stand in Major Templeton's grove, the warm July sun of the early afternoon making his new black store-bought suit seem heavy and uncomfortable. The talks he had made in the home of Jacob Donaldson and others of the Christian Association had been brief and before a few friends. This was different: this was to be a sermon, his first sermon. Before him on the plank benches that seemed to stretch endlessly across the grass under the trees were people who were strangers; some who had come out of curiosity, others who opposed the Christian Association and who would be critical no matter what he said. But there were smiling faces, too: well-wishers, friends who nodded at him and occasionally raised a hand in greeting. He caught sight of Editor Sample, leaning against a tree at the edge of the grove, and of the Reverend Aaron Riddle, and the Reverend Mordecai Anderson, pastor of the Presbyterian Church on Upper Buffalo Creek. His eyes went back to his own family group, seated under the trees on the green rug his mother had brought from Ireland, and catching his father's eye, he smiled, wishing he could somehow share the older man's confidence that his plea for unity would be welcomed by the established churches. Father Thomas had insisted that James Foster preside at this meeting so that he could hear his son as one of the congregation. "He must stand before the Lord alone now," he had said. "But I shall be praying for him."

Suddenly Alexander felt a wave of heat pass over him, and he fidgeted with his high stock, smoothing his cravat. He had hoped Margaret Brown and her family would be here. They must have known he was to speak. He had not seen them since he had been their overnight guest six weeks ago. But the *Reporter* had carried a notice that young Mr. Alexander Campbell, late of Glasgow University, and the son of the eminent Thomas Campbell, would preach his first sermon on July 15, 1810, in Templeton's Grove, eight miles north of Washington. They must have seen it. He resisted the impulse to tug again at his collar as James Foster arose from his seat beside him to open the service, and, folding his hands in his lap, repeated silently the petition of the Psalmist: "Let the words of my mouth and the meditations of my heart be acceptable in thy sight, O Lord, my strength and my redeemer."

While the people stood after the opening prayer, Foster led them in the responsive quotation of the One Hundredth Psalm, and then, as they seated themselves, he said quietly, "Alexander Campbell, candidate for the ministry from the Christian Association of Washington County." He bowed to Alexander and left the platform.

Alexander arose slowly, his pocket Testament open in his hand, waiting, an unconscious dignity upon him, until the last rustling noise had died away. Clearly he read his text from the seventh chapter of the Gospel according to St. Matthew:

"Therefore whosoever heareth these sayings of mine, and doeth them, I will liken him unto a wise man, which built his house upon a rock . . ."

He was almost through his reading when he glanced up. An open carriage was driving into the grove from the Canonsburg road; it pulled to a stop at the far side of the stand and the Brown family stepped out. He finished his text and slipped the New Testament into his pocket and launched into his sermon, thankful that he had memorized it. The next time he glanced in the direction of the new arrivals he saw that they had seated themselves on a blanket to one side of the stand, as close to it as they could get without disturbing others. He turned away, his thick hair slightly ruffled by the breeze, his face flushed by the strain and the July heat, his tall figure unshielded by any table from the full view of every listener.

His voice at first seemed halting, but as the words brought meaning and significance to his mind, the strain lessened. He used no gestures; he made no passionate outcries of exhortation according to the preaching pattern of the day; his tone was almost conversational, but the audience listened quietly, with growing attention, for the half-hour that he spoke. For a few seconds after he had finished he stood before them motionless, his hands clasped behind his back, sensing their approval. He had not mistaken his vocation. And then James Foster mounted the stand and, with hand uplifted, committed them all unto the care of their Lord.

Alexander was trying to slip from the rear of the stand, his legs suddenly weak, when he felt a hand touch his arm. People were beginning to crowd about; a crescendo of voices was reaching him, but they seemed a long way off as he looked into the flushed, excited face of Margaret Brown.

"Papa always insists on hearing young preachers, to help them out, he says. But you didn't need any help, Alexander. You are—" She stopped and corrected herself. "You will be a great preacher one of these days." The teasing glow went out of her eyes and a warmth came into them. And then the crowd surged between them and she was gone.

The next Sunday Alexander preached in an open field near Middletown, this time from the floor of a wagon bed; the following week at the courthouse in Washington, and a week later in a grove near Buffalo. Margaret Brown was seated with her family in the center of the group on a long plank supported by two upturned barrels, and as he brought his sermon to a close he was conscious he had not done well. He had been more aware of her face in its blue pokebonnet with the fluttering lace edge than of his message. It was the same sermon he had preached the Sunday before at the Washington courthouse, but somehow, today, it had not been so effective. Even Margaret had seemed restless and inattentive before he had finished. Father Thomas was right, he thought, as the closing words rolled effortlessly from his lips.

"You'll be serving a warmed-over dish," his father had said, "and that's bad for any preacher. It's laziness. Whatever else it may be, it's not real preaching when you memorize your sermons, and your people will know it."

"But it's a good sermon," Alexander had protested; "the best I've written!"

"And you especially want your friends in the Buffalo community to hear your best?" Father Thomas shook his head doubtfully. "Will you be preaching to please the Lord, my son, or your friends?"

The feeling of failure was still upon him as he sat with Margaret three hours later in the grape arbor in the Brown yard. He and his father had declined the Browns' invitation to go home with them for dinner, remaining, instead, with the group in the grove for a dinner on the grounds, but had promised to stop by on the way home for a glass of buttermilk and cake. Now his father was in the sitting room, talking with Mr. and Mrs. Brown and Jane, who was soon to marry John Stevenson and move to Pittsburgh, and he and Margaret had wandered into the yard to admire the early asters.

"Something's troubling you, isn't it, Alexander?" Her warmly appraising eyes looked at him anxiously as she twirled a purple blossom under her nose.

He crossed his legs on the narrow bench fastened by a rope hinge to the trellis, and stared at her as though debating his answer. "Yes," he said after a pause. "Several things are bothering me."

"Could I help?"

"You have helped me already. You made me realize during the service this morning that I am a vain, pompous, strutting fellow, eager for approval; that I'm a poor preacher."

She laughed. "You're a good preacher," she said. "You—you recite your sermons well."

He put his head in his hands and groaned. "That's just it," he said. "You knew I memorized them!"

"But they're good," she consoled him. "Only—"

"I know," he said. "Only they sound like hollow brass and tinkling cymbals; like they came from a book instead of from my

135

heart." He pulled a leaf from the grapevine and tore it to bits. "Yet I do feel them in my heart; I feel the Lord wants me to be a preacher, a good preacher. From this day forth," he said solemnly, "I'll never memorize another sermon. I'll be a real preacher or none!" He reached out and took her hand. "You see how you've helped me?" He grinned.

"Me? You did it yourself!" She pulled her hand away and shook her finger at him. "So now you have no more problems!"

He ran his hand through his hair. "I wish that were true. I'm afraid our problems, our big ones, are just beginning."

"What do you mean?"

"This morning after the service the Reverend Mordecai Anderson talked with Father and me about making application for the Christian Association to join the Pittsburgh Presbyterian Synod of the National Church of Scotland. Father is inclined to do it."

"What do you think?"

"I hardly know what to think. Most of our members are Presbyterians of one kind or another, and accept the Westminster Confession. But the Nationalist Synod is composed of clergymen as hostile to our insistence on freedom of opinion as the Seceder brethren are. If we were accepted, we would be a thorn in their flesh, and if our application were rejected, it would be another big blow to Father Thomas."

She nodded, understanding, and they sat in silence for a time. The sun was casting long shadows, and Alexander glanced up at the deepening sky.

"Father and I should have been halfway home by now." He arose abruptly. "We find life much too pleasant at the Brown mansion. I apologize."

She arose without a word and placed her hand in the offered crook of his elbow. Slowly they began the walk back to the house, the deepening bond of understanding between them requiring no words.

"It is abhorrent to me," Father Thomas said at last as though they had been discussing the subject all along, "to realize that our Association is coming to be regarded as a separate religious body.

Even my warm friends among the preachers take good care to see they do not give us their approval publicly. They consider us outside the fold rather than reformers within it."

Alexander nudged his horse forward so that they rode in single file for a time, uncertain what to say to comfort his father, who had believed so implicitly that once the call was made, other Christians would be as anxious as he to heal the divisions among them.

"I don't object particularly to the Westminster Confession," Father Thomas continued, as though arguing with himself. "I accept it as a commentary and interpretation of wise and good men upon the Scriptures. What I cannot do is to give it equal authority with the Bible."

Alexander pulled in his horse and waited for his father to ride alongside. "Does that mean," he asked, "that you are seriously thinking of applying for admission to the Pittsburgh Synod?"

"I am."

For a few minutes they rode in silence, Alexander unwilling to distress his father by disagreement and equally unwilling to give him what he considered false comfort. He tried to speak casually.

"The antagonism of the clergy as a whole, and that of the organized church, is a natural enough result, Father. The purpose of the Association is to sweep aside creeds; and since all organized church parties are founded upon human creeds, and the Presbyterians are especially rooted in one, I don't believe the Synod will accept us. From their viewpoint our Association is a Trojan horse. It would be suicidal for them to admit us into their organization."

"I cannot accept that view." Father Thomas reined aside and stood facing his son, his face tense, their mounts nuzzling each other. "The Confession of Faith declares the Bible is the only rule of faith and practice; they cannot reject us because we stand upon that principle. I must deliver my soul! I cannot tolerate the thought that I have in any degree helped create another division within the church! Yes, I shall petition the Synod!"

Alexander attempted to smile, glad that the deepening shadows obscured his face. "I'm afraid it will be useless, but I shall do everything I can to help. May the Lord bless you, Father."

"May the Lord bless us all," Father Thomas repeated hoarsely.

For a moment they sat, staring at each other in the faceless darkness and then, wheeling sharply about, began to jog smartly into town.

Harvest time was on the land. The hum of cider presses devouring pungent mounds of crimson apples mingled with the sound of the scythe and sickle in the fields. Golden shocks of corn arose to stand as sentinels in the long, furrowed rows. A cool softness invaded the hills, and over the countryside hung the pungent odor of apple butter, steaming in bubbling brownness in iron kettles in every yard.

Alexander's duties on the home place increased. Casings of sausage meat were hung in the smokehouse over slow hickory fires. Parsnips were dug and stored in the cellar; pumpkins were dipped in wax to preserve them; turnips and rutabagas were binned next to the Irish potatoes under a thick covering of sand hauled from the river bed.

But Sunday morning always found Alexander preaching, now from a wagon bed or stump of a tree on some farm; now from the rostrum in the Washington courthouse; often in the crude meetinghouse erected by the Association at the Crossroads. The Brown family attended with a regularity that made them seem as members, and Alexander's encounters with Margaret were frequent, each one anticipated and prolonged. The Crossroads was proving inconvenient for many of the members, some of whom had moved nearer Buffalo, and early in the fall another site was selected in the valley of Brush Run, two miles above its junction with Buffalo Creek, on ground given by William Gilchrist. Logs for the new meetinghouse were milled at David Bryant's sawmill, and on September 16, Alexander preached at the new location, standing on a bench beside the foundation the men had erected the day before.

Crowded into his days was the preparation of a formal statement for Father Thomas, applying for admission to the Pittsburgh Synod. His father, he realized, needed his help. Mutterings against the Association had increased, and the older man at times seemed alarmed, uncertain what he had started. As Alexander helplessly watched the lines of discouragement deepen in his face, the resentment which had begun to gnaw in him turned into a smoldering anger against the type of clergyman who revered creeds above Christ and who would build divisive walls about their separate sects.

It was in this mood that he attended the commencement exercises of Washington College on Thursday, September 27, 1810. The four-year-old frontier Presbyterian college, with its half-hundred students, could not in fairness be compared to the centuries-old University of Glasgow, but he was shocked by the degree of license permitted the students in their exhibitions. They had turned the liberty granted them in this land of freedom into a license to behave in a manner inappropriate for any institution of learning, especially one dedicated to Christian learning according to the pattern of John Knox. The caricatures of the Scots and the Irish; the mock trial at the bar; the displays of bare-knuckled boxing for the amusement of the audience; the use of profane language aroused his indignation.

Early the next morning he placed another article on the desk of Editor Sample. It was in the form of a letter to a mythical friend, a devastating criticism of the spectacle written with ironic insight into the moral laxity of the community. Boldly he signed it "Bonus Homo."

"It's better than anything you've given me yet," Editor Sample said as he looked up from reading it, a grin spreading over his face. "If your Clarinda essays raised a rumpus, this will start a war. It will be on the front page Monday." He laid down the sheets of paper and stood up, facing Alexander. "Every subject you touch sparks interest. If you ever quit preaching, I'll make room for you on the paper. Or turn the whole thing over to you. You should have one of your own."

"Maybe I will someday. It would be another way of spreading the Gospel. No Christian can rest at ease in Zion, even if it means stirring up trouble. I never forget that Jesus was the most controversial figure who ever lived."

It was the last day of September, and Alexander again stood on a bench beside the now rapidly rising structure of the new Brush Run meetinghouse, his congregation seated in wagons arranged in parallel rows before him, and at the sides on piles of lumber from the Bryant mill, which would be used in the building. Clouds obscured the sun; the air was damp and chill with a threat of rain; babies cried; children were restless; and just as he got well into his sermon a wind, penetrating and cold, swooped upon them from the north and for a few minutes spiraled his words into the void of the sky. He tried to continue his carefully thought-out metaphysical thesis of justification by faith, but it sounded halting and strained, lacking in either comfort or hope for the earnest, toil-worn men and women who tried to give him their attention. After forty minutes he brought the sermon to a close and pronounced the benediction.

John Brown and Margaret, seated nearby on the leather pad from their carriage, protected from the chill by a blanket, were the first to reach him.

"When a woman like Ann Brown commits a sin like staying home from preaching to work with Holly preparing a meal for a preacher," said John Brown, "she expects him to come and eat it. She says we dasn't come home without you."

As usual there were other friends at the Browns' table. Jane had married John Stevenson and moved to Pittsburgh, but the Hodgens and the Askews and the James Fosters were there, adding to the good talk and enjoying the abundance of food. Alexander's sermon was scarcely mentioned and he felt an unconscious rebuke in their lack of interest in it. Instead, the petition to the Pittsburgh Synod was discussed, and all predicted it would be accepted. Maybe he was wrong about it, he thought as he refrained from commenting. When the talk turned to the commencement exercises at Washington College, he was surprised that no one shared his sense of the improprieties of that occasion. Was he too censorious?

As the group left the table for the sitting room, he made his way toward the door and slipped out of the house, starting across the side yard, unconsciously going toward the grape arbor.

"I'll show you a better place," a light voice said behind him. "It's our favorite spot when Jane or I have anything on our minds. But first I think you need to stretch those long legs of yours. Let's take a walk."

For almost an hour they tramped the fields, talking little, and then he let Margaret lead him down the slope of the hill, toward a live oak, its spreading limbs like a protecting canopy extending over Buffalo Creek, a stream of pools and eddies and suddenly rushing currents; wide and deep, and narrow and shallow by turns; its center deep enough to drown a man.

He made a seat for her in the moss against the tree and spread the afghan she had brought along over her knees, and then sat beside her, their backs against the gnarled trunk. The dappled, cold sunlight of late afternoon filtered to them through the almost bare branches. They watched for a while in silence a whorl of snake doctors along the edge of the stream while the grasshoppers and crickets resumed their nervous chant and bullfrogs began to croak.

"I almost wrote you a letter," she began. "Of apology for what I said about reciting your sermons. I'm sorry, Alexander."

He stared straight ahead, his face impassive, his voice deep with conviction. "You did me a great service, Margaret. You made me realize, well, like another Scot, Robert Burns, once said:

"Oh wad some power the giftie gie us
To see oursels as others see us!
It wad frae monie a blunder free us,
An' foolish notion."

She looked at him solemnly, and after a pause he went on, cauterizing the hurt in his heart.

"I've written a bumptious piece for the *Reporter*, maybe too bumptious. It's an ironical account of the exercises at the college last Thursday. I didn't think the fencing, the boxing, the profane language used in some of the stage plays were appropriate to a college, and I said so, holding the whole thing up to ridicule."

"Is it signed Clarinda?" she asked, a twinkle in her eyes.

He smiled, a grudging, half-smile. "Not this time. I'm through with Clarinda. You guessed I wrote them?"

She nodded. "Maybe I know you better than you think."

He stared at her for a moment without surprise, and then looked away. "I'm signing this one Bonus Homo."

"Where ever do you get such names?"

"Clarinda is from Robert Burns. He wrote some poems to a lady-love by that name and it struck me. But Bonus Homo, well, I felt I was writing for a lot of people, a lot of good men and women who were as disgusted as I was. I realize now I was presumptuous. Perhaps they don't feel that way at all. But I've agreed to write two more of them."

"At family worship the other day." she said softly, "Papa read from Ecclesiastes, the seventh chapter. I'm sure you're familiar with it. 'Be not righteous over much; neither make thyself over wise. . . . For there is not a just man upon earth, that doeth good, and sinneth not.' "

"I know the chapter. Bobby Burns knew it, too. He wrote a poem, an 'Address to the Unco Guid,' based upon it. It goes:

> "My son, these maxims make a rule
> An' lump them aye thegither;
> The Rigid Righteous is a fool,
> The Rigid Wise anither;
> The cleanest corn that ere was dight
> May hae some pules o' caff in;
> So ne'er a fellow creature slight,
> For random fits o' daffin."

He picked up a pebble and threw it far out into the stream, watching the widening ripples, avoiding her eyes, and then he scrambled to his feet. "Burns wrote another one, which just fits you:

> "My love, she's but a lassie yet,
> We'll let her stand a year or twa
> She'll be no half sae saucy yet."

"What would you and your Mr. Burns do if your lassie didn't change, and remained as saucy as before? What then?"

"Very simple," he said.

> "If to change her mind, we canna make her,
> The devil take her!"

She laughed, a mellow, tinkling, far-off laugh like the chimes of tiny bells at a distance. "Why, Alexander!" she said. "You're so unpredictable! One moment you're a self-righteous saint and the next you're fairly human!"

142

He turned to her in final momentous decision that had been forming gradually in his heart for weeks; a timidity upon him now that the time was at hand equaled only by his great need of her; a fear that she would have none of him. He gulped and clutched at the remnant of his courage, his voice hoarse.

"Will you marry me, Margaret?"

"Yes, Alexander."

For a moment he stared at her in bewilderment, as though doubting his ears, and then he reached out and took her hands and pulled her to her feet.

"I must warn you!" He spoke slowly, his voice thick with a mingled dread and happiness at which she could only guess. "Your lot will be a hard one. I shall be a preacher all my life, maybe an unpopular preacher, fighting for a cause most people will oppose. I expect to accept no money for my preaching. Our support must come from farming, teaching, writing—whatever tasks the Lord gives me to do. The world will call me a fool."

" 'The foolishness of God is wiser than men,' " she quoted softly.

"Hardship is all I have to offer you," he went on, "that—that and my love."

"And that, dear one," she said, "is all I want."

His arms went about her like the opening and closing of a gate, locking her forever in his heart and life; a reverent, almost unbelieving joy upon them both. And then, as their lips met, the yard bell began to toll for evening worship.

Chapter 13

ALEXANDER HAD NO OPPORTUNITY TO SPEAK TO MR. BROWN THAT evening but early the next morning he located him at his gristmill. A light freeze the night before had put on Buffalo Creek a thin sheet of ice that was breaking up now, and Mr. Brown and Benjy were pouring sacks of grain into the yawning mouth of the wooden funnel while the huge millstone creaked and the great wooden wheel turned heavily against the thickening slush of water, mud, and ice.

The older man turned around as Alexander approached, and waved him toward the shed that served as an office and weighing room. In a few minutes he came in and closed the plank door behind him. Alexander cleared his throat, wondering how best to begin his declaration, when Mr. Brown sat down heavily on the end of an upturned barrel and ran his hand across his forehead.

"Margaret told us," he said simply.

"It happened suddenly," Alexander said, his voice husky. "It was the hand of God. Neither of us realized it until—"

"I know," Mr. Brown said. "But I expected it."

"Otherwise I would have asked your consent to speak to her. But I didn't know it myself until it happened."

Mr. Brown nodded. He stooped and picked up a a handful of soft red wheat and began rubbing it between the palms of his hands.

"I know it's a lot, asking for Margaret; I love her, but I won't ask her to share my life until I'm able to care for her. I'm a preacher and always will be, but I'm resolved never to take any pay for my preaching and so I'll have to make our living some other way: farming or teaching probably. God will show me the way."

"God has shown the way," Brown said. He threw the handful of wheat back in the bin and stood up.

"What do you mean?"

"We like you, wife and I. And we know you'll make Margaret happy and proud. She loves you. But before we give our consent, you must make us a promise."

"Yes?"

"You must not take her away from us."

"I don't understand."

"Our home must be your home. My stepdaughter Jane has married and gone now, and wife and I can't give up Margaret; at least, not yet, anyway. If she is willing to accept you as a husband, we will gladly accept you as our son. You can help me on the farm or with the mill, or you can conduct a school, but you must not take our daughter away from us. We will live together as one family."

Alexander stiffened. He shivered as though with sudden chill in the dampness of the little shed and began to button his coat tightly about his throat.

"No," he said. "No. It's because you think I can't support her. But I will—only just now the way isn't quite clear."

"Like I said, the way is clear." John Brown spoke solemnly, an anxiety about him. "This will be your home and you will be our son. You see, the Lord is good to both of us. I've always wanted a son."

"I'm sorry," said Alexander. "A promise like that would be like binding the hands of God. I can't bargain for my security as though I didn't trust Him."

Mr. Brown reached out and placed his hand on the younger man's shoulder. "Pray about it, won't you? And whatever you do, don't fly in the face of Providence because of personal pride. For Margaret's sake!"

It was Saturday, October 4, 1810. Alexander leaned forward in the back row of the main hall of Washington College as Father Thomas completed his simple petition for admission of the Christian Association into the Pittsburgh Synod of the Mother Kirk of Scotland. It was the third day of the session, and the hall was crowded with clergymen from the presbyteries of Erie, Hartford, Lancaster, Redstone, and other points; frontiersmen for the most part with the breath of the outdoors about them; forthright men, rigid and uncompromising in their unceasing fight against what they considered evil.

His father finished and stood, hesitant, his slender figure slightly stooped; an expectancy, a hopeful waiting upon him as he scanned the faces of those about him; a gradual wilting in him at what he read there. And then came a shifting of feet, an uneasy shuffling, and a few questions, a vagueness about them, which some of the clergymen felt in duty bound to propound, their minds closed upon the answers before the questions were asked. Within minutes the chairman waved Father Thomas aside, and he made his way, almost stumbling, down the narrow aisle.

Alexander arose as he approached and together they went outside to wait in the yard with the Hanans and the McElroys and James Foster and Abraham Altars while the Synod pondered its decision.

An hour later they were recalled, and Father Thomas, his son beside him, stood before the clerk clinging desperately to hope.

"The Synod unanimously resolves," the clerk read, his face impassive, "that however specious the plan of the Christian Association and however seductive its professions, experience of the effects of similar projects in other parts has evinced their baleful tendency and destructive operations on the whole interests of religion by promoting divisions instead of union, by degrading the ministerial character, by providing free admission to any errors in doctrine, and to any corruptions in discipline, whilst a nominal approbation of the Scriptures as the only standard of truth may be professed, the Synod are constrained to disapprove the plan and its native effects.

146

"And further, for the above and many other important reasons, it is resolved that Mr. Campbell's request to be received into ministerial and Christian communion cannot be granted."

Alexander felt himself tighten with anger as he listened, and he put his hand on his father's arm to lend him support. But Father Thomas did not seem to need support. His shoulders seemed, instead, to straighten as the reading progressed, an unexpected benignity in his face. When the clerk finished, he bowed to the assembly and without a word led the way from the room, Alexander following with flushed face.

"It is God's will." Father Thomas spoke in resignation to the waiting friends in the yard. "Now we shall have no angry, hostile men sitting in judgment; nor need we fear their wrath. We are free, free to march toward our high goal. The Lord's will be done! Blessed be His name!"

"But they were hateful!" Alexander said indignantly. "Why did they have to add abuse to the denial of the application? And they need not have characterized our plea as 'seductive' and of 'baleful tendency.' And what did they mean by 'many other important reasons'? It's an outrage!"

"Easy, my son," said Father Thomas. "We should not look for base motives in everything they say."

"But your enemies will see hidden meanings there," James Foster said. "That last charge, especially, should be corrected."

James Hanan and Abraham Altars nodded. "They will read character defects," John McElroy said; "reasons too dark for record. If there are other reasons you should know what they are."

"We should demand a clarification of the denial," Alexander said firmly. "It will not do to let that charge slip. What are the unnamed 'many other important reasons' which deny us membership in the Synod?"

"Perhaps you are right," his father agreed reluctantly. "We want no aspersions upon the name of the Association. I will ask for a clearance of the record tomorrow."

Alexander and his father sat up until past midnight preparing the request and early the next morning laid it upon the table of the chairman of the Synod. But it was not until late in the afternoon that it was given recognition. Then, briefly, with a finality that was not to be denied, the answer was officially returned:

"It was not for any immorality in practice," the clerk read in his flat, metallic voice, "but in addition to the reasons before assigned, for expressing his belief that there are some opinions taught in our Confession of Faith which are not founded in the Bible, and avoiding to designate them; for declaring that the administration of baptism to infants is not authorized by scriptural precept or example, and is a matter of indifference, yet administering that ordinance while holding such an opinion; for encouraging or countenancing his son to preach the Gospel without any regular authority; for opposing creeds and confessions as injurious to the interests of religion; and also, because it is not consistent with the regulations of the Presbyterian church that the Synod should form a connection with any ministers, churches, or associations; that the Synod deemed it improper to grant his request."

"Blessed are the meek, for they shall inherit the earth," rang in Alexander's mind almost bitterly as he waited, this time in the rear of the hall, and saw his father, his slight, rugged figure outlined against the wall toward the front, raise his hand as if in benediction as the clerk finished. And his whole being filled with a mixture of pity and admiration and anger as he heard Father Thomas admit mildly and without emphasis, as though he knew his words were falling upon deaf ears, that he opposed the Westminster Confession because it contained interpretations not revealed in the Word of God; that the rite of infant baptism was not a matter of indifference but of forbearance among Christians; that many truths could be drawn by fair induction from the Word of God but that no such deduction could ever be regarded by him as equal in authority with the expressed and declared Word of God.

"It is hard to understand," said Father Thomas as they tramped home together in the twilight of the late afternoon, "how Christians can be rejected by any church organization because they have no other rule than the Bible."

"You were not rejected, Father, for adhering to the Scriptures,"

Alexander said indignantly. "You were rejected for doubting the infallibility of their Westminster Confession of Faith. That human creed, and not the Bible, is their yardstick, and you, yourself, are an example of the punishment given those who deviate from it."

For a time they walked in silence along the cinder path leading to their two-storied log house at the junction of Chartiers and Strawberry Alley, Alexander still smarting under a slow, burning rage.

"We must fight back!" Alexander said suddenly. "We must challenge the Synod and all its aspersions and its misrepresentations. I am not asking you to do it, Father, but I shall! I'll answer their insults and innuendoes, and place the truth upon the record. I'll let the people of the community know that their real enemy is the organized clergy!"

"Gently, my son!" said Father Thomas. "These men are in error but they did their duty as they saw it. And they are still our Christian brothers. We shall pray for them."

Within a few weeks the engagement of Alexander Campbell and Margaret Brown became generally known although there was no formal announcement. And as though by common agreement, it seemed to be taken for granted by their friends that he and Margaret would take up residence with her parents. But Alexander had never consented, even at Margaret's pleading, to such a plan. "I'll make the living without any help from relatives," he insisted stubbornly, and cast about for possible teaching positions or farm work. But none offered enough free time for him to continue his studies and preaching, and he refused to press Margaret for a wedding date, or to discuss their plans until he could see more clearly into the future.

His "Bonus Homo" letters were brought to a close early in December. They had served their purpose, Editor Sample said, in arousing public concern regarding the morals of the community. Margaret said little to him about them, but her silence spoke loudly, and when the last one appeared he admitted to her he had been more caustic in his criticisms than the frontier conditions justified. People were made good by precept and example, Father Thomas told him, and not by ridicule and condemnation. And Father Thomas was right.

On Christmas Eve the Brown home was aglow. Bayberry candles gleamed in pewter sconces on the walls; laughing voices mingled with happy music of an itinerant fiddler and John Brown's harmonica. An "Open House" was the annual custom of the Browns on this festive day, and more than fifty friends dropped in to exchange greetings and enjoy the crisp crullers, honey, and ginger cakes, and the sweet grape wine poured by Mrs. Brown from an earthenware pitcher.

As the fiddler struck up the plaintive strains of a waltz, William Sample approached Alexander and Margaret standing by the hearth.

"A cakewalk?" he called. "No harm in a cakewalk, is there, preacher?" He laughed and took Margaret's hand and began stepping high in time to the fiddle music.

Alexander stood watching in half-disapproving silence as other couples joined them. The Browns were good people and a credit to the Lord, but they were going too far when they publicly embraced the worldly follies of the Episcopalians. His sternness gathered itself into a frown as he saw Dorothea and Joseph Bryant arm in arm joining in the laughing processions, followed by Nancy and Andrew Chapman. And then Mrs. Brown skipped by on the arm of her portly husband, her eyes glowing with excitement.

The music came to a stop and the parade of merrymakers dispersed, and Margaret appeared at his side. He plunged his hands into the pockets of his coat.

"Dancing is folly," he said solemnly. "I should reprove you for scandalizing your time in such a fashion."

"Nonsense!" she said, laughing. " 'There is a time to weep and a time to laugh; a time to mourn and a time to dance.' Solomon said that, and he's a wiser man even than you." She looked at him owlishly. "I thought it might shock you!"

He sighed and ran his hand through his hair. "You think I'm self-righteous, don't you, Margaret?"

"I think you're confused," she said quietly.

They had wandered to the far end of the room, and Margaret

seated herself on the sofa pushed against the wall. She motioned for Alexander to sit beside her.

"I am confused," he said. "You are not acting like a girl who is going to marry a preacher. It's time you began to think about more serious things."

"Is it?" she asked. "Do you know that song about the siege of old Troy?" She began to sing softly:

> "I courted as long as the siege of old Troy,
> To win a fair maiden my time did employ.
> But when I asked her the wedding to set,
> The answer she gave me was, 'Time enough yet.'

Only," she turned her face very close to his, "you haven't asked me to set our wedding date. Do you realize that, Alexander? I'm beginning to wonder if you want to marry me at all."

"You've lost your mind!" he said sternly. "You don't know what you're talking about!"

"I've lost my heart." She spoke almost in a whisper. "Which is the only reason I'm humiliating myself like this. You've put sinful pride before your love for me, Alexander. Either that or you don't want to marry at all. Which is it?"

He stared at her, amazed, and then after a long moment took her hand and pressed it to his lips.

"I've been acting my rigid, self-righteous self," he murmured. "Telling God how I wanted things done instead of being willing to accept His way." He bowed his head. "Margaret, I need you to keep me humble. I love you better than my own life, and yet—yes, I've been flying in the face of Providence. We must marry right away, Margaret. It's the pattern of the Lord!"

On Wednesday afternoon, March 12, 1811, Alexander and Margaret were married in the family parlor, with the Reverend John Hughes of West Liberty, a long-time friend of the Brown family, officiating. More than a hundred friends from the Buffalo, Charlestown, and Washington communities crowded the house, spilling over into the narrow, back hallway and dining room and adjacent bedroom, murmuring admiration of the wide-eyed bride in her simple white dimity dress, its wide lace bertha falling in ripples of soft fullness over her shoulders, its long, full sleeves billowing to her wrists.

It was midnight before the bride and groom could flee from the confusion of happy congratulations after the reception and supper. For the first time they were alone together in the room over the family parlor that had formerly been shared by Margaret and her half-sister Jane. Tomorrow, according to custom, they would go to the home of the bridegroom's parents to receive more congratulations, and mingle in friendly intimacy in the bosom of the family for two weeks. But now they were alone.

There were no words between them while he held her in his arms, a dedication and a crowning ecstasy upon them both as they knelt together for their first nightly prayer.

Two weeks later they returned to Buffalo—two weeks of parties and visits and long walks and rides and talks; the beginnings of a growing together, and happiness. On both Sundays Alexander had preached at the Washington courthouse, and Margaret had sat in the front row, her face reflecting her joy of being the bride of such a man of God. She was immediately accepted into the Campbell family as a cherished daughter and sister, an understanding and congeniality among them Alexander could hardly believe possible; from the beginning a submergence of her life into the life of her husband, and a devotion which, Father Thomas told his son, made him one of the blessed among men.

"The Lord guided you well in your choice of a wife," Father Thomas said as he told them good-by. "He has blessed you and He will expect great things from you; more than from most men."

"You are a dear, good man." From her position in the buggy Margaret bent and kissed him again on the cheek. "Father Thomas, I am proud to be your daughter!"

Chapter 14

IT WAS NOT YET SIX O'CLOCK IN THE MORNING OF SATURDAY, MAY 4, when Alexander rode up to the unfinished meetinghouse of the Christian Association at Brush Run. A scattering of buggies, wagons, and saddled horses was already in the little fenced enclosure, and others were arriving. On Saturday the routine of the farmer families was broken, but it was still a day of demanding duties and, when possible, they assembled for church affairs early in order to return to their chores the sooner.

Alexander was tying his bridle reins to the railing when Father Thomas rode up on Zeke, his face a study in conflicting emotions. Alexander waited for him to dismount, the early sun filtering through the first tender leaves of the maples while the lacy vines of the scuppernong grape on the paling fence made sensuous patterns on the ground.

"I remember what Ben Franklin said about the picture of the sun." Father Thomas finished hitching his horse and gave the reins a final confirming twist. He motioned toward the sun patterns. "Is it a rising or a setting sun?"

"That will be up to us." Alexander smiled in understanding. "This is a sad day, Father, and yet it can be a most auspicious and happy occasion. I feel we may be on the eve of great events. Who knows?"

They walked slowly toward the one-room structure, its single center entrance, flanked by two small shuttered windows, still without a door. Inside, members of the Christian Association were gathered, seated on sawhorses and planks, upturned barrels and camp stools, and as they entered, the murmur of voices stopped and faces turned toward them expectantly. The Association had met two days before in its regular biennial meeting in conformity with the provisions of the "Declaration and Address" and, after prayerful discussion, had agreed to meet again today officially to form the basic structure of an organized church.

Father Thomas went to the front of the room, and as the group waited, raised his hand in prayer, a prayer for guidance, his voice throbbing with an intensity Alexander had never heard before. The business was quickly dispatched. Thomas Campbell was elected elder and Alexander licensed to preach; John Dawson, George Sharp, William Gilchrist, and James Foster were chosen as deacons. At the conclusion, as if in obvious relief but with deep thankfulness, they sang the old metrical version of the One Hundred Eighteenth Psalm, a solemn and joyous acceptance and dedication of the new status they were assuming. They were now an organized, separate church body.

"I suppose it's the only thing to do," Father Thomas admitted as he parted with Alexander at the fork in the road to Washington. "No group can function without organization. But we must not let the mechanics of our organization blind us to our ideals and our original purpose." He leaned forward in his saddle, his voice almost pleading. "You're going to give us our first sermon tomorrow morning, my son. Remind us that we have organized not as a new church body but as the oldest one. Emphasize that all Christians are our brothers. Join with me in inviting not only our own members but all Christian believers to participate in the Lord's Supper. And in the afternoon I'll preach, and plead for Christian unity across all party lines. We must never abandon our plea!"

Alexander nodded, his heart filled with understanding and affection, his mind braced with renewed determination to resist all pressures to let the new church become a neat, smug compartment of the world of religious sects.

The crowded weeks passed swiftly. Alexander helped about the Brown farm and preached on Sunday, alternating between Brush

Run and Crossroads for the convenience of the members. But the first flush of enthusiasm for the new church had died down and only the hard core of the faithful came regularly. Mr. and Mrs. Brown and Margaret presented themselves formally for membership and were received, but there were few other additions.

"The movement will die a-borning if it doesn't grow," Alexander told Margaret as they drove home from a midweek preaching service at the home of William Gatwood. "It has never penetrated outside this area. I should make a missionary tour."

"How would you go about it?" Margaret asked.

"I'd be like Peter and Paul, preaching wherever I could find listeners. I'd meet with hostility, I know, just as we have here, but the blood of the martyrs is the seed of the church."

"You're not a martyr exactly," Margaret reminded him playfully. "You love it all too much. But it would be exciting. Why can't I go along, too?"

He pinched her cheek as they drove up to the stile and, tossing the reins to Benjy, he jumped to the ground to assist her from the gig. "It will be no journey for a woman, especially for a young bride. Home is where the heart is, and I want my heart to stay here."

"Your heart will always be first in your work, Mr. Reformer," she said. "I know that and I accept it. But I'll help you all I can."

"You're the most wonderful helpmeet a man ever had!" He pulled her close, astonished to find her thick lashes damp with tears. Tenderly he kissed the tears away, and as they stood Benjy, all unnoticed, led the horse and gig away to the barn.

When John Brown stopped at the West Liberty post office a month later on his weekly trip to the town, the post rider had just arrived and was blowing his horn. He sorted the mail and handed Mr. Brown a thick letter addressed to Margaret, charging ten cents for the postage, which meant Alexander must be more than one hundred miles away.

"It's his travel journal!" Margaret exclaimed when she opened it. "He promised me he'd keep one. Now we can know what he's been up to."

She was seated with her stepmother on the lawn under the live oak tree, their embroidery hoops on their laps.

"Call Holly and Benjy, will you, Papa? I want everybody to hear what this preacher husband of mine has been doing!"

"I'se here, Miss Margaret." Holly appeared suddenly from the summerhouse and ambled across the yard. "Youse dat excited you was screaming and didn't know hit."

Margaret laughed and, controlling her voice with an effort, began to read:

"I set out from home on Thursday, May 16, 1811, and stopped first evening at Lutham Young's, conversed upon the fundamental doctrines of the Christian religion. Next morning, accompanied to the river by Mr. Young, I crossed opposite Steubenville. Introduced myself to Mr. James Larimore and Dr. Slemmons and was received with courtesy. Was introduced by Dr. Slemmons to Mr. Buchanan, lodging at the doctor's. After dining, reasoned with Mr. Buchanan on the general state of religion and argued the principles with him which we advocate; but he would not see. In our discourse a Mr. Boyd of Steubenville interrupted by vociferously taking Mr. Buchanan's side of the argument. Finished in a disorderly manner. Appointed to preach in the courthouse on Sabbath day at twelve o'clock. Proceeded to James McElroy's where I tarried till Friday morning, hospitably entertained. On Sabbath day I preached, according to appointment, in Steubenville. Had a crowded house, notwithstanding Messrs. Buchanan, Snodgrass, Lambkin, Powell, and others."

"That Buchanan argument must have been even better than the one he had with Brother Obadiah Jenkins," John Brown chortled in reminiscence. "I wish I'd been there. 'Lay on, Macduff, and damn'd be him that first cries, "Hold! Enough!"'"

"He'll be home next week," Margaret went on. "In time, he says, to preach at the first worship service in the completed Brush Run Church on July 4." She looked up at her father, assuming a hurt expression. "Do you suppose that's the reason he's coming back—just to preach in the new church?"

"Don't worry!" Mrs. Brown laughed, intent on her embroidery. "Men are all like that!"

"You're married to a Holy Cause all right," Mr. Brown said

156

soberly, "and you might as well get used to it. But he'll always be a good husband, daughter. He loves you, too."

"I ain't nebber seen a preacher yet who warn't hongry." Holly spoke up. "And wid all de talkin' Mr. Alex is done he must be all skin and bone by now. I'll put de big pot in de little pot and fry de skillet. We'll let him eat high on de hog for sho when he gets home."

True to his promise, Alexander arrived home on Saturday afternoon, July 3. He was tired to the point of exhaustion, but late into the night the family sat about the big table in the sitting room, listening to the tales of his journey.

"It's like plowing new ground," he said wearily. "The minds of the people are as hard and as brittle as dry earth." He clenched his fist as though crumbling dirt. "It will take almost a miracle to unite them in Christian bonds of fellowship."

"Don't be discouraged. You just landed among a bunch of hidebound Presbyterians," Mr. Brown said. "They're thick up there around Steubenville. Other places, mebbe, it won't be so hard."

The next morning Alexander sat on the small unpainted rostrum in the Brush Run meetinghouse and looked at the earnest faces before him with an apprehension he could not down. Some who had once been identified with the Association had become indifferent; others had moved away; others were unable to give it financial support or to attend regularly. Only a handful, he reflected, perhaps thirty people in all, could be counted upon to kindle the spark that would sweep the world and unite the warring sects of Christendom.

It was a strangely solemn service, the atmosphere heavy with reverence, as if the significance of the new fellowship had invaded the hearts of the group for the first time, the very smallness of their number drawing them closer together. He and Father Thomas had agreed that no set order of service be regularly followed which might become a pattern for the future, but that always Holy Communion should be offered, not only to the members but to all believers regardless of church affiliation.

After the service Alexander sought out his father. "I noticed

157

Joseph Bryant and Abraham Altars and the Widow Margaret Fullerton didn't partake of Communion," he said, puzzled. "Do they object to a weekly observance of the Lord's Supper?"

"No." Father Thomas kicked at a clump of field grass as though meditating his reply. "They told me before the service began that they wouldn't participate. They had examined themselves and judged they were unworthy."

Alexander stared, and then laughed incredulously. "I know no better people," he said. "What demonic sin do they imagine possesses them?"

"They have never been baptized," Father Thomas said uncomfortably. "They want me to baptize them. By immersion," he added, as though in afterthought. He turned to walk away.

"Wait, Father!" Alexander persisted, a half-smile on his face. "What did you tell them?"

"Of course I agreed to do it," Father Thomas said. "Immersion is an acceptable method of baptism, although certainly not the only form. I can see no objection to it. Equally, I see no need to insist upon that form alone." He turned to his son as though for confirmation, but Alexander looked away, a soberness in his face. After a moment they began to make their way toward their buggies.

Three weeks later, while Alexander was on a three-day preaching tour in the Charlestown area, Father Thomas immersed Joseph Bryant, Abraham Altars, and the Widow Fullerton in a deep pool in Buffalo Creek on the Bryant farm two miles above the mouth of Brush Run. It was an impressive but an awkward ceremony, he told Alexander two days later while on a passing visit to the Brown farm.

"Some of the brethren say it was unseemly that one who had himself never been immersed should immerse others," he said. "But baptism is baptism, whatever form it takes." He spoke almost defensively, as though arguing against his own doubts. "I still say it's a matter of opinion and forbearance."

Alexander made no reply, unwilling to wound his father by open disagreement; uncertain as to his own conviction. As they stood in sudden awkward silence the yard bell rang, summoning them to midday dinner.

The rapidly worsening relations between Great Britain and the United States, which had begun with the impressment of American seamen into the British Navy during the first term of President Jefferson, had extended into the term of President James Madison. Twice a week the stagecoach from Pittsburgh rolled into West Liberty and Washington, bringing dispatches of the mounting tension in Washington City. Alexander felt that as a British citizen his position was untenable, and in September he filed his petition for citizenship in the District Court at Charlestown. In two years he would take his public oath of allegiance to his new country. The knowledge heightened his feeling that he should also take a public oath of allegiance to his God as a minister.

He was a half-preacher, he told Margaret one morning; there was a difference in being licensed to preach and in being set apart by ordination, a public acceptance of a special responsibility to bear witness. And a public ordination would quiet some of his critics and hush the mouths of the clergy who had hurled the charge at Father Thomas that he had "encouraged and countenanced his son to preach the Gospel without any authority."

Margaret's face had clouded at this admission, her light brown eyes troubled.

"I think you should be ordained, as you say," she said thoughtfully. "But not for such a reason. Not just to quiet your critics. There are other reasons." She smiled up at him from the bowl of asters she was arranging and then bent her head and buried her face in the flowers.

He drew a deep breath. "You're right, of course," he said after a moment, accepting the gentle rebuke. "I'll try to forget what men are saying and quench my desire to retaliate. I want to be ordained in order to be better able to serve God. That is enough!"

Alexander preached at Brush Run on the last Sunday of the year, and on January 1, 1812, presented himself for public ordination.

159

In a solemn service for all those who crowded within the little church Father Thomas delivered the ordination sermon and was assisted in the laying on of hands by the deacons of the young church, George Sharp, William Gilchrist, James Foster, and John Dawson.

"You are now an apostle of the Lord," Margaret said as they drove home through the fields thickly covered with a blanket of crunching white. "And you are also"—she snuggled against him and lifted her face, her lips close to his ear—"going to become a father."

He pulled sharply on the reins and brought the horse to a stop, turning to her, speechless.

"How blind you are, darling!" She laughed. "I've known it for months, and so have Papa and Mama. But I thought I wouldn't mention it until after your ordination so as not to distract you."

His free hand cradled her head against his shoulder, still unable to put into words the wonder upon him. "I love you, Margaret; how I love you!"

"Long after you have become a famous preacher and I am dead, I shall be proud that next to the Lord Jesus Christ I was the first in the heart of my husband. You must always love me, Alexander. I love you too much. Sometimes I'm even afraid I love you more than I love God."

When Alexander was admitted into their bedroom late in the afternoon of March 13 he walked on wondering tiptoe. Beside Margaret in the canopied four-poster bed snuggled a red-faced mite of life, its tiny hands fighting the air, its voice rising in a crescendo of bewildered shock.

"She's preaching already." Margaret's voice was faint, barely above a whisper, but a smile crossed her white, triumphant face.

"We won't name her 'John Thomas' for our fathers, after all." Alexander tried to laugh to ease his own bewilderment. "But they will understand. How about 'Jane'?" He bent and kissed Margaret solemnly and then stood unsteadily to peer at his daughter. "Mother would be proud. Although, come to think of it, we really ought to call her Hosanna. She's the most beautiful baby in the world!"

"We can think up fancy names for the other ones," Margaret

said, and turned her head on the goosedown pillow to gaze at her firstborn child. "Jane, Jane, you've got a name, so will you stop howling!"

Almost every day brought friends to the Brown home to see the new baby. Gifts of hand-made dresses and petticoats, some of them two yards long, trimmed with yards of rufflings and lace and bows of ribbon; and offerings of knitted booties and snug caps and sheltering bonnets piled high on the chest of drawers John Brown had fashioned, while coverlets of soft, hand-loomed wool protected the sturdy cradle he had carefully made, testifying to the love of many friends.

The child was six weeks old and Margaret was finishing her bath one morning before the open hearth in the kitchen, wrapping the infant in a thick blanket of white wool, when she suddenly turned to Alexander, sorting seed corn at the table. It was early May, but spring was late and the air was still crisp.

"We haven't discussed the baby's baptism," she said. "Isn't it time? What if we should lose her?"

Alexander did not look up, his eyes and hands concentrated upon his task.

"I know how you feel," Margaret went on. "And I feel the same way. Infant baptism is a matter of opinion." She paused, her voice troubled. "But it's my opinion she should be sprinkled and right away." She looked at Alexander questioningly. "Don't you hear me, dear?"

Alexander pushed the corn into a heavy cotton sack and tied the cord before he spoke. "Yes, I hear you, but I don't want to. Because I don't know what to say. I've been searching the Scriptures for the authority for infant baptism and—well, Margaret, it just isn't there." He shook his head. "There isn't any. Christ said, 'He that believeth and is baptized shall be saved, but he that believeth not shall be damned.' That doesn't any longer seem to me to leave baptism, or the method of baptism, as a matter of our opinion or preference. It's a Divine command!"

"But baptism could be by sprinkling, couldn't it?"

Again Alexander shook his head. He stood up and thrust his hands deep into the short pockets of his leather jacket. "The Greek word, *baptizo*, as used in the original text and translated as *baptize*, can only be defined as 'to plunge, dip, immerse.' New Testament baptism, I am now convinced, is for believers only, and is always by immersion in water."

"Then what must we do?"

"Infant baptism is without Divine authority and we cannot practice it."

Margaret bent her head over the now-sleeping baby. "But what if she should die!"

Alexander placed his hand on her shoulder, his grip firm, his voice warm, tender, understanding. "She would go straight to God who sent her to us. 'Suffer little children to come unto me for such is the Kingdom of Heaven.' Does that imply they are born in sin?"

Margaret raised her head indignantly. "Of course they have no sin. You are right!" She looked him steadily in the eyes before she stood up and kissed him. "And when you go down into the water for your own baptism, my husband, I'm going with you. I want to be properly baptized, too."

"There can be no objection to baptism by immersion for the unbaptized," Father Thomas said when Alexander rode over to tell him of his decision the next day, "but you are already baptized. I see no reason for putting off Christ merely for the sake of making a new profession. You will only be going out of the church for the sake of coming in again."

"Not only Margaret and me, Father, but Dorothea wants to be immersed, too," Alexander said gently, anxious not to disturb him too much. "We had a long talk about it while we were waiting for you and the boys to come in from the fields. And I think Mother, too, is leaning in that direction."

"I wouldn't be surprised." Father Thomas smiled at him. "Your example has an influence upon them. You have made your decision, my son. You must follow your conscientious convictions. I have no more to say, but I think your decision should be publicly announced among our people that they may be informed." After a pause he continued: "Who will perform the ceremony? I somehow do not feel I should do it."

"I had thought of my friend Matthias Luce. He's a Baptist preacher near Washington and of course believes in immersion. But I want to make it plain to him and the world that I am not thereby becoming a Baptist. There will be no recital of a miraculous conversion. I will be baptized only upon a simple confession of faith that Jesus is the Son of God, according to the terms of the Great Commission and the practice of the Apostles and the early church, or not at all."

"Brother Luce will not want to do it that way, my son. He will risk the censure of his church."

Matthias Luce did hesitate at first, as Father Thomas had predicted. Alexander talked with him until past midnight that night before he consented.

"The idea of baptizing a man into Christian fellowship instead of into a specific church," he pondered, "is startling. But it opens new doors into the whole concept of the meaning of baptism. Yes, I'll do it!"

The baptism, it was decided, would be at noon on Wednesday, June 12, at Buffalo Creek on the David Bryant farm in the same deep pool where Father Thomas had performed the service for others the year before.

When Alexander and Margaret arrived at the pool on the appointed day, Father Thomas was already there, with Dorothea, Nancy, Jane, and their mother. Almost shyly he held out a bundle to show Alexander.

"It's a change of clothing for all of us." He nodded at Alexander's inquiring look. "Yes, we are all convinced, my son. Maybe it was partly my cantankerous Scotch stubbornness that has kept me from seeing the truth all along." He smiled as though making a happy confession. "But I think it was also my hope to avoid any points of difference that could hinder Christian unity. We are taking a stand now that may vitally affect our Movement." He looked around at the crowd that had assembled to witness the service. Almost a hundred people, including most of the members of the Christian Association,

163

lined the banks of the stream. "The brethren here should know that we are doing this because we believe that baptism is not a matter of opinion but a Divine command, and that there is only one method of obeying it."

He mounted a little knoll a few feet away and began to speak. With many a pause and troubled expression, he recounted his struggles, his blind devotion to human error, the slow dawning of the truth. And then, in an almost symbolic gesture, he motioned for Alexander to join him. "As my son has led me to see the light, may he lead others."

As Alexander extended the invitation for others to join them, a hush fell upon the crowd, a feeling that for some they had come to a parting of the ways. And then his mother and the girls came forward, and Margaret, and James Hanan and his wife, old friends from Ireland.

One by one Elder Matthias Luce, his hand uplifted, led them into the pool.

Chapter 15

JUNE BROUGHT THE NEWS THAT THE NATION WAS AT WAR WITH England.

"I'm torn between two poles," Alexander told Margaret as he laid aside the Washington *Reporter* containing the announcement. "England is wrong about this war and a part of me says I should help fight her. America is my country now. But a part of me says that all war is wrong. I've been praying about it, but I don't know what to do. I haven't had any answer yet from the Lord."

Margaret leaned forward and rocked the whimpering baby in the cradle between them.

"Maybe you've been listening too hard to the voice of Alexander Campbell." She smiled, the dancing lights in her eyes a little dimmed. "You are sensitive because other young men are leaving and you think their action may be a reflection upon you." She paused as though to give added weight to her words. "Perhaps it requires more courage to stay at home than to go, especially with so many people already so quick to criticize you."

He got up abruptly and began pacing the floor. There was truth in her words.

"Why don't you talk it over with Father Thomas?" she said.

He found his father the next afternoon hoeing in his corn patch behind the house, working abstractedly, his mind plainly not upon his task.

"I understand," he said patiently when Alexander had finished. He turned as though to examine a hill of corn and then straightened, and spoke almost sternly. "You're restless, my son, just as I am, just as most of our group, chafing under the hostility of the community. But Margaret is right. Your pride has become involved. The country is in no great danger and does not need you as much as the people here need you. You are their leader now." He stated the fact simply, an acknowledgment of what they had both come to accept, that the leadership of the Restoration Movement had been transferred, as if by Divine authority at the time of their immersion, from the father to the son.

Alexander looked out over the fields, his head lifted, as though listening. Was the Army of the Lord recruiting to the roll of another drum? "I was thinking only of myself," he said. "I'll stay with our people." He turned as though to end the discussion and then faced his father in sudden recollection.

"Matthias Luce came to see me this morning." He paused as if in doubt whether to continue.

"Well?"

"He wants to propose our Brush Run Church for membership in the Redstone Baptist Association."

Father Thomas stopped hoeing, his face shining. "If they would admit us as we are, we should accept!" he said promptly.

165

"I was sure you would feel that way," Alexander said. "But I am not convinced. It would mean, for one thing, that we would be considered Baptists, at least in name."

The older man turned to lead the way toward the house. "It would also mean we would not be adding to the divisions within the church." He smiled at his tall son walking with long, measured strides beside him. "What did you tell him?"

"I told him we couldn't accept their Philadelphia Confession of Faith any more than we could any other human creed," he said. "But since we've accepted immersion, we are half-Baptist, he says, and he thinks the Redstone Association might admit us even with our 'peculiar beliefs,' as he calls them."

Father Thomas' eyes shone. "It would mean we can yet work within the frame of a great church instead of as another small separate sect," he said. "Matthias Luce is a messenger of the Lord, Alexander. He is a positive sign your duty is here. Think it over carefully, my son. God's hand is in it."

Within a month the remaining members of the Brush Run Church requested immersion, and the Restoration Movement had completed the evolution of its beliefs and practices. At its meeting in November, as though weary of hostility, hopeful of the end of their denunciation as heretics, as a disrupting influence, as a band of fanatics, the group welcomed the offer of the Reverend Luce to propose the Brush Run Church for membership in the shelter of the Redstone Baptist Association.

Yet in what way were they heretical? Alexander went over again in his mind the issues: The rejection of human creeds and hierarchies; the repudiation of infant baptism; the adherance to believers' baptism by immersion upon only a confession of faith in Jesus Christ as Lord; the observance of the Lord's Supper on the first day of every week, with their refusal to "fence the tables" and withhold the symbols from any believer who felt himself worthy to partake— these were the terrible, sinful heresies that set them apart in the religious mosaic of the world. And God grant they would continue to set them apart, he prayed, even within the nominal fold of the Baptist church.

On New Year's Day, 1813, Joseph Bryant, who had marched away to war with William Sample, came back again, no longer shy, and with a lameness in his leg, and on January 13 was married to Dorothea by Father Thomas, and took his bride a half-day's journey away to live on his father's farm. With the spring, Father Thomas, a restlessness upon him, went on a prospecting tour into Ohio, returning with glowing accounts of the town of Cambridge, in Guernsey County. But to Alexander by far the most important event of all was Margaret's second confinement on September 13. She had a difficult labor, and when at last he stood beside her bed and held in his arms another tiny female symbol of their love, he felt a contrition that made him strangely humble.

"Maggie, darling, it's a beautiful baby, but you'll never go through this again," he promised. "I'll never let you."

She smiled weakly, her brown eyes in her white face propped against the pillows like deep pools with the glint of sunlight dancing upon them. "Just because Eliza Ann is going to have a big nose like her papa's is no reason for you to leave me," she said. "How would you like that name, Alexander? For my own mother who died when I was born."

He placed the baby gently beside her and kissed her on the forehead. "It's a wonderful name," he said. "I think it's even better than Hosanna, the one we almost gave little Jane. Remember?"

"Hosanna!" chortled Holly, standing behind him with a pail of hot water. "I loves dat name!"

Margaret laughed softly, cuddling the baby against her breast. "Holly's going to bathe us now," she said, indicating the round tin tub with sweet oil floating in it. "I never taught you to read, Holly, but you know lots of things you could never have learned from books. And I'll make you a promise." She smiled at Alexander. "You can name our first son all by yourself. I won't say a word!"

Six weeks later, on November 5, Alexander sat with his father and James Foster and Abraham Altars in the Baptist Church at Uniontown while the Redstone Association, upon the motion of Elder Luce, admitted the Brush Run Church into membership. It was not a unanimous welcome. A vigorous minority, led by Elder John Pritchard of Cross Creek, denounced them as heretics and sowers of dissension. But as Brother Obadiah Jenkins told him the next day, "It was a great victory for the Lord. Now if the other churches will just follow your example, we'll all get together and have Christian union. We'll all be Baptists then!"

Alexander was standing at the stile in front of the Brown home, talking with his father, when Brother Jenkins rode up. He laughed at the sally even though it nettled him. But when the Baptist preacher had ridden on, he said nothing of his chagrin to his father. Now that the church was in the Baptist fold, however dubious a shelter it might prove, Father Thomas had come by to tell him he had decided to move to Ohio.

"I'm a preacher and a teacher," his father told him, "not a farmer. And not a fighter," he added half-defensively. "I have a feeling there will yet be much tempering of mettle before our plea is understood in these parts. This is stony ground. But if I plant the seed in Ohio, there should be a harvest there for other hands to gather later. It's a newer country than this. Maybe eventually all of our group could move there."

Alexander nodded. His father had the restless spirit characteristic of the pioneer. This was not the first time he had mentioned his desire to move on.

"Will you open a school as well as preach?" he asked.

"Of course," Father Thomas said. "And I'll have plenty of help, too. Andrew Chapman has asked for Nancy's hand. They want an early wedding. I'll marry them before the month is out and they will go to Cambridge with us. Joseph Bryant and Dorothea will go along, too."

Alexander did not try to dissuade him. Cambridge, Ohio, was a full ninety miles away, but he knew his father was right. The Restoration Movement needed a fighting spirit, or its ideals would be lost in the welter of the Baptist hierarchy, and his father was better adapted to the schoolroom than to the firing line. But when the wedding was over and the family gone, he missed them more than he had thought possible. He missed the steadying influence of his mother; the exuberance of the children; the spiritual counsel and gentle restraint of his father. The admitted leadership of the Restoration Movement was his now, and the responsibility was heavy.

Almost impatiently he began preaching at every opportunity, explaining the simple purpose upon which the Restoration Movement was built, pleading for tolerance, for understanding, and Christian love. But he felt he was talking into the wind; that, as Father Thomas had said, his words were falling on stony ground. For against the background of the Baptist fold the differences that set the Brush Run group apart from the others seemed to stand out more sharply than ever. Hostility increased and persecutions multiplied to the point of violence. Frequent attempts were made to break up their meetings; rocks, sticks, clods of earth were hurled into the water during their baptismal ceremonies; claims were made that they were desecraters of the Sabbath, and an aroused clergy, especially among the Baptists, denounced them openly.

It was close to midnight early in March and Alexander was riding home from a service at Bates' Fork. A heavy storm, brewing all day, suddenly broke on the mountainous roadway. The rain fell in sheets and the rising fords made the narrow inclines almost impassable. At the first farmhouse he stopped and asked for shelter. In the flickering light of a candle a woman peered at him from the doorway.

"You Alexander Campbell?" she asked cautiously.

"I am."

"I would as soon give shelter to the devil himself," she said. "My preacher says if you should drown it would be a blessing!" The door slammed in his face.

"I rather admire her," he told Margaret afterward. "She had the strength of her convictions. To her mind I am preaching the devil's doctrine and it would be better if I were dead. What bothers me is that she got it all from her creed-bound pastor, whoever he is." He shook his head. "To think the message of our Lord is in the hands of such men!"

But the incident served to increase the restlessness among the members of the Association. Letters from Father Thomas had brought glowing word of Ohio and, although he said he found it a worldly place, he felt the prospects for the reception of the Restoration Plea were favorable.

It was on little Jane's second birthday, March 13, 1814, that Alexander first mentioned to the family, sitting in the kitchen after supper, the plan forming in his mind.

"It's not only the bitterness against us here which concerns us," he explained to the family. "It's the prospects some of the men see for making a better living than is possible in this rocky hill country. Some think we should move as a colony."

There was a sudden silence in the little circle. Margaret, seated on the bench beside him, held her baby tightly against her, and John Brown, with a slow, puzzled frown, began gently to jostle little Jane on his knee.

"Maybe it would be good riddance for some of them to leave," Mrs. Brown said bluntly. "The church could do better without any deadheads."

"The talk is of moving as a colony," repeated Alexander.

"It will pass," said John Brown cheerfully. "We all talk about moving West occasionally. It's the Ohio fever."

But it did not pass, and in April, at the urging of the group, Alexander called a special meeting of the congregation at Brush Run. As the presiding elder he kept himself apart from the discussion but he was not surprised when it was unanimously voted that a committee make an examination of possible locations within an area of two hundred miles to the west. A week later, at the head of a volunteer committee consisting of Abraham Altars, George Archer, Richard McConnell, and John Cockens, he set out on horseback for an exploratory trip.

"I'm going with an open mind, knowing the Lord will guide me," he told Margaret the night before he rode away.

"Yes, my husband." She sat in his lap and snuggled her face against his, again that teasing light in the depths of her brown eyes. "And when the Lord speaks, be sure you don't fill your ears with the voice of Alexander Campbell."

He pinched her cheek before he kissed her. The Lord's blessings were uncounted. In addition to all the others He had given him a wife who would never let him rest easily in Zion.

They were gone until the first week in June, and when they returned, half-reluctantly Alexander reported their decision.

"We favor moving," he told the family, "near Zanesville in Ohio. Good farming country at cheap prices and close to a growing town where the men can find work during off seasons. I could start a seminary and farm, and preach for miles about."

"Is it near Cambridge?" Margaret asked.

"Not far away. But that would mean nothing, for Father Thomas is planning to return to Pennsylvania. Thomas Acheson has been writing him, urging him to go to Pittsburgh and start a school. A wealthy merchant there, Nathaniel Richardson, would help him."

John Brown started to speak but checked himself, and instead got up abruptly and suggested it was time for bed. As Margaret and her mother were going to their rooms with the children, he turned to Alexander and asked him to come into the attic room he sometimes used as an office. Puzzled and a little disturbed at the soberness in the older man's face, Alexander followed him and watched him light the big candle on the rough oak table with the smaller one he carried in his hand. Then he seated himself on the split-log bench while his father-in-law began pacing back and forth.

"Last week while you were gone," Mr. Brown said finally, "I made up my mind. I haven't told wife or Margaret, but I've had a pounding in my heart that frets me and I get out of breath when I do heavy work like plowing. My rheumatism is getting bad, too. I'm going to begin to take life a little easier. I'm going to quit farming."

Alexander stared in surprised concern. "But the gristmill? You can still run it, sir?"

Mr. Brown shook his head. "There's a mill in Charlestown now, and a new sawmill coming in, too. Mine are too small to compete with them. The appropriation for the National Road has been voted by Congress and the chances are it will come through Charlestown. That means the town will grow. I've thought it all out. I've decided to move into town and run a store, a grocery store. That is"—he looked at Alexander, puzzled—"I had planned on it if you could run the farm. But if you make this move to Ohio, well—" He threw out his hands in a gesture of despair.

Alexander coughed and shifted his feet. "You mean you might sell the farm if I left?"

"That's about it," Mr. Brown said. "I bought this land when it was uncleared forest. My life is in it. It should stay in the family. But I'm not able to manage it any more. Can you do it, son? At least for a time?"

Alexander drew a long breath. Slowly, his face set sternly, as though he were somehow groping for words, he stood up. Affectionately he reached out and placed his hand on the other man's shoulder.

"I've had an uneasy feeling all along about this move to Ohio," he said. "Somehow it seemed we were running away because the task here was hard. I've tried to convince myself it was the Lord's will, but now I see He is plainly showing me my error. It's hard here, a stony, difficult field with the Redstone Association growing more hostile to us all the time. But we grow under a burden." He turned and walked toward the door and back again. "We've planted the seed of the Restoration Movement here, and if it takes root here, it will elsewhere. I know the others will agree with me, especially James Foster. I'll tell them my decision tomorrow." He paused and held out his hand. "I'll stay, of course, sir. You can count on me to run the farm as best I can."

Three weeks later Alexander and Margaret stood at the turnstile as John and Ann Brown climbed into the carriage for the journey to Charlestown. Benjy had driven ahead with the wagon loaded with their personal belongings; a small house had been secured in town and a store building leased. The Brown Grocery Store would open its doors on October 1.

Amid a confusion of farewells and moist kisses and promises of frequent visits across the eight miles which would separate them, Mr. Brown slapped the reins and the carriage pulled away.

They were back in the sitting room before Alexander saw the envelope on the round center table. He picked it up and slowly unfolded the paper. For a moment he stared at it, puzzled, and then his face grew prickly hot.

It was a warranty deed.

In the dim light of the fading afternoon sun he read in the big, sprawling handwriting of his father-in-law:

Know all men by these presents, that I, John Brown, of the County of Brooke and State of Virginia, for and in consideration of the natural love and affection which I bear to Alexander Campbell, my son-in-law, and for the sum of one dollar, receipt of which is hereby acknowledged, do give and grant a parcel of land supposed to contain 300 acres . . .

Alexander folded the paper and placed it back in the envelope, his hand shaking, his mind suddenly filled with the stern admonition of Isaiah: "This is the Way; walk ye in it."

BOOK III

Then the Ear

Chapter 16

THE YEAR 1816 HAD BEEN UNUSUALLY TEMPERAMENTAL, WITH SNOW as late as June and frost every month during the spring and early summer. But today, Friday, August 30, would be uncomfortably warm, Alexander thought, as he glanced down at the low-hanging train of dust raised in the narrow road by their new carriage. Within a year or two, if Congress could be persuaded to route the National Road from Philadelphia through Wellsburg instead of Wheeling, it could well be less than a thirty-minute drive, but even at their gentle pace they would cover the five miles from Wellsburg to Cross Creek and be among the representatives present of the thirty-three churches of the Redstone Baptist Association when the meeting was called to order at ten o'clock.

James Foster and Abraham Altars and many of the others from Brush Run would be there, and Father Thomas, too, with an application for membership from his small, newly organized church in Pittsburgh. Nathaniel Richardson, the wealthy Pittsburgh merchant, had been as good as his promise, and had helped Father Thomas not only to open a school but had assisted him in starting a church, and had even made the first donation toward the erection of a building for the group in Wellsburg when Alexander had told him of the plan on a visit to Father Thomas last fall.

Margaret enjoyed these meetings, with their sincerity and turbulence and general good humor as much as he, but this time, perhaps, he should have left her and nine-month-old Maria Louisa with the other children at Mother Brown's in Wellsburg. The day might be difficult for them, especially for an infant, even if the business session was short and only the new officers elected and the preachers selected for Sunday sermons. He clucked noisily at Maria Louisa staring at him owlishly in her mother's lap.

"I would have named you Joanna Brown Campbell if your mother had been willing," he told her. "I think it's even prettier than Maria Louisa."

Margaret smiled. "We'll use it later, darling," she promised. "But the first name will be John."

He shook his head doubtfully, and then they laughed together, as though they shared a secret.

"I don't think they'll let me preach at the meeting on Lord's day, or any other time," he said. "Elder John Pritchard has never forgiven me for raising that thousand dollars for the Wellsburg building, and he's the host preacher at Cross Creek. The poor man seems to think I want to organize a church in Wellsburg just in order to hurt his Cross Creek Church, which is only five miles away. He thinks I want revenge because he opposed our admittance into the Redstone Association. And now, since we have a thousand dollars in hand for it and Father Brown wants actually to start building in Wellsburg, it's worse than ever. He's made it a family affair."

"Papa is not really happy in that Cross Creek Church." Margaret smiled at the recollection. "He joined them when he moved to Charlestown last summer because he thought he should, it being closer than Brush Run, but he's a member of the Restoration, not a real Baptist. Elder Pritchard should understand that our group in Charlestown simply want a place of worship of their own."

Alexander grinned. "I think he even blames me because the town changed its name from Charlestown to Wellsburg last year," he said. "And why shouldn't they name it Wellsburg? Alexander Wells and his father-in-law, John Prather, practically own the place, and he's very generous with his money. If the townspeople want to pass his name on to posterity, it's their affair. I'm not to blame."

"Elder Pritchard simply doesn't like you," Margaret said. "Maria Louisa and I have a song which will explain it all." She turned the baby about so that the child lay facing her in her lap, cooing at her. "Now, together, Maria Louisa!" She wagged her finger like a tiny baton and began to sing:

> "I do not love thee, Doctor Fell,
> The reason why I cannot tell;
> But this alone I know full well,
> I do not love thee, Doctor Fell.

Now, if you should go on another money-raising tour, he would like you even less!"

Again they laughed together, while Alexander slapped the reins over the gray mare's back, and they jogged smoothly on and lapsed gradually into silence and their separate thoughts. And it had been a wonderful tour, that three-month money-raising trip for the church they expected to organize someday in Wellsburg—his first extended journey at his own expense since Father Brown had deeded him the farm.

By stagecoach to Pittsburgh and Philadelphia and Trenton and New York, and upon his return, his first visit to Washington City, still bearing its gaunt wounds of the war. With Congressman Richard Johnson he had called upon President James Madison, and they had discussed the bounties of Virginia and the wonders of the Scriptures, with never a mention of that war which the President had tried so hard to avoid in 1812, and which had closed so indecisively in December two years later. He had even stopped again with William Penn VI, and at Pittsburgh had visited with Father Thomas and the family, observing the school he had started when he moved from Cambridge four months before, and had preached for the small group meeting in the schoolhouse on Liberty Street which Father Thomas had organized.

As he thought of his father, some of his lightness of spirit left him, and he turned soberly to Margaret.

"Father Thomas is like one of the planets in moving from place to place. He has lived in Washington, in Cambridge, Ohio, and now in Pittsburgh." He paused, a quick, dry humor in his voice. "He will be here tomorrow. I hope he won't tell us he has decided on another move."

179

"He has good connections in Pittsburgh," said Margaret thought-fully. "With a rich merchant like Mr. Richardson placing his son in his school and backing him with his influence, he should do well there. Now that he is preaching, too, he should be happy."

Alexander did not reply, and again they lapsed into silence. Soon now they would be at Cross Creek, and in the midst of the excitement and inspiration of the day. But for the time Alexander's thoughts were far from the scene ahead. He was worried about Father Thomas more than he would admit. The heart and soul of the older man were in the cause of the Restoration Movement he had brought into being, the movement to restore the early church in its simplicity and power based on the New Testament alone; and now that he had passed on to his son the leadership, Alexander knew he felt lost. His love of teaching, at which he was so successful, partially filled the need within him. But Andrew Chapman and Nancy had left him to return to their farm, and with only faithful Joe Bryant and Dorothea remaining at Pittsburgh to assist him, the school would be handicapped and he might become discouraged again.

Alexander shifted uncomfortably in his seat, as though he was himself at fault. Father Thomas must again somehow, someway, find himself useful in the center of the Movement he had begun. Alexander frowned and slapped the check reins against the back of the trotting mare. While he groped for the answer they mounted a ridge in the road and stopped a moment to look into the shimmering valley of Cross Creek below where the Baptists from the intersecting states of Pennsylvania, Ohio, and Virginia were assembling for the annual convention of the Redstone Association.

It was pleasant, Margaret reflected, to sit quietly with her baby amid the other women before the meeting opened, and watch and listen as her husband's friends crowded about him and urged him to be one of their preachers at the convention. He was a handsome man, she thought, appearing older than his twenty-six years in his black suit and high stock and white cravat; almost six feet tall, smiling and slender and alert, and with an unconscious dignity that his light brown, almost reddish hair, his clean-shaven ruddy face, and his long Roman nose, tilted, she thought in amusement, as though about to move to the right, did not lessen. His high, wide forehead was like a bulging dome; his wide, firm mouth expressive. But it was his eyes, deep blue, now twinkling with amusement beneath his craggy brows, now somber in gravity, now flashing in the heat of indignation, which she thought his most striking feature. His hands and feet were too large, and he walked, as he rode, bending a little forward, as though to hasten his speed with the force of gravity—a man whose day was never long enough for all the things to do, and yet who seemed never to lack time to give to others. But he had his enemies, too, she remembered, as she glimpsed Elder John Pritchard standing a little distance apart, conferring with two other men equally lean and unsmiling. Like the woman who had refused Alexander shelter, they probably thought him a heretic and a devil, and a better subject for the shroud than the preacher's coat. She shuddered at the thought, and rose to join the other women as they began to file into the big barnlike meetinghouse for the opening session.

It was after the preliminaries and the election of officers for the coming year that Elder Matthias Luce nominated Alexander Campbell as the principal preacher for the Lord's day, seconded by Elder Henry Spears of Maple Creek.

Elder John Pritchard was on his feet instantly. "We generally follow the rule," he reminded the assembly, "that the host church has the privilege of selecting the preachers for the important Lord's day services, choosing those who have come from a distance. Therefore, as the pastor of the host church, I nominate our good brother, Elder William Stone of Ohio in place of Mr. Campbell. We can have the pleasure"—he spoke the word derisively—"of hearing Mr. Campbell at almost any time."

Margaret's heart warmed as friends of Alexander began to voice immediate objection, and for a few minutes it seemed to her that the meeting might even break up in disorder. And then she saw Alexander rise and whisper to Matthias Luce, who promptly withdrew the nomination.

"It would only have stirred up more bad feeling if it had gone to a vote," Alexander explained an hour later as they drove to Wellsburg. He smiled grimly. "As Elder Pritchard says, they can hear me almost any time. But you may remember that Elder Stone and Elder William Brownfield, who seconded Pritchard's motion, are the two preachers who, with Pritchard, led the fight against us when we were voted into the Redstone Association three years ago. They are not our friends."

"'I do not love thee, Dr. Fell—'" Margaret began.

"It's more than that," said Alexander soberly. "They know their reasons well. I do not preach their kind of Baptist doctrine, and they'll never be content until they throw me out of the Redstone Association. But I would like to preach to them. I would like a chance to explain our views to such men. They are the ones with the closed minds, not the people." He grinned, a sudden fleeting humor in his face. "I might even convert a few of them. But more likely they would brand me a worse devil than before after they heard the new sermon I have in mind."

"You would make a handsome devil," Margaret said, again the dancing sparkle in her eyes.

Quite suddenly his free arm went about her, and for a time they drove in silence, the baby sleeping soundly in its mother's lap.

The ways of the Almighty are inscrutable and passeth all understanding, Alexander thought as he stood Sunday afternoon on the stand erected under the elms in the churchyard because the building would not hold all the people who had come to hear him preach. The sudden illness of Elder Stone had created an emergency, resulting in an invitation for him to substitute, and now he stood looking over the crowd assembled to hear him, singling out the more bigoted of the preachers who had voted yesterday to refuse admission of Father Thomas' little church in Pittsburgh into their Redstone Association. Men, women, and children; farmers and townspeople, at least five hundred of them, from the valleys and the mountains of the three adjacent states, were seated uncomfortably but quietly on the hard, backless benches, some present out of hunger for social conviviality but most of them because of a hunger in their hearts. He had wanted this chance to preach, not only because it meant that the seed of the Restoration Movement would be carried to places he could not go by people he would never have the opportunity to preach to again, but it also meant he could explain to these rigid, letter-bound preachers the fresh, vitalizing concept of the Gospel that had been forming in his mind these past two years.

And the Lord had opened the way, against all expectation or hope.

He breathed a prayer and then, quietly, his high, clear voice seeking out every part of the assembly, began to speak, taking his text from the eighth chapter of Romans: "For what the law could not do, in that it was weak through the flesh, God sending His own Son in the likeness of sinful flesh, and for sin, condemned sin in the flesh."

He no longer wrote out his sermons, but he outlined them carefully, and today he had many notes as this sermon, "The Law," needed them. It was an interpretation of the spirit of the law as against the letter of the law, an interpretation which, rejecting the Old Testament as being of equal authority with the New Testament, many would consider a deliberate blow at cherished beliefs.

He spoke deliberately, his voice vibrant and distinct and compelling but not exhortatory, his logical reasoning making a careful and reverent distinction between the Mosaic dispensation which was ended and the dispensation of Jesus Christ which was forever.

"There is no need," Alexander explained, "for preaching the Law of Moses in order to prepare men to receive the Gospel of Jesus Christ. Christ is the end of the law for righteousness to everyone that believeth. Go into all the world, said Jesus, and preach the Gospel, not the Law, to every creature. Teach the disciples to observe all things whatsoever I, not Moses, have commanded you. In the Acts of the Apostles we see the Apostles and the first preachers proclaiming the Gospel with not one word advocating the ancient Jewish law. We have the substance of eight or ten sermons delivered by Paul and Peter, and not one instance of preaching the Law to prepare their hearers, whether Jew or Gentile, for their reception of the Gospel. Christ and not the Law was the Alpha and Omega of their sermons!"

He paused as he noticed Elder Pritchard abruptly leave his seat and motion for several other preachers to join him on the outskirts of the congregation. Then he continued, like an earnest young schoolmaster lecturing to students who wanted nothing but the truth:

"It follows there is an essential difference between the Law and the Gospel, between the Old and the New Testaments. No two words are more distinct in their significance than 'Law' and 'Gospel.' The Law is denominated 'the letter'; the Gospel is denominated 'the spirit.' In respect of existence or duration, the former is denominated 'that which is done away'; the latter, 'that which remaineth.' "

The packed assembly began to stir; little eddies and swirls of sudden movement; loud-whispered comments. This was an attack upon their cherished doctrines.

An aged woman, seated precariously on a rear bench, pushed her bonnet back on her head and, struggling to her feet, lost her balance and slumped with a gasping cry to the ground. As though at a signal, Elder Pritchard rushed to the stand.

"This heresy must stop!" he called angrily. "Now! Now!"

Others rose to their feet, some shouting for Alexander to stop, others calling to him to proceed. The woman got to her feet and adjusted her black bonnet. Alexander smiled at her and bowed as she resumed her seat and waited until Elder Pritchard, his lean face bloated with outrage and frustration, publicly called for Elders William Brownsfield, Elijah Stone, Peter Dillon, and Ephraim Estep to meet him at the meetinghouse for immediate consultation.

As the wrathful red-faced men stalked away, the audience quieted, some with murmurings, some with curiosity, but most of them with quiet eagerness to hear more of this strange doctrine. Alexander caught the eye of Margaret as he resumed speaking. She was seated with the baby between Father Thomas and Father Brown on a bench beside their carriage, a smiling proudness in her. On John Brown's face was a zest that he reserved for religious controversy while

Father Thomas seemed downcast and dejected, almost a sadness in his brown eyes. Father Thomas would not be preaching this sermon on the Law, Alexander thought. His ways were gentle ways. He would not offend the Association by preaching a view so contrary to their doctrines. He would have preached a sermon like the circular letter he had submitted the day before, a sermon on the Trinity, which would have displeased no one; he would have trusted to other times and places to spread his separate beliefs. But Alexander had waited two years to explain to the Redstone Baptist Association why its Brush Run Church preached only the Gospel of Jesus Christ, nothing more and nothing less.

"The Almighty Father, after the transfiguration, when Christ appeared with Moses and Elias, told all His creatures that 'This is my beloved Son in whom I am well pleased—hear ye *him!*' We find that in all things whatsoever the Law could not do is accomplished in Him and by Him, that in Him all Christians might be perfect and complete, 'for the law was given by Moses, but grace and truth came by Jesus Christ.' "

He paused again, conscious that the spectacle of the preachers in huddled conference behind the building while the people listened willingly reflected a scene enacted on the Palestinian shores long ago. It was the clergy, the priests, not the people who had opposed new truth from the beginning. Quietly he continued.

"Christians live not under the Law but under Christ! Since Christ and His teachings replace and supersede and include all that survives to us from the Laws of Moses, we find that all the arguments and motives drawn from these ancient Jewish laws in the Old Testament, and taught us even by our modern teachers of religion, such as that the disciples of Jesus should baptize their infants; should pay tithes to their teachers; observe holy days or religious feasts as preparatory to observance of the Lord's Supper; sanctify the seventh day; enter into national covenants; establish any form of religion by civil law; all such reasons which would excite the disciples of Jesus into compliance with or imitation of Jewish customs are inconclusive and ineffectual, and repugnant to Christianity, being neither enjoined nor countenanced by the authority of the Lord Jesus Christ."

185

"It was a great sermon!" John Brown told him as they rode homeward two hours later. "A regular declaration of independence of the Christian church against the Old Testament law! But it was worse than heresy to Pritchard and his crowd. It was holy treason, and you'll hear from it!"

"They may call it treason now," Margaret declared warmly, "but a hundred years from now the whole Christian world will recognize it as the truth! They'll be proud of my husband then!"

Alexander joined in the laughter, his thoughts suddenly on Father Thomas riding horseback with his old friends, James Foster and Abraham Altars, fifty yards ahead. They would have a long discussion tonight at John Brown's, and tomorrow Father Thomas would return to Pittsburgh, preaching along the way as he could. But a new restlessness would be upon him because of his rejection by the Association; a feeling that his usefulness was over; that, somehow, he was on the fringes of the Movement he had started. And he would not have preached the sermon on the Law. Alexander looked at him, a slight, gallant, stooped man on his gray dappled horse, a dejection about his narrow shoulders that conscious effort could not hide. Although a committee headed by Elder Pritchard had promised to visit his little church in Pittsburgh and examine further into the possibilities of admittance into the Redstone Association, nothing would be done about it. Despite all his dreams, he and all he stood for had been now twice rejected by the organized church. As Alexander watched him disappear around the bend in the road, he wondered how long it would be before the Brush Run Church would suffer the same fate.

As the winter became spring, ripening into summer, Alexander grew conscious that the Baptist churches in the Redstone Association had grown more hostile since his sermon on "The Law," and he was no longer invited to preach in many pulpits where he had once been welcomed. But a spirit of inquiry was abroad among the people and he felt the fields were white unto the harvest if only he had some helpers. Aside from Father Thomas' church in Pittsburgh there was still only one organized body among his followers, meeting alternately at Brush Run and Crossroads, and the total known ad-

186

herents, including those not yet organized at Wellsburg and Washington, scarcely more than a hundred and fifty persons. They had no trained leaders to carry the message to new groups, and their enemies were increasing.

"Somehow we must do better," Alexander told Margaret as they sat late one night discussing the darkening prospects. "James Foster and Father Thomas and I are not enough. The Movement will stagnate and dry up into nothingness unless we can raise up young Timothys to help us. But how?" He put his New Testament in his pocket and looked at Margaret in the rocking chair beside him, knitting on a tiny woolen coat.

"You will find a way, Alexander," she said gently. "Remember the Scripture: 'Commit thy way unto Jehovah. Trust also in him and he shall bring it to pass.'" She held up the coat for inspection. "For our son, John Brown Campbell. Wouldn't it be wonderful, Alexander, if he could be your Timothy?"

He leaned forward and quieted her flying fingers with his, a deep tenderness in his face. Margaret was four months pregnant again, and the strain of the growing family was enough for her without his worries. He fingered the half-finished coat.

"You want a son very much, don't you, Maggie? Of course he will be my Timothy. We'll train him ourselves, in our own seminary." He smiled at the surprise on her face. "That's the answer, Maggie. I'm going to open a school for boys at Wellsburg to give special training for the ministry, and send them out over the country, preaching the restoration of New Testament Christianity! I've been dreaming about such a thing for a long time."

Instead of the teasing glow in her eyes he had half-expected she looked at him seriously, her hands suddenly tight within his.

"Of course," she said. "The very thing! But why Wellsburg? Why not right here in this big house? At least we could start it here, and when it grew we could add another building right here on the farm. We could make it into a real college eventually!"

He laughed and, rising, pulled her to her feet and kissed her. "A college?" he said. "Now who's dreaming? It's time to go to bed. The details of our seminary can be worked out in the morning."

But in the cold light of morning the thought of a seminary seemed remote and impractical. Margaret was not sickly but her health was frail and she had enough work to do with her household and growing family without having a lot of boys under the same roof, even though they did have space for them. But during the weeks they continued intermittently to discuss it as a hopeful dream.

And then, early in October, they received a letter from Father Thomas. He was moving again, this time to Kentucky.

Chapter 17

AS MARGARET SAID AFTER THE BABY WAS BORN ON JANUARY 17, 1818, the name of John Brown Campbell was not appropriate. Their fourth daughter was named Lavinia.

A week after the birth a letter was received from Father Thomas. He had found the Baptists in Kentucky not only the most numerous of any sect, but a cordial, hospitable people of liberal views, although they seemed accustomed to an emotional style of preaching which reached the heart but which failed to impart knowledge to the mind. The family was settled in the town of Burlington, in Boone County, he said, a village of three hundred people, where he planned to preach each Lord's day to all who would hear him and to conduct a school with the assistance of daughter Jane, since Dorothea and her husband, Joseph Bryant, had returned to Washington to resume farming.

The letter conveyed a contentment that had been absent before, and as Alexander read it, he breathed deep with relief. Now he could give attention to the problem of furthering the Restoration Plea. The seeds were planted but the harvest was late; later than his own lifetime, he sometimes thought, if his work took root at all. Other methods of extending the Movement must be tried.

The possibility of a seminary occurred again and again. While helping Benjy with the chores, while driving to a preaching appointment, while preparing a sermon, the prospect would come before him.

"It could be a boarding school for any boys whose parents cared to send them," he told Margaret. "And from them we could select those best fitted to receive further training for the ministry."

Margaret smiled at the enthusiasm in his face. "You must do it at once!"

"We could start as soon as we could build an addition to the house," he said. "Possibly in the fall or next spring."

"The time to do a thing is when the urge is upon you. There's no reason to wait. We have plenty of room in this house." She held up her hand and counted off the rooms on her fingers. "This sitting room could be the schoolroom, the upstairs would be a dormitory, and the children and you and I could move into the three rooms below. They're dry and airy and next to the kitchen, and with that big fireplace down there, they are warm enough in winter and there's even a window above ground in the main room."

"But you and the children might be there for months," he said doubtfully, "before we get the addition built. And you aren't too strong, Margaret. You have too many colds in winter."

"Nonsense! I'm as healthy as you are!" The words came indignantly. "Please let's try it, Alexander. You could train your young Timothys and I'd be like the old woman who lived in a shoe, except that I'd live in a basement. It would be fun!"

He arose and peered out the darkened window, the heavy winter snow like a white shroud over the earth. He shivered as though at a sudden draft, and then stood before her, uncertainty struggling with the approval on his face.

"It should be for only three months." He spoke slowly, as though to convince himself. "Surely we could build the school addition before the fall quarter begins. But the rains begin in April—"

"Spring begins in April," she amended. "And so does the Buffalo

189

Seminary." She spoke the words with a finality as though to end the discussion and arose and placed the sleeping baby in the cradle with its head under the netting hanging in folds from the wooden canopy. "Isn't she a beautiful baby, Alexander? But I do believe she's going to have your nose. Wouldn't it be a pity if all the children had your nose?" She smiled at him, the dancing lights again deep within her brown eyes. "It's already beginning to tilt a little to the right, just like yours!"

For a moment they stood together beside the walnut cradle, and then, abruptly, he spoke, his voice husky, and reached for her hand.

"I'm ashamed that with all this I should ever become discouraged. The Lord moves in mysterious ways and I am resolved to trust Him. To think this all started because I once went to lend Father Brown a book!"

She raised her face to his, a solemn, impish mischief in her eyes. "It could have been planned that way, m'lord," she said softly. "The minute I saw you coming up the walk I said to the Lord, 'That's my man!' And now to give you some interest on the loan of those books!"

She lifted her face to his, and as he kissed her there was no thought of the school in the minds of either of them.

Buffalo Seminary opened at noon on the first Monday in March, 1818, with eleven boys, ranging in age from ten to seventeen years, as boarding students. The long sitting room was crowded with their families and friends who had come to witness the opening ceremonies. The singing of the Twenty-fourth Psalm, a prayer, and a long, rambling talk on "Christian Education" by Dr. Joseph Doddridge, the venerable Episcopal clergyman of Wellsburg; an outline of the course of study, and announcements, and the Buffalo Seminary was in session.

The Bible, from Genesis to Revelations, would be a daily textbook, Alexander told them; every student would be required to attend the worship services each morning and evening, and to lead in biblical discussion when requested. The classics would be taught, and as the student body increased, other branches of learning would be offered, with English grammar and literature, mathematics and penmanship as the basis for all. Strict discipline would be enforced, with the students rising for morning worship and breakfast at six o'clock, and all lights out by nine at night. Room and board was one dollar and fifty cents a week for each student, with a tuition fee of five dollars for the quarter. Recitations would be heard in the mornings, with the evenings devoted to study, and two hours in the afternoons given to outdoor recreation, or work, according to need. During bad weather all recreation would be indoors, and at all times the boys would be closely supervised with fatherly firmness and attention.

As the school progressed Alexander found that if he had been busy before, his workday now was never done. Margaret, too, was never idle. The basement was comfortable enough, but as the snows melted and a wet spring set in, Alexander noticed that it had an air of musty dampness; the rooms never completely clear of the fumes from the huge cooking fireplace in the adjacent kitchen with its stale air locked inside with the winter's heat. But neither Margaret nor the children seemed to mind, although their skin lost its freshness and Margaret developed a chest cold that persisted with racking intensity for weeks, and in turn passed among the children. But the die had been cast, and when worries over the health of the family seized Alexander, he brushed them aside and redoubled his efforts to find suitable materials and skilled carpenters for the building of the extension to the house to provide for the seminary.

The cornerstone of the new addition was laid on the second Wednesday in May with appropriate speeches by Lawyer Philip Doddridge of Wellsburg, Elder Matthias Luce, and Alexander, and fervent declamations by three of the students. And although Alexander announced that the addition would be completed before the fall quarter began, spring passed and summer came before the major construction actually began.

The front porch was made into a hallway connecting the house with a two-story wing erected on the west, the lower floor to serve as a classroom capable of seating thirty students at desks, the upper floor to be used as a dormitory. In appearance it would conform

191

to the rest of the house, even to the details of hand-tooled moulding and cornices, glass windows, and floors of quarter-sawed oak. To hasten the work, Alexander contracted for the building to be constructed in sections at Pittsburgh and shipped down the Ohio River by flatboat to Wellsburg, and then transported by oxcart to Buffalo. He hired extra workmen, dreading the prospect of having Margaret and the children spend even a partial winter again in the sultry dankness of the basement rooms. And then came a long delay in the delivery of the final siding, and another distressing letter from Father Thomas.

He was moving again.

The family has been happy at Burlington, he wrote, his school flourishing, his preaching well received. But he could not continue to live, nor allow his children to live, in a state that made it a penal offense to give religious instruction to anyone at any time.

On a recent Lord's day he had preached to a number of Negro slaves, idling in family groups in the fields near his school. The next day he had been informed by a committee of citizens that he had violated a state law in preaching to Negroes without the presence of white witnesses, and warned not to repeat the act.

"Is it possible," he wrote, "that I live in a country where reading the Scriptures and giving religious instruction to the ignorant is a penal offense? Can the Word of God be thus bound and the proclamation of the Gospel thus fettered in a Christian land? Whatever the cost, it is impossible for me to live and breathe in a state where I am forbidden to preach the Gospel of the crucified Saviour to my fellow human beings, no matter what their color or condition of servitude. I am closing my seminary, and as soon as I can settle my affairs, I will find another location in a free state."

Alexander laid down the letter and sat for a long moment, pondering again on the inscrutable ways of Providence. He was as opposed to slavery as his father. Even in the Virginia Panhandle, where it was almost nominal, the institution was a colossal evil to be endured only until it could be abolished by legal means. And yet, however lightly and without plan, he was himself bound by its chains.

192

With his marriage to Margaret he had become the owner of the faithful Holiday, a marriage gift from his father-in-law, and the kitchenmaid, Mary, who had such a sullen disposition that had he not been a Christian, he told himself, he would have sold her. And for Holly's sake he had purchased her fifteen-year-old son, Benjamin, when John Brown had removed to Wellsburg four years before. He planned to give them their freedom as soon as they were able to care for themselves and wanted it, but in the meantime he was himself a slaveowner, however much he might oppose the institution.

If Father Thomas refused to live in a slave state, he might also refuse to work in slave territory, even in the Panhandle, where the yoke was light. But if he would, Alexander could use him in Buffalo Seminary, and his father would again feel useful. The need of each of them held the solution of their separate problems.

"Bring the family back North," Alexander wrote immediately. "The Restoration Movement and Buffalo Seminary both need you. You can live in the free soil of Pennsylvania, and resume the pastorate of the Brush Run Church. Without the compromise of any convictions you can teach in the seminary and insure the training of young preachers to follow in your footsteps. This is truly," he added with a flourish, "a call from Macedonia. Please come!"

September found Father Thomas and his family settled on a small farm in Washington County, Pennsylvania, two miles from the village of West Middletown, midway between Washington and Wellsburg, and only seven miles from Buffalo and Alexander's house. He was happier than he had been for years, he told Alexander as he assumed the teaching duties at the seminary and the active oversight of the Brush Run Church. The Lord had led him where he was again needed; he would never move again.

It was early December before the new addition was ready for occupancy by the boys and Margaret and the children could move back into their quarters. The school was progressing well; its success was assured. With Father Thomas and Alexander's sister Jane both teaching, new classes were formed and the student body growing.

193

Margaret was again pregnant, but her health seemed good, and in the comfort of their old living quarters, the children gradually regained their liveliness. Alexander's fears diminished and the future began to glow with hope.

In late January he went to Pittsburgh to settle his account with the Monongahela Building and Construction Company, and to preach for the pastorless church established by Father Thomas which still met regularly in the school building on Liberty Street. And as usual, by standing invitation, he stopped at the home of his friend, the well-to-do merchant, Nathaniel Richardson, at 58 Fourth Street.

As Alexander entered the parlor his host beckoned him to the narrow street window.

"I want your opinion of the young man you will see coming down the street with my son Robert," he said. "He's a young Scotsman much like yourself, and your father's successor in our school here. But I'm a little worried about him."

For several minutes they stood together looking out on the windswept cobblestone street, the snow banked in a long white rampart along its outer edge. Midway down the block, walking slowly toward the house, was the lean figure of fifteen-year-old Robert in earnest conversation with a thick-set young man of average height, both muffled in long woolen coats and shawls, their hands deep in their pockets.

"His name is Walter Scott and he's a good teacher," Mr. Richardson continued, leading the way to deep-bottomed leather chairs before the coal fire in the grate. "Once a Presbyterian like yourself, and from the way he talks also something of a reformer. You should get along well."

Alexander grinned. He seated himself comfortably, facing the glowing coals. "We'll probably try to reform each other," he said. "Is that why you're worried about him?"

"Not at all." Mr. Richardson laughed. "As an Episcopalian observing from the side lines, I realize that that is inevitable, but it doesn't worry me." He leaned forward and spoke rapidly, his face now serious. "Walter came over from Edinburgh about two years ago. Being low in funds, he walked all the way here from New York and began teaching in the school of George Forrester who was, as you know, a follower of your friends Robert and James Haldane, and an immersionist like yourself. Forrester later went into business and young Scott took over the school. After your father left Pittsburgh, we sent Robert there and I must say that next to Thomas Campbell I consider Walter Scott the best teacher I ever knew."

He paused, reflecting, and then went on. "Forrester converted him, as you Baptists say, and rebaptized him by immersion. Walter then began to study the Bible constantly, and went for a while to New York to unite with the Haldanian Baptists there, but eventually we got him to come back. He lives with us now as a member of the family and teaches fifteen pupils every day in his apartment upstairs. My son Robert is devoted to him."

Alexander nodded. "Then why are you worried?"

Mr. Richardson leaned toward him, speaking in low-voiced earnestness as the stomping of the two young men could be heard on the steps leading to the front door. "His friend Forrester was drowned last summer and young Scott turned to religion for solace. He frequently spends an entire night memorizing whole chapters of the Bible. He seems to be searching for something and never finding it, almost like one obsessed. I want you to talk with him."

"The Apostles were obsessed," Alexander said quietly.

The door opened and Robert Richardson and Walter Scott came in, unwinding their shawls, their cheeks glowing from their walk in the cold air.

"Mr. Alexander Campbell!" Walter Scott spoke in a deep musical voice, his hand outstretched impulsively. "I would recognize you from your description anywhere. Greetings, sir!"

"And also possibly because I told you Mr. Campbell was expected today." Mr. Richardson laughed as the two shook hands. "I hope you boys have been discussing something besides religion. Why not politics occasionally? Or even the young ladies? I daresay you both will be interested enough in them one of these days."

Young Robert laughed self-consciously, and then, almost as though

195

admitting a wrongdoing, he said, "We were discussing the four Gospels." His voice was high-pitched and hesitant. He shook hands with Alexander and stepped back, his light blue eyes watching for signs of disapproval in his father's face.

Mr. Richardson spread out his hands. "See?" he said to Alexander. "When I was Robert's age I found other things to talk about besides religion. But not these boys. They're both obsessed!"

Walter Scott smiled indulgently, his brown eyes glowing, his hair, black as midnight, like a skullcap topping his finely chiseled, sensitive features.

"I was only explaining to Robert that in my analysis of the testimonies of Matthew, Mark, Luke, and John I had made the discovery, a new one to me, that their one supreme and specific purpose in writing the life of Jesus was to prove that He was the Christ, the Son of God. This was to them the one and the only essential fact in our Christian religion. And the acceptance of that fact is, to me, the only thing necessary for salvation."

Alexander stared at him. By a different process of reasoning, as he and Father Thomas had experienced when they were thousands of miles apart, this young man had stumbled upon the same truth that was consuming his own thought. He had grasped the substance of what Father Thomas had expressed in the "Declaration and Address"; he had put into words the basis upon which all churches could unite. Here was an apostle of the Restoration Plea.

"You are, indeed, an obsessed man, Mr. Scott," he said after a moment. "I'm delighted to know you!"

When he left Pittsburgh four days later, after arranging for Walter Scott to preach for the church on Liberty Street, he carried with him the certainty that in this young man he had found a new friend and a fervent and gifted ally in the Restoration Movement.

Their fifth daughter was born on February 16, 1820. Alexander had been worried about Margaret's health and, overcoming her objections and ignoring the protests of Holly, had engaged the services of Dr. Henry Warren from Wellsburg. But the doctor was a half-hour late and the faithful Holly was again vindicated.

"Dese ole doctor men doan know any more about birthing babies den ole Holly," she grumbled amicably. "Me 'n Miss' Marget works together fine!"

They named the baby Amanda Corneigle for Mrs. Campbell's mother, and said nothing about a son. But he knew Margaret was more disappointed than he. In the Lord's own good time, he thought. Or never.

From the beginning the baby was puny, as Holly said, and Margaret was longer than usual in regaining her strength. He blamed himself for both. The basement living, the responsibilities of the boys, the confusion in the house—all had taken their toll. The farm was providing a fair income, and if he could increase his land holdings he could soon afford to move the school to Wellsburg.

John Brown still owned an adjoining 136 acres, and in March he paid the older man $1,823 for it. It was hilly land, much of it unsuitable for farming, but it was good pasture.

"Good sheep land," John Brown told him. "There's a future in raising sheep in this country."

Within a week Alexander had purchased a ram and two ewes of Merino strain, the ewes ready to lamb in the spring. As the flock increased, he could afford not only to expand Buffalo Seminary but to explore other methods of spreading the Restoration Movement.

As if in confirmation of his purpose, late in March two totally new and different methods of spreading the Plea presented themselves.

Alexander knew the Baptists had been seeking an advocate of their position on infant baptism to debate with a Presbyterian preacher, John Walker, and in March he began receiving a series of letters from Elder John Birch, urging him to undertake the task. At first he declined. Father Thomas was opposed to public debates on religion; they degenerated, he said, into personalities and only aroused bad feeling. But when the third request reached him, Alexander read it thoughtfully. If some of his fellow Baptist ministers were convinced that he was the one among them best equipped to render this service to the cause of truth, had he the moral right to refuse? He would talk with Father Thomas about it during the noon recess of the classes.

197

But when he sought Father Thomas out in his classroom, he found the older man in a distraught state.

"My neighbor, William Markey, was arrested yesterday," his father said before Alexander had a chance to present his problem. "Arrested and fined four dollars! And for what offense?" Father Thomas rubbed his hand over his eyes as if to shut out the image the words aroused. "Because on returning from worship last Lord's day he picked up a bucket his teamster had left at Wilson's Tavern the day before. He committed the offense of carrying a burden on the Sabbath! It's an outrage! Bigots! Bigots!"

Alexander nodded. It was, he realized, the work of the Washington Moral Society, an organization that had developed in the four years of its existence from a voluntary association for the suppression of vice into a punitive arm of the local law by enforcing its own version of morality upon the people.

"And Elijah Smith was recently fined six dollars because he traveled on a Sunday when he hurried home from Pittsburgh because his wife was sick," Father Thomas went on. "The burning shame of it is that one half the fine goes to the support of the preachers! Why don't you write an article for the Washington *Reporter* about it? William Sample should be glad to print it!"

Alexander's eyes grew reflective. Was God showing him still another way of spreading his views? He had written nothing for publication since his early Clarinda and Bonus Homo articles. He sat for a long minute, saying nothing, watching a butterfly on the window ledge open and close its wings slowly.

"Yes, I'll write something," he said abruptly. He got up and went to the window and looked out. "It's tyranny, of course, and that it is aided and abetted by the clergy is a disgrace. Denouncing it will afford me a chance to speak out against such clerical hierarchies. It will give me the opportunity to plead for a return to simple New Testament Christianity, unfettered by opinionated bigots." He turned and faced his father. "The Lord is opening the way, Father. He has shown me this way and He has shown me another way—that of publicly debating the issues on which we differ with the organized sects."

Father Thomas looked up at him, surprised. "But that can only arouse bad feeling," he said. "Each man goes away more firmly convinced than ever that he is right."

"I'm not so sure," Alexander said. "I've had another request to debate the Reverend John Walker on infant baptism. The very persistence of the requests may be a sign God wants me to try out this method. I am inclined to accept it."

Father Thomas closed his eyes for a moment, and when he opened them his face was serene again. "You must do what you believe to be your duty, my son. Always. God will guide you."

"You will hear from this, Alexander." Margaret looked up from the copy of the Washington *Reporter* he handed her two weeks later. " 'Candidus' is just as clever as Clarinda or Bonus Homo, and on sounder ground. But your words have a sharper sting to them. For instance—" She paused and then read aloud:

When the culprits pay dear for their sins, they will from principles of avarice become morally correct. And what becomes of the fines? Oh, they are given to some pious clergyman, to be applied for the education of young men for the ministry. Go on, therefore, in your misdeeds, ye profane, for the more you sin the more preachers you will have.

"Not all preachers in Washington County favor the Moral Society. Father Thomas doesn't, for instance." She shook her head. "Sometimes, my darling, I fear you are too severe in your judgments."

"The majority of them favor it or it couldn't exist," Alexander said. "The professional clergy is a bunch of stall-fed, self-righteous men, with a hankering for worldly goods and titles. They have already taken from the people the key of knowledge and now, at least here in Washington County, they're taking their personal freedom. I should have spoken out against them long ago!"

Margaret proved a true prophet. The "Candidus" letter created an uproar in the county, and in the next issue of the *Reporter* scores of indignant letters attacked the author. He was an enemy of the church, a friend of corruption, an evil influence. His identity was an open secret.

But Editor Sample was delighted.

"Let me have more of these broadsides," he urged Alexander as the two met before the Washington post office a few days later. "The people are cowed now, afraid of the clergy and the informers. And most of the magistrates and constables are in cahoots with them because of the fees. It'll be a rough-and-tumble fight with no holds barred." He grinned broadly, as one understanding friend to another. "But when it's over, my friend, if you haven't landed in jail by that time, I may desert the Episcopal fold and become a Reforming Baptist myself. I like your principles!"

Chapter 18

DARKNESS WAS FALLING WHEN ALEXANDER MOUNTED PRINCE FOR THE ride of twenty-three miles back to Buffalo from Mount Pleasant. The road was winding and through thickly wooded sections, but he had traveled it often, and Prince, one of three young horses left at the farm by Mr. Brown, was as familiar with it as he. The horse whinnied and he gave it loose rein as he sat back in his saddle, drinking in the beauty of the June twilight, watching the stars come out as familiar landmarks disappeared in the soft darkness. His mind was filled with a strange elation, the sweet taste of victory.

The two-day debate had gone well. Reverend Walker had been an able opponent in his defense of infant baptism, but Alexander knew his own arguments, backed by Scripture, had been unanswerable, and he felt a little awed by the clear perception with which his mind had grasped the new truths revealed to him during the debate. It was almost as if the hand of God had been unfolding the pages. Plain to him now was the strong connection between baptism and the gift of the Holy Spirit. It had come to him with startling clarity in the heat of the discussion; and with it a sense of the awesome importance of the holy ordinance. Baptism, he realized more clearly than ever, was a primary, vital step in conversion.

And from this time onward he knew he would be committed to public debate as a tool in man's everlasting search for the truth. But his delight and skill in logical argument, his persuasive delivery— where had he acquired them? It frightened him a little. And it worried him. Father Thomas was of the opinion public controversy should be shunned in religious matters. Dissensions would be ended, he maintained, if men would stand on the Bible, and it alone. If men were honestly seeking the truth instead of authority for their own preconceived views, the Bible's true sense could be garnered from its words; to think otherwise would be to regard the Bible as having no definite meaning at all.

But as for him, Alexander thought, Father Thomas was wrong. Public debate fulfilled him. It gave him a satisfying sense of power. The clash of mind against mind was as stimulating to his spirit as exercise was for his body, the muscles of his mind responding to the challenge of opposition as the hard strength of his arms reacted to the swing of the ax.

He was glad he had announced at the conclusion of the debate that the proceedings would be published. Salathiel Curtis had taken copious notes, and tomorrow he would secure them and send them to Steubenville by Benjy for printing.

It was midnight when he rode into the barn and led Prince into his stall. Benjy was fast asleep but he had pitched fresh straw into the horse's trough, Alexander noticed as he unbridled the animal and loosed the belly strap and dragged off the saddle. As he started toward the house, through the trees edging the back pasture he noticed the soft glow of a Betty lamp with its spouted saucer and lid in the window of the back bedroom.

Margaret should be asleep. She had looked thinner lately, and tired. The care of the five children was beginning to tell on her, even with the additional help of Susan McElroy, a sister of John McElroy and a member of the Brush Run Church, who had come now to live with them. Holly's time was taken up in the care of the schoolrooms and dormitory and in placating the bad-tempered cook, Mary, and in washing the linens and clothing and helping with the carding and spinning. He must secure more help. He was glad he had built the small schoolhouse on the slope not far from the east side of the house. Margaret could keep her eye on the children there without being disturbed by them. Jane, now eight years old, Eliza Ann, seven, and Maria Louisa, five, and even little Lavinia, not quite four, were all progressing well in their studies under the tutelage of the gruff but able teacher, Miss Jane Eliza Campbell, who had been secured by John Brown in Wellsburg. She was no relation to the family, but she was devoted to the children in her abrupt way, and he hoped she would stay with them until the girls were ready for more advanced work.

Margaret was sitting by the cradle as he entered. Her face, full of anxiety, turned to him.

"It's the stomach complaint again, I think," she said. Her voice was almost a whisper, but it aroused the dozing three-month-old Amanda, and her tiny face wrinkled in an agony of spluttering breath. "Her breathing is so labored. Set the pan of water on the hearth again. I'll try to let the vapors open her throat."

By morning the child was better and Alexander, seeing Margaret somewhat relaxed, told her of the debate.

"Father Thomas was there and rejoiced in my success," he said. "But he is still only half-convinced that public controversy should be used to further the cause of the Restoration Movement."

"But you were only defending the truth!" Margaret said. She was dipping the wick-yard of her lamps in strong, hot vinegar to prevent any odor from the lamps. "Isn't that different from having arguments over opinions or mere speculation?"

"I think it is. And I feel God has given me a gift for it so surely He wants me to use it." He bent over and kissed her. "I will never use it except to spread the truth as I see it," he said solemnly. "I feel a hand is leading me, Maggie, more clearly than ever before. I am strong as I was never strong before. It is as if a door had been opened before me." He paused, almost a puzzled look on his face, and stared at her. "The Restoration Movement is at last starting to spread. I don't know how, but I am convinced that in God's own way it is taking root somewhere, somehow, and in time we shall find out."

She nodded, her eyes full of wonder, and he was grateful for her silence.

Within a few weeks the reports of the debate were delivered from Steubenville, a thousand copies printed on foolscap, and Alexander took them into West Liberty for distribution by Abraham Altars to homes in that community; a second batch he took into Washington where James Foster assumed the responsibility of placing them on the doorsteps. Three thousand more copies were printed, and at Mount Pleasant, Father Thomas hesitated only briefly before he agreed to see they were circulated among all who could read. Others in the Brush Run Church, at Crossroads, and in Wellsburg took them in bundles to distribute by every means available.

Reactions were felt almost immediately. Even the Baptist clergy in the Redstone Association gave grudging acknowledgment of his triumph in defending the Baptist position on immersion although Alexander noted they tempered their approval with acrid comments on his otherwise unorthodox position.

Little Amanda's spasms of difficult breathing and colic increased as the hot, humid summer advanced; her cries of distress punctured the long days and the night hours. On the tenth day in August Margaret was sitting by the bedroom window in the morning sun, brushing the hair of Jane and Eliza, pulling it back tightly and tying it with blue ribbons, while Holly, her voice a croon, held the baby across her lap, tapping with her long black fingers the swollen stomach.

Suddenly the little body stiffened. .

Holly's crooning stopped. "She's done gone to Jesus," she said quietly after a moment. "He's took pity on the pore little thing and took her home."

Margaret dropped the brush, her arms falling limp at her sides, her face white. Her eyes riveted on the small form in Holly's arms.

"Call your papa," she said thickly to little Jane. "He's in his study in the attic; call him quickly!"

The next afternoon Alexander knelt beside Margaret as Mr. Brown and Father Thomas lowered the pine box that Holly had lined with pink muslin dotted with rosebuds into the small grave Benjy had dug that morning in the hillside pasture across the roadway from the house. Margaret looked up at the sky, her eyes wide and unseeing.

"Help us, dear God!" she said.

"Help us to say, Thy will be done," prayed Alexander.

"This is hallowed ground now," Father Thomas said as the family group wound its way down through the orchard that faced the road, sharing their sorrow, and in the sharing finding the grief was lightened.

Margaret stopped and looked back. "It is God's Acre," she said. "No other use must ever be made of it, Alexander."

Alexander paused beside her and studied the hillside. "None will," he said. "I'll have a stone wall erected around the whole slope. It will be set apart forever as God's Acre."

The autumn months crowded upon them. Goldenrod covered the hills and the first frost ripened the persimmons to lushy goodness. The harvest was abundant, and Alexander secured James Anderson, a member of the Brush Run Church and an excellent farmer, to stay on the place and supervise the fields. He was a silent, leathery man, his face hawklike, his piercing eyes reading the soil and the skies as other men read a book. Additional day laborers were secured but Alexander still spent an hour before breakfast every day working with them in the fields: reaping, storing, husbanding the land. By six o'clock he was with his classes, the daylight hours consumed by the school, but nightfall found him again with James Anderson, finishing the milking, bedding down the sheep, now a flock of twenty.

Margaret was again pregnant and Mrs. Brown came frequently from Wellsburg to assist with the care of the fifteen boys now enrolled in the school, more and more often accompanied by Selina Bakewell, a lifelong friend of Margaret's.

As Alexander observed them about the house, Selina Bakewell's short, robust, bustling figure seemed as much in contrast with Margaret's slender, graceful appearance as her literal, unhumorous temperament contrasted with Margaret's lighthearted, natural gaiety. Although Selina was a member of the Presbyterian Church in Wellsburg, he noticed she listened with increasing interest to the discussions on religious issues that took place around the supper table.

"We're not trying to proselyte you, Miss Selina," he said one evening early in May after a lively discussion. "These discussions are a form of recreation with us; we enjoy them."

"I know you do." She smiled faintly and shook her head, her kindly black eyes blinking rapidly. "But I can't somehow. When a soul's in danger of fire and brimstone, it's no time to laugh."

"What on earth do you mean?" He stared at her. Selina took her religion with a solemn austerity foreign to his God-conscious household. But she was a good woman and sometimes, when handling the baby, he had noticed her angular face lose its tightness as she seemed to stand breathless before the miracle of God's love. "Your soul is in no great danger. You are precious in God's sight because of your acceptance of His care."

"But I've never been immersed!" She spoke almost on impulse. "And you said yourself that that is the only true baptism."

"The Lord has revealed that truth to you, not I," he said earnestly. "I am only His mouthpiece. But if you are convinced of the truth about baptism, I shall feel honored to officiate at your immersion."

On the following Sunday, May 31, 1821, Selina Huntington Bakewell was among those immersed in a solemn ceremony at the mouth of Buffalo Creek. Margaret, suffering with morning sickness, did not attend, but she insisted Alexander bring Selina home with him after the service.

"She's like a sister in so many ways," she told him. "I find myself depending on her more and more. And now she's my sister in the church."

It was six weeks later, July 13, and Alexander had dismissed the school for a two-week vacation, glad to send the boys to their homes. He had looked over the group each day with growing apprehension; in none of them could he detect the spark of religious concern. Rather, most of them were boys whom their parents found difficult to handle, intent on mischief.

"I'm beginning to feel I'm wasting my time," he confided to Father Thomas one morning. "I did not plan to run a reform school."

Now he sat on the long portico he had added to the front of the house, enjoying the cool of the early evening, with Margaret reclining on the settee. Holly had quieted the four children and put them to bed. They heard her now at the rain barrel in the yard, getting water to put in the sour milk to clabber it.

"My time will soon be here, my husband," Margaret said dreamily. "The Lord is good; He took away my last baby only to send me another."

Alexander reached out and covered her hand with his own, his throat tight with a compassionate aching. The warm intimacy of the moment was broken as two men on horseback stopped at the turnstile and dismounted. Margaret saw them, too, and got to her feet awkwardly.

The men started up the cinder path, and Alexander went down the steps to greet them.

"My name is Adamson Bentley," one of them said, lifting his broad-brimmed white hat, his high leather boots and the yellow buttons on his dust-colored coat catching the gleam of the lamp from the open door. "And this is my brother-in-law, Sidney Rigdon."

"Travelers caught at nightfall on this remote road and seeking shelter are always welcome." Alexander extended his hand. He had claimed similar hospitality himself in his travels.

"We are Baptist preachers as well." Mr. Bentley smiled. "From Warren, Ohio. And we are caught here by deliberate intent. Your reputation, Mr. Campbell, and your views have penetrated even to to the Western Reserve."

Margaret welcomed them as graciously as her condition permitted and withdrew as Alexander invited them to sit down.

"The Western Reserve covers three million acres, I understand." Alexander laughed. "Do you mean I am known over all that?"

"By those with ears to hear you are," Mr. Bentley replied. "And eyes to read. The settlers in those nine counties in Ohio are ready and ripe for a new look at the old, old story, such as you are providing. They are receptive to the simplicity of a Gospel that will match the simplicity of their daily lives."

Far into the night the three men talked, a feast of kindred minds. They spoke of the ancient order of things and the modern; of the Christian and Jewish dispensations; of faith, repentance, and baptism.

It was past midnight when Alexander at last showed them to beds in the school loft, but by daylight they were up and ready to depart. Both were handsome men, Margaret thought as she helped Holly and Mary serve them a breakfast of hoecakes fried in the long-handled spider, eggs poached in cream, slices of ham, and steaming coffee.

"They want me to come as soon as I can to visit the Western Reserve," Alexander said, his eyes shining, as he stood arm in arm with Margaret watching the two riders wind their way into the hills. "They've organized the Baptist churches there into the Mahoning Association and are eager to have me come and explain more of my views." He lifted his hand in a gesture of gratitude. "Thank God there are some Baptists not in the mood to tear me to pieces. I sometimes grow weary of enduring the rebuffs and cantankerous attitude of the Redstone Association."

"Then why don't you leave it?"

Alexander chuckled. "Nothing would please the Redstone clergy more. I think it may be a streak of my Scotch stubbornness that makes me stay on with them. I'm a burr under their saddle. I feel I shall leave it eventually, but I won't be put out. I'll choose my own time."

"How did these men way off in Ohio hear of your views?" Margaret asked.

"They had read copies of my debate with Mr. Walker." Alexander clasped Margaret's arm and began pacing the length of the porch. "I knew God's hand was guiding me in that debate. Somehow I knew it was the opening wedge to great opportunities. And the power of the printed page, Maggie, is one I have to consider, too, in planning ways of spreading the Restoration."

"You love it, don't you, my husband?" Margaret looked at him with warm understanding, and snuggled against him. "You are God's crusader for the truth. He called you to this new country for just that purpose. Never lose sight of that high calling!"

His arms went about her, holding her close. "I know I can do great things," he said.

She lifted her head, looking deep into his eyes. "Through Him who strengtheneth you," she reminded him softly.

"Oh, Maggie, I need you!" he said after a moment. "I need you to keep me humble. I know my weakness. I glory too much in my own strength. I—" He stopped, staring at her. Her face had gone white. "Margaret, darling, what is it?" He steadied her as she swayed and almost fell. Her head was bent forward, her face writhed in pain.

"Holly, get Holly!" She put her hand in her mouth to stifle a scream.

Her baby was born at noon. It was a difficult birth, and later Alexander sat by the bed for five hours, watching Margaret's white face as she slept, exhausted, her dark lashes outlining the circles under her eyes which had seemed to grow larger and deeper the past year. When, finally, she stirred, he motioned for Holly to bring the baby and put it in his arms. The infant let out a series of piercing squalls.

"She's going to make the welkin ring," he said as he saw Margaret's open eyes appraising the child. "Just like Clarinda. Remember Clarinda? It was Clarinda who gave us our first common bond."

"Clarinda," Margaret repeated very low, and smiled weakly. "She has done it again. This is Clarinda!"

He stared a moment, puzzled, and then laughed. "We'll call her Clarinda, of course." He handed the baby back to Holly and bent to kiss his wife. "And this time you are the author."

It was six weeks before Margaret was able to leave her bed, and a September haze hung over the countryside as she sat for the first time on the portico. Now that she was better, Alexander was leaving for the Western Reserve.

"Adamson Bentley has set up a series of ministers' meetings at which he wants me to speak," he told Margaret. "He says my views have actually broken the shell of the sects in that region."

"Your views or God's truth?" The twinkle in her eyes did not wholly conceal the rebuke.

He kissed her gratefully. "Thank you, Maggie," he said. "I shall remember it is He, not I, who can accomplish miracles."

"But God has raised you up for such a time," she said. "God go with you, my husband."

Father Thomas and Jane stayed at the house during his absence, conducting the school. The boys were raucous and at times unmanageable, and when Alexander returned a week before Christmas, he was genuinely disturbed at the prospect of giving more of his time to the unproductive school. He had toured not only the Western Reserve, but Pittsburgh, Philadelphia, Baltimore, his preaching creating a response that gratified him and gave him new enthusiasm for planting the seeds of the Restoration Plea. The Lord was showing the way; the time was ripe; the flood must be taken at its crest.

"I had thought we could train leaders for our cause," he said almost in despair. "That is my only reason for conducting this school. There is such a need for leaders! The whole country is suddenly receptive! The fields are white and, lo, the laborers— Well, I doubt any of these lads will labor for the Restoration."

He looked intently at Father Thomas sitting by the window in the kitchen, gazing in thoughtful reflection at the setting sun behind the hills, an abstraction about him, a patience Alexander could not share. "I am going to discontinue the school," he announced abruptly.

Father Thomas turned and held up his hands. "I feared you would feel that way, my son. But don't decide such an important move hastily. Give the seminary another year. I agree with you that your task is to be out among the people. You have the gift of persuasion; your mind is tuned to logical reasoning. But daughter Jane and I love to teach, and we'll carry the burden for you. Give the school another year." He got up from his chair, as if dismissing the subject. "How is my little church in Pittsburgh faring?"

"Young Walter Scott is preaching for it. He is married now to

Miss Sarah Whitsitt and they are living with the Richardsons. He is a fine preacher but he needs assistance. I've persuaded my new friend, Sidney Rigdon, to go to Pittsburgh and help him. Rigdon was in our ministers' meeting in Ohio and is committed to our Plea. He is an eloquent man."

"You mean my little church will have the services of both of these men?" Father Thomas inquired, surprised.

Alexander shook his head. "No. I'm using a bit of strategy, that's all. Mr. Rigdon will preach for the Baptist Church in Pittsburgh, endeavoring to bring it into the Restoration Movement. Then we plan to have Walter Scott's group unite with it and form a really influential church in that city. I am greatly impressed with the ability of these two men."

"But you say Mr. Scott is quite young and immature?"

"In a way, yes. He's twenty-five, I'd judge, and filled with enthusiasm, literally on fire for the task of redeeming the church from its rigid ecclesiasticism; to let the pure air of the Gospel flow through it. He is a born evangelist. But"—Alexander ran his hand through his hair—"he needs guidance. I could better invest my time with men like him than with this school, unless the boys improve."

But another year did not improve Alexander's estimate of the value of the school. It consumed more of his time than he felt justified in giving it, and his frustration mounted. The work on the farm grew to demanding proportions as he continued to add to his acreage and enlarge his sheep flock, and in September 1822 Mr. Brown suggested a remedy.

"A Methodist preacher in Steubenville has two fine Negro men in his service," he told Alexander. "He is going South and will not take slaves there. He will place them only where they will receive Christian teaching and know Christian care. You would be doing them a kindness to buy them."

Charlie and Jim Poole were purchased and readily found a place in the life and affections of the family. They were eighteen and twenty years old, respectively, and Alexander promised them their freedom when they became twenty-eight years old. Heartened by this help, Alexander felt more than ever that God was directing his steps into full service for the furtherance of the Plea.

"It's as if I had been guided day by day," he told his father early in October. "I'm under a compulsion to spread the Restoration. The tide of the Movement is reaching the flood stage; it has taken hold slowly here, but in Ohio scores are embracing it; in Pittsburgh and in the South there is eager interest. I am told a Baptist preacher in Kentucky, a man called Raccoon John Smith, holds similar views, and a Presbyterian preacher down there, a Reverend Barton W. Stone, is advocating the return to simple New Testament teachings along our lines, and has quite a following. I want to learn more of their efforts; I want them to learn more of us. I must multiply my voice!"

They were coming in from the back pasture where they had inspected another pair of Merino sheep Alexander had purchased the day before from a young woolgrower, Matthew McKeever. Mr. McKeever had been frequently about the place during Alexander's absences, admiring his flock, and had become acquainted with his sister Jane. Now he had walked on ahead of the two men toward the house, and as Alexander and his father stopped at the cowshed to mend a three-legged milk stool, they saw him helping Jane into his buggy, driving her home to West Middletown. Father Thomas looked at Alexander with a knowing smile.

"I'm afraid the school will be losing daughter Jane," he said.

Alexander looked after them, and then stooped to fix the stool. "Jane has always wanted to have her own school," he said. "And young McKeever seems interested in what she's been doing here. Maybe they will start one together someday."

Father Thomas nodded, and then looked down at his tall son. "What did you have in mind, son? How would you multiply your voice?"

Alexander studied the wooden peg he was forcing into the round hole of the stool seat. He finished the repair and placed the stool firmly on the ground and straightened.

"I'm going to start a monthly paper," he said. "One that will

211

espouse the truth and expose error. It will acknowledge no standard but the Bible, oppose nothing the Bible contains, and support nothing it does not teach."

"You mean," queried Father Thomas gently, "it would be controversial?"

Alexander frowned. "What if it is? I know you dislike controversy, Father, but it can't be avoided when you are fighting a battle such as ours."

"The Redstone Association will not like it." Father Thomas looked worried. "The clergy will think you are fighting them."

Alexander forced a smile. "And they will be partially right for once," he said. "By whatever name they call themselves, religious bigots of all sects must be fought to the bitter end. That's the reason I continued those occasional 'Candidus' letters in the *Reporter* for a time. They helped to smash that Washington Moral Society and now freedom is no longer a joke nor religion a mockery in Washington County. And the experience opened my eyes to the power of the press. What was done county-wise I can attempt on a larger scale with a magazine of my own."

"And the school?"

"I'm closing it the end of December. With the year 1823 I propose to give my time to spreading the Restoration through my magazine and preaching trips."

Father Thomas pursed his lips thoughtfully. "What will you call it? *The Idol Breaker?*"

Alexander laughed. "I think we have a better name, and one equally appropriate. Walter Scott suggested it when I discussed the venture with him in Pittsburgh. What do you think of *Christian Baptist?* Or does that name imply too pertinently that not all Baptists are Christian?"

On November 10 Margaret gave birth to a son.

"We already have the name," she said when her mother leaned over her and told her the glad news. "Papa deserves a namesake. It's Master John Brown Campbell."

But John Brown never saw his namesake alive. The baby's face

212

was blue, and despite all that love could do, the next morning the feeble spark of life flickered, and was gone.

Tenderly, Alexander lifted the pine box and carried it across the roadway, accompanied only by Mr. Brown and Father Thomas, and briefly, compassionately, committed the infant soul back into the hands of its creator and the remains to a sacred spot in God's Acre.

For three weeks Margaret lay in a darkened room, her frame racked with coughing, her eyes blinded by tears, a hectic spot of red flaming on her cheeks.

"Pray for me, Alexander," she told her husband repeatedly, clinging to his hand. "Tell me all is well."

And hours upon end, night following day and day following night, Alexander soothed her with words of comfort and of love.

Gradually plans took shape for the new periodical. With the help of James Anderson, Alexander erected a small shed, sixteen feet square, on the bank of Buffalo Creek back of the house as a printing shop. He secured two double composing stands, a type bank, and a hand press, setting the equipment so near the water's edge that Robert Buchanan, the pressman sent over by William Sample from Washington, could wet the paper for presswork by dipping it directly into the stream. He used a large stone to lay the wet paper on, and another for the dry sheets, while he stood half-leg deep in the water, allowing it to play over his bare feet.

Alexander was thirty-five years old, and he noticed for the first time his hair was becoming streaked with white.

"But I've never felt younger!" he told Margaret, staring at himself in the oval mirror above the washstand as he shaved one morning in February. "I'm just beginning to live!"

"You're beginning to be a great man!" She smiled at him proudly, plaiting her hair and winding it about her head. "And greatness, my husband, brings its distinctions as well as its responsibilities."

"With me, my dear, it's age." Alexander laughed and stopped whetting his razor on the leather strop to shuffle through some letters on the table. "Here's a request I received yesterday that I debate with a Mr. McCalla in Kentucky on baptism. How the doors

213

are opening! And look at this!" He held up a letter postmarked Newry, Ireland. It was a single sheet, folded and sealed, the back addressed in a fine Spencerian hand to Reverend Alex Campbell, Buff Seminary, Brooke County, Virginia."

"It's from my uncle Archibald. He says, 'I gather you have given over all thought of my happiness or at least of ever meeting me on this side of time. But this note is to say Providence has sent me a son whom I have named for my highly respected nephew, Alexander. I have heard of your greatness and it is only what I would expect from one of your natural ambition of character and impetuous passions.'"

"Congratulations!" Margaret clapped her hands happily. "You at last have a namesake. And the honor is well deserved. Your abilities are known clear across the ocean. As well," she added after a moment, "as your ambitions." She looked at him, her eyes teasing, and then fastened a pin at the collar at her throat and came up to him and looked intently into his eyes. "Forgive me, Alexander. It is only because I love you so wildly that I mention such things. God be with you, my darling." She kissed him lightly on the cheek and turned and left the room.

Alexander finished shaving thoughtfully. Margaret knew him as no one else did. Her gentle finger probed his weakness—his love of power, his craving for authority, his desire for leadership. The eyes of her love detected it when he himself was unconscious of it.

He dried his face and slipped into his waistcoat, fastening his cravat with more than usual care. At family worship this morning he would read from the Beatitudes: "Blessed are the meek, for they shall inherit the earth." Dear God, he prayed as he closed the door behind him, burn that message into my heart.

The first issue of the *Christian Baptist* made its appearance on July 4, 1823. The lead editorial caused a lifting of eyebrows among the professional clergy.

"We expect to prove," the statement ran, "whether a paper perfectly independent, free from any controlling jurisdiction except the Bible, will be read or whether it will be blasted by the poisonous breath of sectarian zeal and of an aspiring priesthood."

Succeeding issues carried discussions of the Restoration Movement, pleas for unity of all Christians on the basis of the Bible alone, articles by Walter Scott, replies to correspondents; but in them all the onslaughts were continued. The erection of costly church buildings was attacked, the clerical love of pompous titles held up to ridicule. Stinging comments were made on the methods of selling pews, the sectarian motives of missionary work and Sunday schools, the organization of auxiliary societies.

In vain Father Thomas sought to soften his attacks.

"Missionary work is the scriptural plan for converting the world," he protested with his son. "And Sunday schools are a principal means of teaching our young! You cannot oppose them!"

"I do not oppose them," Alexander said. "I oppose only the abuse of them. They have been perverted to sectarian purposes. Missionary societies are used, not to spread the simple Gospel but to propagate the views of the sect which sponsors them; Sunday schools are instilling into the minds of the young, not the love and knowledge of God, but the theology of the clergy."

He included a piece purporting to be the "Third Epistle of Peter," written in a particularly satirical vein. Calling it "A Looking Glass for the Clergy," he quoted the apostle as admonishing the clergy with such injunctions as:

"Let your dwelling places be houses of splendor and let your names, even your reverend titles, be graven thereon; have you robes of black and robes of white; so shall you show forth your wisdom. When you go to the church to preach, go not by the retired way; you shall be gazed upon by multitudes, and they shall honor you, and the men shall praise you and the women shall glorify you. And let your sermons be full of the enticing words of man's wisdom, beautiful with metaphors and with hyperbole and acclamation and with syllogisms and with sophisms. And take good heed to your attitudes and your gestures, knowing when to bend and when to lift your right hand. Preach not, 'Peace on earth and good will to men,' but preach you glory to the victor. In all your gettings, get money! Now, therefore, when you go forth on your ministerial journey, go where there are silver and gold. For verily I say, you must get your reward. And over and above the price for which you have sold your service, take you also gifts, and be mindful to refuse none, but receive gifts from them that go in chariots, and from them that feed flocks, and from them that earn their morsel by the sweat of their brow. And you shall wax richer and richer, and grow greater and greater, and you shall be lifted up in your own sight and exalted in the eyes of the multitude, and lucre shall be no longer filthy in your sight. And verily, you have your reward."

"Oh, my son, my son!" Father Thomas shook his head. "You must not condemn the clergy so violently! They are good men!"

"Of course there are good men in the clergy," Alexander replied. "There are even good kings! But they are not the only expounders of the will of God. Simple men in the pews have access also to God. Yet the clergy presumes the right to speak for them; even to think for them. In order to raise the people's admiration of them for their own advantage, they have taught them in creeds, in sermons, in catechisms, in tracts, in pamphlets, that they alone can expound the New Testament; that, without them, people are either almost or altogether destitute of means of grace. And they organize societies to usurp the place of the church."

"But organizations are necessary to carry on the work of the church," his father pointed out.

Alexander shook his head. "No, Father. The church can carry on its own work. It is adequate to all purposes which entered into the design of its founder. Every Christian who understands the nature and design of the institutions called the Church of Jesus Christ will lament to see its glory transferred to a human corporation. The church is robbed of its character by every human agency that would ape its excellence and substitute itself in its place. I will stick by the charges I have made, and let the sparks from the fire within me fall where they may!"

The sparks fell with suddenness. Within two months an organized movement against him was set on foot among the outraged Baptist clergy. The next meeting of the Redstone Association would be in September. Systematically the churches in the Association were visited; they were urged to send messengers to vote to refuse the heretical editor of the *Christian Baptist* a seat.

Alexander learned of the impending move from James Foster. The Brush Run Church, of which Alexander was a member and elder, had not been visited, Mr. Foster said, but it was the only one not lined up against him, and its efforts to back him would prove futile against the organized attack.

"I'm more disturbed than I allow myself to appear," Alexander told Margaret a week before the scheduled Redstone meeting.

"But you are not happy in the Redstone group," Margaret reminded him. She was reading to the four children in front of the fire in the sitting room, Clarinda asleep in her cradle. The day had been overcast and chilly with the threat of early winter, and now the clouds had loosened a downpour of rain which beat against the windows with ominous force. "Why should you care greatly if you are no longer a member? Will it mean they will vote the whole Brush Run Church out, too?"

"No, they don't want to exclude the whole church. They plan only to single me out." He stood up suddenly from the cane-bottomed ladderback rocker in which he had been sitting, thumbing his Bible, and laid the book on the table. "I am disturbed chiefly because I have promised to debate with Mr. McCalla next month in Kentucky, and if I go there as an ousted member of my own group, I will appear discredited."

"Then can't you leave voluntarily?"

He ran his hand through his hair, walking with long strides the length of the room and back. "Not if the church of which I am an elder is still a member. And I have no disposition to ask the whole Brush Run Church to leave." He went to the window and stared out at the rain sweeping in gusts across the yard, the wind bending the pine trees like saplings. And then he turned toward the door. "I'm going to ride over to Wellsburg to talk with your father."

Margaret turned a startled face toward the window. "In this storm? The creek must be overflowing its banks by now. Your horse will have to swim over every one of the eight places where it crosses the road!"

He laughed. "It will be worth it."

"But what can Papa do?"

"He has been wanting to organize a church in Wellsburg for

217

a long time. It should have been done before now. If we can or-ganize it at once, what would be more natural than transferring our membership there? We live closer to Wellsburg than Brush Run."

Margaret stared at him, doubt mingling with admiration in her face. "You're using strategy," she said.

He came back from the hall where he had called Benjy to saddle his horse, and gently rumpled the hair of the children. "And why not? The wiles of the clever clergy will be met by the wiles of the clever heretic."

When the September meeting of the Redstone Association was called to order, Alexander sat in the audience, his face innocent of injury, his eyes watching the clergymen in their various maneuvers of political expediency, whispering, conferring, casting dubious glances in his direction, waiting for him to announce himself, as usual, a messenger from the Brush Run Church. It was to be the signal for their vote to deny him a seat.

The roll of the Brush Run messengers was called. The clerk scanned it, puzzled, and then looked over his spectacles at the group from the Brush Run Church seated in the rear of the building with Alexander in their midst.

"Why isn't Mr. Alexander Campbell's name here?" he demanded. "Isn't he your elder?"

Slowly, in the loud silence that followed, Alexander arose. "I regret so much of the concern of your clergy has been spent on so trifling a matter," he said in mock solemnity. "The reason I am not a messenger from the Brush Run Church is that I am now connected with the new Wellsburg Baptist Church, which is not a member, and never will be a member, of the Redstone Association."

"Never did hunters on seeing the game unexpectedly escape from their toils," he told Margaret when he returned home, "glare upon each other a more mortifying disappointment than that indicated by my pursuers on hearing I was out of their bailiwick."

"Out of their bailiwick and into the bailiwick of the unknown," she said gently. "Oh, my husband, what now?"

Chapter 19

FOR SEVEN DAYS THE DEBATE WITH THE REVEREND W. L. MC CALLA ON infant baptism was waged under a blue October sky in a grove in Washington, Kentucky. Alexander had ridden Prince the three hundred miles from Buffalo, thankful for the company of Sidney Rigdon, who had come over from Pittsburgh to guide him into country he had never before visited. As they journeyed together, now discussing the Scriptures, now reveling in the lush countryside, Alexander felt the same warming sense of comradeship he experienced when with Walter Scott. Here, he thought, is a friend, compatible in taste, receptive in spirit, matching in intellect and knowledge and love of the truth his own aspirations. He would make a mighty colaborer in the Movement.

The weather had been fair, the winding road a pathway to a new world, the sky a depthless blue. They passed strings of cattle and bleating sheep, heading for the eastern markets, and occasionally they joined processions of Conestoga wagons, with their six-horse teams and jangling bells, pushing West and South. They stopped their horses to drink at the little spring on Colerain Pike outside Cincinnati just across the Great Miami River, and enjoyed a midday dinner for a levy at Isaac Jackson's log cabin near North Bend, trading happy repartee with the dapper little proprietor with his knee breeches and shining silver buckles, and his hair in a queue bobbing against his spine.

Mr. McCalla had been a lawyer before becoming an advocate of Presbyterian doctrine and a stanch Paedobaptist, and although Alexander had gladly accepted his challenge to debate because of the opportunity it provided to bring the message of the Restoration Movement to the people of Kentucky, as their preparatory correspondence had developed, he sensed a personal animosity.

"Mr. McCalla has questioned my piety," he told Sidney Rigdon as they rode along. "I know I have nothing to boast of, but God alone and not Mr. McCalla is the judge."

Sidney Rigdon laughed. "You will have nothing to fear."

"I hope not," Alexander said. "I wrote him that since he is celebrated for piety and orthodoxy and I for the want of it, a great deal will be expected of him and very little of me."

Sidney Rigdon proved a reliable prophet. As the debate continued, Mr. McCalla's heavy oratorical effort, abundant with bombast, eloquence, and emotion, sounded like the howling of the wind in contrast to the well-documented, unemotional statements of Alexander, which cut into the heart of the subject like a surgeon's knife.

"In the spirit only of truth I contend for the truth," he told the great audience seated in the grove. "With humility and love I open my lips. My design is not to widen the breach or to throw stumbling blocks in the way by inflaming your passions, but to lead you to understand this most important institution of baptism."

He met the personal abuse that interspersed his opponent's arguments by the simple device of ignoring it. More strongly convinced with each reading of the Scriptures of the inseparable connection between baptism and salvation, he concentrated on hammering home the primary importance of the ordinance as a divinely authorized symbol of the remission of sins.

At the debate's conclusion the Kentucky Baptist brethren hailed him in triumph, delighted with his defense of their baptismal position. Few took issue with his interpretation of its design although Alexander knew his view was not held as Baptist doctrine. Instead, invitations to preach in all parts of Kentucky poured upon him.

Alexander glowed with his success, but he was also disturbed. Was he in the anomalous position of being considered an advocate of the Baptist church? The thought repelled him. The object of his life was not to entrench it, or any sect, more securely in the lives of the people, and certainly not to foster a denominational triumph.

"If you knew me better you would love me less," he frankly told a group of admirers at a soiree in the home of Major John Davis the evening after the debate closed. "I have almost as much against you Baptists as I have against the Presbyterians."

He distributed copies of the *Christian Baptist* containing blasts at cherished customs; he explained the "Declaration and Address," and the function of the Restoration Movement at David's Fork, Lexington, Mayslick; he spoke frankly with groups in private homes. But the enthusiasm for him only increased. It was as if the whole state, wearied of denominational strife, was eager to be led back into New Testament simplicity of worship. Everywhere he was greeted by inquiring minds and given a receptive hearing. All Kentucky, he learned, was still feeling the effect of the Great Revival of twenty years ago, and as he listened to accounts of it: the emotional intensity it had created in the minds of the worshipers so that some of them would jerk and bark and roll on the ground and howl for hours on end, he shook his head. Religious faith and love of God could not be built on such insanity, call it by any name they willed.

Emotion alone is not enough, he told himself as he prepared to return to Buffalo. He would come back next year after the people had cooled off and see if their interest was genuine.

A year later he returned. It was autumn again, and for three months he toured the rolling gold-and-scarlet countryside, preaching to ever-increasing crowds, meeting with ever-growing enthusiasm. Leaders in the state's political life were frequently in his audiences; educators conferred with him; Henry Clay of Lexington invited him for an evening's discussion in his home, Ashland; ministers of the Gospel with whose names he had been long familiar—Jacob Creath, James Challen, Barton W. Stone, P. S. Fall, John Smith— sprang into living personalities and sought him out in friendly inquiry.

"At last I've met Raccoon John Smith," he wrote Margaret. "He is somewhat a product of the Great Revival, and has no formal education, but is full of simple-hearted goodness and a pugnacious fighter

221

for the right as he sees it. He seems dedicated to the Restoration Plea, holding out only until I assured him that I, too, believed in such things as 'religious experience,' which his emotional nature embraces ardently. I tried to make it clear to him, however, that I did object to the use made of such emotional upheavals. About Barton Warren Stone—" He paused in his writing and studied the tip of his goose-quill pen for a long minute before continuing. "He is a former Presbyterian minister who, like myself, has turned from the Westminster Confession to the Bible, accepting it and only it in matters of religion. He has a large following in this region, and our views are remarkably similar. He believes in immersion as the only form of baptism, and has rejected all human designations for the church, content with the simple name Christian. He has approached me about uniting our forces." He paused again, and for a moment stared blankly at the page. "Whether he meant I would join him or he would join me, he didn't say. So—" He left the sentence unfinished.

He had been gone for more than two months when Margaret wrote she was not well. She was pregnant, and the baby was expected in December.

Hurriedly he finished his journey. He reached home on the first day of December, coming from Cincinnati by boat up the Ohio River to Wellsburg, as the season was mild and the river open. On December 16 the baby was born, another girl.

"I've run out of names." Margaret's eyes smiled at him.

"Then we'll use your own," Alexander said promptly. "Maybe dress it up a wee bit. How about Margaretta?"

Christmas passed and the storms of winter settled on the little community, holding it fast in an icy grip. Only the twice-weekly trips to West Liberty to meet the post rider were attempted.

The enforced seclusion created a new impatience in Alexander, and day after day he spent writing for the *Christian Baptist*, sometimes at the printing office, more often bent over the table in the attic study.

In the trenchant, compelling style that had become characteristic, he pictured the customs and practices of the early New Testament church, heading the series of articles "The Restoration of the Ancient Order of Things." He outlined the plan of human redemption in a series he called "The Christian Religion." The apostasy of the church he revealed in another series called "Ecclesiastical Characters, Councils, Creeds, and Sects."

Some of his writings appeared at once; some he held for future issues. But always in each issue he vigorously attacked sectarian intolerance, dipping his pen in biting, penetrating sarcasm. The response to his views in Kentucky had strengthened his conviction that the people were weary of the shackles of human creeds.

This became especially apparent following the publication of a piece he entitled "The Parable of the Iron Bedstead" in which he said:

In the days of Abecedarian popes it was decreed that a good Christian just measured three feet, and for the peace and happiness of the church it was ordained that an iron bedstead, with a wheel at one end and a knife at the other, should be placed at the threshold of the church, on which the Christians should all be laid. This bedstead was just three feet in the casement on the exactest French scales. Every Christian, in those days, was laid on this bedstead; if less than the standard, the wheel and a rope were applied to him to stretch him to it; if he was too tall, the knife was applied to his extremities. In this way they kept the good Christians, for nearly a thousand years, all of one stature. Those to whom the knife or the wheel were applied either died in the preparation, or were brought to the saving standard.

One sturdy fellow, called Martin Luther, was born in those days, who grew to the enormous height of four feet; he of course feared the bedstead and the knife, and kept off at a considerable distance deliberating how he might escape. At length he proclaimed that there was a great mistake committed by his ancestors in fixing upon *three feet* as the proper standard of the stature of a good Christian. He made proselytes to his opinions; for many who had been tried on the three-foot bedstead, who were actually four feet, had found a way of contracting themselves to the popular standard. These began to stretch themselves to their natural stature, and Luther had, in a few years, an iron bedstead *four feet* long, fashioned and fixed in his churches, with the usual appendages. The wheel and the knife soon found something to do in Luther's church; and it became as irksome to flesh and blood to be stretched by a wheel and rope to four feet, or to be cut down to that stature, as it was to be forced either up or down to the good and sacred three-foot stature. Moreover, men grew much larger after Luther's time than before, and a considerable

223

proportion of them advanced above his perfect man; insomuch that John Calvin found it expedient to order his iron bedstead to be made six inches longer, with the usual regulating appendages. The next generation found even Calvin's measure as unaccommodating as Luther's; and the Independents, in their greater wisdom and humanity, fixed their perfect Christian at the enormous stature of *five feet*. The Baptists at this time began to think of constructing an iron bedstead to be in fashion with their neighbors, but kindly made it six inches longer than the Congregationalists', and dispensed with the knife, thinking that there was likely to be more need for two wheels than one knife, which they accordingly affixed to their apparatus. It was always found that in the same proportion as the standard was lengthened, Christians grew; and now the bedstead is actually proved to be at least six inches too short. It is now expected that six inches will be humanly added; but this will only be following up an evil precedent; for experience has proved that as soon as the iron bedstead is lengthened, the people will grow apace, and it will be found too short even when extended to six feet. Why not, then, dispense with this piece of popish furniture in the church, and allow Christians of every stature to meet at the same fireside and eat at the same table?

The magazine was circulating now in Ohio, Virginia, Tennessee, Kentucky, and as far away as Georgia, Mississippi, and Missouri. Alexander was told it was read as no other religious paper, and his confidence in it as a medium for the spread of the Restoration Movement was exceeded only by his delight in the uproar it was creating.

With each issue, hundreds rallied to his views as if thirsty for the stream of fresh thought. A flood of applauding letters followed an article he wrote in a vein of rugged honesty, in answer to a reader who identified himself only as "Independent Baptist":

I was once so straight that, like the Indian's tree, I leaned the other way. I was once so strict a Separatist that I would neither pray nor sing praises with anyone who was not as perfect as I supposed myself to be. In this most unpopular course I persisted until I discovered the mistake and saw that on the principle embraced in my conduct there never could be a congregation or church upon earth. This plan of making our own nest and fluttering over our own brood; of building our own tent and of confining all goodness and grace to our noble selves and the elect few who are like us, is the quintessence of sublimated pharisaism.

But the trumpets of disapproval sounded with equal fervor when, with the biting sarcasm he reserved for what he termed the "stall-fed clergy," he wrote:

224

I once went to a Presbyterian meetinghouse, well filled with fashion and beauty. The wooden throne was superb, and in the first boxes sat and reclined the wealthy and proud on seats as soft as sofas. The grave young parson sang and prayed for one hour and six minutes, worshiping, if not in spirit and truth, certainly in taste and elegance. His sermon was forty-five minutes long, and was all built on this clause: "Why will ye die, O house of Israel?" He finished with one song and prayer twenty-seven minutes long, and then blessed the people and sent them home for a week.

Next day I inquired after his stipend and found it was annually $2,000, besides marriage fees and funeral sermons. His sermon on "Why die ye, O house of Israel?" cost the congregation $26. Now, if one clause of a verse cost that people $26, how much would it cost them to have the whole Bible thus explained? I soon found, by the rule of three, it would require more than a thousand years to get once through, and cost one million, three hundred thousand dollars. But the misfortune was that they must all die before they would hear it all explained, and pay all their lives for that which would never be accomplished. But they were amused once a week for their money, and their life was only a frolic throughout, and the parson might as well have some of their money as the play actor or the confectioner.

But I couldn't help contrasting the present state of the Christian congregation with that of the first disciples, and their teachers who were first employed in the work. The same sort of men, and actuated by the same motives, too, now pay dollars instead of stripes for hearing preachers, and the children of those who whipped and scourged the first teachers now contribute by tens and twenties to those who call themselves the successors of those who freely received and freely gave.

Deploring the love of titles and desire for distinction among the clergy, he wrote in a later issue:

I notice two more ministers have been promoted to the high and distinguished honor of Doctors of Divinity. It is apprehended that, owing to the peculiar influence of this climate, in a short time all our divines will grow up into Doctors of Divinity. It is fairly presumable that the Doctors themselves will take a second growth and shoot up into Cardinals. I understand that it is about to be resolved that no collegiate board is ever to sit down, or rather to rise up, without creating two or twenty Doctors of Divinity. What an army—where there are no privates or subalterns, but every man is a Captain or a Colonel or a General! How Satan will tremble when attacked by a whole army of Doctors of Divinity!

The demand for copies of the paper taxed the capacity of his small printing shop, and the mail became so heavy that Benjy took extra gunnysacks to West Liberty to meet the post rider. Someday Buffalo must have its own post office, Alexander determined, but first its name must be changed. Two other communities in the state were using the name of Buffalo and the confusion had become annoying. The name of "Bethany" appealed to him as appropriate to the rolling countryside, so similar in contour to the Judean hills, and he petitioned the Statehouse in Charlestown for the change.

"The preachers are on the warpath but the common people hear me gladly," he marveled to Father Thomas who drove over from West Middletown one morning in April when the road was open.

"And you are doing much good, my son," his father replied. "But I fear your perspective has become warped. You need to get away for a time. Get the feel of the people; talk with the preachers about their problems; visit with men who have no contact with the church and get their viewpoint."

Margaret agreed with Father Thomas.

"The great General Lafayette is to be entertained at the Globe Inn in Washington in a few days. David Morris, the proprietor, has asked us to drive over for the festivities. It will do you good to get away."

Alexander shook his head. "We're both men of war, but the general's methods are not mine. I abhor force and violence; God's method is by persuasion."

"But persuasion through love, not bitter reproach," Father Thomas said. "You are rushing in where angels fear to tread."

"Well, the angels will soon join me," Alexander replied, unabashed. Nevertheless, he agreed to make a brief trip into eastern Virginia.

It was not a happy trip. He found his father was right. Hostility among clergymen who had once been friendly was more pronounced than he had suspected. Some refused to open their pulpits to him; others avoided him; some openly attacked him. He discovered he was alienating some of the very men he had hoped to convert to his views. In Richmond, Bishop Robert Semple of the Methodist party received him coolly.

"As a man you are mild, pleasant, and affectionate," the bishop told him frankly. "But as a writer, you are rigid and satirical beyond all bounds of scriptural allowance."

It was an unexpected, stinging rebuke and Alexander felt it.

He considered going into Ohio, where the ministers in the Mahoning Association on the Western Reserve would receive him more kindly, but instead he took the stage for Pittsburgh. The family of Nathaniel Richardson, he knew, was away, but Walter Scott and Sidney Rigdon were there and would salve his wounds. The two churches they led had joined forces, as Alexander had hoped, and the new united group promised to be a strong spearhead for the Restoration Movement in western Pennsylvania. A visit to it would be balm to his spirits.

But Mr. Rigdon, he learned when he reached the city, had gone to Ohio, his imagination captured by a new concept of supernatural gifts and miracles. It was rumored, he was told, that Rigdon had read the manuscript of a romance concerning a fanciful account of the settling of North America by the ten lost tribes of Israel, written by a former Presbyterian minister, Solomon Spaulding, and was negotiating with a Joseph Smith in Palmyra, New York, for its publication.

"Rubbish!" Alexander exclaimed, scarcely able to believe he had lost the friend upon whom he had built such hopes. "Where is Walter Scott?"

But Scott, he learned, had departed for Steubenville, where he was opening a school. The church upon which Alexander had counted was in bitter strife.

He continued by stagecoach to Wellsburg and, unannounced, walked up the coal-ash walk of John Brown's brick house. The door was opened by Father Thomas. It was Friday morning.

"I came over to preach here on Sunday," his father explained when the greetings were over. "The folks at Brush Run have decided that that location is inconvenient and the church has disbanded. Some of them live nearer Wellsburg and will put their membership here and want me to preach for them. But most of them want to start a church at Buffalo."

Alexander loosened his cravat and sat back heavily on the sofa, his long legs stretched in front of him. He ran his hand over his face.

"That means, then," he said after a pause, "until the Buffalo group is organized this church in Wellsburg is the only one we have." He put his head in his hands, weary beyond all expression.

"That is enough," his father said gently, his voice warm with understanding. "We had no desire, anyway, to add to the catalogue of sects. We want only to bring about a condition where all Christians can feel in fellowship with any group which gives allegiance to our Lord."

"You are right, Father," Alexander said. "Thank you for reminding me; sometimes I forget and lose sight of our purpose." He told him of the strife in the Pittsburgh Church. "I fear I started it with my articles on 'The Restoration of the Ancient Order of Things.' I meant, of course, we should return to things sanctioned by the early church, such as the weekly breaking of the loaf, the fellowship, the simple order of public worship, the independence of local groups."

"Didn't they want to accept those procedures?"

"Want to do it!" Alexander fairly shouted. "They wanted to go even further! They wanted to adopt such things as the holy kiss and feet washing!" He got up and clasped his hands behind his back and began pacing the floor. "The Pittsburgh Church can be saved after this turmoil dies down, but it has taught me a lesson." He turned and faced his father. "I've learned many things on this trip, Father."

For three hours he talked, three hours of soul-searching in the humility of repentance.

He was up before daybreak the next morning to continue on to Buffalo. The weather had been stormy but today promised to be fair.

Holly met him at the door, her face contorted in grief. "De Lawd musta sent you, Mr. Alexander," she said between sobs. "Hurry up de stairs to Mis' Margaret. Lit'le Chile Margaretta hast jest died! Oh, Lawdy! Oh, Lawdy!"

Chapter 20

IT WAS SEVEN O'CLOCK MONDAY MORNING A WEEK LATER. MARGARETTA, seventeen months old and sickly from birth, had developed a constriction in her throat, Alexander learned, and had died in convulsions. Early the next morning her body had been laid to rest in God's Acre. And now the thread of life was again picked up. The children were in the schoolhouse; Holly was using the pressure iron in the kitchen; Margaret was in the yard, trying to conquer her sense of shock and loss as she gathered tiny rosebuds and bunches of sweet alyssum to place on the mound of fresh earth across the roadway.

Alexander had been up since four, going over copy for the paper. He would continue the series of thirty-two articles he had planned on "The Restoration of the Ancient Order of Things," but he would make it clear that in pleading for the restoration of the pattern of the New Testament Church he was pleading for it only as the basis upon which Christians could unite. He would work the series over carefully. Now he went into the sitting room and picked up the farm ledgers he kept in the escritoire. For two hours he checked them. James Anderson had done well in managing the place. The hay and barley had realized a sizable profit; the apples sold in the Steubenville market last fall had brought four cents a pound, and the sheep had yielded a clipping of almost a thousand pounds. He would increase the flock even further.

The Negro, Jim Poole, spoke from the doorway.

"They's a gentleman riding up to de stile," he said. He peered out through the half-open door. "Now he's comin' up de walk."

Alexander met him on the porch steps, both hands extended. "I am honored," he exclaimed. "Mr. Henry Clay, welcome!"

The tall, slightly stooped man with clear gray eyes smiled at him.

"I'm inspecting the National Road," he said. "Hearing your home was on this proposed route, I felt I must stop. Are you preparing another one of those fine sermons I heard you deliver in Lexington?"

They seated themselves on the porch, Mr. Clay crossing his long legs in their tight dust-colored linen trousers strapped under his boots while Alexander told Jim to bring refreshment for the traveler. For an hour they talked of general matters.

"You must stay for dinner and the night," Alexander said finally.

Mr. Clay shook his head. "Time is of the essence," he said. "I must be in Wheeling tonight and back in Washington by July."

"Wheeling?" Alexander echoed. "Wellsburg should be your destination. The National Road should have been routed through Wellsburg, not Wheeling. Now that it is in such a sad state of repair, I assume, of course, you are realizing that fact."

"I wish I could agree with you." Mr. Clay spoke slowly. "But your Panther Mountain on the Wellsburg Pike presents too great an obstacle. And besides, the tollgates and milestones are still in good condition on the old route. It would mean increasing the toll from a bit to a fipenny bit if we changed the route now."

"It will cost you more than that in votes from this community," Alexander said, his eyes twinkling, "if you should run again for a national office."

William Sample was writing frequently in the *Reporter* of Mr. Henry Clay's renewed ambitions to become president.

Mr. Clay stood up abruptly, as if unwilling to discuss either his ambitions or the National Road.

"I'll be riding on," he said, and extended his hand. "I see you have some Merino sheep." He began walking slowly toward his horse hitched at the stile. "Do you have any for sale? I'm looking for a pair."

Alexander looked at the sheep grazing in the pasture near the creek.

"I'm not disposing of any this year," he said briefly. "I'm wanting to increase my own flock. I suggest A. R. Dickenson in Steubenville; he could ship them down by river, provided we have some rain. The river is low this year."

Mr. Clay looked out over the fields. "You have fine holdings here," he said. "The preaching business must pay."

Alexander felt his face flush. "I accept no pay for my preaching in any form," he said. "And never shall. I do not believe in a paid clergy." He hesitated, and then added, "Although I realize some men, not so fortunate as I, must have some recompense."

When the visitor had gone, Alexander walked thoughtfully back to the house. It would mean great things for the Buffalo community if the National Road could be rerouted through that section as it pushed farther into the West, but Mr. Clay's inspection of the alternate route was only a token gesture. He plainly did not have an open mind on the matter. More powerful forces had influenced him; manufacturing plants were opening in Wheeling, and it was even rumored that another great factory for blowing glass would soon be started there.

Politics was a sad business; Christian men should take more part in it. Perhaps he should participate in public matters. The next morning, when Charlie Poole returned from West Liberty with the four-day-old copy of the Richmond *News,* he felt the compulsion even more strongly. The country had lost two of its leaders, John Adams and Thomas Jefferson. Both men had died on the same day, July 4. Who would replace them? Men like Henry Clay?

Alexander ran his hand through his hair and picked up an armful of books. He went out into the smokehouse, heavy with the odor of ham and hickory ash, and called Charlie Poole.

"Find me a table and put it in the downstairs bedroom," he said. "Something large enough for me to spread out a dozen books and papers."

He met Margaret in the hallway as he returned.

"I must build myself a study," he said. "I'm finding it difficult to concentrate in the confusion of the printing shop, and the attic room is not suitable. I'll try the bedroom for this work."

231

"What is it?" she asked. "Copy for the paper?"

"No," he said, and paused. "I'm undertaking a translation of the New Testament."

Her eyes widened. "Oh, my dear!" she exclaimed. "You are not tampering with the Bible!"

He laughed. "The tongues of earth are continually changing and we need a version in the plainest and best style of the present day. Besides, there is need to clear up the inaccuracies in the old versions."

"Your boldness leaves me breathless, but I admire it," she said, shaking her head. "What a task!" She pulled her shawl closer about her shoulders although the July day was sultry.

Alexander noticed the gesture and put his arm about her, thinking again how frail she seemed.

"Yes, it's a task," he agreed, "but it is a matter of paramount importance to provide an accurate account of the Gospel story if all Christians are ever to unite. The Bible is more than a collection of stories of the past; it is a living oracle."

"A living oracle," Margaret echoed. "What an expressive term!" She looked up at him, her eyes wide. "What a fine name that would be for your translation!"

"It's not altogether my translation. A great deal of work has already been done on it by others."

"Who had done it? Qualified men?"

They had gone into the bedroom and Alexander laid his books on the long table Charlie Poole had set up before the back window.

"I think they are," Alexander said, sorting his notes. "Dr. George Campbell, principal of Marischel College in Aberdeen, has worked on the four Gospels; the Pauline epistles have been translated by Dr. James MacKnight of Edinburgh; and Reverend Joseph Doddridge has worked on the Acts of the Apostles and Revelations. An edition of their labors has been published in London but they've been unable to have it brought out in America. I'm going to undertake it on my own press. And," he added thoughtfully, "I think I shall call it *The Living Oracles*."

Through the heat of August, September, and into the golden days of October Alexander spent every hour he could spare from other duties hunched over the long table, working on the translation. He arose at four each morning and spent two hours in the printing office down by the creek, writing now a stinging, satirical reply to a critical comment; now an impassioned plea for tolerance; occasionally an interpretation of a profound spiritual theme. At six he returned to the house for breakfast and morning worship, and consultation with James Anderson about the farm work, and at seven o'clock he was at the long table, dipping his pen in the ink he watched Holly carefully make for him from extract of logwood, bechromate of potash and cloves, boiling the mixture in soft water in an iron pot in the yard.

Sometimes patiently, more often furiously, he checked, documented, compared, wrote, aware of the misleading meaning of many English words since the translation of the King James Version in 1611. In Luke 18:16 he substituted "Permit the children to come," for "Suffer little children to come." In Acts 17:3 he changed "alleging" to "evidently showing." He used "behavior" in I Peter 3:1 instead of "conversation," and in I Timothy 2:9 he inserted the word "modesty" for "shamefacedness." All the pronouns, "thee," "thou," "thine," and "thy," he changed to the more familiar "you" except when applying to prayer, and after wrestling with his conscience, finally deleted in Acts 8:37 the account of the baptismal confession of the eunuch, the passage which most vividly supported his own views on baptism but which he discovered was not in the ancient Greek manuscripts. But in all other references to baptism he boldly and with unabashed honesty substituted the word "immersion" for the less graphic and less specific word "baptism."

In late October the work was nearing completion. But he needed, as he said, to "let it cool"; to get away from it and see it from a new perspective before he gave it to his printers.

Margaret's coughing spells had grown more severe.

"Why not take a trip with me?" Alexander suggested to her one morning. "You should not be subjected to the rigors of the winter here. Kentucky and Tennessee are warmer states. You would benefit there."

"But the children," she protested. "Who would look after them?

233

Susan McElroy is getting married next week and leaving, and Miss Eliza is not well."

He hesitated. In July his sister Jane had married the young wool-grower, Matthew McKeever, and they had opened a school for girls in their home in Mount Pleasant, not far from West Middletown. Father Thomas and his wife were living with them.

"Daughter Jane is almost sixteen," he said, "and of the age to enjoy a trip. She could accompany us. Both Eliza and Maria Louisa could enter their aunt Jane McKeever's school. The two babies, Lavinia and Clarinda, are of course too young to be put there. Why not ask your friend Selina Bakewell to stay here with them? She could oversee the household and we could provide additional assistance by securing Elizabeth Patterson from Wellsburg to help out."

Within a few days it was arranged. With her mother's help Margaret assembled a fitting wardrobe. They made three trips to Steubenville and Wheeling, and soon the needles were flying—two dresses of alpaca for travel, and one of silk for Sunday wear, steel-colored with an underskirt of blue silk trimmed with quilling of ribbon. For daughter Jane they made a serviceable green wool for traveling and a dark red merino for Sunday trimmed with black velvet edged with white; and a cloak of velvet with a small hood.

"I feel better already," Margaret told Alexander as Benjy drove them into Wellsburg for an overnight stay at the Browns' two-story brick house. Her light brown eyes seemed to hold flecks of gold, he thought, twinkling with their old-time gaiety. Selina Bakewell had gladly agreed to stay at the house and give it supervision, and Alexander was further heartened by the arrival of an excellent printer from Cardiff, Wales, a portly, genial man named William Llewellyn, who came so highly recommended that he put him in charge of the printing shop, and left in his care a collection of church songs which he instructed him to compile into a book during his absence.

"This shop is the fountainhead of information, inspiration, and influence for the restoration of New Testament Christianity," he told the new foreman the day before he left. "Guard it well. I prize it as I do nothing else in my possession."

The next morning, in brilliant October sunshine, they boarded the stage which was to take them through Ohio. It was a Troy coach, the body suspended by leather springs, the outside a brilliant red and gilt, the interior fitted in leather and velvet, with a boot on the rear for mail and baggage.

Four male passengers were their companions on the crowded seats while three more rode outside beside the driver, all trappers, scouts, surveyors, Margaret thought, studying them. They made ten miles an hour through the beautiful rolling hills of Ohio.

Margaret and Jane sat with wide-eyed interest observing the change of horses every twelve miles, watching for the postilions with horses which were ready to assist them up the long hills, enjoying the riot of autumn foliage on all sides. But each nightfall they welcomed the sound of the long horn as the driver pulled to a stop before the watering trough of the tavern which would shelter them, gladly climbing out of the coach at the hitching post identified by its "rum" strap. They were fascinated by the common rooms with their enormous fireplaces and six-foot pokers hanging over the hearths, but as the rooms were crowded with men, rough with the breath of the frontier, Alexander ordered their meals served in their bedrooms.

At Cincinnati they stayed at the Avery's Inn, obtaining two adjoining bedrooms and a small sitting room. No sooner had they refreshed themselves than a knock was heard at the sitting-room door, and Alexander opened it to see a short, slender youth with light brown hair that fell in soft curls about his ears.

The young man bowed with courtly dignity from the waist. "Am I addressing Mr. Alexander Campbell?" he said, a shy smile lighting his fine, sensitive features.

"You are," Alexander replied.

"Then I consider this the proudest moment of my life," he said, extending his hand. "I am David Burnet. I read in the *Christian Baptist* of your proposed visit and calculated you would reach Cincinnati on this day."

Alexander shook hands with him, puzzled. The name was vaguely familiar. "You are the mayor's son?" he asked.

The young man nodded. "But the distinction in which I take most pride is that I am a preacher of the Gospel, the primitive Gospel as advocated by you."

Alexander's eyes widened. "Now I remember," he said, "you are the Boy Preacher!" He reached out and put his arm affectionately about the youth's shoulder. "I have heard of you. Come in and let's get acquainted." He led the way into the sitting room and introduced the visitor to Margaret and Jane.

For an hour they talked together. David Burnet, they learned, was eighteen years old but had been preaching since his immersion in the Baptist church two years before. He had refused an appointment to West Point in order to enter the ministry, disappointing his father, the mayor of Cincinnati, and his distinguished uncle, Judge Jacob Burnet, who had obtained the appointment for him.

"You are of the stuff of which great leaders are made," Alexander told him when he arose to leave. "Let me hear from you often. The Restoration Movement will have use for you."

The next day they visited the open-air markets on Sycamore Street. None of the apples, Margaret remarked, could compare with the apples on their own farm, and certainly not with the new strain of golden fruit their neighbor Henry Grimes was developing on his farm. Two days later they went to the Public Landing and boarded the steamer *Wheeling Packet* for the one-hundred-forty-one-mile run to Louisville. Fascinated, Margaret and Jane watched from the deck the activity of the singing stevedores, loading molasses in hogsheads; the roustabouts pulling tierces of tobacco and salted meat; the friends waving to incoming packets; the roistering of beer drinkers at the Over the Rhine Tavern just across the cobblestone road from the dock.

Louisville, Versailles, Lexington, passed in swift succession. They met men and women whose names had become household words.

"So this is Mr. Barton Stone!" Margaret said graciously when introduced to a rather small, thickset man with graying upright hair one evening after a preaching service in the meetinghouse of the new sect, "Christians," in Georgetown. "My husband has told me of your similar views."

Mr. Stone's blue eyes, deep-set and piercing, brightened. "Our views are so very close," he said, "the Lord willing we may someday unite our efforts. Your husband is a very great man, ma'am."

The next morning at breakfast in the tavern dining room, Alexander showed her a copy of the new paper Mr. Stone was publishing.

"He's calling it the *Christian Messenger*," he said, "and it already has a wide circulation."

"More than the *Christian Baptist?*" Jane asked, looking up from her plate of flannel cakes.

Alexander shrugged. "I think not," he said.

"That is, you hope not," amended Margaret, smiling. "Anyway, my dear husband, the country can use another good religious periodical. I glanced over one while waiting for you in the common room at Avery's Inn, and in one column it told the way to heaven, and in the next how to graft trees, make canals, raise revenue, and clean black silk. On another page was a fine devotional message, followed by directions to find a barber."

"The *Christian Baptist* will never be used for any purpose but the cause it represents," Alexander said. "And I doubt Mr. Stone will allow his paper to be perverted."

"Mr. Stone seems to have a large following here," Margaret observed as they arose to leave the table. "Has he been preaching these views long?"

"For twenty years," Alexander replied. "He wrote a stirring defiance to the Presbyterian church, called 'The Last Will and Testament of the Springfield Presbytery,' when he withdrew from that body in 1804, appealing for one church, one name, one source of authority, the Bible, and he has been preaching that doctrine ever since."

"That sounds like your views all right," Margaret said thoughtfully. "I like Mr. Stone. I hope you can work together."

On through Tennessee they journeyed. In Nashville they were greeted by Philip S. Fall, a short, stocky man with a perpetual smile. He had been the first Baptist preacher in Kentucky to take his stand openly for the principles of the Restoration Movement. They were introduced to the Ewing family, wholehearted advocates of the new Movement. In the three weeks they tarried in Nashville, Jane's brown eyes held a new light as she saw the sights of the bustling city in company with the young son, Albert Ewing.

The winter snows had melted when they returned in March. The change of climate had stimulated Margaret, but the rigors of travel had also taken their toll, and as spring advanced her condition noticeably worsened. For Alexander the days became a succession of blurred activity. Selina Bakewell had proven a good foster mother during their absence, even if she had created a stifling atmosphere of piety, and more and more she began staying at the house as Margaret weakened. "Aunt Betsy" Patterson was a stanch and cheerful helper and agreed to stay on, and James Anderson had continued to manage the farm well. It was showing another heartening profit.

It meant financial freedom, Alexander thought as he went over the ledgers. It meant he was a wealthy man, a wealth which was only a trust, he reminded himself. He tried to restrain the surge of pride that swept over him. He cast about for additional land and bought one hundred and fifty-six acres from Caleb Jones and forty-two adjoining acres from James Robinson, some of which he put under immediate cultivation, some he kept for pasture for his growing flock of sheep.

The hymnbook was off the press; William Llewellyn had done a good job. He ordered immediate printing of the new translation of the New Testament, calling it *The Living Oracles*, and made frequent trips to Steubenville to buy paper from the John B. Bayless Company, staying overnight each time with the volatile, enthusiastic Walter Scott.

"I pretend my interest here is to see the two new rag engines and four moulding vats used in making paper stock at the Bayless mills," he told Walter on the second visit. "But it's really to feel your friendly handclasp and listen to you play the flute."

Walter laughed, the keen intelligence of his dark eyes mellowed by affection. "And to persuade me to quit my school and my small church here and go into evangelism." He shook his head of heavy black hair. "We have three babies now and Sarah needs me at home."

"But you are a born evangelist!" Alexander remonstrated. "Your place is out on the firing line, battling for the truth. The revolution-

238

ary stand you took against Calvinism in the articles you sent me for use in the *Christian Baptist* convinced me of that."

Walter's eyes brightened. "I still get hot under the collar when I think of Calvinistic foolishness—all such talk of grappling of souls in agony, wrestling with election and damnation and enabling grace before a man can be saved. It's nonsense!"

"But people are saying we have gone to the other extreme—we make it too simple; that we believe there is some efficacy in the water itself to save souls."

"That's likewise nonsense!" Walter Scott exclaimed. "Without a previous change of heart, baptism can avail nothing!" He got to his feet and began pacing the floor.

Alexander smiled, a knowing grin. "I can see you'll be taking the stump soon," he said.

Alexander returned home to find unexpected good news. A dispatch from the Statehouse in Charlestown informed him that his petition to change the name of the village of Buffalo to Bethany had been granted.

He folded the notice and put it away thoughtfully in a box in his bedroom. The acquisition of the new name gave him a strange sense of destiny. Forces were congealing that could have far-reaching significance. And Bethany had given them birth.

"Bethany!" He spoke aloud to himself as he went outside and stood on the porch and looked about. With Bethany the center, the Mecca, the heartland, of a vast Christian brotherhood, who knew what the locality could become?

"The name Bethany suits this place," Father Thomas said the following day when he drove over with Alexander's mother to visit the ailing Margaret. "The quiet of the hills, the seclusion; a place of retreat such as Jesus would have loved."

"It's a retreat for mapping out strategy for the Army of the Lord," Alexander laughed, "not for leisure. I'm about to declare war on whatever is causing the lethargy among the preachers in the Western Reserve. They seem to be taking their ease in Zion. Have you seen the last report of the Mahoning Association?"

Father Thomas nodded, his eyes clouded. "Only thirty-four baptisms in the whole year," he said. "And with thirteen exclusions and fourteen dismissals and four deaths. Well, it will take a long time to convert the world at that rate."

The two men had walked out on the porch, leaving Alexander's mother with Margaret in the darkened bedroom. Alexander turned to his father.

"They've neglected evangelism in their zeal for biblical knowledge. They're absorbed with studying the Word of God instead of preaching it. There is not a single itinerant preacher in the field. That's the trouble!" He tore a rose from the vine on the porch trellis and studied it for a moment. "When we go to the annual meeting of the Mahoning Association next month," he said finally, "what do you think of taking Walter Scott with us? He has the power and the fire they need. If they hear him preach, I think they could be persuaded to employ him as an evangelist."

On August 20 Alexander set out on horseback with Father Thomas for the annual meeting of the Mahoning Association at New Lisbon, Ohio, with Walter Scott astride his sorrel mare between them. It had taken little persuasion to convince the young enthusiast he should look over the field, ripe unto the harvest for restoring the New Testament church.

As the horses jogged along the dusty road, Father Thomas holding a linen shawl across his narrow shoulders, the end brought over his head and flapping over his white hair in protection against the sun and dust, both Alexander and Walter shielding their eyes with their broad-brimmed Panama hats tilted low over their foreheads, Walter talked excitedly of his growing conviction of the necessary steps in conversion.

"You have insisted that the New Testament is the constitution of the Kingdom of God," he said to Alexander. "But how does a man get into the Kingdom?"

"You don't think it takes a long, agonizing process?" asked Father Thomas. "You don't think a man must wait for the Holy Spirit?"

"No, and you don't either, sir!" Walter Scott fairly shouted. "A man is saved, or becomes a citizen of the Kingdom, or comes into full membership of the church, whatever you want to call it, by simply obeying the commands of Jesus Christ!"

"And what are those?" Alexander prodded happily, aware they might be crystallizing a formula which could prove a foundation plank in the still evolving platform of the Restoration Movement.

"There are five clear steps," Walter said, drawing up his horse sharply.

The other men drew rein, and together they sat, the dappled shade of a roadside maple making a pattern of light and shadow upon the little group.

"Jesus states them over and over again all through His teachings," Walter said. He held up his hand, counting off on his extended fingers. "Faith, repentance, baptism, the remission of sins, and then, and not until then, the gift of the Holy Spirit. After that a man enters into eternal life."

He spoke the last words solemnly, and for a minute they sat, a pregnant silence upon them. Some geese across the roadway chattered and clucked, and in a distant field a dog barked.

"There are three things, then, that man must do," Alexander said at last. "Believe, repent, and be baptized. Then there follows three things God has promised to do: Remit our sins, bestow the Holy Spirit, and grant eternal life."

"And that," Father Thomas said gently, his voice shaking with emotion, on his face the dawning of a new wisdom, "is the beginning and end of salvation."

As Alexander had hoped, the Mahoning Association was enthusiastic over the preaching of Walter Scott. He was employed as an evangelist in the Western Reserve to rekindle the fires of enthusiasm for the Restoration Plea started by Alexander on his first visit to the territory seven years before, and assumed his duties at once.

Back home Alexander plunged into the demands of the farm. The harvest was again abundant and five additional day laborers were hired to help in the fields. Selina Bakewell had assumed charge of the household, with Aunt Betsy's help, which left him grateful and humble.

"If ever you should need another wife," Margaret whispered to him one morning as they were finishing breakfast at her bedside, her eyes half-joking, half-serious, "don't overlook Selina. I would consider her a worthy successor."

Alexander arose abruptly, and then bent and kissed her forehead, his eyes blurred. "Don't ever mention such a thing," he said hoarsely. "No one can ever take your place with me."

His daughter Jane was receiving letters from young Albert Ewing in Nashville by every post. In October, Alexander himself received a carefully worded communication from the young man, asking for her hand.

He went into the darkened bedroom where Margaret lay. "They want to be married in January," he said as he finished reading the letter to her. He took her thin hand in his and, leaning over the bed, looked anxiously into her face.

His wife was dying of consumption. The thought had gnawed at the corner of his mind for months but he had never before allowed it to take form. Now it stood out, cold, naked, sharp. Margaret was dying.

"But Christians do not mourn as those without hope." How often he had quoted the words to those in sorrow. "But this, dear God, is different! This is Margaret!" The spectacle of the open grave yawned before him, terrifyingly close, poignantly real. How cold was the comfort now of his cherished logic; how empty his ponderous words; how meaningless his absorption in doctrine, theology, fine phrases. "O God, put Thy healing hand upon my heart! I need Thee now!"

He sat down on a chair beside the bed and bent his head until it rested on their clasped hands. What had caused this dread disease? The winter in the basement while he conducted the seminary? Was it exacting its toll? He should have refused to allow her to make the sacrifice, but in his ambition, his blind enthusiasm, his desire to "make little Alexander Campbells," his common sense had been overruled. "O God! O God!"

"January is a symbolic month." Margaret's voice was low but clear. "The start of a new year, a clean, unblemished sheet, a fresh life. Yes, call Jane to us, Alexander. We should give her our blessing."

The first copies of *The Living Oracles* were off the press in October. Orders that had accumulated before the final printing were being filled; others came with each post, and the printing shop was alive with activity.

For the pre-publication copy, Alexander charged $1.75; to later subscribers, $2.00. He had a few copies superbly bound in calf and gilded which he sold for $3.00. But he found the distribution a problem. The postage on single copies amounted to $2.75 for a distance of more than one hundred miles. He encouraged orders in larger quantities, and these, six or ten copies, he put up in strong boxes and delivered to a commission merchant in Wheeling for delivery at the expense and risk of the purchaser.

Postage on the *Christian Baptist* was also mounting as the subscriptions increased, and now that the name of the community was distinct, and mailings from Bethany running into thousands, he made application for the community to be further identified by a post office. Within a week the request was granted, and he was named postmaster. The advantage of the new office was more than one of convenience. The franking privilege he would enjoy as postmaster would aid in circulating the printed matter he was issuing.

Alexander opened his eyes on Monday morning, October 22, to find daylight already streaming in through the half-closed blinds. He lay for a moment on the cot he had occupied in their bedroom since Margaret's condition had worsened, a strange detachment upon him, as if he had wandered into a new heaven and a new earth. It must be six o'clock; he should have been up two hours ago. But still he lay, a sense of foreboding clutching him. He heard Holly in the kitchen and Selina's steps on the stairway, and then the familiar noises of the children in the room above him, dressing, romping, laughing. But a sound was missing. What was it? And then he remembered. Margaret was not coughing. He arose and went to her bed.

She was awake, her eyes open, listening, as he had been, to the warm, familiar stirrings of the house. She smiled faintly and opened her lips, but the effort to speak was too great and he motioned her to silence. Rapidly he dressed and went into the kitchen.

"We'll have morning worship in here," he said to Holly bending over her new Empire stove. "Miss Margaret is very weak. The voices in the dining room would disturb her."

Holly looked over at him, her eyes rolling in apprehension, and then turned abruptly back to the stove without speaking, as if words were useless, her broad shoulders shaking.

It was ten o'clock, but still he lingered in the sitting room, thumbing his Bible. He should be at the printing office attending to the binding of *The Living Oracles*; he should be working on the essay he had started on "Spiritual Blindness" for the *Christian Baptist;* he should be inspecting the new pair of Saxony sheep James Anderson had introduced into his flock this fall; he should be writing Walter Scott out on the Western Reserve.

But still he lingered. At ten-thirty he went into the bedroom, a strange compulsion upon him. Margaret was breathing evenly, her long white hand fingering the coverlet, her eyes closed. The red spots on her cheeks were no longer noticeable. The children were at their studies in the schoolroom; Selina had left for Wellsburg to fetch Mr. and Mrs. Brown; Aunt Betsy was upstairs, her quick footsteps tapping back and forth, straightening the rooms; an occasional clattering of pans, quickly subdued, indicated Holly and Mary were busy in the kitchen.

Without speaking he fell to his knees by the bed. He was not conscious of the passing of time; he was not conscious of forming clear thoughts; no prayer worded itself in his mind and arose to the throne of grace and mercy. He knelt in an attitude of pure communion with his Lord. He felt, as never before, to be in the luminous presence of God.

When he lifted his head the clock in the hallway was striking eleven. Margaret was dead.

Chapter 21

Jane's marriage to Albert Ewing in the sitting room on the morning of January 24, 1828, with Alexander officiating, was a quiet and
solemn occasion. Only Selina Bakewell was present besides the relatives. Holly and Benjy, with Charlie and Jim Poole, stood in the
doorway, and as soon as the benediction was pronounced, showered
the young couple with handfuls of rice brought by John Brown
from his store in Wellsburg. For the first time since Margaret's death
in October the house rang with laughter.

Three hours later, after a wedding dinner supervised by Mrs.
Brown and Selina Bakewell, the young couple left for Wellsburg to
begin the long journey by boat to Nashville, and Alexander felt
again almost as bereft as he had at Margaret's death. Jane was mature
beyond her years and had taken the place of a mother in the lives of
her younger sisters more than he had realized. Now the role would
be assumed by fourteen-year-old Eliza Ann, but the responsibility
of the family was his, tempered and lightened though it was by the
constant efforts of "Aunt Betsy" Patterson and the faithful Holly, and
the well-meaning intervention of the relatives. And the demands on
his time and strength were relentless.

Reactions were pouring in to *The Living Oracles*. Many condemned the translation as heretical and unsound; others were as
emphatic in praise. The first edition had been sold out and the second
was almost exhausted. The hymnbook was also selling well, and he
planned to enlarge it. The *Christian Baptist* was still the subject of
furious contention, but the target of Alexander's wrath had shifted,

for the time at least, from the creed-bound clergy, whom he considered the enemies within the church, to the enemies without the church, the small but articulate group of infidels whose voices were increasingly rising in a crescendo of criticism of all religion.

Their leader seemed to be Robert Owen, a wealthy manufacturer from New Lanark, England, who had established a socialistic colony at New Harmony, Indiana, where the goddess of reason was enthroned, religion barred, and atheism encouraged. Alexander was dismayed in March to learn that a challenge hurled by Mr. Owen to debate his system of moral and religious philosophy with any clergyman in the country had gone unanswered.

In the April issue of the *Christian Baptist* he boldly accepted the challenge. He wrote:

Mr. Owen says in his challenge that he proposes to prove that all religions of the world have been founded upon the ignorance of mankind; that they are directly opposed to the never-changing laws of our nature; that they have been and are the real source of vice, disunion, and misery of every description; that they are now the only bar to the formation of a society of virtue, of intelligence, of charity in its most extensive sense, and of sincerity and kindness among the whole human family; and that they can no longer be maintained except through the ignorance of the mass of the people and the tyranny of the few over that mass.

Now, be it known to Mr. Owen, and to all whom it may concern, that I, relying on the Author and the reasonableness and the excellence of the Christian religion, will engage to meet Mr. Owen at any time within one year from this day at any place equidistant from New Harmony and Bethany, such as Cincinnati, Ohio, or Lexington, Kentucky, in a public debate of his propositions before all who may choose to attend.

Within a month the agreement was confirmed by a personal visit to Bethany of the renowned philosopher. Alexander found him to be a friendly, affable man, hearty and genial, and in spite of the differences in their views, he felt a warm friendship for him. The debate was planned for the following April, to be held in Cincinnati.

No sooner had Mr. Owen left than Jacob Creath arrived at Wellsburg on the steamer *Triton* from Cincinnati, a fine new boat carrying forty passengers, and made an overnight visit with Alexander.

"This big house needs a mistress." Creath spoke to him in fatherly

246

fashion as he made his departure. "Your children need a mother's care. And you, my son, need a wife's companionship and counsel. Mortal man was not made to live alone."

Alexander nodded. What Jacob Creath said was true. But no woman would ever take the place of Margaret in his heart.

On the last Sunday in June he preached at Wellsburg and after the services accompanied his father-in-law to his home for dinner. Seated across the table from him was Selina Bakewell.

He had not realized, he thought as he smiled at her, how the close association with her in his home during Margaret's last days had accustomed him to her presence. He had seen her only briefly since Jane's marriage, but now he realized he had missed her. Her forthright personality, which at first had seemed to him hard, at times even brittle, now seemed engaging, and behind the stern demeanor of her bearing he knew now was a heart as tender as it was loyal. If she seemed to lack compassion it was because her sympathies were too deep for ready articulation. Had Margaret's father and stepmother planned this meeting for a purpose?

The thought persisted all afternoon as he sat with them on the lawn of the brick house under the maple trees facing the river, discussing the morning service, the coming debate with Robert Owen, the children, now visiting their Grandmother Campbell at Mount Pleasant, and the declining moral conditions of the times. The Browns had visited him frequently since Margaret's death, and had often taken the children for a stay in Wellsburg. They were as grieved in their own way as he; but they well knew the void in his life created by Margaret's passing. They were wise, wonderful people, devoted to their grandchildren and to him. They were giving him a hint to the future.

When Selina arose in the late afternoon to return to her brother Horatio's home across town, where she was living with her mother, Alexander arose with her. Without comment he helped her into his buggy. And as though all her life had been in training for this moment, she sat beside him, as easily and naturally as though she belonged there. Together they turned at the roadway for one last smiling farewell wave to the aging couple on the porch, and then began to jog steadily through the dusty street, a companionable, understanding silence between them.

They were married on the morning of July 31 at Horatio's home, with Dr. Edward Smith, pastor of the Presbyterian Church at West Liberty, an old friend of the Bakewell family, performing the ceremony. Only the Browns and the members of the two families were present, with Jane and Albert Ewing coming up from Nashville for the event. After the wedding dinner they went directly to the green-shuttered house on Buffalo Creek, and three days later left the damp heat of the hills for the cool green of the Ohio countryside to attend the annual meeting of the Mahoning Association at Warren.

They went by carriage, with Jane and Albert accompanying them on their return to Nashville. Arriving in Warren, the first to greet them was Walter Scott.

The thirty-one-year-old evangelist had produced astounding results in the Western Reserve. He had roamed the hills and broad valleys, preaching the simple terms of salvation he had outlined to Alexander that day on the road: faith, repentance, baptism, remission of sins, and the gift of the Holy Spirit, and had inspired Adamson Bentley, Jacob Creath, William Hayden, and scores of other preachers to new heights of enthusiasm. The Bible was not only being read as never before but was being studied. Lives were being changed. Almost a thousand baptisms were reported for the first year's work, and many churches were pledged to abandon their creeds and adopt the Bible only as their rule of faith and practice. Ministers, lay preachers, whole congregations of Baptists, Methodists, Presbyterians, were joining the new Movement to restore the simple practices of the New Testament church. Forces had been swept into motion which meant, Alexander knew, a clean break sooner or later with the Baptists; the formation of a church which, properly directed, could sweep like a tidal wave into the future.

"Yet it is not a new church we are forming," he repeatedly counseled the preachers in their enthusiasm. "We are not adding to the catalogue of sects. We are restoring the church as it was originally

248

formed by the Apostles, ridding it of the barnacles encrusted by time and men's opinions."

It required only a few days after their return from Warren for Selina to adjust to her new role of wife and mother and settle into the routine of daily living.

The Lord has truly blessed me again! Alexander thought in growing affection as he watched her one morning early in September going over the household supplies with Holly.

She was not so tall as Margaret, nor so pretty. Her face was plain, almost angular, with small black eyes which were quick to flash above her long nose and thin, firm lips. Frugality and piety seemed ingrained characteristics. But the shell of her severity would crumble in time, he felt, in the atmosphere of the happy family group, and more and more she would make herself indispensable in his daily living, until at the last he would wonder how he could ever have gotten along without her. He shivered at the certainty of the process and moved to walk away when she stopped him, pointing to a two-gallon, iron-hooped wooden keg in the corner of the kitchen.

"Oysters. The best." Her voice held a note of pride. "Put up by Thomas Elliott and Company in Baltimore. Now that it's oyster weather again I had Jim Poole pick up a keg for you at Mr. Brown's in Wellsburg yesterday."

"How did you know I liked oysters?" he inquired.

"I notice you eat your share whenever you have the chance." Her eyes held a glint of amusement, and for a moment he thought she was going to embrace him as she came and stood beside him, but instead she looked at Holly and turned away. "But they're expensive, I'll have you know!" Her voice was almost tart. "They cost plenty. Raw ones delivered in tin canisters, and pickled ones like these in kegs, are $1.85 a gallon." She shook her head. "Maybe it's sinful, such extravagance."

He laughed good-naturedly. "You must not be too frugal, Selina. We have plenty. I'm buying more land all the time. I've just paid $2,338 for two hundred and thirty-six acres of the Richard McClure

249

farm. It will enable me to increase my sheep flock. I'll soon be one of the largest landowners in the state; and I'm already the largest woolgrower."

Selina gave a little clucking noise, as though in doubtful agreement. "I always thought it was a sin to be rich," she said, wiping her hands on her apron. "But I reckon you know what you're doing."

Alexander smiled, a trace of annoyance on his face. "I'm using the money in the service of God; that's my reason for accumulating it." Without waiting for her reply he moved on, his conscience suddenly uneasy. Why shouldn't he acquire wealth? He went up the stairs, two at a time, to his attic study. He must get to work on the Owen debate.

Public debates were a popular pastime and drew large crowds, but this debate, he knew, would attract more than the idle curious. Robert Owen was a man of international stature, an authority on social reform, the acknowledged champion of infidelity in the United States and Great Britain. A debate with him would be no matter of splitting theological hairs; it would swing upon basic philosophies of life. Alexander would be in the role of Defender of the Faith; he would be in the public eye as never before.

It was early in November that Selina told him she was pregnant.

He had returned from Wellsburg to find his reference books back on their shelves in his study, and the loose manuscript of his opening remarks at the debate neatly stacked in little piles. It was not the first time Selina had attempted to straighten his desk. It took him an hour to sort out his papers and reassemble his books as he wanted them, and before he was finished he had made up his mind.

"I've decided to build a study, a separate one-room building across the road in the apple orchard," he told her that evening when they had finished discussing her coming confinement. "I'd planned on doing it someday, and now that the family is growing is the time. It will give you more room in the house; maybe the attic study can be used as a nursery."

"I thought of that when I was up there today," she said. "Or it could be used for my mother's bedroom." She nodded at the surprised look on Alexander's face. "Mama is not getting on too well with Horatio's wife in Wellsburg; she wants to visit us some, and with the baby coming and all, I would be glad to have her. When can you get started building your study?"

"I'll draw up the plans," Alexander said, "and James Anderson can start building it while I'm in Cincinnati for the debate in the spring." He stood up abruptly and then bent over and kissed Selina on the forehead. Selina had meant well, straightening his study. But at times her efficiency startled him, and he knew it terrified Holly and Benjy. Holly was getting too old, he reflected, to adjust to change. Her hair was completely white now and she walked with difficulty.

He was not surprised when she came to him a week later.

"I'se misery in my joints," she confided to him. "Why cain't I go work for Mis' Brown in de city?"

For a moment he looked at her loyal black face, lined now with a painful decision and a concern lest she hurt him. And then he looked away. Holiday Bethesday Brown had been a wedding gift to Margaret from her father. She had been the midwife and nurse and friend to all their children. But Selina's ways were not her ways, and she was troubled.

"I know how you feel, Holly," he said slowly. "Of course you may go. I'll set you up with a pension in a little house all your own in Wellsburg, and you can work for Father and Mother Brown for wages, or for other people if you like. You'll be a free woman."

Selina had no objection when he told her of the plan. She had never worked with Negroes before and admitted she found it difficult to adjust to their leisurely ways. "Aunt Betsy" Patterson and the other white women they secured from time to time as day workers were better suited to her disposition.

Cincinnati, Ohio, in 1829 was a city of twenty thousand people, a lively manufacturing and river town, and, with its public and private schools and churches that dotted the skyline with their piercing steeples, was, according to the weekly newspapers, the *Chronicle* and the *Whig*, the most religious-minded and cultural city in the growing West. Whether this claim was accurate made little differ-

251

ence, Alexander thought, as he looked out over the audience at the Old Stone Church of the Methodists on East Fifth Street, the largest in the city, on Monday morning, April 13.

The church held twelve hundred people, and already it was filled. Visitors were present from as far away as New York and New Orleans, attracted by the novelty of the occasion. He recognized in a front pew Mrs. Frances Trollop of England, the eccentric Englishwoman already beginning to be well known throughout the country for her fabulous bazaar on the Public Landing.

Father Thomas was seated in the place of honor behind the pulpit, a venerable figure with his snow-white hair, a benignity about him; Alexander's brothers, Archibald and Thomas, young men of twenty-seven and twenty-four, married and well anchored in their medical profession at Wellsburg and Pittsburgh, were midway of the audience. Behind him, and to the left on a separate raised platform, were the seven moderators, three of whom had been chosen by each debater with the seventh chosen by the moderators themselves. Robert Owen had chosen Colonel Francis Carr, Henry Starr, and the well-known preacher and writer, Timothy Flint, publisher and editor of the *Western Monthly Review*. Alexander had selected Colonel Samuel W. Davis, Major Daniel Gano, and David Burnet's uncle, Judge Jacob Burnet of the Ohio Supreme Court. The moderators had selected the Reverend Oliver M. Spencer, and elected Judge Burnet as their permanent chairman. Charles Sims was appointed by the moderators as the official stenographer to record the speeches for publication.

Alexander glanced over the audience again as Judge Burnet arose promptly at nine o'clock with gavel in hand. The pews were packed now, with people standing in the aisles, the men and women separated according to sex by a four-foot wooden partition which ran the length of the church. Only in the house of God, Alexander thought, were families so rigidly torn asunder by self-righteous bigots eager to frustrate even by outward symbol the design of the Almighty. Religion as practiced by most of mankind had much to answer for, and persons such as Robert Owen were scourges of God to shock men from their lethargy and awaken them to the true value of their faith.

Alexander flushed self-consciously as Mr. Owen, seated on his right, turned to him, his plump face beaming, before he arose to his feet in response to Judge Burnet's introduction for his opening statement.

"May the truth prevail, Mr. Campbell," he said.

Alexander leaned slightly forward, his eyes on the famous stocky figure. How had he, Alexander Campbell, an unknown young preacher from the foothills of the Alleghenies, been drawn into the role of Defender of the Faith? What strange force had compelled him to answer this mighty man's challenge? This was no sermon before the Redstone Baptist Association, or an appearance before the Synod, or a friendly debate with another preacher on some scriptural interpretation. He was the spokesman now of all Christianity, and upon his efforts souls yet unborn might live to curse or to bless him.

All morning the two men spoke, alternately, for thirty minutes at a time, presenting their basic positions. But at the beginning of the afternoon session, Mr. Owen asked the indulgence of his opponent for more time and began the reading of a two-hundred-page manuscript which he called "Twelve Facts or Fundamental Laws of Nature," and which consumed the rest of the day.

"I noted his points carefully," Alexander commented as he and Father Thomas sat with David Burnet in their room at Avery's Inn that night after supper. "These facts, or Laws as he calls them, are mere truisms. I'll admit them all without debate and they have no application whatever to any of the propositions in Owen's challenge. I hope we've heard the last of them and can come to grips tomorrow with the real issues."

David Burnet laughed, his booming, resonant voice in his short, thickening body like the sudden roar of a cannon in the little room.

David was twenty-two now and mature in mind and heart. He was soon to marry Mary Gano, he told Alexander with warm feeling. He had been preaching for a Baptist church in Dayton which he had brought into the fold of the Restoration Movement but was now giving most of his time to nurturing a new church on Sycamore Street in Cincinnati, devoted wholly to the new teaching.

"You're right, sir!" he said heartily. "Owen's facts are universal and no man would dispute them." In a sudden droll mimicry of the Welsh philosopher he ran his hands through his curly hair, now clipped short, and took from his vest pocket a sheaf of notes. "Here they are, the great twelve fundamental laws of nature as only recently discovered by that renowned atheist, Robert Owen!" Slowly, in mock solemnity, he began to read:

"One: That man at his birth is ignorant of everything relative to how his own organization functions, and that he has not been permitted to create the slightest part of his natural propensities, faculties, or qualities, physical or mental.

"Two: That no two infants at birth have yet been known to possess precisely the same organization, while the physical, mental, and moral differences between all infants are formed without their knowledge or will.

"Three: That each individual is placed at birth, without his knowledge or consent, within circumstances which, acting upon his peculiar organization, impress the general character of those circumstances upon the infant. Yet—"

"Read no more!" Alexander interrupted with a laugh. "The other propositions are equally truisms and have as little to do with the truth or falsity of Christianity as with any other religion. As we go along, surely we can begin the real issues of the debate."

But as the days passed it became clear to Alexander that Robert Owen, kind and genial and witty and the soul of courtesy, was ignoring the real issues, concentrating wholly upon explaining his "Twelve Laws" which, once understood, he declared, would relieve man, who, he claimed, was wholly the victim of his circumstances, from any moral responsibility, and would make unnecessary either religion, marriage, or private property, and bring about Utopia.

Alexander listened with mounting dismay.

"Our problem is not," he cried in rebuttal, "the ordinary affairs of this life, the fleeting concerns of today; it is not whether we shall live all freemen or die all slaves; it is not the momentary affairs of empire—nay, all these are but the toys of childhood contrasted with the questions: What is man? Whence came he? Whither does he go? Is he a mortal or an immortal being? Is he doomed to spring up like grass, drop his seed into the earth, and die forever? These are the awful and sublime merits of the question at issue! It is not what we shall eat, nor what we shall drink, unless we shall be proved to be mere animals; but it is: Shall we live or die forever?" He turned to Mr. Owen. "Your Twelve Laws, sir, are as applicable to a goat as to a man! Let us discuss the real issues!"

But Mr. Owen persisted with imperturbable good nature to read and expound his "Laws," detailing the perfected social system which would follow their adoption. On Friday evening he completed reading his manuscript for the twelfth time and in a gesture of magniloquence offered to Alexander the privilege of speaking uninterruptedly.

The next morning the house was even more crowded than usual. People stood in the aisles, sat on the steps of the rostrum, perched on the window ledges. Alexander began to speak slowly, choosing his words with care. He presented the historic evidence of the Christian religion, its prophetic evidences, its genius and tendency, and its effect on the social system. Two hours went by and the audience sat tense, absorbed in his words.

"Pure Christianity," he declared, "aims not at reforming the world by a system of legal restraint, however excellent; but its immediate object is to implant in the human heart a principle of love. Here is the grand secret! The religion of Jesus Christ melts the hearts of men into pure philanthropy." He paused and looked steadily at his opponent. "No social compact has as yet existed without the doctrine of responsibility, obligation, or accountability. Mr. Owen lays the ax at the root of all obligations, and would have society hang together without a single attraction save animal magnetism."

Four hours passed, and still the audience listened. Five, six hours passed. A short recess was declared, and Alexander resumed speaking.

"No unrestrained freedom can compensate for the immense robbery of the idea of God and the hope of deathless bliss. The worst

255

thing in such a scheme as Mr. Owen presents which could happen, or even appear to happen, would be success. But as well might Mr. Owen attempt to fetter the sea, to lock up the winds, to prevent the rising of the sun, as to exile the idea of God from the human race. The proofs of His existence are as numerous as the drops of dew, and everything within us and without us, from the nails upon the ends of our fingers to the sun, moon, and stars, confirms the idea of His existence."

At the end of ten hours another recess was declared, and at its conclusion the house was again crowded. For two more hours Alexander explored and exposed the false principles on which infidelity rested. He presented the Gospel as a series of connected facts, decrying the evils attendant upon human creeds, and pictured a glorious era for humanity based not on idle human schemes, but on God's own plan for the brotherhood of man.

When he sat down, wet with perspiration, weary beyond expression, he had spoken for twelve hours. For a long moment the audience sat silent, and then it rose to its feet almost as one body in a ringing, prolonged tribute to the Defender of the Faith.

On Sunday night, after preaching twice that day to packed congregations at the Old Stone Church, Alexander sat in his room at Avery's Inn, writing to Selina, a feeling of deep loneliness upon him. This was the inn where he and Margaret had stayed on their trip South a year before her death, and it was crowded with memories.

"We never really got to the points at issue in the debate," he wrote hurriedly. "Robert Owen is in many ways a great and good and benevolent man, and it is a disgrace to Christianity that such a man was repelled in his youth against all religion by the clamorous and disruptive claims of the contending sects."

He dipped his new metal nibbed-point pen again in the jar of ink, and sat a little more directly under the flaring candle cluster over the table, uncertain how best to phrase the thought in his mind. This was his first long separation from Selina since their marriage, and before they met again she would be a mother. And it might be difficult for her. Even at twenty-seven, no longer a young girl, a

256

wife had reason to expect her husband to be near at such a time. He felt a sudden pang of conscience.

But Selina would not be the first wife who had brought a child into the world while her husband was elsewhere on duty. Her mother would be there, and a well-ordered household, headed by "Aunt Betsy," would take from her any onerous duties. She had courage. She would get along. And she had urged him to go ahead with the debate; a cancellation or even a postponement, she had rightly said, would have been construed as timidity on his part in defending Christianity against its world-famous defamer.

"I should be at home before the middle of next month," he resumed. "May the good Lord who has always been our strength and our refuge preserve and keep thee, my dear, dear Selina. Your affectionate husband, A. Campbell."

He hesitated a moment before he added the postscript. "If the baby is a girl, what would you think of naming her Margaret Brown?"

Chapter 22

It was Friday, May 1, before Alexander left Cincinnati. There had been much to do. He had received a letter from a group of admirers in Brooke County urging him to become a delegate to the approaching Virginia State Constitutional Convention. Occupied with the debate, he had come to no decision about it, but now he must give it some thought before returning home. Robert Owen, anxious to begin a trip to England, had left for New York after selling to Alexander his publishing rights to the stenographic report of the debate as transcribed by Charles Sims, and the copy needed editing. Many people who had been won to Alexander's religious views during the debate requested baptism, and both Alexander and Father Thomas were kept busy performing this happy service. Alexander also took advantage of the opportunity to discuss with David Burnet, Jeremiah Vardaman, Jacob Creath, James Challen, Timothy Flint, and other friends, the advisability of discontinuing the *Christian Baptist* and replacing it with a monthly journal of a milder character.

Although not a month had passed since the paper first appeared in July 1823 but that new readers had been added, Alexander felt more and more that it represented an era in his thinking that was rapidly coming to an end. For him the time of the iconoclast, the breaker of idols, was passing. It was the time now to build up.

There was no doubt that the *Christian Baptist* had shaken the religious world into which it penetrated from its apathy and had developed a spirit of inquiry among the people. But Margaret had been right. He had been too caustic. Even the *Northern Whig* of Belfast, Ireland, an erudite and stanch supporter of his views, had said of the *Christian Baptist* in its November 4 issue, which had reached him just before he had left for Cincinnati: "It might do more good provided it were written with less bitterness. It is a mixture of pepper, salt, and vinegar, served up with a dash of genuine Irish wit—but with a good deal of instruction." His attacks, for instance, against a paid clergy could well be a reason why more young men were not responding to his calls for the ministry. Few preachers, he admitted, had the opportunity to serve without pay. How much better, Alexander found himself frequently thinking, if even the Apostle Paul could have been freed from his tentmaking and had devoted all of his time to the cause of Christ. Coupled with the thought was the disturbing doubt that his own work might be more effective if he gave less time to his business affairs. But he pushed the doubt to the back of his mind.

Yes, the times were ripe, his friends agreed with Father Thomas, for a periodical with a milder tone, that breathed more of the love of God and less of His wrath; a true harbinger of the glad tidings.

The Restoration Movement was congealing as a religious force in the country with each passing day; it was breaking gradually, steadily, irrevocably, from the Baptist fold; and it was well now to allow the healing power of tolerance to play its part. As Jeremiah Vardaman had quoted to him from the third chapter of Ecclesiastes:

To every thing there is a season, and a time to every purpose under the heaven:
A time to be born, and a time to die; a time to plant, and a time to pluck up that which is planted;
A time to kill, and a time to heal; a time to break down, and a time to build up.

When he rode up the serpentine bridle path to the green-shuttered house at Bethany eight days later and tossed to the grinning Benjy the reins of the black stallion he had borrowed from John Brown for the ride home from Wellsburg, it seemed to Alexander that he had been away much longer than five weeks.

Selina met him in the doorway, the severity of her angular face softened by a glowing welcome as he stepped forward, stooping a little to kiss her. In her own stern way she loved him more than anything in her life, he knew, and while he had been away she had given him a daughter.

She returned his embrace awkwardly. "Margaret Brown Campbell is waiting for you in the sitting room," she said almost shyly. "She's asleep, but you can see her. Mama is there, too. We've been expecting you every day," she chided gently, and then more boldly, "Where on earth have you—" She left the question hanging and Alexander felt a sudden self-reproach and at the same time a little irritation.

Without comment he followed her into the sitting room. "Aunt Betsy" Patterson and Mrs. Anna Bakewell sat beside the baby sleeping in the walnut cradle that John Brown had made for his first grandchild seventeen years ago.

A hasty handshake with the short, fat older woman who watched him with black, pecking eyes, her face expressionless, and a word of greeting to "Aunt Betsy," and he stooped over the cradle for a long time, his eyes riveted on the tiny, still-puckered red face, the

259

soft tuft of brown hair at the top of the head, the tiny pink clenched fists outside the coverlet. This was his eighth daughter and his ninth child. Margaret Brown Campbell. He raised his head and met Selina's eyes, and saw a pride in them that surprised him. A warmth of affection for her came over him. Laughter and running feet sounded from the schoolhouse beside the shed kitchen. Miss Eliza was dismissing her pupils in order that they might greet their father, fresh home from the wars. Miss Eliza had been a good teacher but was leaving in a month, Selina had written him. Mrs. Bakewell motioned him toward the outside, her round, fat face puckered in protest at the noise. He nodded at her and then slowly placed his arm about Selina.

"You're a wonderful woman, Selina. A thoughtful, considerate, wonderful wife and mother. And that's a beautiful baby!" He kissed her on the forehead, and she flushed and glanced at her mother, embarrassed, before she reached up and boldly put her arms about his neck, and for a moment rested her head on his chest.

It was after supper and evening worship, before he told Selina and the girls about the debate, and showed them the newspaper reports he had brought with him, or mentioned his plans for the new magazine. Somehow it seemed to him, as they sat together in a family circle in the big sitting room before a hearth fire just big enough to drive away the spring chill, that his children were growing up about him almost as friendly strangers; interested and affectionate and yet with a distance between them which had not existed in his father's family.

Selina began reading aloud to the girls from the half-page editorial in the Cincinnati *Chronicle and Literary Gazette* for April 25:

"It will be recollected that Mr. Owen proposed to prove that all the religions of the world were founded in the ignorance of mankind, that they are the only source of vice, disunion, and misery, and that they are the only bar to the formation of a society of virtue, of intelligence, and of charity in its most extended sense. To sustain these positions, Mr. Owen produced and read his 'Twelve Fundamental Laws of Nature,' and considered their pertinency so great that he read these twelve laws twelve times to the audience. They constituted, indeed, the sum and substance of the philosopher's argument. But that he has succeeded in impressing their truth upon a single one of his hearers, it would be hazarding too much to admit; and so far from having established or even sustained to any extent the several positions in his challenge, we believe when we say that in the opinions of nine tenths of his audience a greater failure has seldom been witnessed on any occasion. All admit that the talent, the skill in debate, and the weight of proof were on the side of Mr. Campbell."

"Hear! Hear!" called Alexander suddenly from his chair, his voice vibrant. "You will make me quite vain, my dear, if you read any more in my presence. And I wouldn't have my daughters think their father is not a humble man!"

The girls laughed as if at a joke, and after a moment he joined them, a joy in his heart that he was home again in the bosom of a family who loved him enough to laugh with him at his faults.

Maria Louisa clapped her hands for attention. "I've been studying history, Papa. You are like Henry the Eighth. You can be called 'Defender of the Faith' just like the king!"

"Hush, child!" said Selina. "Your father is not at all like that wicked, murdering king! Don't ever mention them in the same breath again."

Alexander joined in the uncertain smiles, and then, suddenly, began to talk of things of general interest. The state of Virginia was going to hold a convention to draft a new constitution, he told them. It would convene at Richmond in October, and it was important that thoughtful, well-meaning men serve as delegates, pushing aside their own business for a time to draft a good basis for the state government. But it was not until the rest of the family had gone to bed that he told Selina of his decision to campaign actively for the election.

"I am allowing my name to be offered as one of the four delegates from our district because this is no mere political task. The organic law of the state is to be amended at this convention and I want something to say about it," he explained to her.

Selina sighed. "I don't like politics," she said.

Alexander smiled. "I had hoped I wouldn't have to campaign. But I learned today when I came through Wellsburg that Congressman Philip Doddridge has been campaigning hard, for both himself and his lawyer friend Sam Sprigg of Wheeling. He was one of those who wrote me in Cincinnati, urging me to run as a delegate, but I think he found since then that I'm opposed to slavery, as though that's any secret. At any rate, I must take to the hustings like any politician and fight, or I'm defeated!"

Selina frowned, and then she lifted her head, a proud lifting. "You'll fight, Mr. Campbell. And you'll be elected. I wouldn't be surprised if you don't run ahead of even Congressman Doddridge. You're a great man. You could even be governor if you wanted to!"

During the next three weeks Alexander spoke in each of the five counties of Ohio, Brooke, Tyler, Monongalia, and Preston, comprising the Seventeenth Virginia Senatorial District. Wherever he appeared, he made votes, and after the election on June 2 found, to his surprise, that in the field of nine candidates he had placed third, after Colonel Charles Stephen Morgan of Monongalia and Congressman Philip Doddridge of Brooke County, with Eugenius M. Wilson of Monongalia elected as the fourth delegate.

Colonel Morgan was an old friend, and in August Alexander wrote him, confiding in him a plan for the abolition of slavery he had long been holding in his mind:

I have always been of the opinion that some one day ought to be fixed in the new Constitution as the last day on which any person should be born a slave. In other words, that from the 4th day of July, 1840, or 1835, or 1850, or some such period, all persons born within the country shall be born free.

I hope we will pull together on this one. Tell me what you think of it.

In the greatest dispatch, please excuse this miserable scrawl. Your friend, A. Campbell.

As Alexander confided to Father Thomas, he was not surprised at Morgan's reply, received two weeks later:

You are young, and inexperienced in politics. Before you propose to abolish slavery by outright constitutional amendment, it will first be necessary to change the organic law permitting the iniquitous mixed basis of representation which gives the slaveholders an additional vote for every three slaves he owns. As you theologians say, let us put first things first. Once we break the stranglehold of the East, with its multiple slave votes, we can then proceed with this reform.

But by all means let us discuss the matter when we get to Richmond. We think much alike. I must leave this week with my Methodist preacher-brother William, and will be waiting for you. We of the West must pull together, or we will accomplish nothing.

Alexander had a genuine respect and friendship for Charles Morgan, for four years now the state senator from the Seventeenth District, a man of principle and integrity and sound judgment who knew his way in politics. But he was wrong, he felt, about the amendment to abolish slavery. If Virginia could lead the way, the other southern states would in time follow her example and a cancerous corruption which could yet ruin the country would be eliminated once and for all.

He found himself busier than he had been in a long time. He would be in Richmond three months or longer, and before he left he had to finish the preparation of the debate for publication as well as make plans for the remaining issues of the *Christian Baptist* to appear concurrently with the opening numbers of the new magazine which was to succeed it.

He wrote to Walter Scott in Canfield, Ohio, a week before he began his ride to Richmond on September 20:

Why do I not keep the good name of *Christian Baptist* which you helped so much to name and nourish, in its fight for truth? It is a good name and well established, known and loved among many people. But hating sectarian names as I do, I am resolved to prevent the name of *Christian Baptist* from being fixed upon us as many people are trying to do. It is true men's tongues are their own, and they may use them as they please, but I am resolved to give them no just occasion for nicknaming advocates for the ancient order of things.

He knew many people were referring to his followers as "Campbellites," and to the cause he advocated as "Campbellism." And although he knew Walter Scott could never be guilty of using such a term, before he closed his letter he unburdened himself of his deepest feeling on the subject:

"Campbellism" is a nickname of reproach, invented and adopted by those whose views, feelings, and desires are all sectarian; who cannot conceive of Christianity in any other light than an "ism." These "isms" are reproaches on those who originate and apply them. He that gives them, when they are disclaimed, violates the express law of Christ. He

263

speaks evil against his brother and is accounted a railer and a reviler, and placed along with the haters of God and those who have no lot in the Kingdom of God. They who adopt them out of choice disown the Christ and insult Him; for they give the honor which is due to Him alone to the creature of the devil. If Christians were wholly cast into the mould of the Apostles' doctrine, they would feel themselves as much aggrieved and slandered in being called by any man's name as they would in being called a thief, a fornicator, or a drunkard. If we are to be called by any name other than that of Christ, let us be known as Disciples.

The rapid expanse of the Restoration Movement, the union of so many different religious parties in the revival of the Ancient Order of Things, the assurance he felt in his heart that the church being formed was not another sect but simply a restoration of the first church, leaving no need for any succeeding religious reformation— all gave him a sense of the Movement's niche in destiny. The religious world could well be on the eve of tremendous happenings.

"I shall call the new magazine the *Millennial Harbinger*," he told Selina the night before he left on Miss Fanny, his new black mare, for his ride to Richmond. "It will be a harbinger among the people of the glad tidings, the Gospels, which prepares mankind for the second coming of the King of Kings, the ultimate triumph of the Kingdom of God on earth!"

At fifteen minutes past eleven o'clock, on the second night of his arrival in Richmond, tired but with an exhilaration in him at the events of the day, Alexander sat in his room on the upper floor of the Swan Tavern on East Broad Street and began a letter to Selina. He had grown accustomed to sharing with her, he realized, the happenings of each day, and he missed her companionship, her patient habit of listening to each detail, her insight into his problems, more than he had thought possible. In large, sprawling letters he printed across the top of the first sheet:

First Letter from Richmond, 1829

Richmond, Oct. 5, 1829

My dear Selina:

I arrived safely here yesterday evening at two o'clock and preached at seven to an immense congregation. I was hailed on the street two or three times before I got to a tavern. I have been welcomed by preachers and people, civil and religious. My mare was no more apparently fatigued when I arrived in Richmond than when I left home. She is, however, dangerous to ride. Very scary, and she well nigh pitched me off. I felt much fatigued but a good deal rested today.

We met at the Capitol at twelve o'clock and organized the convention. I sent the particulars to Mr. Sample for his paper. Mr. Monroe, ex-president, was nominated by James Madison, ex-president, for president of the convention and was unanimously elected. It was a most imposing spectacle and will command great veneration. No body ever met on this continent more venerable. I can find time only to inform you of my safe arrival and to send you all my warm affection. It is not with me out of sight out of mind. But I need not write about it. Please remember me most affectionately to all the children, to my father and all the household, and keep the balance of my affection for yourself.

Your affectionate husband,
A. Campbell

Write immediately.
Have you heard from Mr. Ewing?

Even as he added the postscript he felt he knew the answer. His old friend, Greville Ewing of Glasgow, the one man next to Father Thomas who was literally his "father in the faith," was dying. He had heard only last month of the accident which had caused the death of Mrs. Ewing at the Falls of Clyde the summer before, and the paralysis of her husband from which there was no recovery except in the eternal. Any day now could come a letter from his uncle Archibald at Newry that his old friend had been released from bondage. The old order passeth; the new order comes upon the scene, and lingers for a little while and passes on. All is change. Only God is immutable and everlasting.

He sealed the letter to Selina and propped it on the table beside his bed. He would post it the first thing in the morning. For a moment he stood in the center of the room, rubbing his cheek. Then, wearily, fatigue descending upon him like a blanket, and a sudden humility, he sank to his knees and began to pray.

The ninety-six convention delegates met daily in the crowded Hall of the House of Delegates in the Capitol, and as time passed, Alexander found himself caught up more and more in the excitement of the history-making days. It was an honor to be a delegate to this convention, to be a part of the group of men reshaping the organic law of the state of Virginia; a great responsibility. And he liked Richmond, the broad, tree-lined streets, the friendliness of the people, the hospitality of the public places, the taverns and the boarding-houses, swollen now by the arrival of the delegates and their families to twice their normal capacity, with many visitors forced to seek lodgings in private homes. He liked the two-storied frame Swan Tavern at 812 East Broad Street, a typical inn within a stone's throw of Capitol Square, with its long front veranda, its two wings extending in the rear, and its half-dozen outbuildings sprawling over the block between Eighth and Ninth streets on Broad. It had once housed Thomas Jefferson, and other great men, and was still considered one of the finest taverns in Virginia.

But he was more deeply impressed by the men he was meeting, all delegates to the convention, many of them leaders of the nation. James Madison had been the Chief Executive when Alexander had arrived with the family from Ireland in 1809. Now he was a venerable figure in black, seventy-nine years old, his voice low and almost inaudible, and on the rare occasions when he spoke before the convention, the other delegates gathered about him as children about an aged father. And James Monroe, elected president of the convention by acclamation, was even more infirm than either Madison or Chief Justice John Marshall, who seconded his nomination. He was frequently absent because of his poor health, but Alexander soon realized he exercised great influence in the deliberations. Chief Justice Marshall he found to be a hale and hearty old man of seventy-five years, his tall, lean figure, his black, penetrating eyes lending weight to his singsong voice. The three men were all deeply conservative, intensely earnest, greatly and genuinely respected.

Congressman John Randolph of Roanoke was a consummate actor, Alexander thought, feared by friend and foe alike whenever his slender figure arose to its full six feet to unleash in barbed, resonant words the fury of his sarcasm. As the days passed he came to know such men as United States Senator John Tyler, tall, graceful, with conciliating manners and a Roman nose; United States Senator L. W.

Tazewell; Governor William B. Giles; and discovered, to his satisfaction, that he could hold his own in discussion with them all.

His reputation, he found, had preceded him. He was the only preacher among the delegates, and his liberal theological views, as well as his recent triumph over the renowned Robert Owen, focused the spotlight upon him. The attention gratified him more than he would admit to Selina in his frequent letters. He tried to write with restraint of his pride in being appointed to the important judicial committee, under the chairmanship of Chief Justice Marshall, but he told her frankly that he was sought after at social gatherings and that he had received more invitations to preach in the pulpits of the city than he could accept. Margaret, he thought, would have lifted a warning finger, but Selina was different. She was beginning to enjoy her position as the wife of a great man. He smiled at the thought. She no longer chided him about accumulating more land, and he noticed she was buying nicer clothing for herself and the children. The last time they had been together in Wellsburg she had flushed with pleasure when a merchant had addressed her as Mrs. "Bishop" Campbell.

But as the days wore on his hopes faded that he could propose an amendment to the state's constitution which would lay the foundations for the gradual abolition of slavery.

"The basis of apportionment of representatives will first have to be amended," Colonel Morgan reminded him time and again. "East of the Blue Ridge Mountains there are almost four hundred thousand slaves, and each slaveowner is entitled to three votes for every five slaves he owns. West of the mountains where we live there are only about fifty thousand slaves. So the East has the voting advantage. We'll have to change that before we can hope to accomplish anything on the slavery question itself."

In lieu of the amendment for the placing of a limit and the time when any person could be born a slave in the state, Alexander agreed first to present a resolution, sponsored jointly by Mr. Doddridge, "that in the apportionment of representation in the House of Delegates regard should be had to the white population exclusively." This resolution was the first topic called up for discussion after the routine committee reports, and although Alexander expected opposition, he had not anticipated the solid hostility of the eastern delegates that resulted.

"It is not the increase of population in the western part of the state which the gentlemen in the eastern part ought to fear," he declared in the heated debate. "It is the energy which the mountain breeze and western habits impart to the emigrant. They are regenerated, politically I mean, sir. They soon become working politicians, and the difference, sir, between a talking and a working politician is immense. The Old Dominion has long been celebrated for producing great orators; the ablest metaphysicians in policy, men who can split hairs in all abstruse questions of political economy. But at home, or when they return from Congress, they have Negroes to fan them to sleep. But a Pennsylvania, a New York, an Ohio, or a western Virginian statesman has this advantage: that when he returns home he takes off his coat and takes hold of the plow. This gives him bone and muscle, sir, and preserves his republican principles pure and uncontaminated."

John Randolph, seated to his left, said in a loud stage whisper: "That man even rewrote the Lord's Holy Scriptures. Nothing this convention can do will satisfy him!"

Instantly Alexander turned to him.

"Mr. Randolph," he said, "you are right! Nothing can satisfy me but the abolition of slavery. I expect to introduce an amendment to the constitution of this state to abolish slavery altogether. I should be well satisfied with its speedy passage."

"You would do well, sir, to wait until this issue is settled first," Mr. Randolph replied. "As Lord Beacon said, 'Time is a great innovator.'"

"No doubt you also remember, sir," Alexander replied, "the full quotation from His Lordship: '*Maximus innovator tempus; quidne igitur tempus imitemur?*'"

While Chief Justice John Marshall rapped for order, the convention broke into admiring laughter and applause. Alexander flushed with pleasure. He had acquitted himself well.

Late that night the four delegates from the Seventeenth District sat in conference in Alexander's room at the Swan Tavern.

"I seldom agree with John Randolph," said Philip Doddridge. "But this time he is right in principle despite your victory over him in repartee this afternoon. Any amendment introduced at this time to abolish slavery would only jeopardize what little chance we have to secure a more equitable representation between eastern and western Virginia. If we can do that, then you can proceed with your free-the-slaves idea. But not now!"

"Doddridge is right," said Colonel Morgan earnestly. "Jeopardize that chance and even the western delegates will turn against you. Why not concentrate now on some of these other issues: the extension of suffrage to all white male citizens over twenty-two; the reform of the county court system; the matter of public education? Direct your fire, my friend, where it can hope to do some good, not on some utopian scheme which would imperil every reform we hope to accomplish."

Alexander knew they were right. Emancipation would come eventually, and while he felt increasingly a compulsion under God to help bring it about, he must bide his time. Perhaps he should begin closer to home. He should free his own slaves. The thought hit him with the force of a physical blow and almost involuntarily he winced. But long after the men had gone the thought persisted.

In order thoroughly to familiarize himself with each issue before the convention, Alexander arose at four every morning and spent three hours in going over the reports and resolutions. All day he sat in the convention hall, but every night, and each Sunday during his stay in Richmond, found him preaching not only in the various pulpits of the city but in Petersburg and other adjacent communities, pleading for a return to the simple practices of the early New Testament church as the basis upon which all Christians could unite. He was making friends and advocates who would in good time be powerful supporters of the Restoration Movement.

His Richmond services were attended by scores of the convention delegates as well as the townspeople. Former president James Madison came to hear him repeatedly. John Randolph, with whom he seldom

269

agreed, sat in the audience night after night. He formed a warm friendship with the delegate from the Twelfth District, Philip C. Pendleton of Louisa, and after the evening services the two men frequently sat for long hours in earnest conversation, drinking coffee in the common room at the Swan Tavern. One evening they were joined by Mr. Madison, and when they arose to go to their rooms, the venerable former president of the United States laid his hand in fatherly affection on Alexander's arm.

"You have ability as a statesman, Mr. Campbell," he said. "But you have made no mistake as to your calling. You are one of the ablest and most original expounders of the Scriptures I have ever heard."

Mr. Madison was right, he thought grimly as the days passed and he saw the issues he advocated go down one by one in defeat. A cobbler should stick to his last. His plea for the extension of the franchise to all white male taxpayers over the age of twenty-two was compromised to extend to leaseholders and householders, but it left 30,000 otherwise qualified males of legal age who owned no property without the right to vote. His plan for the reform of the court system in the western counties of the state was defeated. The magistrates still had the right to appoint their own successors, violating, he claimed, the very Bill of Rights itself of the Federal Constitution.

Late in December, after a session in which he seemed to have accomplished nothing, he sat down in a mood of discouragement to write to Selina. He had lost every major effort. The basis of representation remained the same. The convention had refused even to consider his resolution for adequate state support for a system of public education. He dipped his quill pen in the inkpot and began to write, slowly, almost laboriously.

Richmond, Dec. 23, 1829.

My dear Selina:

It is now in the twelfth week since I arrived in this city and about fourteen weeks since I left home. I am worn out with fatigue. I have not been a free man since I came here. It puts me in mind of going to school. I am under tutors and governors, and I do not like it. I need not tell you that I am homesick. But when I am dismissed, I will have to take a circuitous route home which will keep me much longer than I could otherwise go home, say two weeks longer. I have done all I could consistent with duty and circumstances to promote the welfare of my country and my fellow man. But our success has not been equal to our exertions. But in the "good cause" I have been more successful.

He wrote a while longer and then, in sudden impatience at his discouragement, pushed the pen and paper aside and, walking to the window, stood for a long time looking out upon the tree-lined street. It was two days before he finished the letter.

The vote on the constitution was taken on January 14, 1830. It was approved by the narrow margin of 55 to 40, with only Philip Doddridge from Wellsburg not voting because of illness. The document would now be submitted to the people for ratification. Alexander would do what he could to defeat it. The conviction was on him that great opportunities had been missed, and he felt a strange foreboding of tempestuous consequences.

The next day he left on horseback for home, preaching along the way as he had opportunity. Almost four weeks later he rode up the familiar bridle path to the Bethany house. He had been gone five months.

Chapter 23

IT WAS GOOD TO BE HOME AGAIN, ALEXANDER THOUGHT AS HE AWAKened the next morning in the big four-poster bed. He lay for a moment, his eyes piercing the pre-dawn darkness, touching each familiar object in the room.

Selina had managed the household well during his absence, even with the care of the new baby. And the past months had not been easy. Miss Eliza, the children's tutor, had given up her position and Eliza Ann, now sixteen, Maria Louisa, fourteen, and Lavinia, twelve, had been placed in the care of their aunt Jane McKeever at her Pleasant Hill Seminary for Young Ladies near West Middletown, with only eight-year-old Clarinda at home. But an epidemic of measles had broken out in the school in the early winter, and they had returned home. Selina had tried to maintain a school of sorts for them but visitors had been frequent, the household supervision demanding, and the children's routine broken and their instruction haphazard. The McKeever school would not reopen for another year; Alexander must make some other plans for the children's schooling.

He arose and dressed quietly. It was not yet four o'clock and Selina was still asleep with the baby in the cradle beside her. He left the room and made his way out of the house and through the paling gate to his study across the roadway.

A mound of accumulated mail was on his desk. He sat down and began sorting through it: correspondence from his readers; reactions to his debate with Robert Owen; letters from churches, pleading for a visit from him; heartening words from Kentucky and Tennessee where the Movement was spreading like a grass fire; letters from Walter Scott in the Western Reserve where hundreds were being won and where the Mahoning Association, the last vestige of the Movement's tie with the Baptists, had resolved into a simple annual meeting, discarding all sectarian nomenclature. He paused at the sight of a letter from his cousin, Enos Campbell, in Ireland. He would read it later. He started to lay it aside, and then on impulse loosened the flap and spread out the sheet.

Enos wanted to come to America, and if Alexander could use him, he wrote, he would help in teaching and supervising the children. Alexander read the letter again slowly, and then closed his eyes, the wonder of God's care filling him. He pulled a sheet of paper toward him and scrawled, "Come at once, dear cousin," and signing it, addressed the back of the sheet, folded and sealed it.

William Llewellyn came in at six o'clock. For more than an hour

Alexander sat with the stocky, cheerful little Welshman, discussing the format of the new magazine, plans for another edition of *The Living Oracles*, arrangements for a more inclusive hymnal.

William Llewellyn shook his balding head. The shed by Buffalo Creek was small; it could no longer handle the volume of work.

"Then a new building will be erected," Alexander said in sudden decision. "We'll put it about a mile farther from the house, in the village near the site on which the new Bethany Church will be built in a year or two." It would be a two-storyed structure, it was decided, providing facilities not only for publishing and mailing the thousands of copies of printed matter Alexander was now issuing, but space also for the Bethany post office.

Back at the house, morning worship with all the family gathered about the big dining-room table, and the servants seated or standing in the hallway or by the doors, was heartwarming. These twice-daily periods of Scripture reading and prayer were more than formal, routine occasions. They were spontaneous expressions of deeper impulses that characterized the family, rich in spiritual insight and wisdom. God was a personal friend and to talk with Him was as natural to all of them as greeting a companion.

After worship lanky James Anderson appeared and the work of the farm was discussed. Two more field helpers had been obtained; the stand of wheat promised to be abundant; new acreage was being cleared to be sown to barley and oats, and a new strain of tender golden corn was being planted. The winter had been cold and the wool clip, Anderson estimated, would amount to well over five thousand pounds. It was rumored spring lambs would bring $1.50 apiece.

"You should give thanks to God, Mr. Campbell," his farm manager said, his thin lips compressed in a tight smile. "You're a rich man."

Alexander looked away, uneasy. "I should give thanks for God," he amended.

After James Anderson had left, Selina handed him a letter from her brothers, Horatio and Theron Bakewell. Horatio had started a glass factory and pottery in Wellsburg, and Theron was operating

273

a boat store on the Ohio. Both were inexperienced in business and had written Selina, asking her to secure advice from Alexander on handling money while traveling or by post.

"Write them something like this," Alexander said, impatient to get back to his desk and his work on the new paper. "Tell them that Mr. Campbell is of the opinion it is unsafe to remit money via postmaster receipt. The best way, he says, is to make deposit in banks and get drafts, payable at home or some place near to, say, Pittsburgh or Wheeling. To carry your money you had better privately make a small pocket in your drawers. Only take care when you get into the water. This way Mr. Campbell advises as being the safest. Never leave money in your trunk when absent from the boat."

Back at his desk he found a letter among his mail from an old friend, William Tener, in Newry, Ireland. The Restoration Movement had taken root in Ireland, Tener wrote, and was spreading to England and Scotland. The "Declaration and Address" had been circulated widely in those countries, and the *Christian Baptist* was read by hundreds. Alexander's eyes grew moist as he read. The seed was sinking into ever deeper soil; the message was spreading in ever-widening circles. Of a group that had been organized in Newry, all his old friends and relatives had joined except his uncle, Archibald Campbell. Alexander smiled at the recollection of the Scotch stubbornness of his Presbyterian uncle. The closing lines in the letter from Tener stabbed his conscience. Why, his old friend asked, had he stepped aside in his religious duties to enter the political arena? Alexander frowned. He had no liking for politics and the implication that he had embraced it at the expense of his paramount task nettled him. He picked up his pen and answered at once:

You ask, what business had I in such matters? I will tell you. I have no taste or longing for political matters or honors, but as this was one of the most grave and solemn of all political matters, and not like the ordinary affairs of legislation, I consented to be elected; and especially because I was desirous of laying a foundation for the abolition of slavery.

He was even more frank in a letter to Colonel Morgan, who had remained in Richmond some time after the convention had adjourned, and had forwarded him some pamphlets he had left behind. He wrote:

I am glad that I have got nearly done with politics. When I finish writing some essays against the adoption of the Constitution for the Wheeling and Wellsburg papers, and finished talking against it, I shall claim a discharge from that war, for it is to me a barren theme. I never could bring my energies to bear upon a matter so barren and unfruitful as politics.

In a few years it will not matter a grain of sand who is President, nor who was King, nor under what government he lived or died.

I am conscious that many are infatuated with the charms of political life. It has none for me, and never will have. I view mankind in a higher relation than as a subject of taxation, or a defender of the country, on a muster roll. I view him as one who may be immortal, a citizen of heaven and a priest of God. Men are in pursuit of shadows, catching after baubles which glisten to the eye but are filled with wind.

I have more pleasure in thinking on men's eternal destinies, or in reading one section of the Oracles of God, than in all the splendid schemes of earthly ambition and political grandeur.

Please give my kind respects to your brother William, who proclaims the Gospel. Tell him, his lot in this life, if he acquit himself well, is in my judgment much more honorable than thine, more happy and a thousand times more useful.

In the meantime, excuse my great haste, and accept the assurance of my personal friendship.

A. Campbell.

Can you obtain a few subscribers to the *Millennial Harbinger?*

But Alexander was not done with politics. At meeting after meeting of aroused citizens in Brooke County he spoke upon the principal features of the proposed state constitution, making no effort to conceal his disappointment in it, clinging to the hope it would be rejected. And although the state-wide vote when the referendum was held was 26,055 to 15,563 in favor of its adoption, it was found that his efforts in his own county had not been in vain. Brooke County voted 370 to 0 for its rejection.

The agitation over slavery continued to grow. As a public declaration of his stand, Alexander took immediate steps to free his own three slaves.

"I'm warning you, they will run away and cause all kinds of

trouble." Philip Doddridge spoke grimly as he handed Alexander the certificates of freedom he had prepared. "And under the law you are responsible for any damages they may incur for the next ten years. It's an action which you'll live to regret."

Alexander folded the papers carefully and put them in his pocket. He did not particularly like Philip Doddridge, although on most important issues they had voted together at the convention. He was a good lawyer, and a popular congressman, the oldest son of the venerable Episcopal rector, Joseph Doddridge, and no one had ever questioned either his courage or the integrity of his convictions.

"If you would join me," he said, "we might start a general movement which in time would enable the state of Virginia to lead in the fight for racial freedom as she did for political freedom in '76."

Doddridge laughed, his tone harsh. "And have thousands of freed Negroes congregating in every town like maggots about a bone? When freedom comes to the slaves, if it ever does, it must come in slow stages so that they will be prepared for it. You'll have a civil war on us if other people followed your example."

"We will have one if they don't," Alexander replied, shaking his head. "This is an issue no Christian can ignore." He paused as though in indecision. "It's the one thing that would force me into another venture in politics!"

Unexpectedly, Doddridge stood up and held out his hand, a conciliatory grin on his broad red face. "I don't agree with you, Campbell, but for the sake of my own political future, I want you to stick to your preaching." He lifted his hand in mock surrender. "Start any movement in theology you like but stay out of politics. I want to keep my seat in Congress for a while longer! But watch those Negroes, like I said, or they'll cause you trouble!"

Jim and Charlie Poole and Benjy Brown dated their freedom from the next afternoon. They became hired servants in the Campbell household; loyal, steady, dependable, causing no trouble, slackening not a whit in their labors.

Copies of the new paper began rolling off the press, meeting with immediate acclaim. Churches were springing up everywhere in support of the Restoration Movement. In October Alexander left

276

for a tour through the South. Eliza Ann was almost seventeen years old and in love with a Wellsburg law student, John Campbell. Letters from her sister Jane Ewing, in Nashville, urged her to come for a visit before she married and settled down, so Alexander secured a gig and took her with him.

They journeyed through Ohio, Alexander preaching at almost every village to Baptist churches, to newly organized bodies which had embraced the new Movement; to family groups, to civic gatherings, meeting everywhere with hospitality. They went on into Kentucky, staying at the Galt House in Louisville, and then to Lexington, where they were entertained by the president of the great Transylvania University, and Alexander spoke to classes of students. Eliza Ann was alive with enthusiasm for all she saw. Christmas was spent with the Ewings in Nashville, a happy reunion, a joyous holiday, a holy occasion. Jane had not been well, Alexander learned. A dry cough had begun to bother her and she was running a slight fever.

"But the visit with you and Eliza has made me feel better already," she told him as he was hoisting his trunk on the rear of the gig for the return journey. He noticed it was showing wear. It was a wooden, paper-lined trunk, covered with calfskin, and the original hair was now completely worn away.

"If these tours keep up," Jane laughed, "you'll wear out a dozen more trunks. But if you do as much good everywhere as you've done here in Nashville, it will be worth it!"

Alexander smiled. More than thirty persons had been added to the Restoration Movement during his preaching that week, and the group was greatly encouraged. "More important than making converts," he said, "is changing lives. And only God can do that. I am merely His instrument." He kissed Jane good-by, lingering over the farewells, thinking how much she resembled Margaret.

He was back in Bethany in March, in time to welcome Cousin Enos from Ireland. Enos was a hearty man, ruddy-faced and genial, a larger edition of the happy-go-lucky youngster Alexander had known as a child.

"You're a blessing straight from the Lord, Enos," Alexander told him as he helped him unpack his boxes in the upper back storeroom

Selina had turned into a bedroom for him. In the bottom of one box was a fiddle. Alexander smiled and picked it up. Gingerly he plucked at the strings. The Christmas party at the Brown home when he had been engaged to Margaret echoed in the softly twanging chords. A cloud passed over his heart, and he gently laid the instrument on the cot. "Selina does not care for music greatly, Enos," he said.

With Enos installed as the happy, robust teacher of the Campbell children, other children from nearby families joined the schoolroom and the place resounded with activity. Preachers and other friends Alexander had made on his trips were frequent and lingering visitors, and the house was always crowded. Selina's mother was spending more and more time with them, returning to Wellsburg for brief stays at the home of her son Horatio, until trouble with his wife would send her scurrying back to Bethany.

"There's not a spare corner in the house tonight," Selina remarked one evening as they were preparing for bed. "If another guest should come, we'd have to put a pallet in the kitchen."

Alexander was slowly unbuttoning his shirt. He finished and slipped the garment off before he answered her. "Since I put this addition on twelve years ago for the Buffalo Seminary, the house is so large I understand some people are calling it the Campbell Mansion," he said, grinning. "But I can see we need still more space. On the west side of this room, for instance, we could add another wing. I'll see about it soon."

"What do you mean, soon?" Selina questioned.

Alexander shrugged. "Next year, possibly."

Selina tightened the silk ribbons she was now wearing at the throat of her long flowered flannel nightgown into a neat bow, and came over and stood beside him.

"Next year," she said, "is not soon enough. We are expecting another child, Mr. Campbell."

For a moment he stared at her, and then drew her to him and kissed her. "We'll start adding to the house tomorrow!" He laughed in genuine pleasure at the news.

She pulled away. "Don't promise things you've no mind for doing. Tomorrow you are going to Wheeling," she reminded him. "It's the tenth of April, and young Dr. Robert Richardson is to be married. Had you forgotten?"

"Not at all. And I am to officiate at the ceremony," he said. "You must go with me. But the house will get my attention soon, I promise you."

He drove to Wheeling alone in the buggy the next day as Selina was suffering from morning sickness.

Robert Richardson, the young lad he had first met in Pittsburgh ten years ago, was now a doctor, practicing in Wellsburg, and had become a frequent visitor in the Campbell home. It was comforting to see him when the children were sick, riding up to the turnstile in his Prince Albert coat and beaver hat, walking with the slow dignity of his twenty-six years into the house, his saddlebags over his arm bulging with his instruments and bleeding bowl. He was not only a skilled physician but a genuine Christian, Alexander often reflected, dedicated in mind and heart to the restoration of the New Testament church. A year before he had broken all formal connection with the Episcopal church and had ridden horseback two hundred miles to Ohio to be immersed by his old friend, Walter Scott. Since then he had preached occasionally and had written frequently for the *Millennial Harbinger*, articles in which Alexander detected not only penetrating insight into the distinctions on which the Restoration Movement was based but promising literary ability.

The wedding was a quiet affair. Rebekah Encell was only fifteen years old but had budded into beautiful young womanhood, and as she stepped from the side of her widowed mother in the parlor of the Encell home in the river town of Wheeling, bustling with new industry, and placed her hand in that of the tall, awkward young doctor with the high forehead and weak eyes, half-closed now against the noon sun, Alexander felt an upsurge of emotion. The marriage would establish another fine family in the Wellsburg Church.

Spring flowed into summer with hastening rhythm. In July Alexander pondered on the strange coincidence of the death of the third former president of the United States, James Monroe, to occur on July 4. August brought its promise of another rich harvest.

"I guess it isn't as sinful as I once thought to be wealthy," Selina remarked one morning when Alexander showed her the deed to thirty-four additional acres of cleared land he had purchased from Harry and Elizabeth Gist. "I know it's mighty convenient." She motioned for him to follow her outside, past the back yard where the housegirl, Susannah, was making lye soap in an iron kettle, to the barn. On the walls hung three new sidesaddles. "I had my brother Theron order them for the girls. I also had him order a new kind of high chair for the baby; it's gilded and has roses painted on it."

Alexander started to speak but checked himself and smiled, nodding. Selina was entitled to whatever she considered fitting; she was prudent by nature and would never go to excesses. But he must deliver his own soul from the thought of using his wealth only for his own welfare, or even the happiness of his family.

"Our wealth is God's way of setting me free to spread His truth," he said thoughtfully. They went back to the house, Selina, heavy with child, walking awkwardly. "I must never forget it, Selina. I am trusting you to remind me of it, as I shall remind you."

"And may I never depart from the truth of God," he said to himself an hour later as he sat at his desk and read a letter from Walter Scott confirming the disquieting word about their mutual friend, Sidney Rigdon. It was true, Walter wrote, that Rigdon had embraced the queer sect called Mormonism which advocated polygamy as a Christian duty. He was actively promoting it on the Western Reserve. Alexander recalled the rumors of Rigdon's enthusiasm for the strange manuscript written by Solomon Spaulding several years before. Sidney Rigdon would have made a great leader for the Restoration. He had unusual facility of speech and a brilliant mind. But no one tainted with the grotesque new sect, Alexander thought grimly, could ever be even remotely trusted within the fold.

On October 14 Selina presented him with a new baby, a healthy, lusty-lunged boy. Her face was radiant with a joy Alexander had never seen in it before as he stood by the bedside gazing into the infant's half-opened eyes. He fingered the blanket spread over the child, dyed from butternut hulls he had watched Selina brew in an open kettle in the yard.

"At last," Selina said, her short, thick fingers smoothing the blanket into place, "you have a son! A little Alexander!"

He bent and kissed her. "Thank you, Selina," he said, his voice thick, his mind whirling with memories best laid aside.

They talked for a few minutes, and then he walked with Dr. Richardson to his horse at the stile, helping him adjust his saddlebags. The young doctor was leaving within a month with his bride to live in Carthage, Ohio, drawn there by his friendship for Walter Scott. The frontier town could use another physician, Mr. Scott had written him, and opportunities abounded for spreading the Gospel.

Eliza's hand had been requested by young John Campbell, but no marriage was planned until he finished his law studies. Maria Louisa told her father at Christmastime of her love for Robert Henley, and because Selina was not yet strong enough to supervise a large wedding, they were married quietly in January 1832, in the parlor on the same spot on which Jane had married four years before, the same spot on which Alexander and Margaret had been united now twenty-one years ago. For a wedding present Alexander presented them with the farm of thirty-four acres he had purchased the spring before. The acreage adjoined the back pasture in the hills not far from the rear of the house, and it would mean Maria Louisa would be close to home.

A cholera epidemic was sweeping the country. By spring most public places were closed by government order; stores and business houses were padlocked; streets in many cities deserted. Alexander had large placards printed in his new printing shop, giving remedies for the malady and pointers for the care of the sick, and had them posted all over Wellsburg, Washington, and Bethany. Business was at a standstill, mails were delayed, and it was midsummer before Alexander learned full details of momentous events that had transpired in Kentucky in February.

Chapter 24

THE NEWS CAME ONE MORNING IN A LETTER FROM RACCOON JOHN Smith.

"We decided," the hearty, forthright evangelist wrote, "to be no longer Campbellites or Stoneites, New Lights or Old Lights, or any other kind of lights, but to come to the Bible and to the Bible alone as the only book in the world that can give us all the light we need. A union of your followers and those of Mr. Barton Stone has taken place in Lexington, Paris, and Georgetown, and it is spreading to other localities."

The letter went on to give details of how Mr. Stone and John T. Johnson, John Rogers, and himself had planned a series of meetings of the two groups during the Christmas season to culminate in a formal union after the first of the year.

Alexander read the letter twice before he called Benjy. "Take the buggy to West Middletown and fetch my father," he said.

By early afternoon Father Thomas had arrived and together the two men sat in the study the rest of the day and far into the night, discussing the news.

"It wasn't unexpected, Father," Alexander said, pacing the floor. "Mr. Stone has made several overtures to me on the matter, and when I was in Kentucky last year I learned the two groups were frequently meeting together as one body. Several have written of such a possibility, as you know, and I've printed their comments in the *Millennial Harbinger*. And Stone has written repeatedly of it in his paper. But I had no thought of it being so imminent." He stopped and rubbed his forehead. "It is so unceremonious! There is danger it has not been thought through. Yes, I fear it is premature."

"But we are together on the essentials, son," Father Thomas said. "The followers of Mr. Stone believe as we do in immersion as the only form of baptism; they reject creeds, reject infant baptism, believe in uniting all Christians upon the Bible alone, and—"

"The fact that they oppose creeds," interrupted Alexander, "and accept only the Bible does not mean we are in complete agreement. Many persons have inveighed against creeds and dogmas!" He stood before his father, his hands thrust deep in his pockets, his face flushed. "Our Movement is something entirely new in ecclesiastical history! It is not only anti-creedal, it has unveiled the light on the ancient Gospel. Yet Mr. Stone seems to feel we are only preaching a doctrine he began preaching thirty years ago!"

Father Thomas looked at him closely. "Are you sure, my son, you are not letting pride of spirit color your reaction to this news?" he queried gently. "Are you not squinting at some sort of precedence or priority in the claims of Mr. Stone in having first discovered the principles of the Restoration?"

Alexander sat down heavily in the high-backed chair before his desk. Suddenly he covered his face with his hands.

"It is startling," Father Thomas went on, his voice low, vibrant with understanding and sympathy, "for a man to discover he cannot control the forces he has set in motion."

For a full minute silence filled the little room. And then Alexander looked up. "We tread a curious path to holiness," he said. He turned to his desk and again picked up the letter. "They are sincere men, all of them. Barton Warren Stone," he said the name slowly, "knows that to convert a man is not merely to baptize him; he knows it is not enough to give a man the name 'Christian,' or to induce him to protest against human creeds. He knows a man must turn from darkness to light, from the power of Satan to the power of God, and that he must do all that the Lord has commanded. And John Smith, John Rogers, John Johnson," he mused, "all well bear the name of John the Apostle.

"I think we have reason to thank God and take courage," Father Thomas said, "and bid the union Godspeed."

"We will need God's blessing," Alexander said. "The Baptists regard Mr. Stone's group as even more heretical than ours, and the prospect of our united strength will cause their trumpets and those of the other sects to sound the battle cry again. We'll be accused of starting another church party. We must stress now more emphatically than ever that we are not another church, but the early church restored; that we are nothing more or less than disciples of Christ."

"Disciples of Christ," Father Thomas repeated, a new wonder in his voice. "We are already being called by that name by some. I wonder if that is how we should be known?"

Alexander shrugged. "We are called also 'Reformers' and 'Reformed Baptists,'" he said.

"Mr. Stone's groups are called 'Christians' and the church is called 'Christian Church.' I somehow favor that name," Father Thomas went on. "The disciples were first called 'Christians' by Divine appointment at Antioch. It signifies a radical relationship to Christ, and it is consistent with our purpose in restoring primitive Christianity in letter and in spirit."

Alexander shook his head. "But the disciples were also called 'Disciples' in Judea, Galilee, Samaria before they were called 'Christians' at Antioch. In the Book of Acts, the term 'Disciple' is used thirty times and the term 'Christian' but twice. It seems to me it is more descriptive and less confusing; many people, including the Unitarians, call themselves 'Christian.' But the name will probably evolve as we grow. It is a matter, I should say, of subordinate importance just now."

Each post brought additional news of the union. There was no written contract between the two groups, but the contagion of fellowship spread, and as local congregations realized that the similarity in doctrine and purpose which made them practically indistinguishable from each other had been recognized, unions took place in Tennessee, Georgia, Virginia, and even faraway Indiana and Missouri. In Kentucky and Ohio entire churches, many of them Baptist, came over to the new united group and hundreds of individuals,

284

some of them unchurched and some already members of the denominations, joined in a streaming procession.

But with the phenomenal growth of the new body, new problems arose. Disputed points of doctrine seemed to usurp the Gospel; a muddled conception of the plan of the New Testament church was evinced by its self-appointed leaders; jealousies were created; friction developed; and at times it seemed to Alexander that the simple plan of the whole Restoration Movement was in chaos. But in the darkness of his thinking always would come a fathomless sense of assurance that there was design beneath the chaos.

He stayed at his desk all year, keeping in touch with the progress of the union, sifting its issues, clearing moot points, evaluating its effects. Sometimes he spoke softly, sometimes like rolls of thunder in the pages of the *Millennial Harbinger*, and by the spring of 1833 the confusion was subsiding.

The early fall brought heavy rains and the Ohio River was overflowing its banks. The town of Wellsburg voted to raise $25,000 by lottery to erect two flood walls. One morning Horatio Bakewell rode over from Wellsburg with the news that his pottery and glass factory on the bank near the edge of town had been swept away by the rising water. Alexander inspected the loss the next day. To aid in salvaging the stock, he agreed to lend Theron Bakewell funds to buy a new boat store to take the load of recovered earthenware and glassware down the river to sell.

In December the new Bethany meetinghouse was completed, a stone structure near the two-story printing office. It was simple in design and adequate in size for the small village. Many members of the old Brush Run Church who had been worshiping with the Wellsburg group immediately transferred to the more convenient location, but Father Thomas declined to move his membership.

"Wellsburg still needs me," he told Alexander, "particularly since Robert Richardson has moved to Ohio. He was a tower of strength in that group and is sorely missed."

He was missed, too, in the Campbell house. Selina was expecting her third baby soon.

In January the baby was born, another girl, and was named for the state of Virginia. The day after her birth Alexander received a letter from Nashville. His eldest daughter, Jane Ewing, was not well; she was showing symptoms of the disease that had taken her mother: a dry cough, fever, pallor of the skin, and loss of weight. Alexander wrote her cheerful, encouraging letters but in his heart he feared the dread consumption would take its toll. In June word came of her death. Her bereaved young husband, Albert Ewing, brought her wasted young body to Bethany for burial in God's Acre. He lingered after the services, reluctant to leave and, thankful for his help, Alexander turned over to him the supervision of the book bindery in his printing office as well as the preparation of another new and more inclusive edition of the hymnal.

Reliable men were scarce, he was finding, not only in business but in the ministry. Too many of the preachers who had rallied to the plea of the Restoration were willing to accept the protection of the new Movement and disclaim its obligations. They were swept along by the tide of enthusiasm until the crest was at its peak, but when interest slackened, their efforts lagged. In a stinging rebuke Alexander wrote in the *Harbinger:*

In what way are we reformers? We hope in practice! Get out and work, you preachers. So many have but one talent, the talent of taking care of themselves! Bring the question home to yourselves: Wherein am I reformed?

To bolster his confidence in the leadership, he made a trip to see Walter Scott in Carthage, near Cincinnati. The eloquent, hard-working evangelist was still winning souls with his logical plan of salvation, and for long hours the men sat before the fireside, sometimes with Dr. Richardson and his wife, Rebekah, now the parents of two children, discussing the problems created by the growth of the Movement and by its union with Barton Stone's followers. David Burnet came over from Cincinnati and joined the discussions, bringing a maturity of viewpoint and judgment that matched the dedication of his heart.

The men agreed the confusion over the principles of the Restoration Plea should be clarified by a statement of belief.

In January 1835 Alexander issued a three-hundred-and-fifty-four-page exposition. To prevent his traducers from characterizing it as a creed, he offered it as merely a statement of his personal convictions, labeling it: *The Christian System, in Reference to the Union of Christians and the Restoration of Primitive Christianity as Pleaded in the Current Reformation.*

The entire Christian system, he explained in the document, divided itself naturally into three parts: "The principles by which the Christian institution may be certainly and satisfactorily ascertained; the principles on which all Christians may form one communion; and the elements or principles which constitute original Christianity."

"It is an excellent exposition of the scriptural teachings, my son," Father Thomas assured him. "But the opposing brethren will now think they have you in a trap. They will call it 'Campbellites' Creed,' propounded by no less a personage than the arch-heretic himself. You must be prepared for it!"

"Ridiculous!" scoffed Alexander. "No one will believe such a charge. The whole religious world knows by now that no man among us can speak for another, that we take the Bible and nothing but the Bible as the foundation of our belief. Christ alone is our creed."

And as though in demonstration of the strength with which the Restoration Movement had made its principles known, Alexander was proved right. A few efforts were made to brand the *Christian System* as a written creed, but since the truths propounded were applicable to all Christians of whatever sect, such a claim made no progress even among the most sectarian minded. As a concise statement of religious belief, the book rapidly became a welcome manual for all articulate followers of the Restoration Movement and within a year went into a second edition.

And then in April death unexpectedly claimed Alexander's mother, and for a time the pride and luster of life were again dimmed for her eldest son. For a week he stayed with Father Thomas.

"She was not only a mother but a symbol of mothers," he told his father as they sat together in the back yard of the McKeever home in West Middletown, sharing their memories. He lingered over the days in Glasgow, the voyage across the ocean, the night of the shipwreck. Gallant, courageous, his mother's presence ran like a golden, shining cord through it all. At the end of the week he had made up his mind.

"You must go home with me, Father. You must make your home hereafter with me," he said. "Jane and Matthew are plainly crowded here and need all the space in this house for their school."

"But what would I do there?" Father Thomas asked almost plaintively. He was seventy-two years old. His eyesight was failing, and his memory at times was faulty. "Maybe I should live around with each of the children. I don't know, I don't know." He stretched out his hand as though for reassurance and Alexander took it firmly in his own. The other children were all married, with responsibilities of growing families. Tommie, married to Sarah Speer, had taken a medical course in Pittsburgh and had a practice of sorts there, but his restless, erratic temperament brought him frequently to Wellsburg to stay with Archibald, and occasionally he rode over to Bethany unannounced and stayed for a night or for a month, as the mood seized him. Archibald, steady, dependable, conscientious, had a growing medical practice in Wellsburg. He had married Phoebe Clapp and lived in a two-story white frame house on Main Street, a block from Alicia, who had married Phoebe's brother, Matthew Clapp.

"No," Alexander said. "You should have a settled home. And I need you, Father, more than you realize." He looked out across the freshly plowed furrows of the adjoining field. "I know I seem confident and strong but—" He paused, hesitating, groping for words.

"I know," Father Thomas said. A soft breeze lifted his long white hair. Alert to a need, he at once became the comforter. "Life is hard. Success is a mirage; the dream is ever far off; the goal ever receding. But God is with us, son, even when we tread the wine press."

That summer Alexander turned his small frame study across the road over to his father and, securing carpenters from Pittsburgh, added the new wing to the house which he had promised Selina and built a new study for himself in the cluster of pines he had planted west of the house. It was an octagonal brick structure, the doorway facing the road, the walls solid brick and lined with bookshelves, the only light coming from a cupola at the top.

Both the new wing to the house and the study were finished in time to be viewed by friends who attended the marriage of Eliza Ann to John Campbell in October. The young lawyer from Wellsburg had finished his studies and friends predicted for him a brilliant future in the courts.

The wedding was the most elaborate any of the girls had yet enjoyed. For weeks before the date Selina had been supervising Jim and Charlie Poole in cleaning the house. The hearth bricks were washed with redding and milk, rubbed with a paste of powdered stone, and polished with lamp oil. Great branches of pine and cedar and masses of autumn foliage decorated the rooms, and although it was not yet twilight when the ceremony was performed in the old sitting room on the spot where Alexander and Margaret had married, Selina insisted upon lighting her new Argand-type lamps with their circular wicks and broad-bottomed bases, burning whale oil instead of bear oil. The air was crisp with October's hint of winter, and every fireplace in the house was aglow. Coal instead of wood was burned for the occasion, although it cost four cents a bushel. More than a hundred friends crowded the sitting room, spilling over into the hall-way and new parlor, and even the capacity of the new brick kitchen, connected to the house by a dogtrot, was taxed to provide the great freezers of ice cream and four-tiered cakes, and steaming kettles of black coffee.

As the weeks passed, Father Thomas' presence was a comfort to Alexander and his counsel a tempering influence, but he could do little to lighten the work load. Maybe God had planned it that way, Alexander frequently reflected; maybe each man was destined to use his gifts and then release the burden.

Theron Bakewell had sold his boat store and opened a general store in Bethany, consuming Alexander's time with his need for advice, soliciting his help in printing handbills advertising cassinettes, jeans, cloth, queen's ware, and knives. He moved into rooms in the rambling log house of his brother, Edwin Bakewell, Selina's younger brother, to whom Alexander had rented some of his acreage in exchange for his help on the farm. Mrs. Bakewell became a permanent fixture in the Campbell home, moving in with four trunks and two birdcages after a particularly stormy session with Horatio's wife in Wellsburg, unloading her imagined griefs into Selina's sympathizing ear, taxing Alexander's patience.

Alexander purchased one hundred twenty-seven additional acres of partly cleared land from Lewis Jones to use as pasture for his sheep, now grown to more than six hundred head. He instructed James Anderson to purchase at an auction in Wellsburg ten new sows with their litters, paying $10 apiece for them, and seven cows with calves for $14 each. Prices were rising, business was brisk all over the country; the only ominous note besides the slavery issue was the unrest of the labor group. The new General Trades Union, Alexander reflected as he looked over the dispatches, should be watched.

But all was not peace in Zion. Hostile leaders among the sects, aroused as Alexander had anticipated they would be at the sweep of the united church, blasted at it from pulpits and press. David Burnet sent him from Cincinnati a pamphlet entitled, "Campbellism Exposed, or Spurious Gospel Unmasked," one of the most bitter and misleading attacks he had yet seen on the Restoration Movement.

"I consider this pamphlet so misleading it will defeat itself," Alexander wrote Burnet upon his insistence that it be answered. "To mention it would only be to gratify the vanity of the author, whoever this Dr. W. W. Sleigh might be."

"Dr. Sleigh is a moral defective," David wrote in reply, "and should be exposed." He enclosed a clipping from the New York *Sun* written by the highly esteemed Origen Bacheler, telling of Dr. Sleigh's swindle of a music teacher's life savings of $1,800, and a pamphlet detailing his career as a religious humbug. "You should warn our people against him."

In the next issue of the *Millennial Harbinger* Alexander printed the warning, quoting from Mr. Bacheler's article.

"But it is not enough to answer one man," he told Selina one morning in December. "I should be out defending our position. Our leaders are for the most part inexperienced; many of them are bewildered, unable alone to meet these onslaughts. Our churches are young; they need bolstering."

"Why don't you go on a tour then?" Selina asked. She had developed a way of pinning him to the wall with his own arguments. "I can manage the house, and James Anderson has the schedule for the farm worked out for the spring and summer. I heard him tell you about it."

"Getting editorial help is more difficult," Alexander replied. "That's what worries me. A new edition of the hymnal is in progress and Albert Ewing is too inexperienced to handle it even with William Llewellyn's help. *The Living Oracles* should go into another printing. Orders for the *Christian System* have to be filled as they come in, and the *Millennial Harbinger* needs constant supervision."

"The Lord will provide someone," Selina said. She did not bother to look up from the baby she was bathing.

Alexander felt a slow irritation mounting in him. Selina had grown more understanding and sympathetic, but while her piety had lessened, her faith in God's care was implicit, and her placid assumption of Divine help was at times annoying. He went out of the room and closed the door sharply behind him.

A fresh stack of mail greeted him on his desk as he stepped into his study. It had been increasing with each post since the union with the Stone forces had been consummated, and the task of reading and answering pertinent communications was enough to occupy one man's full time. It was out of the question for him to go on a tour among the distressed churches, as much as they needed him, unless he had help.

He sorted the letters almost absently, worried, doubtful of where his duty lay. He stopped as the postmark, "Carthage, Ohio," caught his eye. A letter from Walter Scott. He sat back in his chair to enjoy it.

But it was not from Walter Scott. It was from Robert Richardson.

Ever since Alexander's visit to Carthage the year before, the doctor wrote, he had been feeling the compulsion to take a more active part in the growing task of the Restoration Movement. The vicinity of Wellsburg needed a physician as much as the Ohio country into which tides of new arrivals each day were bringing fresh talents and skills. Could Alexander use him in any way if he returned to the Wellsburg community?

Alexander got up and took from the shelves the back copies of the *Millennial Harbinger* which had carried essays and letters by the young man, and critically scanned them. The doctor had ability in using words, his reasoning was clear, his convictions strong. He put the volumes back on the shelves and looked up, staring out at the sky through the bubbled glass in the roof of the cupola. Selina and her faith, he thought, and closed his eyes, enveloped in a wave of humility. Quickly he sat down at his desk and wrote:

Come to Bethany next April. I will find you a comfortable wigwam which I have built since you were here, a frame building, one story, containing three apartments on one floor, thirty feet in front by ten in width, having under the same roof a folding room for the *Harbinger*, and I will guarantee you five hundred dollars for the year. I may want your assistance and supervision of the affairs of the press for a part of your time, say three or four months of the year while I may be absent on some tours. There will be a garden connected with the house. I have rented the premises to Edwin Bakewell from whom you can find pasture for a horse and cow. I need not be further particular. You will freely and familiarly communicate all your views on these points as soon as possible.

Four days after Robert Richardson reached Bethany the next March, Alexander packed the smallest of his leather saddlebags.

"I must not take that much." He waved aside the pile of clothing and his new broadcloth suit Selina had laid out. "No more than a change of drawers; no more than I can carry myself. I'm going to war!"

Methodically she continued packing his portmanteau. "War or no war, you're going to look like a gentleman should."

Before he left he scrawled a hasty insertion for the next issue of the paper:

All letters containing queries, difficulties, or disciplinary matters are, during my absence, to be attended to by Dr. Robert Richardson. From these letters which require the attention of the public, or of particular churches, he will write such essays as will engross the matters, or he will directly reply, according to the wisdom given him.

He arranged for the hymnbook to be combined with one prepared by Walter Scott and John T. Johnson, and left orders with Dr. Richardson and Albert Ewing to include in it some of the hymns he had written himself: "On Tabor's Top the Saviour Stood"; "Come, Let Us Sing"; " 'Tis Darkness Here, but Jesus Smiles."

For three months he traveled, carrying the bulging portmanteau Selina had packed, as if driven by a relentless force, as if time were running out; crowded, blurred days and sleep-hungry nights. He spoke ninety-three times, for two hours or more at a time, hardening himself to rebuffs, praying for wisdom, pleading for an understanding of the ideals of the Restoration Movement. His route led him through the East, where hostility was the most pronounced, traveling by steamboat, stage, Conestoga wagon; on horseback and sometimes on foot; in snow and rain, and sometimes in oppressive heat; to Cleveland, Rochester, Buffalo; then to Syracuse, Saratoga Springs, into Vermont; on to Boston and New York, and down again into Pennsylvania.

It was late on the afternoon of Saturday, August 2, 1836, when he stepped from the steamer at Philadelphia. The docks were crowded; stevedores jostled for advantage; the heat was oppressive. Weary to the point of exhaustion in body and more fatigued in spirit, hungry for a friendly hand, Alexander scanned the faces of the perspiring, indifferent crowd.

"James Hazlett!" His cry was spontaneous as two tall, smiling men in Panama hats and black frock coats walked from the crowd with outstretched hands. "And Dr. Morrison! How thoughtful of you to meet me!"

The encounter with the old friends he had not seen since his visit to Philadelphia two years before was interrupted by the approach of a stranger, a tall, lean man, his long face creased by a frown of doubt and displeasure, a three-point star gleaming on his dark shirt. He spoke directly to Alexander.

"You are Alexander Campbell of Bethany, Virginia?"

Alexander looked at him, surprised. "I am, sir. And you?"

"Sheriff Andrews of Philadelphia County." He handed Alexander a folded paper. "This is a warrant. I have orders to place you under arrest."

Chapter 25

IN THE STUNNED SILENCE THAT FOLLOWED ALEXANDER READ THE DOCU-ment. He was charged with criminal libel in a suit filed by Dr. W. W. Sleigh, the spurious religious leader whose record he had exposed in the *Millennial Harbinger*. The courthouse was closed for the weekend, the sheriff explained, his stern face lightened by a quick respect for Alexander, but he could accept an appearance bond for $10,000. Thirty minutes later it was all settled. The outraged Hazlett and Morrison were accepted as bondsmen and the officer left the dock.

"You see what mine enemies think of me!" Alexander laughed a trifle grimly as the three friends sat that night in Morrison's home on Mulberry Street, discussing the matter. "It's flattering to learn my paper is so effective. Dr. Sleigh must have been following my movements closely. He evidently knew I was scheduled to arrive here today, and by demanding such a large bail, hoped he could land me in jail. And in a way I feel I should not have imposed on you two. If a man's pledged word is not sufficient bond at any time for his appearance, he should go to jail."

"And play into the hands of pious frauds?" said Hazlett. "I read that pamphlet, 'Campbellism Exposed.' You should have sued Sleigh for libel yourself!"

Alexander shook his head. "It would only have brought him into more public notice. I printed his record in the *Harbinger* only because I felt it my duty to warn our brethren the scoundrel was on the loose, and to beware. This is a nuisance suit, brought only to discredit our work, to throw a stumbling block in its progress. He knows he was not libeled."

But yielding to the urgings of his friends, Alexander permitted them to engage for him two of Philadelphia's leading attorneys, James R. Broom and J. R. Ingersoll. On Monday morning a reduction in his bond to $4,000 was secured by them, and with the case set for hearing in November, Alexander preached, as planned, in the Musical Fund Hall for the next three nights, the room crowded to capacity.

When he reached Bethany on the morning of September 6, the air was heavy with the threat of storm. He had gone to Baltimore from Philadelphia, and then had returned by stagecoach to Pittsburgh and taken a steamer to Wellsburg where he had been met at the boat landing by his father-in-law, John Brown, with the news that Mrs. Ann Brown, Margaret's stepmother, had died in June. He stayed overnight with Mr. Brown, sitting with him on the porch of the brick house he now occupied alone, discussing far into the night their undimmed hope of immortality; recounting the stirring events of bygone days; the dreams, the disappointments, the struggles, the triumphs the years had brought.

John Brown was driving his wagon to Wheeling the next morning to purchase supplies at a wholesale grocery house, and Alexander was up before daylight to make the trip with him as far as Bethany. The Campbell house was a mile past the turnoff at Point Breeze for the Wheeling road but, although Mr. Brown gladly drove the extra distance, he shook his close-cropped graying head when Alexander insisted he come in for breakfast.

"I had coffee in the kitchen while you were shaving, and I'd best be on my way," he said. "It's a fair piece to Wheeling and I want to be back before sundown. Besides," he looked up at the house, insistent honesty in his misty eyes, "the old place is still alive with memories. I'd rather not disturb them. God go with you, son." He gripped Alexander's hand hard in parting.

At the door Alexander met his cousin Enos just coming out, his fiddle under his arm.

"Welcome, welcome!" Enos' hearty voice boomed, thick with Irish brogue. "It's time ye were a-comin'!" And then his voice lowered. "The bairns are not a-stirrin' yet, it's that early, so I'm tiptoeing up to the Henley barn to play me fiddle. It's the only chance I'll be gettin' today."

Alexander laughed. "Nonsense! Play it for us after breakfast. I'd like to hear you." He paused as Enos put his finger to his lips.

"Your wife has no mind for fiddle music," he said, almost in a whisper. "She thinks it's not fittin' to be comin' from the house of the bishop!"

Alexander started to laugh but thought better of it. Selina had her hands full, keeping the family together, carrying the responsibility during his long absences. If she had strange whims and notions, he would respect them.

"Off with you then!" He slapped Enos' shoulder. "I'll hear all about how the school has been going after supper tonight."

By midmorning the cherished reunion with the family, the exchange of news, the lingering worship service about the breakfast table were over, and Alexander got up to go to the printing office. The children had been wide-eyed at the account of his arrest, and Selina's long face had reflected her indignation.

"How could they dare do such a thing," she said, "treating you like a criminal! I'd like to tell that humbug a thing or two!"

"I'm not taking it too seriously," Alexander replied. "It's purely a malice suit, filed for the purpose of causing me humiliation by landing me in jail for a few days. Failing that, the man may drag it through the courts as long as possible. We'll see."

He dismissed the matter from his mind and when he reached his office began scanning copies of the *Harbinger* issued since he had been away. Robert Richardson had done well. His eye ran over the young doctor's essay, "Inspiration of the Scriptures," and then he picked up the copy and went out by the side of the building and sat on a log in the shade of a maple tree, and read it again. Here was the kernel of the whole Restoration Plea, the beginning and end of the whole matter. Since the return to the early church depended on the return to the Bible, belief in the inspiration of the Scriptures and reliance on their promises were keystones in the arch of the Plea. A rustle of leaves behind him, and Dr. Richardson's thin hand was on his shoulder.

After the greetings were over the two men sat together on the log, welcoming the slight breeze that broke the heavy atmosphere, discussing their common task.

"You have hit upon a cardinal thought here," Alexander said, tapping the *Harbinger* containing the essay. "I am convinced more than ever that the weakness of Christianity and the ineffectiveness of the church, the strife and dissension and misunderstandings among us all, are due to the fact we simply do not read the Bible as thoroughly as we should. People depend on what others say about it, upon a preacher's interpretation of it, instead of reading it for themselves. Yet it is the constitution of the church." He passed his hand thoughtfully over his face. "I ran into more ignorance of the Bible on this trip than I had ever encountered before, and into more men who thought they had all the answers themselves."

Dr. Richardson smiled. "More than that, the Bible is a practical guide, and an indispensable one, to our moral and spiritual life," he said.

"It is our only one!" Alexander exclaimed with more than usual feeling. He got up and began pacing the ground. "Why isn't it a textbook in our schools? Our country is founded on the truth it reveals. Yet it is not even read, much less studied, in many public schools. And not a single college in our country lists it as a textbook!"

"That may be due to the Catholic influence," Dr. Richardson said thoughtfully. "There is a tide of Catholic immigrants now coming to our shores, and they not only oppose teaching the Bible in the public schools but are not favorable to public education of any sort."

Alexander frowned. His own Huguenot ancestors had fled from France to escape the Great Persecution of the Catholic Church and he had no tolerance for any attempt to fasten the religious system on this new country. "I know," he said. "It may mean trouble eventually. The Catholic hierarchy makes intellectual slaves of its subjects."

"You don't think they are under orders from the Pope, do you?" Dr. Richardson asked, a twinkle in his pale blue eyes, shielded now against the slanting rays of the sun by his thin hand.

"I think our democratic institutions are in the path of the Pope's ambitions," Alexander replied with obvious annoyance. "Further than that I won't say. Certainly I am opposed to the incidents of mob violence against Catholics we have had in some of our eastern cities. That must be avoided at all costs. There is room in this country for us all, and freedom of religion above everything else must be preserved." He stopped squarely in front of Dr. Richardson. "What would you think of starting a college here in Bethany? Not another boys' school, such as I attempted with Buffalo Seminary, but a real educational institution."

"A college?" Dr. Richardson echoed doubtfully.

Alexander extended his arms as if to embrace the rolling hills, their thick greenery now shading into yellow and crimson, their crests lost from view in the lowering clouds.

"Where could young men be better fitted for the task of leadership in this Movement than in these hills which gave it birth?" he cried. "Where the Bible would be a textbook, and no sectarian doctrine would ever be taught?"

Dr. Richardson smiled, and stood up. "You and Walter Scott," he said, "my two spiritual parents—how closely your minds run together! I suppose you know Mr. Scott has undertaken the presidency of the new Bacon College in Georgetown, Kentucky?"

Alexander nodded. "He wrote me about it. I regret he is leaving the evangelistic field but he said it would be for only a short time, to get the college on its feet. He feels as strongly as I do that the moral training of young people is being neglected in our colleges. In Bacon College he plans to make it a matter of paramount concern."

"I'm sure he will, but he plans also to have the college give training in the technical fields," Dr. Richardson commented. "A well-rounded college should."

"I give my vote for learning in all branches of useful knowledge," Alexander agreed, "but I would not give morality for them all." For a moment there was silence, and then he said, "Yes, when that school is well established and our churches begin to support it, I shall plan definitely on one here at Bethany. We must begin right now to accustom our people to the idea of undergirding our Movement with a strong educational program."

He stooped and picked up a pebble and tossed it at a clump of grass. "You know, Robert," he said, "I find my views changing on many things. Perhaps that's the way the Lord works through people—first the blade, then the ear, then the full grain in the ear."

Dr. Richardson nodded. "It's the law of life," he said. "But not all things obey it. Some men refuse to mature; it takes courage to grow."

Alexander tilted his hat to the front of his head, shading his eyes from the sun. "You're right. I still believe each church should be autonomous on local matters but I'm beginning to see the need for a closer tie among them, something even stronger than our yearly meetings. Take the support of such an undertaking as a college, for instance, or the task of distributing the Bible—we can do comparatively nothing without cooperation." He pushed his hat to the back of his head. "But that will come in time." Abruptly he changed the subject. "Tell me, how have you been, Robert?"

"Well enough," Dr. Richardson replied, "except for my eyes. I spare them as much as possible. Only half of my time is given to editorial work, as you know; the rest I give to my medical practice."

"The people love you as a physician as well as a friend." Alexander spoke hurriedly as a roll of thunder, a sudden gust of strong wind, brought a spattering of rain that hurried them toward the shelter of the printing office. "And I cherish your services as an editorial assistant. So spare your eyes, young man; they are needed. I value your judgment and patience in working out details, a task for which I have little talent."

"Now that you are back," Richardson said hesitantly, "I hope to be relieved of some—"

Alexander turned about at the door of the building. "Now that I am back," he interrupted him, "only means that I am off again. That's why I had you come here, so I could be on tour more often. I leave next month to speak at the College of Teachers in Cincinnati. I am vice-president this year." He stared at the younger man standing just inside the door, holding it open for him to follow. "Mrs. Campbell will accompany me. She has carried a heavy load, too, during my absence, and needs a change. We are to be entertained at David Burnet's new home. So please do not speak of being relieved just now."

He spoke more sharply than he had intended, and Dr. Richardson rubbed his hand across his face as if smarting from a rebuke.

"I enjoy this work," Dr. Richardson said, "and feel God has called me to it. Of course I shall carry it on during your absences. I hope to make it my lifework, with my medical practice becoming more and more a side line. As long as my eyes permit, sir, you can depend on me."

Alexander looked away, ashamed of his impetuous outburst. "Thank you, Robert," he said finally. Turning up his coat collar, he started back to the house.

Selina at first was reluctant to make the trip to Cincinnati. But as plans developed her interest increased and within a week she began packing a portmanteau.

"Since we're staying with the Burnets," she told Alexander, "I'll take my new brown alpaca and yellow knitted shawl." She secured a paper carton from Theron and carefully packed it with her brown bonnet edged with blonde. Her mother could supervise the children, and "Aunt Betsy" and the girl, Susannah, could care for the house.

They traveled by the river steamer *Ohio Belle,* and Selina was astonished at its luxury.

"I don't think it's sinful, do you, to have pretty things about?" she mused the second day as they walked the deck, making their way among roistering men and handsomely gowned women parading its length or lolling in deck chairs. "I stood on a stool this morning and examined the scrolls on the walls and ceiling of our stateroom. They are covered with real gold! And imagine having bathing space in each room!" They passed the portholes opening into the men's saloon, and after a glance through the apertures, her eyes widened and she tugged at Alexander's arm. "I do believe they're drinking hard liquor in there," she said. "I know *that's* sinful. We should return to our stateroom."

David and his young wife, Mary Gano Burnet, were hospitable hosts, and Alexander watched with amusement as Selina's bright, sharp eyes took in every detail of the brocaded draperies and velvet carpets, and the queer fixtures on the walls for the new illuminating gas which would soon be available in Cincinnati. The culture of the wealthy and prominent Burnet family was reflected in this home, a home more pretentious, Alexander reflected, than that of any other preacher he knew of in the frontier country.

"David Burnet has become a power for the Restoration Movement in this section," Alexander commented to Selina that night in the privacy of their bedroom. "The prominence of his family has helped him, but he had real ability himself."

Selina stopped braiding her hair and looked at him knowingly in the mirror. "He talks sometimes like he started it," she said in a stage whisper. "He sounds like he thinks he's the leading man in it, with his big plans and all."

Alexander laughed quietly. "He does have some grandiose dreams for the future of it," he said. "He and Walter Scott are often together and one seems to inspire the other. They envision a great national brotherhood, the churches bound together by organizations, and colleges, and societies for this and that." He slowly loosened his cravat. "And a powerful publishing house," he added. "Their enthusiasm may need to be held in check."

"I like the copy of his new paper he showed us, the *Christian Preacher*, even better than I like Mr. Scott's *Evangelist*," Selina admitted, adding hastily, "but neither one can compare with the *Harbinger*. It is befitting of him, though, to have printed that compilation of your best articles from the *Christian Baptist*. That shows he knows well enough who's who."

"Hush! Hush!" Alexander cautioned as he blew out their candles.

The next morning David Burnet insisted that he visit the new paper mills. "Cincinnati has all the facilities for any publishing effort," the young man told him. "It's a coming metropolis. A fellow reading law in my uncle's office, Nicholas Longworth, recently paid my uncle $5,000 for a cow pasture! Think what faith he has in the future of this town. And our brotherhood needs a central point for the issuance of its printed matter."

Alexander raised his eyebrows. "I secure my paper stock at Steubenville," he told him, adding, after a moment, "Our area, too, has fine facilities for all publishing efforts."

Driving home from the mill of Christian Waldschmidt, Alexander noticed David raise his hat as they passed a battered carryall, the clumping feet of its white horse resounding on the cobblestone streets, the driver sitting bolt upright, his stern, lean face relieved by thick white sideburns. He lifted his tall beaver hat in return of the salute.

"That is Dr. Lyman Beecher," Burnet explained when they had passed. "He's creating a stir here not only as president of Lane Theological Seminary but as pastor of the Second Presbyterian Church. He's something of a heretic himself. He has a large family, and his seven sons, people say, are all destined for the ministry."

Alexander nodded. "I heard of him frequently while in New England last summer. He had a run-in with the Catholics, for which I admire him, and I also agree with his slavery position. Although he's an Abolitionist, he's a discreet one."

When they returned to the house Alexander found a letter sent by special messenger from his lawyer, James Broom, in Philadelphia. Dr. Sleigh, as permitted by Pennsylvania law for either litigant in such cases, had transferred his damage suit from the trial court to a Board of Arbitration to be appointed by the court.

"This means that instead of settlement by an early trial, the case can be dragged out for years," Alexander explained to David and the others. He laughed ruefully. "I'm in for a long siege. This Dr. Sleigh means to be a real nuisance, but there's no help for it. At least my experience will be an exercise in Christian patience which the Lord well knows is not my strongest virtue."

"Perhaps that's the reason he sent Dr. Sleigh your way," said Selina soberly. "Everything works together for good for those who love the Lord. This old humbug may be just what you need to develop your sense of patience with your overambitious brothers."

David laughed, and Alexander looked at Selina sharply, and then relaxed in quick appreciation, a ready smile tugging at the corner of his lips.

The auditorium was crowded the next night when Alexander and Selina with the Burnets entered the First Presbyterian Church for the opening session of the annual assembly of the Western Literary Institute and College of Professional Teachers, popularly known as the College of Teachers. Educators and public leaders from the adjoining states were in the audience, and the Burnet party found seats in the second row at the far left. Then Alexander went up on the platform to deliver the opening prayer before returning to sit beside Selina and to listen with mounting approval as the speaker, Dr. J. L. Wilson, advocated the Bible as a universal textbook. He was pondering on the similarity of the theme with his own recent thinking when he was startled to hear the position challenged from the rear of the room. A Catholic priest had arisen in protest.

"Bishop John Baptist Purcell," Burnet leaned over and whispered to him as the protest continued. "Born in Ireland, ordained in France, and consecrated Bishop of Cincinnati Diocese in 1833. A ready speaker and a fearless one, too."

"And an audacious one," Alexander replied in low tones, "to come to a Presbyterian meetinghouse and expound such views."

Long after they had returned to the Burnet home, Alexander tossed in his bed, nettled by the incident. Was Protestant America to be influenced by the Catholics in planning its program of public education? Was freedom of thought to be harnessed; freedom of religion jeopardized? Were no Protestant voices to be lifted in reply?

The sessions continued for two days, and Alexander attended regularly, but his mind was not on the speeches. The significance of the incident was growing in his mind. The threat of the Catholic influence upon public education loomed as something to be avoided, averted now, while the country was young, before the mould had become set.

He was scheduled to speak at the close of the second evening, and when he arose a decision which had been forming in his mind took solid shape. He folded the notes of his prepared outline and, slipping the sheets into the tail pocket of his Prince Albert coat, began, instead, to trace with logical, deadly precision the connection between Protestant freedom of thought and human progress.

"Man is by nature a thinking being," he declared, "and he ought not only to think, but to think for himself. To the inculcation of this obligation, more than to any other precept in the religious or moral code, was Martin Luther indebted for that eminent success which elevated him to the highest order."

"The fat's in the fire!" Burnet exclaimed in evident delight as they drove home. "The Catholics will burn you at the stake!"

"The fat's been in the fire before." Selina spoke quickly from the rear of the two-seated carriage where she sat beside Mary Burnet. "And Mr. Campbell has never been burned!"

Alexander turned and gave her a grateful look, the soft radiance of the full moon making her, for the moment, almost pretty.

But David Burnet was right. The implication of the address brought quick and heated response from Bishop Purcell.

"The Protestant Reformation has been the cause of all the contention and infidelity in the world!" the bishop thundered in rejoinder the next evening.

Early the next morning Alexander and Selina were finishing breakfast with the Burnets when Walter Scott rode up to the house. As president of Bacon College, he was forced to spend much of his time in Georgetown, Kentucky, but his family remained in Carthage, as he expected to return to evangelistic work within the year. Learning Alexander was in Cincinnati, the impetuous evangelist had ridden horseback from Georgetown to Cincinnati, hoping the Campbells would return to Carthage with him for a visit, and that Alexander would preach at the small Carthage church.

But great issues were at stake, Alexander told him, and David agreed. For a week the three men talked together, meeting with Protestant leaders, counseling, advising, as charge followed charge and public interest flamed. And when a citizens' committee of fifty-six called at the Burnet home one evening, urging Alexander to meet the bishop in formal debate of his charge against the Reformation, they agreed he should accept.

"Much as I deplore their views, I had no idea of becoming embroiled in a debate with the Catholics," Alexander told Dr. Richardson when he returned to Bethany. "I didn't court it and I don't want it, but I'm going to have to undertake it."

The debate was held in January 1837, and captured the imagination of all Cincinnati as the battle raged at the Sycamore Street meetinghouse, swinging as its pivotal axis about six questions Alexander raised concerning the fundamentals of the Catholic faith.

"You're a brave man," David Burnet told him the evening before the debate opened as he looked up from reading the points Alexander intended stressing. Aloud he read:

"1st. The Roman Catholic institution is not now nor was ever catholic, apostolic, or holy, but a sect, an apostasy from the only true church of Christ.

"2d. Her notion of apostolic succession is without any foundation in the Bible.

"3d. She is not uniform in her faith or united in her members.

"4th. Her notions of purgatory, indulgences, transubstantiation, and such things are immoral in their tendency and injurious to society.

"5th. Notwithstanding her pretensions to have given us the Bible, we are independent of her for our knowledge of that book.

"6th. The Roman Catholic religion is essentially anti-American."

He folded the sheet and stood up, a deep respect and admiration on his round, thoughtful face. "Mr. Campbell, I repeat what I said when you took up the gauntlet against the atheist, Robert Owen: You are a brave man. I know of no other Protestant preacher in America who would so boldly stand up to the Catholic Church!"

Cincinnati was a strong Catholic community, and from the start of the debate the passions of the people were inflamed by editorial comments in the *Daily Gazette*. Its editor, Charles Hammond, was a master of satire. On the morning of January 12 Alexander read:

We understand Alexander Campbell is in the city, prepared to demolish not the Cathedral and Chapel which the Catholics have erected in our city, but the whole fabric of Catholic superstition. Rebecca Read has had her day; Maria Monk is on the wane; Mr. Campbell comes in at the death, as Hector put the finish to the life of Patroclus.

We have no reporter engaged, but I purpose myself to look in on the Great Debate to exterminate Catholicism and if I find there is aught of general interest, as I understand it, to play the part "a chiel's among them takin' notes, and faith, he'll prent 'em."

For eight days the debate continued, with crowds so dense that the editor of the *Gazette* was soon forced to admit he feared the galleries might collapse under the pressure. It became the chief topic of conversation about Cincinnati dinner tables. Voices were raised from public platforms, from the pulpits of the city, on the streets; some condemning, other condoning Alexander's onslaughts on every vulnerable point in the framework of the Catholic church. But as the spectacle neared its close it became clear that no decision could be made; no victory could be claimed by either side.

Alexander Campbell is a learned and intellectual man, but in respect to church affairs he is the greatest heresiarch of the great Mississippi Valley.

Alexander read the final comment of Mr. Hammond in the *Daily Gazette* as he rested in his cabin on the steamer on his return to Bethany. He laid down the paper and went into the lounge. He selected a table near an open porthole, and pulling a sheet of paper toward him wrote in reply:

You say I am a heresiarch. Everyone active and earnest in the cause of religion is a great heretic or heresiarch in the eyes of Satan or somebody else. Might I say to you, you do not at all understand my views and my efforts? I have for many years been seeking to unite all Protestant Christians on one great bond of union, as catholic as Protestant Christendom; and even on the subject of baptism (for which I have your sincere aversion) I am perfectly catholic. I contend only for that baptism which the Greek, Roman, and English churches equally admit as apostolic and divine, and I regret only that which is sectarian because it alienates and divides great and good men.

Selina was pregnant again, he learned when he reached home, and Robert Richardson's eyes were giving him grave trouble. In June the young doctor was forced to give up all close work and leave for

306

Kentucky to regain his health. Alexander was confined to the editorial desk, relieved occasionally by his brother Archibald, who helped out as the time spared from his medical practice in Wellsburg permitted.

Business in the country was at a low ebb, and as summer drew on a financial panic seemed inevitable. The 1836 harvest had been poor; grain was being imported from Europe. Banks were being drained of specie and on May 10, 1837, suspended payment. Manufacturing almost stopped in the East and thousands were thrown out of work; bankruptcies were rampant.

On June 24 Selina gave birth to another son. He was a particularly handsome boy with brown eyes, wide-spaced and sparkling, a high forehead, and a well-shaped head. Alexander held him up proudly.

"He looks like the English reformer, John Wickliffe," he said.

"Then let's name him Wickliffe," Selina replied.

All summer repercussions of his debate with Bishop Purcell continued to reach Alexander. It had created strife and bitter controversy, he learned with a heavy heart, and although it had strengthened the Protestant position as the bulwark of democracy, the victory was not a sweet one.

"I never fought for victory but for the truth as I see it," he told Selina one morning after reading some of the reports. "The debate did something to me. I think it awakened me to a danger of which I was unaware. In the turbulence of defending our Plea—answering the critics, wrestling with the petty hostility, fighting off the pin-pricks—I've been in danger of forgetting that all those who follow Christ, regardless of how bitterly I differ with them, are bound to me by love."

"You mean you feel that way even about this Catholic bishop?" Selina's voice was tart but her eyes reflected her wonder at the largeness of the soul of this man she had married, at the depth of a compassion she could never understand.

"I feel only friendship for Bishop Purcell," Alexander said. "Despite our different views, I have a sense of relationship to him. We must never allow difference of opinion, or even the hostility of our tormentors, to cause us to lose sight of our great objective. All of us are brothers in the Lord and someday we shall work and worship that way."

It was true. Despite the continuing hostility of many leaders among the sects toward the Restoration Movement, Alexander found his reactions undergoing a subtle change. He no longer felt the compulsion to dip his pen in vitriol and lash out at his tormentors. All were brothers in the Lord.

He almost spoke the words aloud one morning as he was shaving. He looked at himself in the split-spindle mirror in the bathing room. The ingrained habit of living in the presence of God had put its stamp on his face. All who are followers of the meek and lowly Jesus, all who kneel at the same cross, all who live in the hope of life beyond the grave, he thought, are my brothers.

It was only five o'clock and the family was not yet stirring. He dressed quietly and went to his study. Sorting through a pouch of letters Jim Poole had brought in late the night before, he picked up one from Lunenburg, Virginia, signed by a woman whose name was unfamiliar. She wrote:

I was much surprised today while reading the *Harbinger* to see that you recognize all Protestant parties as Christian. You say you "find in all Protestant parties Christians." Dear brother, my surprise and ardent desire to do what is right prompt me to write to you. I feel well assured, from the estimate you place on the female character, that you will attend to my feeble questions in search of knowledge.

Will you be so good as to let me know how anyone becomes a Christian. What act of yours gave you the name of Christian? At what time had Paul the name of Christ called on him? At what time did Cornelius have Christ named on him? Is it not through that name that we obtain eternal life? Does the name of Christ, or Christian, belong to any but those who believe the Gospel, repent and are buried by baptism into the death of Christ?

Alexander read the letter three times. Its sincerity was manifest; the confusion of the writer genuine. Slowly he spread it beside him on the desk. He folded his arms and bent his head forward in thought, the first rays of the sun striking the east window in the cupola above him, shining in a slanting ray on his almost-white hair. For a long time he sat immovable, remote, a sense of detachment about him, all awareness stilled. It was as if his mind had opened to the mind of God. Finally he lifted his head and picked up his pen.

"Who is a Christian?" he wrote slowly, thoughtfully, and paused for a long minute. And then he continued:

I answer, Everyone who believes in his heart that Jesus of Nazareth is the Messiah, the Son of God; repents of his sins and obeys Him in all things according to his measure of knowledge of His will. I cannot make any one duty the standard of Christian state or character, not even immersion.

It is the image of Christ the Christian looks for and loves; and this does not consist in being exact in a few things but in general devotion to the whole truth as far as he knows. There is no occasion then for making immersion, or a profession of faith, absolutely essential to a Christian, though it may be greatly essential to his sanctification and comfort. I cannot be a perfect Christian without a right understanding and a cordial reception of immersion in its true and scriptural meaning and design. But he that thence infers that none are Christians but the immersed, as greatly errs as he who affirms that none are alive but those of clear and full vision.

He wrote on and on, clarifying his points, explaining his views, and when he laid down his pen at last the yard bell was tolling for breakfast and morning worship.

A new day had begun.

BOOK IV

Then the Full Grain in the Ear

Chapter 26

THERE SEEMED LITTLE DOUBT THAT REGULAR STEAMSHIP NAVIGATION across the Atlantic was now firmly established. In April 1838 two new British steamers, the *Sirus* and the *Great Western*, arrived in New York waters, and before the year ended four steamers were operating on regular schedule between Liverpool and Boston, with passenger travel and mail between the two continents increasing at a fantastic rate. With each post Alexander received letters from followers of the Restoration Movement in Great Britain and Ireland, telling of new churches formed without benefit of human creed, affirming the Bible in its simplicity and power as their only authority. The letters offset the occasional communications from his uncle, Archibald Campbell, in which the stubborn Scotsman never failed to criticize the new Movement. But all clamored for a visit from him. Someday, he decided, he would make the journey.

But things closer at home were demanding attention. The dream of establishing a college at Bethany persisted and, as the summer wore on, his concept grew into a giant educational plan. It would be more than a college, he decided; it would begin in the nursery and extend to the family, school, college, and church, and be so designed as to adapt itself to the whole physical, intellectual, moral, and religious phases of training young men.

As he walked the roads and roamed the fields, the dream merged into a conception of Bethany as the permanent, powerful focal point of the great national brotherhood into which the Restoration Movement would one day evolve; the center of its strength, the heart of its educational life, its missionary efforts, its organizational functions, its publishing ventures. Here, in the stony hills which had given it birth, the Movement would be anchored forever.

A new vitality filled him; a new restlessness consumed him.

"There is so much to do I hate to take the time to eat," he told Selina one evening in July as she came down to the study to remind him that supper was on the table. "The Movement is spreading so rapidly, we are embarrassed by our success. We must somehow train more leaders or we shall have bedlam on our hands!"

It was true. Since the union with Barton Stone's followers, churches were springing into existence like weeds after a rain, all claiming to be a part of the Movement but some of them with little conception of its basic principles, led by laymen with no theological background and some with little formal education. Confusion was rampant, with doctrinal points in dispute, local church procedures assuming a variety of forms, and even a common name still unsettled. In some localities they were known as "Christians," creating confusion with the "Christian Connection," a group of Barton Stone's followers who had not merged with the new Movement; in other places they were called "Churches of Christ"; in still other communities the groups referred to themselves as "Disciples of Christ."

Selina tapped her short fingers impatiently on the back of a chair, waiting for the turbulence of his emotion to subside.

"Look at these letters," he went on, indicating the papers on his desk. "They're all from a man in Painsville, Virginia, a Dr. John Thomas. A sincere man but utterly confused about the simplicity of our Plea."

"How do you mean, confused?" Selina asked. "It seems to me it's plain enough what we stand for."

"He is convinced of certain things in relation to the mortality of man, the resurrection of the dead, the destiny of the wicked, and he's preaching his views with a vengeance, unaware that they have nothing whatever to do with salvation. There are hundreds like him, still mistaking their own opinions of the Gospel for the true facts as revealed in the Bible."

314

"Hasn't he the right to his own opinions?" Selina asked.

"Of course he has!" Alexander said sternly. "But he has no right to force such opinions upon the churches as necessary articles of faith. Opinions on all subjects not revealed in the Bible are merely personal opinions, and no citizen of Christ's kingdom has a right to propound them with any authority whatever!"

"Then if he holds views which are contrary to yours," Selina announced, "he should leave the church. Come on to supper, Mr. Campbell."

"Oh, my dear! My dear!" Alexander said almost in despair. "That is precisely the attitude we must avoid. Even though Dr. Thomas' viewpoint does not coincide with mine, we can still remain in full Christian fellowship in the same church. We may differ on many things, but if we are united on essentials, we can still work and worship together. As each of us demands liberty for ourselves in interpreting the Bible, so must we give that same liberty to others."

He got to his feet and picked from his desk a stack of periodicals. "I want to look these over," he said, "and see——"

"Please, not now!" she said. "Supper's ready."

"Then I'll take them up to the house," he said. "You will be interested in them, too. They're periodicals all claiming the message of our Restoration Movement, circulating now in almost every state. Here!" He handed one after another to her. "Here's Barton Stone's *Christian Messenger;* he has left Kentucky, you know, and moved to Jacksonville, Illinois, but he's still publishing his paper, a sensible, level-headed editor, too, for whom I thank God. I wish I could say the same for all of them. This *Apostolic Advocate* is edited in Richmond by John Thomas, and here is the *Gospel Advocate,* put out by John T. Johnson and Alexander Hall in Georgetown. David Burnet is still doing a fine job with his *Christian Plea,* and John R. Howard in Paris, Tennessee, is putting out this one, the *Christian Reformer,* he calls it. Even in the seemingly impregnable North and East we have these two papers, the *Christian Investigator* in Eastport, Maine, edited by William Hunter, and in Auburn, New York, Silas Shepherd is bringing out this one, the *Primitive Christian.*"

Selina looked at the stack of papers, now heavy in her arms, and her eyes widened. "You don't expect to read all these, Mr. Campbell, in one evening?"

Alexander smiled and took the bundle from her. Selina's reading was confined to the Bible and *The Ladies' Repository*, although she frequently tried to concentrate on perusing the *Millennial Harbinger* out of loyalty to him, and his constant habit of carrying reading material with him wherever he went continued to baffle her.

"Every line," he said. "Because in none of them is the message the same." He followed Selina out the door and closed it behind him, matching his long stride to her short step as they walked toward the house. "There is disagreement and heated contests on all points. The seed has been planted but it needs nurturing and cultivating, and this means I must free myself from all other matters as much as possible in order to help do it. I am trying now to settle the Sleigh case, and I think I can do it."

"Well, I should think that would be a relief," Selina said. "It's been a nuisance all right."

Alexander laughed. "Nuisance is right! After almost two years and twenty-odd meetings of the arbitrators, my gadfly doctor has proposed to dismiss his suit if I will pay only the costs of the litigation and withdraw two statements quoted by me from Origen Bacheler's pamphlet. He doth protest that he was never arrested for swindling, and my lawyers tell me that is technically true. His arrest in Cincinnati was actually the result of a civil action filed by a woman for recovery of money she had lent him and which he had denied receiving."

"Tweedledee and tweedledum, I call it," Selina said.

"He also claims," Alexander went on as they neared the house, "that the statement I quoted from Bacheler to the effect that the London *Weekly Lancet* contained an account of his running away from England after embezzling some funds of a hospital was technically incorrect. It seems the charge was in the form of a certificate signed by a number of London gentlemen and appeared on an outside cover of the *Lancet* and not inside the magazine."

"Rubbish! And he wants you to explain all that in your paper?"

"Of course I won't take up valuable space doing it. But I've instructed Broom and Ingersoll that I'll pay the court costs and with-draw the statements if Sleigh will dismiss the suit and stop bothering me with it. I'm sick and tired of the thing and have other more im-portant business than brushing aside this little man's waspy stings."

Two weeks later Alexander was notified that Dr. Sleigh on August 4, 1838, had not only dismissed the suit but had also filed in the Penn-sylvania Supreme Court a release forever discharging Alexander from all future action, and had taken himself off to London.

"The wheels of the gods grind slowly but they have ground out a great victory!" Attorney Broom wrote him.

Whatever the nature of the victory, Alexander thought as he filed away the boxes of correspondence on the matter, at least in the lan-guage of the lawyers a nuisance had been abated. From the day of the threatened arrest until the day of dismissal, the case of William W. Sleigh vs. Alexander Campbell had dragged through the legal labyrinths for exactly two years less two weeks.

Robert Richardson returned to Bethany late in the fall and settled down with Rebekah and their four children on a farm of sixty-seven acres on the Wheeling Turnpike, two miles from Bethany village. His eyes were improved, and although he could not undertake full-time editorial work, he consented to give oversight to the *Millennial Harbinger*. So on October 8 Alexander left for a tour through the South, planning to go where the need for his counsel seemed greatest.

The weeks drew into months; Christmas came and went and he was still on tour. Virginia and the Carolinas, Georgia, Alabama, New Orleans, passed in succession. On January 16, 1839, he wrote Dr. Richardson from the steamboat *Tapaloosa* as he was traveling up the Alabama River:

This has been with me a sermon of three months' continuance, inter-rupted only by the stages of a journey of some 3,000 miles. My public addresses have been in Virginia thirty-four, in South Carolina twenty-three, in Georgia twenty, in South Alabama ten, besides some hundred fireside sermons. I am a wonder to myself in enduring fatigue.

In Woodville, Mississippi, he remained two days at the home of Mr. and Mrs. William Stamps, captivated by their two young sons,

317

Isaac and William, Jr., with whom he tramped the cotton fields, the dry stalks rustling now in the winter wind.

"What do you raise way up there in the North?" young William asked.

"Why don't you come up and see for yourselves?" Alexander countered.

"Could we?" Their faces shone at the prospect.

That evening Alexander sat until past midnight with his hosts about the fireside, discussing his plan of education. Both Mr. and Mrs. Stamps were enthusiastic; they would see that their sons were among the first to enroll when the college was opened.

Mrs. Stamps' soft brown eyes gleamed warmly as she shook hands with him the next morning at the boat landing. "I wish my brother, Jefferson Davis, could meet you, Mr. Campbell," she said. "He is a lonely widower, living at his place Brierfield, on Davis Bend, down the river a piece. He needs the strong anchor of the Gospel in its simple purity, just like you've explained it to us."

On up the broad Mississippi River Alexander traveled, reaching Louisville late in February. There he received word that his sister Alicia, the wife of Matthew Clapp, had died on January 16. And there, as February turned into March with its burning memories, he wrote Selina on March 12, the anniversary of his marriage to Margaret:

My dear Selina:
This day, twenty-eight years ago, I gave my hand, and my heart accompanied it, to your amiable and excellent predecessor in the holy bonds of matrimony. Heaven lent me that precious gift more than sixteen years, of the value of which I never did form an overestimate. But more than eleven years since He called her to Himself, and more than ten years ago appointed you to fill her place in my affections. . . . I have, my dear Selina, found you worthy of all the affection and esteem which were due to her who desired to bless both you and me by nominating you to be her successor.
You may be assured that if, either by my long absence from you, or any apparent neglect that at any time I may, in my studious hours, have exhibited toward you, it would seem that I did not truly appreciate your excellences, I would have you know it is the offspring of the frailties of human nature. You are my fellow soldier, my true yokefellow, my partner in all my labors.

I do not intend ever to leave you so long again. Meanwhile I trust, as the Lord has kindly borne with my frailties—and I am aware they are neither few nor little—that He will send His angel before me and restore me to your bosom and that of my family in due time.

Meanwhile, my beloved Selina, constantly, as I know you do, pray to the Lord for me that I may be humble. . . .

Yours ever, in nature and in the Lord,
A. Campbell.

From Louisville Alexander went to Frankfort by stagecoach, a distance of fifty-four miles. The day was warm for early March, the road was rough, the swaying coach crowded and uncomfortable, and after twenty-two miles of jostling he was glad to have midday dinner at Shelbyville. In Frankfort he was met at the stagecoach stop by Philip S. Fall, now conducting a school for young ladies in addition to his preaching.

"Yes, I am weary," Alexander told him in answer to his greeting. "Preaching is hard work." He picked up his bag and followed Mr. Fall to his waiting surrey. He would preach that evening in the new Frankfort Christian Church and spend the night in the home of the dapper, robust little man who had been the first Baptist preacher in Tennessee publicly to take his stand with the Restoration Movement, now almost fifteen years ago. He had cherished a warm affection for Philip S. Fall and corresponded with him frequently. "But it is the most important work in the world; and next to it is teaching." He handed Mr. Fall his bag to put on the back seat.

Mr. Fall climbed into the driver's seat and picked up the reins. "But the content of what we preach and what we teach is what makes it important," he said.

Alexander stopped with his foot on the surrey steps. Philip Fall had said a volume in a single sentence. Alexander stared at him curiously. "It makes all the difference in the world," he agreed as he climbed into the seat beside him.

The horse started its slow jog and Alexander leaned back. "Philip, what is the supreme end of education?" he asked.

Mr. Fall pursed his full lips thoughtfully, and after a moment's reflection replied, "It should contribute to the development of both men and women in all attributes of their complex beings."

319

"Including the moral character and the culture of the heart," Alexander said. He smiled, a broad, happy grin. "I will tell you this evening of my plans along that line."

Alexander reached Bethany on March 28, and plunged at once into the task of putting on paper his dream of a fourfold educational structure. He had talked of it at length with Philip Fall and later with Walter Scott as he came through Ohio. Mr. Scott had relinquished his work at Bacon College in Georgetown to David Burnet, who planned to continue with it only until it was further established on a firm basis.

"The uniqueness of the plan," he told Dr. Richardson as they went over the matter, "is that this school must be more than a system of imparting knowledge; it must serve in the formation of character. There is everywhere more of a readiness to reform the creed than the heart; to rectify the understanding rather than the affections; to exhibit sound tenets rather than godly lives. Good works are much more wanting than good notions."

For the next issue of the *Millennial Harbinger* he wrote:

Having now completed fifty years and on my way to sixty, the greater part of which time has been engaged in literary labors and pursuits, and imagining that I possess some views and attainments which I can in this way render permanently useful to this community and posterity, I feel in duty bound to offer this project to the consideration of all friends of literature and morality and unsectarian Bible Christianity. I am willing to bestow much personal labor without any charge in getting up this institution, and also to invest a few thousand dollars in it; provided only our brethren—the rich and opulent especially, and those who have children to educate—will take a strong hold of it, and determine to build up an establishment that may be made to themselves, their children, and many others a lasting and a comprehensive blessing.

Alexander was sitting at his desk in the study on July 7, papers scattered before him with plans for the college, when he glanced out the open door to see his son-in-law, John Campbell, riding up to the stile, his horse covered with lather. He watched as the young man flung the reins over the post and came almost on a run to the study.

"Eliza Ann is dying!" The words came in a breathless gasp as John stopped in the entrance.

Alexander sat motionless, speechless. Eliza Ann and John had been at the house for dinner only last Sunday, laughing, alive, vibrant with youth and love. Their first child was due in two months and they were starry-eyed with the wonder of it.

"The baby was born yesterday. Eliza Ann has been in convulsions ever since. Dr. Archie says she cannot live!"

Without a word Alexander slipped to his knees. For a long minute silence filled the little room, broken only by the heavy breathing of the men as their wordless petitions ascended to the throne of mercy. Then, quickly, Alexander scrambled to his feet.

"I shall go with you at once," he said quietly.

Eliza Ann died two days later. Following the burial in God's Acre, John Campbell lingered on at the big house as though drawn irresistibly to the company of his father-in-law. For long hours the two men roamed the fields, inspecting the crops, or sat in silent communion on the porch, or talked in the study, a deep bond of friendship slowly cementing their lives.

"God moves in mysterious ways," Alexander said at the end of the week when the younger man was preparing to return to his law practice in Wellsburg. "Through our common grief we have been drawn closer to one another. I must not wait for sorrow to bring me closer to my other sons-in-law. My plan for the educational institution is built on the foundation of the family. What is more natural than that my own family should consolidate in making it a reality?"

John shook his head. "As you know, I think you are visionary, Bishop." He used the term endearingly—a term the countryside was using with increasing frequency to distinguish Alexander's family from other Campbells in the area. "You cannot start a college on just an idea, no matter how comprehensive it is. It takes money, lots of money."

"The money will come," Alexander said patiently, as if he had answered the same question in his own mind many times.

John smiled. "I'm a hardheaded lawyer," he said. "I try to tackle

321

a problem realistically. Why don't you first raise some money, or at least find out if the churches will be generous enough to support such a scheme?"

"I have, in a way, felt them out," Alexander persisted. "On my last tour I had that in mind everywhere I went. I didn't present detailed plans, but whenever I spoke of the need for trained leaders, I met with instant response. Everyone knows we need them." He got up from his desk and began pacing the study floor. "I'm a hardheaded businessman, too. I'm not inclined to impractical ventures. Sometimes I think I'm not willing enough to walk by faith. You can well realize that—look at all this land I've accumulated, all this wealth I have to back me up. I give my time to preaching the Gospel without pay because I feel that is the way the Gospel should be preached. But I am frank to admit, John, if I did not know where my next meal was coming from, well—I doubt I could do it on faith as many of our preachers are doing—men with little education or training but, Almighty God," he said reverently, "what faith!" He paused and looked for a long minute out of the open door. "I sometimes wonder," he said thoughtfully, "if my wealth has limited my faith."

"Many men with your resources would be lured to other fields," John said. "I think you underestimate yourself. I feel if you had not a dime to your name, you would still fare forth on these preaching tours. Your faith along that line has simply never been put to the test."

"That's just it!" Alexander said. He turned and sat down heavily. "That is why, in this education venture, I propose launching out on faith. I feel somehow God wants to take the measure of my trust in Him. It is something like a spiritual mission. He has shown me the need exists, and if the need exists, I must rely on Him to provide the means of meeting it."

John nodded solemnly. "Well, if that's the way you look at it, sir, I'll have to go along with you. But in every spiritual mission there are worldly tasks." He drew his chair up to the desk. "First of all, such an institution must be chartered by the state. I can at least do that for you."

Alexander smiled at him. "I am fortunate in my in-laws. Each of you has a particular talent to give to this venture. I'll get us all to-gether and we can begin talking out the problems."

Work was in progress on another enlargement of the house. The dining room was being extended, the flooring of oak planks with their wooden dowels running at right angles to the other flooring; a storeroom added, and a "company" parlor built on to the west wing at the far end off the bedroom. For the new parlor Alexander ordered wallpaper from France, the design depicting the story of Telemachus, the story he had been reading in French as a boy in the pasture in Ireland when he had fallen asleep and allowed a cow to destroy the book. He had seen the wallpaper design in the beautiful home of Andrew Jackson in Nashville on his last trip South and had learned it was the only such design then in America. But Mr. Jackson had graciously told him where it could be obtained.

By September the new wing was completed, and all during the fall and winter the family gathered at frequent intervals about the hearth in the old, intimate sitting room, to discuss the new educational project: Father Thomas, his rocker pulled close to the fire, hugging his gray woolen shawl about his narrow, stooped shoulders, offer-ing nuggets of wisdom only long experience could furnish; John Campbell, realistic, practical, still dubious but giving freely of his legal advice; Matthew McKeever, speaking out of his hard, searing experience in operating with his wife, Jane, the Mount Pleasant Sem-inary for Young Ladies at nearby West Middletown; Albert Ewing and Robert Henley, voicing the views of businessmen conscious of the responsibility involved in undergirding such a venture.

As Alexander outlined his plan he realized that not only to John Campbell but to the others as well it seemed spectacular. Time and again he went over it: a home school for boys under fourteen years, much of their instruction to be correlated with their play interest; a college preparatory school; a college; and, at the pinnacle, a church. He watched anxiously for signs of approval in their faces, but only Father Thomas nodded in understanding. It was loyalty of the others to him, he realized, which held in check the increasing anxiety with which they viewed the formidable proportions of the new institution.

"It's a magnificent dream, son," Father Thomas encouraged repeatedly, his near-sightless eyes staring into a space as empty as the silence that greeted his words.

"I don't see how the church becomes a part of it," Matthew McKeever said one evening, scratching his head.

"It will not be the church as we think of a church," Alexander explained patiently. "That is, there will be no series of set meetings given to Bible reading, Bible lectures, sermons, church order; instead, these virtues will be practiced daily. This church will be in session seven days a week."

"But Bethany is so inaccessible." Robert Henley spoke up, shifting his position as if uncomfortable. "Back here in these hills, on narrow mountain roads, not even on a stagecoach route." Then he smiled and shrugged his shoulders. "But the very audaciousness of establishing a college here may be a distinction that will insure its success."

Alexander hit the table before him with his open palm. "It will have much more to distinguish it, never fear! There is not a literary college in America that has in it a department of Sacred History and Biblical Literature, do you realize that? Not a single college on American soil in which the Bible is honored with a place on the curriculum to be publicly read by all students. That, my dear family, is the real distinction Bethany College will possess!"

Month after month he wrote of the project in the *Millennial Harbinger*, explaining its structure, clarifying its purpose, urging support. "With me," he wrote, "the formation of moral character and education are identical. We contemplate a scheme in which, in one word, the formation of moral character, the cultivation of the heart, shall be the Alpha and Omega, the radical, regulating, and all-controlling aim and object."

But the response from the churches came slowly. The need for the school was acknowledged, and its location in the seclusion of the Bethany hills proved, as Robert Henley had foreseen, an arresting distinction. The natural beauty of the place was well known among the churches from the frequent descriptions Alexander had given in his paper and from accounts spread by visitors from every section of the country who had responded to Alexander's open invitations to come by for a visit. And in the minds of many people the hills, reaching almost the proportions of mountains in their rugged, unspoiled grandeur, matched in majesty the purpose and lofty plan of the college. But the cost, the practical difficulties, aroused misgivings. The churches were poor, struggling with their own obligations, each bent on its own support, and no organization existed among them to promote a common cause. Months passed, and with each post Alexander watched for word that a financial contribution would be forthcoming.

Early in March the group met one morning in Alexander's study, an air of solemnity, an almost frightened hush about them. John Campbell had just returned from a second trip to the state capital in Richmond.

"The charter has been granted," he said. His voice held a note of grim finality. "We are in business!"

In the silence that greeted the announcement, broken only by a shuffling of nervous feet, he pulled a document from his pocket and began to read:

"That there be, and is hereby erected and established, at or near Bethany, in the County of Brooke, in this Commonwealth, a Seminary of learning for the instruction of youth in the various branches of science and literature, and the useful arts, agricultural, and the learned and foreign languages. And be it further enacted, that the said Seminary shall be known and called by the name of Bethany College."

On and on he read, pausing after a provision specifying that the Bible be taught as a textbook; pausing again when he read a provision prohibiting the establishment of any theological professorship.

"There it is!" As he finished he laid the papers on the desk. He ran his hand through his thick brown hair. "On paper! A beautiful dream, we all agree, Bishop. But not a silver dime on hand to buy a wooden peg except what you give yourself."

Alexander looked about the group. The eyes of the others avoided him. A worried frown deepened further the lines on Father Thomas' face; Matthew McKeever leaned his head on his hands, covering his eyes as if reluctant to face the others; Albert Ewing coughed and

325

looked up at the cupola where rain was beginning to patter against the pane of glass. What had he started? A plan without substance? A formless, vaporizing dream? An institution without form, a mockery?

Suddenly Alexander arose and went to the door and threw it open. He stood for a moment, feeling the spray of rain on his face, looking out across the hills like a man searching for that one miraculous, transcending token that he was doing God's will. Then he returned to his chair by the desk and dropped to his knees. One by one the others followed.

Softly at first, and then like rolls of the distant thunder that began to reverberate through the hills, his voice filled the room. "Guide us, O thou great Jehovah." On and on he prayed, ending in soul-searching humility, "Not our will, O Lord, but thine be done."

The men had scarcely risen to their feet when a knock at the half-opened door was followed by Jim Poole's apologetic face in the opening.

"Mis' Bishop said I get this letter mixed wid hers," he said, extending an envelope to Alexander. "She done opened it and said you gentlemen would want to see it quick."

Alexander took the envelope. It was postmarked Benvenue, King and Queen County, Virginia. Puzzled, he extracted from the torn end a single sheet of paper, silence filling the room as he scanned it. Then, slowly, he raised his eyes.

"It's a communication from George M. Pendleton of Virginia," he said, a mixture of wonder and awe on his face. "His brother, Philip B. Pendleton, who was a fellow delegate of mine to the Constitutional Convention ten years ago, died in December. He had read of the college plans in the *Harbinger,* and in his will left $1,000 to the new institution."

Chapter 27

"IT IS THE YEAR OF OUR LORD 1843." ALEXANDER SPOKE ALOUD TO HIM-self as the hands on the clock in the study moved silently past the hour of midnight. He placed the Bible he had been reading in the drawer beneath the seat of the high-backed writing chair the family had given him for Christmas, and leaning forward, turned out the bear-oil lamp on his desk. In the darkness he got up and drew on his fur cap and greatcoat, and walked outside, closing the door carefully behind him. For a moment he stood stockstill, staring in reverence at the stars; abandoning himself to the beauty of the night.

Smoke curled from the chimneys in the big house, and the pines stood tall and dark in the white light of the three-quarter moon. Laughter and happy voices came to him through the cold air. The young people were returning from a sleigh ride for the hot oyster stew Selina would serve around the dining-room table to welcome in the New Year. All the family were together for the first time in several years, and the house was running over with young life: Lavinia, married two years before to young William K. Pendleton of Louisa County, a member of the faculty of the new college; Clarinda, a handsome young woman of twenty-two, more demure than Lavinia but equally popular; Margaret Brown, now fourteen, who had entered Philip Fall's school for young ladies located now in Nashville in the fall but had come home for the Christmas season; young Alexander, twelve, irresponsible but feeling himself a man; Virginia, nine; and Wickliffe, six, an especially charming lad who had inherited his father's sensitivity to the things of the spirit and who promised to follow in his footsteps; and the two daughters of his brother Thomas—Lavinia and Mary Jane, who had joined the family group a year ago following the death of both of their parents. Maria Louisa had died two years before, another victim of the dread consumption. Her young husband, Robert Henley, continued to live on their nearby farm and was at the house tonight as was his other widowed son-in-law, John Campbell from Wellsburg, and several students from the college. It was a congenial, God-loving, God-fearing family, and it was still growing. Another baby, named Decima because she was the tenth girl, had been born two years before, and Selina was again with child, due to be delivered in the spring.

Suddenly Alexander pulled his fur cap closer about his ears and turned up the collar of his coat. A brisk walk under the stars would be good for him. With long strides he covered the distance to the road and, on impulse, vaulted the fence in one quick leap.

"Not bad for fifty-five years!" he chuckled to himself, and then the thought sobered him. The years should be reckoned by more than physical vigor. He walked rapidly, the white road, hard packed with snow, stretching into the horizon as endlessly as his holdings of land stretched in all directions; as endlessly as the new church established by the Restoration Movement was spreading.

Christian churches, dedicated to the unity of all believers in the lordship of Jesus Christ, were organized now in every state in the nation, their spires and steeples or simple, rough meetinghouses accepted marks on the religious skyline. The membership numbered almost a hundred thousand; state organizations were assuming permanent form, binding the groups together for cooperative effort; periodicals were still springing up, some to die overnight, some to flourish; and colleges were being started with surprising, and of late disturbing, frequency.

He reached the bend in the road from where he could see the dark outline of the square new four-story Bethany College building and the equally imposing Steward's Inn, and stood looking about, his mind flooded with memories, his heart reeling with emotion. Three short years ago it had been a dream, but now it stood, mute testimony to God's guidance, all doubts evaporating in its shadows, the faith of its founder crying aloud in its strength.

The time had been right. The decade beginning with 1840 was, according to the Millerites, to mark the destruction of the world. Instead, it was proving one of startling progress. The tide of immigrants from across the Atlantic was swelling the population to more than twenty million. The invention of the telegraph had proven practical and communications were being sent daily over the wires crisscrossing the land like ribbons, like the rails for the steam cars, spreading in all directions. The future of the college was as bright as the promises of God.

The two buildings had cost $23,000, and after the initial start of actual construction, the money had come with an ease that surprised even Alexander. He had given $10,000 and ten acres of land, and from the churches had come almost $26,000 in pledges, half of it now paid in cash. His original concept of a fourfold educational plan had narrowed as the school was put into operation on two practical levels: the college itself, already a tangible reality, and a preparatory school for boys up to fourteen years of age, also in operation on a limited basis in a building on the hill at Point Breeze, caring for fourteen boys and with a capacity for twenty-five.

The college had formally opened in November 1841, with Alexander as president and chairman of the board of trustees, and with a faculty of five men. On the opening day, 101 students had registered, coming to the remote community from nine states. Some had ridden horseback, some had been brought by their parents in the family carriage. Those coming by river had been advised to stop at Mrs. Miller's Tavern in Wellsburg; while those traveling by stage from the East had been cared for at Mr. Lawson's Stage Office in West Alexander, Pennsylvania, until arrangements were made to bring them in the school hack driven by deaf-and-dumb Sam, a free Negro who had taken refuge on the Campbell farm, to Bethany. Five courses of study were offered. Alexander taught sacred history; Andrew F. Ross, languages; Charles Steward, mathematics; William K. Pendleton, natural philosophy; and Robert Richardson, chemistry.

329

Selina's brother, Edwin Bakewell, served as steward, supervising the boarding, lodging, and laundry of the students, for which, with tuition, a fee of $150 a year was charged.

Alexander looked toward Steward's Inn where the boys were lodged, his thoughts for the moment upon the rules he had so carefully formulated. They were simple but they were enforced, and discipline, at first a minor problem, was now excellent. The rising bell sounded at dawn, with classes starting at six-thirty. The dress of the students was uniform, of dark gray with the coat single-breasted, the collar bound with braid and bearing in each end a star worked in black silk. No student was allowed to keep weapons, gunpowder, dogs, or servants, and smoking cigars was forbidden. The student body had grown in the three years of the school's existence to 156, although fifteen boys had been dismissed the second session because of indolence, and one student, William Stamps of Mississippi, the seventeen-year-old nephew of Jefferson Davis, had been accidentally killed by a fall while skating on the ice on Buffalo Creek. A strong college spirit was developing. Two literary societies had been organized and chartered by the state, proudly boasting the new college seal: "Truth bears the quiver but Science gives it the bow."

Robert Richardson had designed the seal, and Alexander felt a tinge of emotion as he thought of the awkward, shy, kindly physician. He and the polished, courtly William Pendleton, trained in the law, had become like his own flesh and blood. Robert's precise, analytical mind, mystical and yet scientific in its meticulous attention to detail, supplemented William Pendleton's accurate scholarship and logical thinking, and together, Alexander realized, they balanced his own tendency to envision truth in bold, panoramic, sweeping strokes. He often wondered if he could carry his growing responsibilities without the two men. Both were not only skilled in their professional fields but stalwart aides in securing support for the college and both shared his dedication to the Restoration Movement. William was serving also as bursar for the college, and he and Lavinia had built a house on the rising ground which had been a wheat field adjoining the campus, calling it "Pendleton Heights." Robert was continuing to help with the *Millennial Harbinger*, and as Alexander

330

started to retrace his steps back to the house, he reflected gratefully how the young doctor's recent articles on "The Spirit of God" had tempered his own too coldly rationalistic views of this awesome mystery. Although he still felt that the Holy Spirit was not "poured out" upon believers but came as a result of faith established by searching the Word of God, he realized such a view could lead to a mechanical literalism, and he was thankful Robert Richardson's mystical nature was keeping him in balance.

The New Year moved swiftly. In February a sheep buyer called at the house. When he introduced himself simply as John Brown, Alexander felt an immediate interest in him.

"I feel very close to another man named John Brown," he told the gaunt, angular fellow as they stomped across the field, inspecting the sheep. "If there's anything in a name, we should become great friends."

Brown laughed, the stern lines of his face softening under his tawny skin. "I'm a friend to all who love the Lord, sir," he said. "And I feel it my duty in these parlous times to break the jaws of the wicked and pluck the spoil out of its teeth. That's my real mission in life."

Alexander looked curiously at the close-cropped head, now uplifted to the sky. The fellow resembled one of the Old Testament prophets. "You are a student of the Bible, I see," he said.

"I am that," Brown replied. "I could match you in quoting it any day, Bishop Campbell." He turned his light blue eyes upon Alexander and seemed to study him. "I used to be a good church member, but I'm beginning to think the church may not be the real temple of God. Too many of the parsons I know are defenders of the slave system."

Alexander pursed his lips thoughtfully. "Many of them also denounce it. I have freed what slaves I had. The system is a colossal evil and will be abolished someday."

Brown nodded. "Someday," he said, "someday—" He shook his head as if to clear his thoughts. "But today I'm a sheep buyer, just now building up a strain for Captain Heman Oviatt of Richfield, Ohio. Let's see what you have in this back pasture."

331

The yard bell rang and Alexander knew it meant a summons to the college. He pulled off his thick mitten and held out his hand. "Continue looking over the flock, Mr. Brown," he said, "and select the pair you want. You'll find my farm manager, Mr. Anderson, in the shed by the barn. He'll handle the sale for me. I'd like to continue this discussion some time."

As he trudged to the house across the frozen furrows of the cornfield, Alexander looked back at the gaunt figure walking toward the back pasture. Yes, the man did resemble an Old Testament prophet, ready at any moment to break into thundering denunciation of the evils of the day.

In May, Alexander was presented with another son whom he named William Pendleton for his son-in-law and co-worker at the college. Selina was scarcely out of bed three weeks later when late one afternoon a carriage drove up to the turnstile. Alexander was just coming out of his study, and approached the dusty vehicle curiously.

"We've come over mountain, hill, and vale!" called the big man in the front seat, pulling in the reins and waving his Panama hat.

Alexander laughed in recognition and extended both hands in welcome as he went toward the carriage. It was Jeremiah Sullivan Black, the well-known lawyer, and his family from Somerset, Pennsylvania. As he reached into the carriage to shake hands, he recalled with what interest the thoughtful legal mind of this man, imbued with Presbyterian doctrine, had grappled with the simple plan of salvation as he had presented it the last time he had preached in Somerset. Like the rich young ruler, this young lawyer, prominent in politics, devoted to good works, had been almost persuaded. Now, unannounced, he had driven his wife and baby, with the nurse, in the family carriage, over the Allegheny Mountains, through Pittsburgh, across the Monongahela River, to remote Bethany, a long, arduous trip. Why?

For a week the visitors lingered, Selina and Mrs. Black exchanging household views, immersed in happy woman talk, developing a mutual fondness for each other, while the two men conversed for long hours, sometimes while roaming the farm, or walking to and

332

from the college, sometimes in the study, of politics, of farming, of education, but mostly of God and His plan for the world.

"We must leave in the morning," Mr. Black said finally. "We have tarried with you long enough."

"What is long enough?" Alexander countered. "Nothing is ever finished until it is finished right."

The next morning was cloudy with the threat of storm. As the family group sat about the big breakfast table following the meal, Mr. Black slowly arose to his feet.

"Could we conduct morning worship down by the creek?" he asked. "And thus conclude our visit properly—with my baptism?"

The fourth day of July had continued to seem a date of divine significance to Alexander, and to counteract the tendency to make it a festive holiday he arranged to have the college commencement exercises each year on that date. This year, 1843, the second such observance would be held.

The exercises attracted more than fifteen hundred visitors, crowding the village of Bethany and spilling over to Point Breeze and into Wellsburg. Tents were erected in pastures adjoining the campus, and pallets covered the floors of the Campbell house, with plank tables set up in the shade of the maples in the yard at the rear of the house for serving meals.

The ceremonies began with prayer, followed by the reading of the Declaration of Independence, establishing a tradition that Alexander hoped would continue through the years. For five hours the audience sat on backless benches, on wagon beds, or on blankets spread on the wide expanse of thick, cool grass in the dappled shade of the great pines and beech trees in front of the college building, giving patient attention to seven speeches. No degrees were conferred, but to the students who had completed the two years' study at the new college Alexander said with warm feeling: "You are the buds and blossoms of Bethany College's future hope. She is struggling into life; and as she is ambitious to be distinguished not merely for her literary and scientific standing amongst American colleges but for her supreme regard to moral culture and moral eminence, you will be inspected with a jealous eye by her friends and by her enemies. Honor her by your virtue!"

Alexander had promised Selina that after the last visitor had departed he would take some rest, but the next day's post brought a letter from a group of Presbyterian clergymen in Kentucky.

"They want me to debate the issues which separate our two bodies," he told Selina. "The Christians now outnumber the Presbyterians in Kentucky four to one, and they're naturally disturbed at the inroads we're making on their members. They say they want to clarify their position in relation to us, but in reality they want to take a whack at me."

Selina was knitting a blue shawl for herself. She had received the yarn and the intricate pattern as a present from Mrs. Black following their return to Somerset, and she wanted to finish it in time to wear to church on the first cool fall day. But she laid it aside and looked resolutely at Alexander.

"You're killing yourself, Mr. Campbell," she said. "A man can stand just so much. Let the Presbyterians stew in their own juice."

"Oh, my dear, my dear!" Alexander shook his head in amusement and impatience.

"Well, you said yourself the Christian church is growing fast enough. So why do you want to try to convert any more Presbyterians? Let them be!" She picked up her needles, as if to end the discussion.

Alexander got to his feet. "My thought is not to increase our own ranks but to help the sects by pointing them to the truth as I see it." He started down the steps of the porch where they had been sitting to go to his study. "I don't care whether a single man comes over to join us, I still feel it my duty at every opportunity to make our position understood. In that way I can strike a blow for Christian unity."

His opponent would be Dr. John C. Young of Center College, the committee wrote when he replied, accepting the invitation. But the next mail brought a correction. Dr. Young could not undertake so formidable a task, they said.

Alexander smiled at the implied compliment. And then his eyes

334

widened in thoughtful surprise. Dr. Robert J. Breckinridge would be his opponent, the letter went on to state.

"He is a brilliant man," Robert Richardson commented when Alexander told him, "one of the most able Presbyterian preachers in the state, a man influential in political circles, too. His brother, John Breckinridge, is being spoken of as presidential timber."

A week later word came that Dr. Breckinridge had refused.

"I will never be Alexander Campbell's opponent," he had said in declining. "A man who has done what he has to defend Christianity against infidelity and to defend Protestantism against the delusions of Catholicism I will never oppose in public debate. I esteem him too highly."

"Now what will they do?" Alexander laughed to Dr. Richardson and William Pendleton as they sat in conference in his study. "Shall I be left talking to myself?"

Not until he was preparing to leave for Lexington in October for the engagement did word come that an opponent had been secured. It was Dr. Nathan L. Rice, of Paris, Kentucky.

"I would have preferred Dr. Breckinridge," Alexander commented with meaningful brevity to Robert Richardson.

Dr. Richardson smiled and shook his head. "I don't blame you. I heard this man Rice in debate with several of our preachers while I was in Kentucky some years ago, and I feel he has been sharpening his claws for you. He's a fluent speaker, with a rapierlike wit."

"It isn't his fluency I mind," Alexander said. "I've read his speeches, and his type of thinking is not mine. He loves the minutiae in fact and detail, and gives little heed to the over-all picture of God's plan of salvation. He debates for victory, not for truth."

The new Main Street Christian Church in Lexington, erected by the united body of Christians the year before, was crowded on the morning of November 15 for the opening of the debate. Lavinia and Clarinda had accompanied their father to the Kentucky city, and Margaret Brown had come up from Nashville with her teacher, Philip S. Fall. David Burnet had arrived from Cincinnati, and now the three girls, with Mr. Fall and Mr. Burnet on either side, were seated in the front row as Alexander mounted the rostrum.

He smiled at them, and let his eyes rove over the audience before

335

he sat down in the high-backed pulpit chair and crossed his legs, spreading carefully the tails of the new broadcloth coat with its satin lapels and black silk vest that Selina had insisted he have made by the Thomas Hughes tailoring firm in Wheeling. Posters had placarded the whole countryside, announcing the debate with Henry Clay as the chief moderator, and many visitors, he learned, had arrived from Pennsylvania, Indiana, Texas, Missouri, braving the hazards of winter travel to attend.

"I'd like to think this crowd is a tribute to an increasing interest in religion." He leaned over and spoke to Mr. Clay, seated at the moderators' table on his far left between the two other moderators, Judge Robertson and Colonel Speed Smith. "But I think the eminence of you moderators has something to do with it."

Mr. Clay laughed and shook his head. "It is the intellectual stature of you two debaters," he said in a loud whisper. "People are expecting to see giants grapple."

But the debate was not a battle between giants. Rather, it took on the aspect of a quarrelsome, nagging haggle. Stacked on the stand before Dr. Rice were all of Alexander's public utterances as recorded in any printed form, and statements out of context, early views divergent with his later opinions, remarks irrelevant to any of the agreed issues to be debated, were presented by the wily debater with relish and ridicule.

Time and again Alexander sought to return the debate to the issues involved: the method and design of baptism; the divisive tendency of human creeds; the place of the Holy Spirit in conversion. But Dr. Rice refused to separate the facts on these points as revealed in the Bible from his opinions about them.

"My opponent is confusing religion and theology," Alexander stated. "A man's essential religion consists of his faith in what is revealed in the New Testament; his theology, on the other hand, consists of his opinions of what is only partly revealed or not revealed at all. I did not come to debate opinions! I am entitled to mine; you are entitled to yours. It is only upon such ground that we can ever achieve Christian unity."

The wrangle continued for sixteen days, and as it neared its con-

336

clusion Alexander knew it had been a failure. There had been no honest attempt to debate the agreed points; no effort to clarify the Presbyterian position in relation to the new body of Christians. Rather, Dr. Rice's repeated thrusts at the position of the Restoration Movement, misleading, inaccurate to the point of absurdity, filled Alexander with a slowly mounting rage. On the last day of the debate he himself abandoned all pretense of sticking with the points of the debate and launched out in defense of the Movement.

"We preach the Gospel only as promulgated by the Apostles in Jerusalem," he cried. "We use the exact words of inspiration. We command all men to believe, repent, and bring forth fruits worthy of reformation. It is not the object of our efforts to make men think alike on a thousand themes. Let them think as they like on any matters of human opinion, provided only they hold the head to be Christ, and keep His commandments. I have learned not only the theory but the fact, that if you wish opinionism to cease, you must not call up and debate everything that men think or say. You may debate anything into consequence, or you may, by a dignified silence, waste it into oblivion." He paused and looked about. Henry Clay was unconsciously bowing in assent, his hands waving in a characteristic gesture of approval.

"We receive men of all denominations under heaven," Alexander continued, dropping his voice almost to a conversational tone in the hushed attention of the audience, "of all sects and parties who will make the good confession on which Jesus Christ built His church. We propound that confession of the faith in the identical words of inspiration so that they who avow it express a divine faith, and build upon a consecrated foundation, a well-tried cornerstone. On a sincere confession of this faith we immerse all persons, and then present them with God's own book as their book of faith, piety, and morality."

He paused, suddenly aware that never before had he put into words so clear and penetrating the basic position of the Restoration Movement. The awareness struck him with a startling sense of illumination; light from the throne of heaven had been shed upon his mind.

337

And with it came a clear rebuke. He had been trying to debate the issues that separated two bodies of Christians. But God's mind had been in him, turning his mind instead, gently, firmly, to a glorious summation of the things upon which all Christians could unite.

A mist came over his eyes; the audience became blurred. The debate—all debate for him—was over.

Chapter 28

DESPITE THE ACCLAMATION THAT GREETED HIM AFTER THE DEBATE, Alexander returned to Bethany with a heavy heart. A sense of having sown sectarian strife haunted him. The bitterness of Dr. Rice's ridicule, his trivial witticisms which had so delighted the audience would be remembered, widening the sectarian breach. Only the printed debate, if it were widely enough circulated, could alleviate some of the harm, carrying Alexander's logical arguments for the points at issue, and his plea for unity, for readers to study in the quiet of their homes.

"In all the annals of the most swaggering braggadocios and vaunting knight-errants," he told Selina when he returned, "I have met with no one superior to Dr. Rice in the science of egotism, in the rare endowment of unblushing self-congratulation, and in the art of making the worse appear the better reason."

"You are just tired," Selina said, her face reflecting a gentleness which had come with the years. "Lavinia tells me you held the people enthralled every time you spoke. They were delighted."

"It is not enough to delight people," Alexander said. "My purpose was to enlighten them."

He was still smarting under the sense of the futility of the debate, heightened by a sense of guilt in participating in it, when guests arrived on Christmas Eve to sing carols in the new parlor. Robert and Rebekah Richardson came early, their faces glowing from the seven-mile horseback ride in the cold night air. Robert was susceptible to nausea in any wheeled vehicle, and Rebekah had learned to ride behind him on his plodding mare, her arms about his lean waist. John Brown also rode horseback from Wellsburg, reporting Buffalo Creek frozen solid at each of the eight points it crossed the road. William Pendleton and Lavinia came down from their big house, Lavinia's dark chestnut curls, falling almost to her shoulders from a velvet bandeau encircling the top of her head, sparkling with snowflakes from the run down the hill.

Selina busied herself in the dining room, setting out honey cakes and sugar wafers on the table and filling great crocks with hot chocolate, ladling it into earthenware mugs for the guests, her voluminous gray silk skirt rustling as she walked. Laughter and singing voices mingled with the plaintive sound of Cousin Enos' fiddle, which Selina had come to accept, and the clear notes of Robert Richardson's flute. Alexander sat in the big walnut armchair for a time, enjoying it all, and then got up and wandered into the old sitting room, and sat down before the fire, his mug of hot chocolate in his hand. In a few minutes Robert Richardson joined him.

"Christmas is the time for glad tidings," Dr. Richardson said, laying his flute on the mantel and sitting on the sofa beside Alexander's chair. "I heard from David Burnet today. He is jubilant over the outcome of the debate."

"David is always jubilant." Alexander smiled faintly. "He is irrepressible. But as to the outcome of the debate, I can't share his enthusiasm. I read the other day that the Presbyterians are honoring Dr. Rice with the title of Doctor of Divinity as a result of the debacle."

Dr. Richardson laughed. "It's the church's way of soothing his wounds. I remember they did the same for Mr. McCalla whom you worsted."

Alexander smiled. "I should be flattered, I suppose," he said, "to

339

be the means of effecting the theological promotions of my opponents. Yes, McCalla was dubbed D.D. after his debate with me, and even Bishop Purcell is much nearer the papal throne, I understand, since our encounter."

"Mr. Burnet said he had been studying your final speech," Dr. Richardson went on. "He is convinced that in it you clearly defined for the church a body of doctrine which we lacked. We have no creed, but at last we have a body of beliefs specifically stated." He paused and stared at Alexander. "He feels a thoroughgoing national organization is now all that is lacking to make the Movement into a permanent institution."

"I know, I know." Alexander stood up and placed his mug of chocolate on the mantel. "It is inevitable. We must have more cooperation among the churches. We need it for general efficiency as well as mutual understanding and encouragement. But—" He hesitated.

"Mr. Burnet thinks we should organize a Bible society soon," Robert went on after a moment. "He feels we can do more in a year through our own society than in a century through the Baptist Missionary Society which we are working through now. I feel his argument has merit. Perhaps we should exhibit our attachment to the Bible by having our own society for its circulation."

"And we should have a missionary society, too," Alexander agreed almost in exasperation. "Many people still misunderstand my attitude on such organizational efforts. I am not opposed to them; I am opposed only to using them to extend sectarian views."

"Then why not encourage Mr. Burnet in his efforts?" Robert queried.

"There are several reasons." Alexander paused and poked at a log in the fire. "For one thing, we are straining every effort just now to gain support from the churches for Bethany College. Think how two or three additional appeals on a national basis would undercut our requests for the college!"

The door opened and William Pendleton came in. "I have a feeling you two are talking church business. Don't you realize it is Christmas Eve?"

340

"There is no more appropriate time," Alexander replied. "You're still young, William, inclined to be coltish; that's your trouble."

"I'm all of twenty-eight," William Pendleton replied, sitting down and extending his long legs comfortably toward the fire. "Although right now I feel forty!"

Dr. Richardson laughed. "Forty is not old! I'm almost there myself. I was thirty-seven in September."

Alexander sighed. "And I am fifty-six." He looked at the two men, reflecting. "What a chain we form of viewpoint, experience, and training. That, with the common passion we share, gives us a unique opportunity to serve the cause of restoring the first church." He looked into the fire and poked again at a glowing log. "The cause that was born in these hills," he went on, almost to himself, "the cause that is centered in Bethany. I'm frank to say I'm wondering," he turned abruptly to the two men, feeling their questioning eyes upon him, "if there is danger in all this talk from Cincinnati that our cause is about to be centered elsewhere?"

The winter passed into spring, and with it came absorbing duties. Walter Scott wrote he was leaving Carthage, Ohio, after giving thirteen years to evangelizing in the Western Reserve, and moving back to Pittsburgh. In April he arrived at Bethany on horseback, his family traveling on to Pittsburgh by boat and stage, and for three days he visited with Alexander.

"I plan to publish a weekly paper," he said, his face still alive with enthusiasm. "I'll call it the *Protestant Unionist* and circulate it through the Pittsburgh area. I'll preach at Alleghany City and Pittsburgh. I won't be idle."

"Wherever you are, Walter," Alexander said, placing his hand on the thick shoulder of the shorter man, "I know you'll be doing God's will. That can't be said of many men. Personal ambition gets in the way; pride; love of power; lots of sinful traits." He smiled ruefully as the dark eyes of the evangelist looked into his, puzzled, probing his heart. "Yes," he nodded, "meaning me!"

The *Millennial Harbinger* was circulating in the thousands, but subscribers were slow in paying. Alexander went over the records one morning and was dismayed to find more than twelve hundred had not paid anything in four years; three hundred had not paid in fourteen years, and more than a hundred subscribers had never paid. He made plans immediately to employ several agents to aid in collecting and in securing new readers.

As Dr. Richardson had predicted, David Burnet continued to agitate for a cooperative society among the churches and agreeing with him in substance, Alexander wrote frequently in the *Harbinger* acknowledging such a need, but always with a note of restraint.

He pleaded for time; he pleaded for more support from the churches; he pleaded for more understanding of the Restoration Movement's aims, purposes, ideals. Where would it lead? His mind groped for the answer as if in a fog. But David Burnet persisted, relentlessly pushing for such an organization. He had become a power among the churches as the pastor of the dominant Sycamore Street Christian Church in Cincinnati, the first man to hold a settled pastorate in the new Movement, and his voice was increasing in weight and influence.

In February 1845 Alexander received a lengthy letter from him. It had happened. A Bible society had been organized by the four Christian churches in Cincinnati. It was to be projected on a national scale, David wrote frankly. It would seek support from all the churches.

Alexander sat motionless for a long time with the letter before him. And then, slowly, the apprehension in his heart turned into a flame of hot indignation. David Burnet was presumptuous; he was defiant. Sick at heart, he picked up his pen.

"It is premature, to say the least," he wrote the younger man, trying to hold his anger in check. "Your 'society' does not represent the whole brotherhood. Other claims come first, yes, such as Bethany College!"

The reply came swiftly, stinging, unrepentant. "Was there a convention to establish Bethany College, the claims of which must now be heard, and until they are heard the Bible Society must die in despair? Do you mean this Society, composed of some hundreds, cannot ask for aid of their brethren, but Bethany College, called into being by one man, may?"

Alexander was still smarting from the retort when news came a few days later that the Cincinnati brethren had organized, not only the Bible Society, but also a Sunday School and Tract Society. The Tract Society, he learned, was for the publication of church literature.

For four days Alexander secluded himself in his study. Since the day he had mounted the crude platform at the Brush Run meetinghouse to preach his first sermon, the mantle of leadership had been on his shoulders. He had called into being the Restoration Movement; its roots were in his heart; its fruits were his to claim. He was "The Bishop," "The Sage of Bethany"; and Bethany was the heartland of the Movement; his publication house the acknowledged fountain head for its national literature. Now other voices were being raised from Cincinnati, speaking for the churches, speaking for the brotherhood of the Church of Christ, the Disciples of Christ, the Christian Church. Called by whatever name, it was the early church of the New Testament Apostles, and he had been the leader in restoring it. And now?

With a sense of compulsion he could not define he wrestled like Jacob with his angel, pleading for a blessing, praying for humility. He must gain this victory, the final decisive victory over himself. He remembered the admonition of Raccoon John Smith. "The love of God," the forthright old man of God had said to him, "shed abroad in our hearts will more effectively unite us than all the wisdom of the world combined." Alexander needed the love of God in his heart.

Gradually he gave a tacit blessing to the new societies. But he could not yet encourage them.

"If it be God's will their plans succeed, time will reveal it," he said in March as he left Bethany on an extended tour through Virginia. As spring advanced he planned to turn his face West, to Illinois and the Missouri country beyond the Mississippi River. He would forget all else but the furtherance of the Restoration Movement. William Pendleton was made vice-president of the college to preside during his absence, also taking over, with Dr. Richardson, Alexander's classes.

Alexander reached Richmond on March 23 and preached for a week at the old meetinghouse on Eleventh Street, a guest in the home of the pastor, his good friend James Henshall, and his wife. Elder Henshall was a hearty man, genial and God-fearing, and his kindly, tolerant spirit eased Alexander's hurt.

Alexander was preparing to leave on the morning of March 31 to take the cars to Charleston and thence proceed West, when a sheriff's deputy appeared at the door of the Henshall house. A damage suit had been filed against him by an Allan B. Magruder in the Circuit Court, charging libel and defamation of character in the amount of $12,000.

"It seems my value is going up," he told Henshall with a laugh. "When Dr. Sleigh sued me at Philadelphia nine years ago, before he ran back to England, my price was only $10,000. At least my alleged libels are not decreasing in value. The *Harbinger* is still being read."

Henshall's round eyes reflected his amazement. "But how does the man feel he was libeled?"

"Magruder has been discredited as a lay preacher and member of the church at Charlottesville and dismissed from its ranks," Alexander explained as they made their way to the courthouse to post bond. "I called attention to the fact in the *Harbinger* only because he claimed to be representing our cause at a Lord's day convention in Baltimore last January at which he created quite a disturbance. His behavior cast such unfavorable reflection on the Movement I could not allow it to pass without correcting the impression that he represented our views. He wrote me at length, objecting to my statement, but I had no idea he felt injured to this extent. I suppose I should see a lawyer. I'm scheduled for dozens of speaking engagements ahead; I can't afford the endless time lost in court procedure."

"By all means," agreed Henshall. "I suggest you see the Honorable

344

James Lyons. He's a real Christian if I ever knew one, a tower of civic strength here in Richmond, and a fine lawyer."

But James Lyons could not take the case.

"Christian people should settle their differences without the notoriety of public hearings," he told Alexander plainly. "Besides, Allan Magruder is a personal friend and has already asked me to represent him. He feels his reputation has been injured. The *Harbinger* is a powerful instrument of public opinion, Mr. Campbell. I'm an Episcopalian, but I read it regularly myself."

"But what does the man want?"

Mr. Lyons shook his head. "He doesn't want the money. He wants an apology."

"An apology!" Alexander cried. "I shall never apologize for writing the truth! I made a simple statement of recorded fact which I had the duty to do. The *Harbinger* is a news organ as well as a journal of religion."

"But there was much to be said in explanation of the recorded fact," Mr. Lyons said patiently. "Mr. Magruder will be satisfied if you will do that."

"But how?"

"Print in full the letter he wrote you which explains his behavior at both Charlottesville and Baltimore."

"Why didn't he say that's what he wanted!" Alexander said in exasperation. "A simple request from Magruder would have saved us both the expense and embarrassment of this public lawsuit. I shall set the matter straight in an early issue of the *Harbinger*."

"These libel suits by preachers are becoming monotonous," he told Henshall after they had left the lawyer's office. "If this ever happens to me again, I'll make no bond, or allow any of my friends to make one for me. I'll go to jail if necessary and stay there until the judgment of the court is rendered. I'll rest everything in the hands of the Lord and be done with it!"

From Virginia Alexander went by stagecoach to Cincinnati and there, without any delay or any attempt to contact the brethren, boarded a Mississippi steamboat bound for St. Louis.

At St. Louis the levee was crowded, the cold, frosty air alive with activity. At least fifty steamboats were taking on and discharging passengers and wares; barrels of flour and great sacks of corn, hogsheads of tobacco and molasses were stacked about the docks. He stayed in the bustling city only long enough to arrange for transportation by stage and horseback into the raw, unsettled frontier country, and two days later was in Columbia, speaking before the annual meeting of the 150 Christian churches in Missouri, representatives of the more than fifteen thousand adherents of the new Movement in the state.

On through Missouri he went, preaching, visiting, counseling, listening, immersing himself in the sheer, naked joy of spreading the Gospel, pushing to the back of his mind the sense of sinful pride that haunted him, wearing himself to exhaustion each day and welcoming at night merciful sleep.

A flood of memories crowded over him as he alighted from the stagecoach in Hannibal. A light rain had fallen and the streets, rutted from wagon wheels pressing West, held little pools of muddy water reflecting the wavering glimmer of the bear-oil lantern swinging at the entrance to the Cow Pony Tavern. He stood for a moment looking about, a sense of wonder and recollection flooding his heart, warming his spirit.

Barton W. Stone had died in this village scarcely six months before while on a preaching tour from his home in Jacksonville, Illinois. His kindly spirit seemed now to hover about Alexander; his simple faith in God's care to engulf him. Barton Stone had been willing to be a humble instrument of his Lord. No haughty pride had tortured him; no vaulting ambition; no lust for power. He was content to be used wherever the Lord had need of him, confident of God's wisdom.

"I know in whom I have believed." Alexander spoke softly into the darkness. They were the words Barton Stone had repeated on his deathbed. " 'And am persuaded that he is able to keep that which I have committed unto him against that day.' I know that my Redeemer lives!"

Inside the tavern he scrawled his name on the buckram-bound

ledger at the long counter beside the stairway, and then sat down heavily on the wooden settee and unfastened his greatcoat while a Negro boy took his bags to his room. Beside him lay a magazine tossed by some traveler. He picked it up. The *Messenger and Advocate*, he read, and turned to the index page, his eyes widening in surprise. It was edited by his old friend, Sidney Rigdon. For a moment he closed his eyes to blot out the image of the man, sensing again the grief, the disappointment, the aching loss he had felt in the desertion of this once-trusted friend to the queer cult of Mormonism. He turned the pages of the paper idly. In a corner of the third page his eye fell upon an editorial comment:

What will come next? "Protestant Unionist!" Queer enough! The Calvinists protest against the Methodists; the Paedobaptists against the Baptists; the Unitarians against the Trinitarians; and the Campbellites against all!

Staring into space, Alexander laid the paper down. *Et tu, Brutus!*

Back in St. Louis by December, he took passage on the packet steamer *Brooklyn* for Wheeling, tired and half-sick. Cold, sleet, and snow followed the boat down to Cincinnati where ice on the river compelled him to make his way across the state by sleigh and horseback. It was Christmas Eve when he reached Bethany, and he found the house strangely quiet. He had been gone nine months and had traveled more than seven thousand miles.

Margaret Brown, as he knew, had married during his absence. Her young husband was John Ewing of Nashville, a nephew of Alexander's widowed son-in-law, Albert Ewing. But he had not been told that Lavinia had become seriously ill. Selina was making daily trips to Pendleton Heights, keeping a teakettle filled with whiskey and hot water boiling in the sickroom over the fireplace, allowing the vapors to penetrate the room, hoping they would relieve the chest congestion. She was applying plasters of horse-radish and mustard leaves to Lavinia's chest, and as a demulcent drink kept on hand huge pitchers of comfrey and spikenard, with sassafras pith and slippery elm.

And Father Thomas was not well. To relieve Selina of his care, Alexander took him in February to West Middletown to stay for a

347

time with Jane and her husband, Matthew McKeever, hopeful that the change would benefit him.

The college affairs were running smoothly; William Pendleton had done well. Support was increasing; the student body growing. The records showed that almost $40,000 had been contributed to the school. Robert Richardson's eyes were again giving him trouble, and to relieve him of some of his editorial work on the *Harbinger*, Alexander appointed William Pendleton as co-editor, increasing the size of the magazine to sixty-four pages.

Spring came slowly, the days damp, the chill penetrating. Lavinia died in May. William Pendleton seemed like a man bereft of his senses. For days he remained in seclusion in Pendleton Heights, seeing no one, refusing to meet his classes, eating nothing. He tendered his resignation to the college, and Alexander refused to submit it to the trustees.

"Give yourself time, William," Alexander told him early in June. "Get away from this house for a while."

William agreed he was right. "I suppose I could be doing some good raising money for the college. I'll go on a tour for it."

"You need more of a change than that," Alexander said. "Why not a sea voyage? Go to Europe; forget the problems of the college and of the *Harbinger* for a time."

William shook his head. Tall, erect, his courtly figure seemed stooped now, his aristocratic face somehow gaunt. "No," he said. "Work is the answer. I need more work. And I don't need to forget the college; I need to forget myself."

Alexander put his hand on the younger man's shoulder, his heart filled with a quiet, understanding sympathy. "You need to get away for a while," he repeated. "Mr. and Mrs. Thomas Semple of Pittsburgh, our good friends, wrote me recently that they were planning a trip to Europe and suggested that I let Clarinda go with them. Why don't you go along, too?"

On the twentieth day of July the party sailed, and soon the mails were bringing happy accounts of the journey. Alexander read each letter with mounting satisfaction. Death could never be the victor. Life must go on.

The mails also brought disturbing word from the churches. The two societies organized by the brethren in Cincinnati were running into trouble. They were soliciting support on a national basis with resultant confusion as to their status. Who had authorized them? Who was defining their functions? Who was overseeing their expenditures? David Burnet wrote Alexander in frank despair, pleading for his help in clarifying the situation, urging his cooperation, soliciting his counsel. But Alexander remained adamant.

"We must move carefully in these matters," he said to Robert Richardson one morning as they discussed the matter. "More than we need a cluttering of societies, each seeking support, we need a strong, central national convention in which all interests should be cared for which meet the approval of the churches."

"It is being rumored," Dr. Richardson said, shifting his feet as if embarrassed, "that your support is withheld for other reasons."

The two men were in Alexander's study, going over copy for the *Millennial Harbinger*. Abruptly Alexander pushed his chair back from the desk and stood up.

"That I am jealous of Bethany as the focal point of leadership?" he asked with equal candor. "That I fear the mantle of authority is passing to the shoulders of David Burnet? That a rival publishing house in Cincinnati may usurp my own publishing ventures?" He stared at Robert, the pain on his face only half-concealed. "That the claims of Bethany College may no longer have priority among the churches?"

He turned and walked to the open door and stood looking across the fields while Dr. Richardson sat silent, his lean face compassionate, his eyes reflecting his understanding of the torture of this great soul. Only the humming of a bee against the glass in the cupola and the sound of men working in the adjoining field broke the stillness in the small room.

When Alexander turned again to face his companion, the lines in his face had softened, and his deep blue eyes under their craggy brows held a new strength.

"My constant prayer, Robert," he said as he resumed his seat, "is to be able to say with John the Baptist, 'I must wane that thou may

349

wax.' " He looked at the younger man almost with pleading. "Help me to remember that, Robert! Help me to do it! Because I love David Burnet like a brother."

An organization of woolgrowers had been formed by the sheep buyer, John Brown, now a frequent visitor at the Campbell home, and Alexander had been requested by him to serve as its chairman, with William Ladd, a Quaker farmer of Richmond, Ohio, acting as secretary, at a meeting in June at Springfield, Massachusetts. Brown had established a commission wool depot in that New England town, in partnership with Simon Perkins of Akron, Ohio, and although Alexander recognized the sound work the man was doing to grade raw wool adequately and establish fair prices for the growers, he also detected an increasing instability about him. His obsession over slavery dominated his thinking. He was a pronounced Abolitionist and Alexander found himself taking frequent issue with him over the violent methods he proposed to achieve that end.

During the summer Bethany was laid out as a town, with lots marked off and sold as new business houses opened despite an epidemic of smallpox that broke out in October in Wellsburg. Theron Bakewell arrived for a visit with his sister Selina and stayed at the Campbell house until after Christmas. He had given up his store boat and was living in New Martinsville, Virginia. Edwin Bakewell had grown restless in his job as steward at the college and was anxious to move on West. Alexander offered him the use of a farm he had acquired in Illinois, and in November he resigned from the college as steward, and left with his wife Julia and their four children for the new country, agreeing to farm the acreage on shares for Alexander.

And then in December there came another letter from Alexander's uncle, Archibald Campbell, in Newry, Ireland.

Alexander smiled ruefully as he opened it. Uncle Archibald was one of the most learned and influential elders of the Presbyterian church in North Ireland. His heated correspondence with Alexander for more than twenty years had never wavered in reflecting his violent objection to Alexander's rejection of infant baptism and his own

350

stanch, stubborn, loyal adherence to Presbyterian doctrine. But now he wrote:

I read your debate with Dr. Rice through the medium of your Dungannon friends. I consider him a much more wily antagonist than either McCalla or Walker. I would not be surprised if the popular cry would be in his favor. But, notwithstanding his ingenuity and wiles, I am now at last constrained to give up infant baptism!

There was more to it but the lines became blurred as emotion filled Alexander's heart. He put the letter in his pocket and that night, in the privacy of their bedroom, he read it aloud to Selina.

"Such a man's testimony weighs more with me than that of many scores of others," he said as he finished. "If the essence of our Plea has penetrated into Uncle Archibald's mind, I think the cause of primitive Christianity is ripe for cultivation in that country."

He sat down and began unfastening his boots as Selina sat silent, braiding her hair.

"Yes," she said finally, as if they had been discussing it all along, "the Lord is preparing hearts in the old country for a personal visit from you. I hate to have you go so far away, but I feel, Mr. Campbell, the time has come!"

Chapter 29

WITHIN A FEW DAYS IT WAS DECIDED THAT ALEXANDER SHOULD VISIT the fledgling churches in Great Britain. He was not unmindful that the trip would give him opportunity to contact relatives and old friends, returning to the land of his birth after forty years as an acknowledged religious leader, a man loaded with honors, wealthy beyond the dreams of his youth. But in moments of deeper reflection he reminded himself that he would go as Paul had gone to the churches at Ephesus and Corinth and Philippi, spreading the glad tidings of the Gospel, making more firm the foundation of the Movement which had followers now in many countries and organized church groups in all the major cities of the English-speaking world.

He wrote of his plan in the *Harbinger*, and no sooner was the copy in the mails than he received a letter from Elder James Henshall in Richmond. Henshall, too, had relatives in Great Britain; he, too, had been desirous of making such a trip. Why not join forces?

Alexander heartily agreed. He liked James Henshall, a quiet, good-humored, self-effacing man; a conscientious Christian, an able preacher, and a loyal friend. He would make a good traveling companion.

Alexander left Wellsburg on April 2 by stage for Baltimore where the two men met by prearrangement. Alexander preached twice at the church on St. Paul Street and then they went on to New York by stage, both men preaching along the way.

The news of his journey had preceded him and wherever he stopped, demonstrations of affection and voluntary gifts of money for "the deserving poor of Ireland" warmed his heart. But no incident gave him more pleasure than the renewal in New York of his friendship with Robert Owen, whom he had not seen since their debate in Cincinnati in 1829. He wrote the family:

The old gentleman shows as few of the scars of time upon his face as any man of his years I know. His unyielding good nature and peculiar indifference as to public opinion, with his pleasing enthusiasm, seem to soothe his mind amidst the reverses of fortune and the universal failure of all his utopian schemes of human improvement. He never alluded to the scenes of Cincinnati, but with the most perfect courtesy and kind feelings, inquired after everything interesting to me, and especially after the health and happiness of my father. I am sorry for the honor of sectarian Christianity but glad for the honor of human nature, to state what you may have heard on other occasions, that of all my opponents in debate, the infidel, Robert Owen, was the most candid, fair, and gentlemanly disputant I have yet met with; and a saint in morality compared with some of my opponents.

With James Henshall he visited Trinity Church, marveling at its magnificence, its cost of $386,000, its seating capacity of 1,000. "We are just as proud of worshiping the Lord in a fine cathedral as in living in a fine mansion ourselves," he said to Henshall. "We have three kinds of prides, and not any one of the three is spiritual pride: personal pride, family pride, and church or meetinghouse pride. It means, 'I am a big man, belong to a big family, live in a big house, and worship in a big church under a very high steeple.' This is to speak sincerely and without hypocrisy, and explains many a strange notion."

At noon on Tuesday, May 4, 1847, the two men boarded the *Siddons*, and with mingled exhilaration and apprehension Alexander stood at the ship's rail and watched the boat lift anchor and wind its way out of the crowded harbor.

The *Siddons* was a sailing vessel of the Liverpool Dramatic Line, launched at New York nine years before, its length almost one hundred and fifty-eight feet, with a beam of thirty-five and a half feet and a depth of twenty-one feet in its hold, and carried twelve cabin passengers, the largest ship Alexander had ever been on, although its furnishings were not so splendid as most of the river steamers on which he had traveled. But it was comfortable, and its master, the well-known Captain Edward B. Cobb of Liverpool, invited Alexander to preach each Lord's day. The voyage took twenty-five pleasant, uneventful days, and on May 29 they dropped anchor at Liverpool.

Alexander was not surprised to find John Davis and his wife Mary, of Millington, awaiting them at the docks. Davis had been for years one of his most steady correspondents. At his own expense he had stereotyped and scattered throughout England and Wales a special edition of *The Living Oracles*, and had been instrumental in introducing Alexander's other publications into Great Britain. After stopping to permit other friends to greet them at the Customs House, Davis drove them to his residence in the valley of the Dee, seventeen miles from the city.

For the next month Alexander and Henshall preached at Chester

353

and Liverpool, at Shrewsbury, at Nottingham, at Leicester. Journeying on to London, they obtained housekeeping rooms on Surrey Street on the Strand, and remained for three weeks, Alexander preaching at the Disciples Meetinghouse on Elstree Street, as well as in the Mechanical Institute, the Alvetian Rooms near London University, and in both Baptist and Unitarian churches. The American ambassador, Mr. Bancroft, invited them to visit with him the Houses of Parliament where they heard Lord Brougham and the Duke of Wellington speak.

"Of all the incongruities I have seen in the whole development of legislation," Alexander confided to Henshall that night, "that of the bishops sitting in lawn or in their white sleeves, and legislating as ecclesiastico-political peers of the realm, with the lords temporal, caps the climax!"

Henshall laughed. "You're quite right," he said. "Where do you think it will lead?"

Alexander slowly unfastened his heavy boots. "I pretend to no gift of prophecy, Friend Henshall, but one or two events appear probable: Many of the English clergy will go over to popery, or the church and state will be separated. Nothing can save the Protestantism of England from decay but the disseverance of church and state."

The last week in July Henshall went to Stockport to visit his relatives, and Alexander crossed the English Channel to Paris. He lingered a week in the French capital, absorbed in the beauty of the public grounds and gardens, visiting the art galleries, observing the gay infidelity of the people. Louis Philippe, he thought, was a clever man and a popular king, but not to be compared with Queen Victoria and her consort, Prince Albert.

Glad to return to England, he rejoined his companion at London and the two men left by easy stages for Scotland, preaching along the way at Banbury, Manchester, Wigan. Timothy Coop, the leading spirit among the Wigan group of Christians, urged them to stop at Sunderland.

"There's a shipbuilder there, Jonathan Douglass, who is such a great advocate of the Restoration Movement," he told them, "that he has given the name 'Alexander Campbell' to one of his vessels."

354

Mr. Douglass proved a hearty host, and for three days they visited among the members of the church in Sunderland, Alexander preaching three times and Henshall twice to the group assembled in the long shed on the shipyards.

It was the fifth day of August, almost thirty-eight years to the day from the time Alexander had left the country, that they reached Edinburgh. The religious climate of Scotland had changed. The Burghers and the Anti-Burghers, as Alexander had known them, had been reabsorbed into the Church of Scotland, and the Independents, whom he had admired under the leadership of the Haldane brothers and the great Greville Ewing, were now divided into two quarreling groups, the Morrisonians and the Congregationalists. Greville Ewing was dead and the aged Haldane brothers were away.

"I've had quite an experience," Alexander greeted Henshall a few days later when Henshall returned to their lodgings from a sight-seeing trip. "Three of the ministers of the Morrisonians called upon me—a Reverend Kennedy, a Mr. Hunter, and a particularly obnoxious character named James Robertson."

"No doubt they wanted you to preach for them?" Henshall removed his thick cravat with a flourish.

Alexander laughed. "Their thoughts were on anything but the furtherance of the Gospel, from what I could gather," he said. "It seems they hold views quite similar to ours, but they are fiercely jealous of their foothold in Scotland. They resent our coming here. They as much as told me so. They've lost several members to a group of our brethren now meeting on Nickleson Street, and are fearful of the inroads the Restoration Movement will make as a result of our visit."

"And just what do they propose to do about it?" Henshall inquired, sitting down.

"I think," Alexander said, "they will attempt to discredit me. They questioned me closely concerning my attitude on slavery, and when I told them I did not approve of using force to abolish it, they insisted I state that view publicly in a lecture."

"Did you agree?"

"Of course not," Alexander replied. "I told them I did not feel I

355

could contribute anything to the settlement of the slavery issue in America by discussing it on the public platform in Scotland. My purpose here is to preach the Gospel. Our preaching commitments extend through September, and I have no free time before we sail on October 6."

"You'll probably never hear of it again," Henshall said.

"I'm not so sure. I have a feeling they will do anything to stop my preaching, or to discredit it. They said they'd be at the Waterloo Rooms tomorrow night when I speak there, for what purpose I don't know, as I'm sure they have no interest in hearing my sermon. They consider me an intruder, bent on proselyting their people, and their feeling seemed so intense I think they'd burn me at the stake if they could, particularly the man Robertson."

As Alexander and Henshall approached the entrance to the Waterloo Rooms the next night, a group of men reading a placard moved aside for them to pass and the placard, posted beside the low entryway, came into view, the words leaping at them in the semigloom of the Scottish summer evening:

Citizens of Edinburgh
BEWARE! BEWARE!
The Reverend Alexander Campbell of Virginia
United States of America
Has been a Slaveholder Himself and Is Still
A Defender of Man-stealers!

Alexander felt his face drain of color, and then become prickly hot. James Henshall stopped, staring at the poster, unbelieving. He turned to Alexander, but Alexander motioned him to silence and led the way into the hall.

The long, narrow room was crowded, men and women sitting quietly but tense, an undercurrent of excitement, of rising indignation about them, an unspoken questioning in their attitude. A few had come out of curiosity, seeking excitement, but most of them were God-fearing, simple people who had come to hear the Gospel proclaimed in its original purity and power. The slavery issue did not exist for them except as a remote, rumbling monstrosity, unthinkable as a Christian practice. That any minister of the Gospel

356

could be contaminated with it was beyond the bounds of their reason, but they were fair-minded and they waited now for him to speak.

Similar placards, Alexander learned from the chairman, had been posted in all parts of the city, and as he arose to speak the room quieted as though all the noises of the assembly had been swept aside with a broom. Quietly, as though he were speaking to his own students at Bethany, he denounced the placard as untrue.

"If these posters are true, it would be as if the capital of Scotland had been invaded by the devil himself," he said. "But they are not true. They are as false as they are treacherous in design. In view of this attack, tomorrow evening I shall give you my full view of the problem of American slavery." He paused for a moment, sensing the stirring in the crowd, and then quietly began his sermon on the Holy Spirit.

Alexander was almost through shaving the next morning when Henshall answered a knock at the door and came back with a square sealed envelope.

"By special messenger," he said, handing it to Alexander. "I can guess who it is from. Our friends are determined that you shall remember them."

"Our friends?" Alexander smiled grimly. "We are better known for the enemies we make." He scanned the contents. "It's a challenge from Robertson, a challenge as insulting as the placards. He says he is prepared to prove that my position and opinion on slavery are at once unholy, unchristian, and inhuman. He wants publicly to debate with me."

"But you told him you had no free time," Henshall said. "We have booked ourselves solidly until we leave."

"He knows that," Alexander said, nodding. "That's the reason he is challenging me. He will use my refusal to discredit me." He stood for a moment and then slapped his towel across the tin water basin. "But I'll accept! I'll debate him in the public press!"

Mr. Henshall looked doubtful. "You will be tangling with an unworthy opponent, and from what I've seen of his methods, an unscrupulous one. I wouldn't do it."

357

But Alexander appeared not to hear him. "We could exchange, say, three essays, each to appear simultaneously in the Scotch Anti-Slavery magazine, the *Christian Messenger* in England, the Abolitionist paper in Washington City, and in the *Millennial Harbinger*. We could cover every issue he has raised. He claims to have some connection with the Anti-Slavery Society here and I'd be glad of the chance to set myself straight with it."

As Alexander pushed his way through the crowd that night to mount the rostrum at Waterloo Rooms for his announced address on slavery, groans and hisses and stomping feet greeted him. He looked out over the hostile sea of faces, listening to the jeers. His enemies had done their work well. The people were plainly prejudiced against him before he spoke. Then he held up his hand for silence.

"I come here not to defend slavery," he said, "but to condemn it. To make clear my position which has been so wickedly misrepresented. I am as much opposed to this evil institution as any man alive. But I am opposed also to force and violence. That is the point on which my enemies are hanging their attack. Slavery in America must be abolished, but it must be done by lawful, peaceful means, and it can be if we allow God's wisdom to enter our minds and direct our thoughts. God's way is by persuasion, not by force, and that is why I am as much against the extremists among the Abolitionists in America and in Scotland as I am against the defenders and advocates of slavery itself!"

He talked for an hour, summarizing the history of slavery in America and the world, and the progress being made to end it, interrupted now and again by hisses, jeers, and a few times by a scattering of applause.

"But the question under discussion," he said frankly in conclusion, "was not activated by my accusers out of sympathy for the slave. It was from hostility to the Restoration Movement now in progress; it was from fear of the inroads this Plea is making in their own sects. To discredit this Plea, they have agitated the slavery issue, defaming me, not to benefit the slaves but to turn away the ears of the people from the truth I preach."

At the rear of the room Alexander saw James Robertson's bulky figure rise, his arms waving, his voice shouting threats and insults. Others joined him, and the room became a whirlpool of tumult with Alexander at its calm center.

"I will debate you, sir," he said when he could be heard above the uproar, "if you—"

"You've changed your unholy mind then, have you?" Robertson yelled, interrupting him. "Or has somebody done it for you? 'Tis a pity you're not a free, independent Scot like myself, loving the Lord and hating a hypocrite!"

"Mr. Robertson, sir!" Alexander said, with difficulty holding his anger in check, "I leave by steamer early in the morning for Aberdeen. As you well know, I have engagements scheduled until I leave the country. I can debate you only in the public press!"

"Hoot! Hoot! I'll nae be put off in that fashion!" Robertson shouted. "You are opposed to the abolition of slavery, you, a minister of the Lord's Word, and I will force you to say so on the public platform, that I will!"

"I'm opposed to making any man's stand on slavery a condition of Christian communion, if that's what you mean," Alexander shouted back, now thoroughly exasperated. "If you refuse to meet me in the public press, that is all I have to say to you." He began to gather his books and papers. "Good night, sir!"

"We haven't heard the last of this," Henshall said as they reached the safety of their lodgings. "Robertson has lost face with the very people he has tried to impress. He'll hound you like a baying dog!"

"I'm afraid you're right," Alexander said. "The man's a religious bigot of the worst kind. He'll do anything to keep me from preaching."

And he was right. In Aberdeen, Banff, Montrose, Dundee, Alexander found himself denounced by placards more and more violent until at Dundee the virulence of the attack seemed even to him to go beyond the limits of Christian patience and endurance. He had seen the same placards before in Banff, but the viciousness of it stung him when they passed it on the public market place while on the way to the Baptist meetinghouse where he was to speak.

People of Scotland, Beware!

Mr. Alexander Campbell and his colleague, Mr. Henshall, from Virginia, USA, are at present lecturing throughout Scotland on Christian Union

and

The Apostolic Commission—the Obedience to the Gospel

or

How to baptize a family one day into fellowship of the American Baptist church and to sell them the next by public sale, or otherwise, to the highest bidder as they do the horse, the ox, or the ass; tearing asunder "those whom God hath joined together." This is the Campbellite "Obedience" to the Gospel!

"A lie often enough repeated is believed by many," Alexander observed to the presiding officer, Mr. Malcolm Malcolm, at the close of his sermon that night. "I am beginning to feel I should make arrangements to debate publicly the instigator of these placards before I leave Scotland. I can schedule a debate the last of September on a free day I was hoping to devote to personal business."

"You know who the man is?"

"Yes, he's a man named James Robertson, a former Baptist preacher, now gone with the Morrisonians, the most intolerant of all the sects in Scotland, I am told."

Mr. Malcolm looked thoughtful. "I wonder if he is the same James Robertson who was publicly censured and dismissed by the Baptist church for abusing his mother?" he said. "I understand that fellow went over to the Morrisonians."

A gleam appeared in Alexander's eyes. "You think he could be?" He stared at Mr. Malcolm, and then shook his head incredulously. "Surely a man who had been publicly censured by his own church, and for such a reason, would not dare challenge the Christianity of another!"

"This man would," Mr. Malcolm said. "He's avid for publicity, and seems bent on mischief wherever he can cause it, although he's pretty shrewd with it all."

Alexander sat late that night, working on a letter to the editor of the Edinburgh *Journal*. Logically, step by step, he stated the biblical and Christian view of slavery, and the attitude of the United States Government toward it. And then he wrote:

360

A word or two on the challenge tendered me from the Reverend
Mr. Robertson: I will meet Mr. Robertson provided only that he be
not that Reverend James Robertson who was publicly censured and
excluded from the Baptist church for violating the fifth commandment
in reference to his mother, of whom I have heard something in Dundee.
All of which is most respectfully submitted to the citizens of Edinburgh, especially to the Scottish Anti-Slavery Society, by their most
abused but unresentful friend,

A. Campbell of Bethany, Virginia.

He folded the letter and sealed it, marking it for posting. If the
exposure was justified, it should quiet Mr. Robertson; if not, it would
give Alexander the opportunity to shout the truth of his slavery
views in refutation of the lying placards. Tomorrow, he reflected
as he blew out the cluster of candles on the table, he and James
Henshall would be in Glasgow.

Chapter 30

GLASGOW WAS A GREAT METROPOLIS NOW, ALEXANDER THOUGHT AS HE
sat in the two-wheeled cart beside James Henshall and listened to
Alexander Paton, the leader of the little Glasgow group of Christians who had met them at the station, point out the spots of interest
on the way to their lodgings. The once-familiar streets held few of
the landmarks he had known. New buildings, some of them four
stories high, had replaced the rows of shops with their half-doors
and overhanging balconies. The streets were still crowded with
hurrying people, but carts and two-wheeled cycles now pushed
through the crowds, and horse-drawn conveyances holding as many
as twenty persons clattered down the brick paving that had replaced
much of the cobblestones. Even the University had changed. In-

dustrial Glasgow had crowded in to impair the beauty of the old seventeenth-century buildings and a movement was on foot, Mr. Paton said, to sell the site to the Union Railway Company and move the University to Gilmorehill on the outskirts of the city. Only the National Cathedral, Alexander thought as he glimpsed it at the corner of High Street, remained the same, as changeless as the Gospel it proclaimed.

They passed the Presbyterian meetinghouse on Ann Street where Alexander was to speak the following night, and abruptly Mr. Paton leaned forward and slapped the reins as if to hurry the horse, his thin face a mask. But Alexander's quick eye caught sight of the placard beside the entrance.

"My enemies have followed me here, I see." He tried to put a chuckle in his voice.

Mr. Paton shook his head and looked away, as if embarrassed. "Those placards are all over the countryside. But they have only aroused more interest in your visit. You'll have greater crowds to hear you because of such persecution." He turned to Alexander, his wide blue eyes staring at him in sober intensity. "We believe in you, Mr. Campbell," he said. "And we're prepared to stand back of you."

"Thank you," Alexander said.

"This persecution is turning into a boomerang," Henshall said. "Since it started, greater crowds than ever have poured out to hear Mr. Campbell. He's had a chance he otherwise would never have had to spread the Restoration Plea."

"But that result was evidently not foreseen by my tormentors," Alexander said, "and as a consequence they've become increasingly inflammatory. But I've offered now to debate publicly with their chief instigator and we're waiting for their next move."

For ten days Alexander and Mr. Henshall preached in Glasgow and the surrounding area—at Kilmarnock, at Ayr, at Irvine, at Paisley; confronted at each place by placards denouncing them, heard everywhere by great crowds of people, some curious, some hostile, but most of them sober-minded, concerned primarily with hearing the Gospel.

They returned to Glasgow on Monday, September 6, for Alexander's final sermon before their departure the next day for Ireland. A month's visit in the land of his birth, a busy round of preaching appointments among the scattered churches there, and they would sail on October 4.

"I have a premonition." Alexander spoke soberly as he removed his boots and prepared to stretch out on the bed for a brief rest before the evening meeting. "Some calamity has happened or is about to happen, Friend Henshall. I can't shake off the feeling."

"Nonsense!" Henshall said. "You're just tired. I'll go down and order some hot milk for you while you rest."

But in a few minutes Henshall was back, his round face flushed with excitement. He came in and closed the door quickly behind him, standing with his back pressed against it.

"The calamity has happened!" he said almost in a whisper.

Alexander opened his eyes. "What do you mean?"

"There's an officer below with a warrant for your arrest!"

Alexander swung his feet to the floor and sat up. "Arrest?" he echoed blankly. "On what charges?"

"Libel!" Henshall came over and began helping Alexander put on his boots. "From what he told me I gather James Robertson claims he was not the Robertson who dishonored his mother; you libeled him in insinuating it." He straightened and shook his head. "Instead of ridding yourself of the man, Mr. Campbell, you've given him another string for his bow."

When the hearing in the magistrate's office was over, Alexander sat in final conference with Joseph Clark, the barrister Alexander Paton had hastily secured for him. This was not the first time he had become embroiled in the law, but this time the accumulated torments of the past weeks smoldered into a sense of outrage and injustice he had never experienced before. He forced himself to listen as the barrister went on speaking.

"The suit is for 5,000 pounds," he was saying, "but it was not filed with any real hope of collecting that amount, or any amount. It is plainly an effort to force a final public humiliation upon you."

"It's a disgrace to all Scotland!" Alexander Paton declared.

"Did I commit libel?" Alexander asked frankly.

363

"Not in my opinion," the barrister replied. "You were entirely within your rights in your letter to the Edinburgh *Journal* in specifying you would not debate the Robertson who had dishonored his mother. There were three Baptist preachers by that name in Edinburgh at the time, and this Robertson could be the one. But even if he is not, your statement is not libelous in the opinion of either the magistrate or myself."

"Then why can't the suit be dismissed at once?"

"The magistrate doesn't want the responsibility of dismissing the warrant on my demurrer. A demurrer is a question of law which he justly considers should be passed upon by a higher court. So we must wait the action of the Superior Court on our appeal. That will require a few days, and in the meantime, of course, you can make bail and proceed on your way."

Alexander shook his head. "I will cancel my engagements in Ireland."

"What!" protesting Henshall. "You have hundreds of friends here who will gladly go your bail!"

"I will go your bond myself," said Paton.

"The magistrate of his own volition has reduced the damages claimed by Robertson from 5,000 pounds to 200 pounds," explained Clark, "which shows well enough how trivial he feels the charges are. The warrant invoked in your arrest is called *in meditatione fugae,* and was designed solely to prevent the escape of fraudulent debtors; it is rarely used, never in cases like this. There's no reason why you should not make bail and go on to Ireland for your engagements."

Alexander stood suddenly erect. "Gentlemen, this is the third time I have been sued for libel. I have let my friends make bond to keep me out of jail for the last time. To prison I'll go!"

"You haven't seen our jails, Mr. Campbell," Mr. Clark said quietly. "It may require ten days or so before our appeal can be heard by the Lord Ordinary. That is a long time to remain in a prison cell during a Scottish winter."

Alexander shook his head. "I don't relish the prospect but I am not unmindful"—he paused and looked about at the earnest face of

James Henshall, sitting in rigid protest in a high-backed chair against the wall of the little room—"that such a move will give increased emphasis to our cause. I will not be exactly a martyr but at least I shall be a witness of the lengths to which religious bigotry leads!"

Mr. Henshall got slowly to his feet. "I love you, Mr. Campbell," he said slowly, "but you are acting unwisely. You are a stubborn man, and a proud one. Your incarceration will be an effective sermon but, frankly, I think you are acting like a fool!"

" 'We are fools for Christ's sake,' " Alexander reminded him quietly. "With the immortal Paul, in nothing am I behind the very chiefest Apostles, though I be nothing."

Ordinarily Alexander went to sleep readily, but tonight he remained awake a long time in his prison hammock. The cell was cold, the air stale, the thin blanket over him felt clammy. He began swaying the hammock from side to side on its giant iron hooks, but on one side it bumped against the wall of the six-foot cell, striking on the other the small table and three-legged stool that reminded Alexander of the milk stools at the farm, the room's only furnishings. He maneuvered it to a stop and lay motionless, staring wide-eyed at the blackness about him, for the first time an apprehension in him that he may have acted too hastily. He was a stubborn man, and a proud one, as Henshall had said. He should not have compared himself to the Apostle Paul.

The case attracted wide attention, as Alexander had foreseen it would. Each day brought visitors to the prison, curious men and women hopeful for a glimpse of the white-haired zealot who stood so stanchly for freedom of religious opinion; puzzled men from the Anti-Slavery Society who questioned him closely on his slavery views and went away satisfied; friendly members of the churches who brought comforting gifts of food and warm bedding. It was ten days before the case was called for a hearing in the court of Lord Murray. Within a few minutes the warrant, *meditatione fugae*, was dismissed for lack of evidence.

"This man Robertson must indeed be a lunatic," Mr. Clark said after His Lordship had left the courtroom. "He is still not satisfied!

365

He is appealing to the Courts of Sessions. That is madness, as it will only increase his court costs and litigation fees. He knows there is no ground for this warrant, as the court has just held. But you are free and your worries are over, sir; the case is virtually closed."

Alexander coughed, a deep-chested rumble, and put his hand to his head. He felt hot and chilled by turns, aching with the cold he had caught in the damp cell. "Then I shall preach at Paisley tomorrow afternoon as I had planned, and here in Glasgow tomorrow night," he said.

"You're still a stubborn man, Mr. Campbell." Henshall smiled wearily, taking his arm. "The thing for you to do is get rid of that cold or we'll never be able to sail for home on the *Cambria* next month."

The next few days passed like a troubled dream for Alexander, and as his cold worsened, he regretted he had not taken his friend's advice. His sermon in the crowded Baptist Church at Paisley could scarcely be heard because of his rasping hoarseness; back in Glasgow he attempted to preach but his voice failed completely, and for three days he stayed in bed, burning with fever.

At the end of the week he had recovered sufficiently to make a quick trip of six days through Ireland, highlighted by a tenderly reminiscent visit at Newry and Market Hill with Uncle Archibald Campbell. On October 4 he was beginning to feel more like himself as he stood beside Henshall on the deck of the steamer *Cambria* and watched the shore fade gradually into a purplish haze.

The *Cambria* carried 110 passengers, and her owners, the Cunard Company, boasted she was the fastest ship afloat. Built only two years before, she regularly made the passage from Liverpool to Boston in eleven days. But it was the morning of October 19 when she nosed her way into Boston Harbor.

"We're four days late, but even at that we've actually crossed the ocean in two weeks!" Alexander marveled as he and Henshall made their way into the Customs House to claim their baggage and pick up mail awaiting the incoming passengers. "It took us fifty-four days on the *Latonia* thirty-eight years ago. The sailing vessels, I fear, are doomed!"

They were at the mail desk and Alexander turned aside to shuffle through the packet of letters handed him. He had been gone now for five months and Selina had never failed to write him each week. But there was nothing here from her. Twice, three times he sorted the letters, and then tore open one from Clarinda. As he read it the color drained from his face; his heart became a stone in his chest. He reached out his hand for the arm of his friend, his voice choking. "My son Wickliffe," he said, staring at the letter incredulously. "My son Wickliffe was drowned!"

For a long time that night Alexander walked the streets with the faithful Henshall, rebellion in his heart, unburdening himself in little unexpected bursts of confidence, grateful for Henshall's silence. Tragedy had invaded his home many times, but not since the death of Margaret had he felt so completely bereft. Consumption gave a warning, casting its shadow many months before taking its toll, but to lose this young son so full of hope and promise and by accident was almost more than he could bear.

"It was such an unnecessary death," he said again as they entered their room at the Astor House long after midnight. "To catch himself under the apron of the mill dam in Buffalo Creek so close to the house, and drown in three feet of water! It's hard for me to say, Thy will be done!"

Henshall made no reply as he closed the door. He felt he could never learn really to know this strange complex man whose austere manner and sometimes caustic tongue concealed such great loneliness of heart. He was a willful man, filled with conviction, consumed by a great cause; at ease among any group of men and yet a solitary figure. And he was bereft now, a bleakness in him which the strain of the recent months did not lessen.

"God will give you peace, sir," Henshall said at last quietly. He turned away.

Alexander seated himself on the bed and stared at his friend, the deep-set blue eyes burning with a faith and a conviction which no words could utter. He spoke slowly, hoarsely, as though the words were pulled from him with an effort. "Though He slay me,

367

Brother Henshall, yet will I trust Him!" He dropped his head in his hands. "But I still do not understand!"

Back at Bethany, his grief-filled, clinging reunion with the family made each one of them seem dearer and closer to him than ever before. Because of his imprisonment he found he had acquired the status of a hero-martyr in the eyes of the Bethany College students, and their approval of his course of action under attack warmed his heart. He was still weak, and the new bereavement was an agony that slowed his recovery. But time's healing process began its slow work, and as the weeks passed he gradually picked up his tasks. In December he received an exultant letter from Alexander Paton in Glasgow. The Lords of the Court of Sessions at the November term had not only confirmed the judgment of Lord Murray in dismissing the *fugae* warrant, but had assessed all costs of the action against Robertson.

"Your friends here," Paton wrote, "earnestly urge you to authorize a civil suit in damages against this man for false imprisonment. Only thus can justice be done and the world conclusively shown that you were entirely blameless in this disgraceful action."

"He's right!" Alexander's son-in-law John Campbell told him when he read the letter. Robert Richardson and William Pendleton agreed.

Alexander hesitated. He would not be motivated by revenge. "I'll do it," he said finally, "only to clear my name completely. But I'll accept not one penny in damages from the man."

"Bethany College is always a worthy supplicant," William Pendleton said with a quiet chuckle. "And as a good Christian, Brother Robertson would no doubt like to make a contribution."

Four months later news came that a judgment of 2,000 pounds sterling had been awarded Alexander by the courts. To escape payment, Robertson had fled to France.

"I regret now I authorized the suit," Alexander told John Campbell the next time he went into Wellsburg. "I don't want to see the man's life ruined. I will gladly forgive the debt and forget it. I

368

hope I never hear of it again." And as he rode toward home an hour later he knew in his heart he never would.

The Treaty of Guadalupe Hidalgo ended the war between the United States and Mexico on February 2, 1848, and the country became wildly jubilant over the acquisition of vast territory. But as Alexander read the news he felt a new dread. Was the heart of the nation becoming corrupted by the spoils of war? Was martial glory blinding men to its horrors? Was this a mild forecast of what could happen if the tensions over slavery resulted in civil strife? Vainly he tried to dismiss the disturbing thoughts, but they crept into his activities by day and haunted his fitful sleep by night.

Death again invaded his home. Selina's mother passed away in May, and in October his daughter, Margaret Brown Ewing, died of consumption. But the hurrying rhythm of each day's events pushed him on, crowding to the background personal grief.

The country was sick. Violence was beginning to flare; a national crisis seemed imminent. Alexander's conscience became tormented by the realization that he had never spoken out publicly against the demonic method of settling disputes called war. In early November he arranged a speaking engagement in Wheeling at the Lyceum, and for two hours spoke against the evil, tracing the history of warfare, demonstrating it as unjustified under the teachings of Jesus, denouncing it as the greatest of all human curses. The hall was crowded and the audience listened intently, but only a perfunctory round of applause rewarded him.

"It was a brave effort," Father Thomas told him the next day, his sightless eyes staring out the window of the sitting room at the snow which had fallen during the night. He pulled his shawl closer about his shoulders. "It's chilly, son. It's as if I feel a cold wind from somewhere."

In March 1849 a letter came from Henry Clay.

"The senator is reviving one of my early dreams," Alexander told Selina as they sat before the fire that evening after the children had

369

gone to bed. "He's offering a provision to the new constitution of Kentucky similar to the one I tried to propose for Virginia twenty years ago."

"The one about freeing the slaves?" Selina asked, looking up from her knitting.

Alexander nodded. "He's proposing that all slaves born after a certain date, in this case 1855 or 1860, would be automatically freed when they reached the age of twenty-five."

"I always did think you had a good idea in that plan," Selina said. "It would take care of the slavery question all right. Only I wish you had been the one to propose it instead of him. You were just ahead of your time, that's all."

Alexander stood up. "I don't care who gets the credit for it," he said, "I think it should be done. If Clay can do it in Kentucky, perhaps other states in the South will follow his lead. I'm going to help him if I can."

After his classes at the college were over the next morning he went immediately to his desk in the study.

"It's a 'Tract to the People of Kentucky,'" he told Dr. Richardson when he handed him some closely written sheets late that night for insertion in the *Harbinger*. "Kentucky occupies a special niche in my heart because the first great impulse to our cause was given there. My heart burns to see our friends there rid themselves of slave labor—the most expensive and least productive labor in the world as even a casual comparison between Kentucky and her neighboring free state of Ohio will prove. One single clause in their new constitution would do it."

"This may throw you into the political arena again," Dr. Richardson warned as he looked over the sheets.

Alexander smiled. "I may also be thrown into hell for acting like a coward. I agree with Edmund Burke that all that is necessary for evil to triumph is for good men to do nothing."

The "Tract" appeared as the leading article in the May 1849 issue of the *Millennial Harbinger*, and was also distributed in pamphlet form throughout Kentucky. Alexander felt he had many

Christian friends in the state who might be influenced and at the close of his long, vigorous statement he appealed directly to them:

But what is the duty of a Christian citizen of Kentucky? The time has come when no citizen of that state can say, I can neither prevent nor perpetuate the indefinite continuance of slavery in Kentucky. I did not put it upon the state, nor can I take it off.

By a single clause in the new constitution you may put an end to it beyond a given day. The Ruler of Nations in His providence is now conferring this power on every voter in the state through this convention for the new modeling of the constitution. By his vote every citizen may from and after a given day be regarded as an instituter or annuller of slavery in Kentucky.

The time has come in Kentucky when the Christian population will speak and vote like Christians at the polls and demonstrate its love of liberty and right, by extending them to everything in the form of man that breathes its air or treads its soil. It will be her greatest honor, as I am sure it will be her greatest interest, to be first in this great work.

The "Tract," as he had anticipated, produced immediate response. Henry Clay was warmly appreciative, but although he was hopeful he did not appear optimistic of the outcome.

"Alas!" he wrote to Alexander, "masters sometimes as well as slaves hug the chains that enslave them. But we shall endure. God bless you!"

A month later he received a communication from his old wool agent, John Brown, now in Akron, Ohio. He enclosed a pamphlet bitterly denouncing the "Tract," entitled, "A Defense of Southern Slavery Against the Attacks of Henry Clay and Alexander Campbell." It was anonymously signed, "A Southern Clergyman."

Across the front of the pamphlet John Brown had written in bold, scrawling letters, "Welcome, Bishop, to the ranks of the Abolitionists!"

Chapter 31

It was tuesday morning, october 10, 1849. alexander lay perfectly still, his eyes roving the bedroom, a rawness in his throat and a flush in his face which had not been there the evening before. Selina must have arisen early; her place beside him was vacant. His black alpaca traveling suit was hanging on the costumer in the corner, his beaver hat on the table beside it, his high boots stood beside the low rocker. In the corner was his portmanteau, still open but packed with his personal toilet articles and notebooks. Alexander, Jr., was to drive him and William Pendleton in the buggy to Wellsburg at noon, to catch the afternoon steamer for Cincinnati.

He got up and went to the washstand and dashed some cold water from the pitcher on his face and ran a comb through his white hair, but his long cotton nightshirt, open down the back and fastened only with two stout cords at the neck, felt cold flapping against his legs and, suddenly weak, he climbed back into bed.

"It's almost seven o'clock." Selina spoke from the doorway, her tone a mixture of surprise and annoyance. And then her black eyes peered more closely and she came into the room and put her hand on his forehead. "Open your mouth," she said gently. She pressed down his tongue with her strong thumb and looked at his throat. "You're feverish, and your throat is red. I'll make up a weak solution of chloride of lime for you to gargle." She pulled the bedclothes up around his neck. "You're staying in bed, Mr. Campbell."

"I can't," he protested. "I have to go to Cincinnati! It's the meeting to organize the Convention!"

372

"You're sick from overwork," she replied. "You're killing yourself, what with worrying about the country and all. Those preachers can organize the Convention without you." She paused at the door. "Mr. Pendleton is here. I'll let him come in if you promise not to talk too much."

Alexander sighed and closed his eyes, and when he opened them the tall figure of his son-in-law was standing by the bed. Twice his son-in-law, Alexander thought, looking at him. Lavinia's widower and now married to Clarinda. The two girls had been closer than any of his children, inseparable in their play, sharing their work, pacing each other in their studies; their disappointments a common burden, their triumphs a common joy. And now Clarinda was taking her sister's place in the heart and life of this man. He held out his hand.

"Selina says I must stay in bed," he said. "And perhaps she's right. With a sore throat and fever I have no business in a town just rid of cholera. You can write me about it, and bring back a full report. It will be a historic meeting."

William Pendleton gripped his hand. "Shall I give them your blessing?"

Alexander smiled. "Tell them to follow God's guidance, not mine." He cleared his throat and when he spoke again his voice was firm. "Tell them I believe a national convention should be formed. But it should never replace the work of the local church; it is only for performing services the churches cannot perform single-handed." He stared intently at the tips of his fingers. "Just because there is no New Testament authority for such an organization does not mean we are acting in an unscriptural manner. I am beginning to realize, William, that to ask for a positive precept for everything in the details of the church is as irrational as to ask for a uniform standard of apparel for all persons in the church." He laced his fingers together and folded his hands across his chest. "No, in all things not of faith, piety, or morality, the church in its aggregate character should be free, unshackled by any apostolic authority. Tell them that." He closed his eyes and swallowed, as if in pain. "And, yes, give them my blessing."

In three days Alexander's fever was gone and by the end of the week he was again at his desk, scanning the mail. The Convention had assembled as scheduled on October 23, William Pendleton wrote, at the old Sycamore Street Church where David Burnet preached, now moved to the corner of Eighth and Walnut streets and called the Christian Chapel. More than a hundred churches from eleven states were represented, with the messengers numbering 156. An organization had been effected, a name chosen: "The General Convention of the Christian Churches of the United States of America," and officers elected. Alexander had unanimously been chosen as the first president.

Alexander laid the letter aside and sat for a long time, his mind going back through the years, touching the milestones, reviewing the changing concepts that gradually, almost imperceptibly, had worn away the corners of the simple blueprint for the restoration of the early Church drawn up forty years before.

Instead of a leaven within the lump of the organized sects, working silently, steadily, mightily for unity, the Restoration Movement was now openly and unabashedly a separate church party, a distinct entity numbering almost two hundred thousand adherents. The focus of the body had shifted away from Bethany, away from the man who had nurtured it, who had led it like Moses out of the wilderness of confusion and the threat of chaos into the wide plains of an ordered plan. But the change was more than that of locality. It was wider and deeper than that of mortal personalities. It was more real than that of academic speculation. The Movement had now little of the original simplicity it had so fervently sought to emulate in the early New Testament church. Machinery was clanking; societies were functioning; planning committees, responsible, authoritative bodies were set up with rules, regulations, resolutions.

Maybe it was all according to God's blueprint instead of his, Alexander mused, as each mail brought more news of the progress of the new body. He pondered each decision that was being made: the encouragement of Sunday schools as a feature of every church; the more meaningful content that was to be given to the ordination of ministers; the recognition as delegates of all who attended regardless of whether they had been officially designated by their local churches; the emphasis on missionary endeavor.

"The missionary fervor of the churches is at such a high pitch," William Pendleton wrote, "that we have formed a specific society for that purpose, calling it the American Christian Missionary Society. And we are beginning work at once. An able man, Dr. Judson Barclay, has volunteered to go to Jerusalem in order that we may obey the scriptural injunction, 'First in Jerusalem,' and has been appointed to journey to that field as soon as feasible."

"God has guided them in that decision," Alexander commented to Selina as he read her the letter that night. "A missionary society is vital to any body of Christians working to spread the Gospel. But, aside from the Convention itself, it is the only organized society we need at this point in our development. We will weigh ourselves down with machinery. I hope David Burnet will see the wisdom now of not insisting on maintaining his Bible Society, and especially his needless Tract and Publication Society. I think I'll remind him," he added with dry humor, "that great men change their minds."

"You've certainly been ready enough to admit you've changed yours," Selina said. "That shows, like you said, Mr. Campbell, you're a great man yourself!"

"At least I do have that one qualification, don't I?" He chuckled. "However, it may be that my youthful intolerance has been merely distilled into something like understanding. It may even be that I've grown a little wiser. I hope so."

Selina sighed. "People should realize that and not be always throwing up to you what you wrote in the *Christian Baptist*."

"It is ironic," Alexander said. "Many of our brethren today would bind the churches to every view I once advocated in the *Christian Baptist*, ignoring my current convictions. They don't realize that the view in which I have changed the most completely is that in which I deluded myself with the fantasy that I could reform the church without reforming the individuals in it."

The weather in the spring of 1850 seemed especially bad. Rain fell in torrents, turning the dirt roads to rivers of mud. Buffalo Creek flooded its banks and the Ohio River was on a rampage. Week after week storm clouds hovered in the skies, reflecting the mood of the nation.

California, gold mad, was clamoring for admission to the Union with a state constitution already adopted and a state government set up without consent of the national Congress; Kentucky rejected Henry Clay's emancipation proposal and continued as a slave state; the boundaries of Texas were in dispute; territorial government for Utah and New Mexico was being debated, and through all the clamoring ran the note of internal strife over the slavery issue, increasing in its ominous rumble.

"Never in the history of our nation have we so needed Divine guidance," Alexander said one evening in May, laying aside his copy of the Richmond *Enquirer*. "Civil war appears inevitable unless Christians of all sects can be persuaded to stand united against it." He got up and went out on the porch, staring up at the stars. The odor of new-turned earth hung in the soft spring air. The maple trees were just coming into leaf, their branches making dancing patterns on the ground as the moon sailed in and out among the scattering of clouds. All nature obeyed God's laws; every living thing responded to His commanding voice. Why was man's duty not made as clear? He walked down the porch steps and started for Pendleton Heights. A talk with William would clear his confused thinking.

The next day Alexander began making preparations to tour the country. William had agreed that his duty lay in spreading words of peace. The younger man consented to take over his college classes for the rest of the school year; forthcoming issues of the *Harbinger* were prepared in conference with Robert Richardson. Within a week he was gone, turning his face to the East. In Pittsburgh, Philadelphia, Baltimore he spoke to great crowds, the atmosphere at each gathering tense with foreboding.

As he concluded his sermon before the Baltimore audience on Sunday, May 26, and stepped from the platform, a short, stooped man extended his hand. He was George Tingle whom Alexander had met in Columbus, Indiana, now living in Washington City and a member of the House of Representatives.

"I've come to Baltimore just to see you," Mr. Tingle said, his round face beaming. "To ask you to preach before Congress in the Hall of Representatives next Lord's day."

Alexander smiled, pleased but puzzled by the unexpected invitation. "Is it customary," he asked, "for Congress to assemble on the Lord's day for religious services? Is this an official meeting?"

"It's not an official meeting, but many members of both Houses are most desirous of hearing you," said Mr. Tingle. "God's guidance, we feel, is sorely needed in our national life."

Alexander nodded. The hand of the Lord was upon his shoulder.

The mood lingered all week as he prepared his sermon, and was still upon him as he arose before the assembled legislators on Sunday morning, June 2. He had come down from Baltimore that morning in the cars, accompanied by twenty of the brethren, seated now in the rear of the crowded hall. The trip had taken two hours, the jerking cars meandering through fields and pastures, stopping now and then to clear the track of pigs and cows. Alexander had sat by a window, a sense of detachment upon him, watching the clusters of Negro cabins spotting the roadway, the families sprawled in Sunday idleness about the bare dirt yards. In Washington the atmosphere was heavy with the scent of the catalpa trees. The rains of the spring had spent their force, and as the party drove by the colonnade of the Treasury Building, past the white-marble front of the Post Office facing the austere Patent Office, past the 180-foot-square gray marble shaft which had already cost two hundred thousand dollars and would someday be a monument to George Washington, the dirt on the streets sent up little spirals of dust.

He looked about the hall. Reconditioning for the summer would soon start; some of the carpeting had already been removed. More dismantling would have been done, he had been told, had it not been for the sudden death on Wednesday of Senator Elmore of South Carolina, who had been appointed only the year before to fill out the unexpired term of John C. Calhoun. The funeral had been

377

held on Friday in the Senate chambers and all work in the capitol had stopped.

His eyes ran over the faces of the audience, crowded together now like attentive schoolboys in the House of Representatives: Daniel Webster of Massachusetts was in the front row; beside him William Seward and Daniel Dickinson of New York; nearby Henry Clay sat beside Salmon P. Chase, and in the rear of the room he recognized Jefferson Davis and Stephen Douglas. On the other side of the aisle were grouped men from the House of Representatives: Horace Mann of Massachusetts, whose educational views he followed with interest, sat near the front, and back of him Alexander recognized Thaddeus Stevens from Pennsylvania as well as Richard Parker and James Beale from Virginia.

He was introduced by Congressman John S. Phelps of Missouri, an ardent follower of the Restoration Movement, and turned at once to his text:

" 'For God sent not His Son into the world to condemn the world,' " he read quietly from his pocket edition of *The Living Oracles,* " 'but that the world through Him might be saved.' " He paused for a moment and let his eyes sweep the crowded hall. A God who would give His son because He loved the world would not abandon it now; and a people who could crowd such a hall as this on such an occasion could never be without hope. For an hour and a half he spoke, using few gestures, scarcely raising his voice, radiating a confidence in God's care and everlasting love; implanting faith, reviving courage. And as he preached he could feel the mood of the audience lift as if hungry men were being fed; parched throats were receiving water. A stir of deep, almost physical satisfaction ran through the crowd. At the conclusion, as the assembly rose to its feet and raised its voice in a great hymn of praise, Alexander knew with a certainty that the Almighty Father had again used him as His instrument.

It was late in July when he returned to Bethany. The college commencement exercises on July 4 had been attended by more than a thousand visitors, straining the capacity of the village, thronging the campus, friends of the 140 students enrolled. Alexander scanned with pride the list of graduates Dr. Richardson showed him.

"Young John McGarvy is a fine lad," he commented. "He will make a showing in Kentucky; I'm glad he's returning there to preach. And I'm happy we could confer the M. A. Degree on Charles Loos. He has done well with the preparatory school. Although we're not justified in maintaining it, he is the type of man we want to keep in the Restoration Movement."

The heavy rains of spring had produced another fine harvest. God's mercy endureth forever, Alexander reflected as he looked over the fields. His flock of sheep was now the largest in the state and his agents were finding good markets for the wool. He stayed on the place all summer, keeping in touch with the national situation, conferring with visiting preachers on brotherhood problems, supervising his publishing projects, roaming the fields, pausing often to watch the geese fly low over the woods.

Selina responded to his mood, and he was grateful for her understanding. But she seemed careworn; the responsibilities of the household were heavy.

"I've been invited to address the Bible Union in New York next month," he told her one morning in September. "Why don't you go with me?"

It was a happy, memorable trip. Virginia, budding into young womanhood at sixteen years, accompanied them. They went in the cars and drove from the New York station in a hansom cab to the Astor House, Selina sitting bolt upright, restraining her impulse to direct the driver as he maneuvered the vehicle through a herd of cattle being driven along the streets.

As they sat at breakfast the next morning in the ornate dining room of the Astor House, Alexander looked up from his copy of the New York *Daily Tribune.* "Listen to this," he said, and read: " 'The great feat of telegraphing was accomplished yesterday between here and New Orleans. New York's news was received there and published in the evening papers at the same time as in this city.' Now, that's progress!"

"It's progress, all right," Selina said. "But it's inconsistent. Look at the way the drovers let cattle wander through the streets here! It's as bad as Bethany!"

Alexander smiled. "We're inconsistent and irregular in our material progress as we are in our spiritual growth," he replied. "We lay hold on God and yet we still cling to old habits. Resistance to change, even for our own good, is an instinctive weakness of mankind."

Jenny Lind, "the nightingale from Sweden," was singing at Tripler Hall, but Selina shook her head when Alexander suggested they hear her. "It's too much like a stage play," she said firmly. She glanced askance at Virginia, seated on her right. "Anyway, I'd rather go to the Grand Fair. We can see the latest inventions there."

For a whole day they walked among the booths at the Grand Fair. Alexander stood for an hour inspecting the new McCormick reaper, a device for harvesting wheat. The one displayed was on its way to the World's Fair in London as a present for Prince Albert, but soon the reapers would be on the public market. He thought of Charlie Poole, laboring in the heat of a Virginia summer with a scythe, and resolved to purchase one of the first machines available.

Selina was fascinated with Dr. Lyon's new insecticide and germicide, guaranteed to kill any insect and not harm even babies; she purchased two jars of the mixture to take home. The new dress material, armure, a combination of silk and wool, caught the eye of Virginia and she persuaded her mother to purchase several dress lengths for herself and Decima.

At the meeting of the Bible Union Alexander presented a recent translation he had made of the Book of Acts, for inclusion in the new version of the Scriptures being prepared by the Union.

"Why didn't you make the translation for our own Bible Society?" Selina asked him that evening in their hotel room. "David Burnet would have been glad to have it."

"David Burnet is not even interested in my complete version of *The Living Oracles*," he said grimly. "But I plan to attend the Convention this year. It will be held in Cincinnati again, on the twenty-fourth of this month. If his Bible Society seems a wise thing for our brotherhood to have, I'll do what I can to strengthen it; otherwise,

380

I am in favor of conserving our resources by abolishing it and working through this Bible Union, that is, as long as it remains out of the control of the Baptists."

"We're such a big-talking people about relying on the Bible and all," Selina said, "seems to me we should be doing everything we can to promote the circulation of it."

"You're right," Alexander said quickly. "Next to Bethany College, there is no task nearer and dearer to my heart than circulating the Word of God. But I feel we can do it better through this great Bible Union, which is already established and working well, than through our own feeble society."

From New York the party journeyed on to Canada, visiting former Consul James Buchanan in Montreal, and then down through Ohio and back to Bethany. Alexander left again almost at once for Cincinnati, arriving late for the Convention but presiding as its president over the last two days' sessions, hearing with increasing apprehension the reports of the struggle of the Bible Society and its fellow Tract and Publication Society. Little had been accomplished by the two organizations, and confusion abounded as to their functions and the limits of their authority. But to avoid an open conflict he kept his peace, and continued on to Indianapolis for a series of speaking engagements.

The Indiana state legislature was assembling for the purpose of revising the state constitution, and the legislators attended his second lecture in a body. At the close of the service a committee from their ranks invited him to open their deliberations the next morning. For the remainder of his stay in the city, his friends had difficulty securing a hall large enough to accommodate the throngs who gathered nightly to hear him.

He reached home in December to learn that Clarinda was seriously ill in the big house overlooking the college. A hectic flush covered her cheeks; her pulse was rapid and night sweats, he learned, were frequent; all symptoms, he knew, of the dread consumption that had so grievously decimated his family.

On January 10, 1851, Clarinda died, only twenty-nine years old, the last of his living children by Margaret, and again the family and friends gathered with aching hearts about an open grave in God's Acre.

As they walked back to the house across the frozen roadway, Alexander voiced to the man beside him, twice his son-in-law and twice widowered, his sense of punishment. God was not mocked; whatsoever a man sowed, that a man also reaped. Was this retribution for his pride, his arrogance, his love of power, of worldly success?

William Pendleton made no reply, a well of doubt and grief in his own heart that choked him.

"God is a god of love," Father Thomas, holding on to Alexander's arm, said quietly in his gentle, quavering voice. "We cannot wander from His love and care. Not even in death."

"Death?" Alexander stopped and stood for a moment, looking back at God's Acre. Gray clouds had overcast the sky, but as he stood a shaft of sunlight struck for one miraculous moment on the stone wall encircling the sacred spot. "There is no death!"

Chapter 32

LATE IN JUNE ALEXANDER WAS NOTIFIED THAT HE WOULD NOT BE reappointed as postmaster at Bethany. The position had been an onerous one, filled with petty details for which he had no liking, and he was not loath to relinquish it. But it meant he would lose the franking privilege for his publications which had been his renumeration for holding the post. The same month he found that the *Millennial Harbinger* had edged into troubled financial waters, and that funds for the college were alarmingly low. In July word came that Henry Clay died on June 29. Peace had lost its most powerful voice, he felt as he read the news, and he had lost a personal friend.

"The task for me, my brother, is here," he wrote Alexander Paton at Glasgow in reply to an urgent invitation to revisit the scenes of his labors in Great Britain. He could give no serious thought to acceptance. "The need grows greater day by day, and the time is short. May God help us!"

He made plans for an immediate tour to solicit increased endowment for the college.

Selina accompanied him as far as New Lisbon, Ohio, where they attended the annual meeting of the Ohio churches and enjoyed a visit with Walter Scott who had come over from Pittsburgh for the twenty-fifth anniversary of his first preaching effort in the Western Reserve. The years rolled away as Alexander listened to the evangelist preach under a great crowded tent in the same grove in which he had started his labors. He seemed afire with the same youthful eloquence, and Alexander was moved to emotion.

"The brotherhood may never realize how much we owe this inspired man of God," he said to Selina after the sermon. "He is the most gifted of all our preachers, and my devoted friend and fellow worker. I thank God upon every remembrance of him."

Selina returned by stagecoach to Bethany and Alexander continued on his tour, soliciting funds for the college, counseling with young churches new in the Restoration Movement, preaching the love of God to men and women who were increasingly bewildered and confused in the thickening atmosphere of the national climate. Indignation flamed in the North over the Fugitive Slave Law and discussions were waged in bitterness; Kansas was aroused to civil strife as the Kansas-Nebraska Act opened new territories to slavery. Families were divided; friends grew hostile. But the anchor of God's word held firm; His love and care the common, healing touch to which all men turned. Alexander burned with a compulsion he had never known before to preach without ceasing, to storm the gates of heaven with his prayers. He stayed on tour all summer, returning to Bethany in September for only a brief respite.

"Everywhere I went I heard talk of a new book, *Uncle Tom's*

Cabin," he told Selina. "It's an anti-slavery novel, and seems to be stirring up the people as no secular book has done in my lifetime. It's inflaming both the North and the South."

Selina was sitting by the window of their bedroom, sewing, her pincushion and scissors dangling from her waist. She stopped her hand in midair as she was reaching for the scissors. "You didn't read a novel, Mr. Campbell!" Her face reflected honest shock.

He smiled. "I did look through it," he admitted. "At Brother Coleman's in Throopsville, New York. It was first published last year as a serial in the Abolitionist paper, *National Era*, in Washington City. I fear it is doing an immense amount of harm." He started out the door and then stopped and came back and put his hand on her shoulder. "There are worse things than merely reading novels, my dear," he said kindly.

Her mouth tightened. "Like what, for instance?"

"Like keeping silent when men are hating each other, looking for the worst in each other." He straightened and ran his hand through his white hair. "My only release from the torment of this situation is to keep busy preaching the only remedy for it I know."

Selina had been mending his undershirt. She snipped the thread off and folded the garment on her lap, pressing its creases firmly with her finger. "I know what you mean," she said, her voice suddenly warm with understanding. She looked up at him. "When are you leaving again, Mr. Campbell? I've got your clothes all ready."

Alexander looked at her a moment, and then bent and kissed her on the forehead. "The Illinois and Missouri brethren are urging me to visit them, and the governor of Missouri has invited me to address the Legislature in Jefferson City. I'll try to get away day after tomorrow."

He returned from the Missouri Country after seventy-eight days, weary and apprehensive, in time to perform the marriage ceremony of Alexander, Jr., to Mary Ann Purvis of Louisiana on December 30. The bride had graduated from Jane McKeever's Mount Pleasant Seminary the year before.

"I knew you had talent as a teacher," he told Jane when she and

Matthew McKeever came over to welcome him before the wedding. "But I never knew you would operate a matrimonial agency. If it weren't for your seminary I don't know where our Bethany lads would look for their wives. I hope you've picked one of the best for my son."

"He had the good sense to pick her himself," Jane said. "And she is one of our finest."

In the spring Alexander, Jr., moved with his bride to Concordia Parish, Louisiana, to operate a plantation near her home, leaving only Virginia and Decima and nine-year-old William Pendleton of all his fourteen children still at home.

As the year drew to a close Father Thomas began visibly to fail. With difficulty he made his way each morning to the little study across the roadway, supported by faithful Charlie Poole, but usually by ten o'clock Selina heard his hand bell pealing, which meant he was ready to return to the house. On the last day of the year he remained in bed, the first time in Alexander's memory his father had not been up and about the house. For three days he lingered, quoting Scripture in his delirium, his quavering voice trailing off into the mumbled refrain of a beloved hymn. He died on Wednesday, January 4, 1854.

The family was grouped about his bed as his physician-son, Archibald, folded the thin hands and pressed down the lids over his sightless eyes, and then Alexander, kneeling by the foot of the bed, arose and wiped his eyes, his hands trembling. One by one they joined hands, Dorothea and Jane and Archibald and Alexander, suddenly bereft but stalwart in their father's faith, while Joseph Bryant and Matthew McKeever and Selina and the grandchildren stood behind them with bowed heads. In a low voice Alexander began to pray.

After the funeral Alexander tried to push to the back of his mind the national dilemma. The problems of the churches needed his attention. Funds to support the enterprises of the Restoration Movement were slow; many suggested methods of solicitation among the brethren were hotly debated, but no organized method of raising money could be agreed upon. David Burnet still clung to his Bible Society and his Tract and Publication Society, siphoning support

385

from the American Christian Missionary Society, the only one of the three to which Alexander gave his full endorsement. In addition, colleges were springing up everywhere, challenging the claims of Bethany for support from the churches: Franklin College and Burritt College in Tennessee; Kentucky Female Orphan School at Midway, and Bacon College at Georgetown; Western Reserve Eclectic Institute at Hiram, Ohio; Walnut Grove Academy, and the new Abingdon College in Illinois; in Missouri were Camden Point Female Seminary, Christian College for Women, and the new Christian University which claimed to be the first institution west of the Mississippi River to welcome women students on a par with men.

Horace Mann, now the president of Antioch College in Yellow Spring, Ohio, was a frequent visitor at Bethany, discussing for long hours with Alexander the educational problems of the country, and to him Alexander poured out his troubled reflections. Was education jeopardized by so many weak colleges instead of a few strong ones? Should more church colleges concentrate on training teachers and leaders, leaving the undergraduate field to secular efforts? What, then, would become of the moral training of youth? But the educator had no convincing answers.

In June 1855 John Brown, Alexander's father-in-law, died, and for months the spirit of the beloved man seemed to hover, with that of Father Thomas, near him. Almost audibly he could hear their voices, whispering caution, warning against personal ambition, turning his mind to the eternal source of wisdom.

But the tension grew among the churches as the fate of the enterprises seemed to hang in the balance. Suggested methods of reorganization came in every mail; William Pendleton took up the cudgel in the pages of the *Millennial Harbinger*, openly denouncing David Burnet's two societies as unnecessary and unwanted. For a time warfare seemed inevitable. And then Alexander learned, suddenly, unexpectedly, David Burnet surrendered. The two societies would merge into the framework of the American Christian Missionary Society.

"And you, Alexander Campbell," David Burnet wrote him in

386

Christian love, "are our unanimous choice as president of this one, inclusive organization."

But Alexander felt no joy in the victory.

"You're brooding," Selina told him one morning in the early summer. "You've always told me I was the worrying kind; now look at you! If it's not the state of the country it's the bickering from Cincinnati."

Alexander shook his head. "I'm afraid it's my conscience," he said. "It is a terrible thing to win a battle—and lose a war."

Selina looked up from the butter she was moulding. "You're talking nonsense," she said. "You need to get away for a while. Why not take a trip up North, you and Decima and me?"

It was a leisurely trip by cars and canal boats and as the days passed Alexander seemed to regain his old spirits. A week at St. Catherine's Springs in Canada seemed to benefit his rheumatic pains which he had begun to suffer, and visits with friends in Toronto and Montreal heartened him.

They stopped in Detroit in August on the return trip, guests in the home of Elder Richard Hawley. A small dinner party of congenial friends had been arranged for that evening, Mr. Hawley told them, and as Alexander and Selina descended the stairway after refreshing themselves and entered the drawing room the first person Alexander's eye fell upon was David Burnet. He and his wife, Mary Gano, were on tour from Cincinnati and had by chance contacted the Hawleys.

The two men met in the center of the room, their hands in a firm clasp, and as if the mantle of Christ's spirit suddenly enveloped them there was a warmth in their reunion that removed forever any sting of their differences. In amiable companionship they spent the evening, discussing the eternal verities, relegating to outer darkness the vexing matters of earthly concern.

The next day was Sunday, and Alexander consented to preach at both the morning and evening services. The task was a happy one but it left him exhausted, and at the close of the evening meeting he was about to step gratefully into the Hawley carriage beside Selina and Decima when a gaunt, beak-nosed man with close-cropped bristling hair stepped forward abruptly, as though he had not planned it, from close beside the building, and came toward him with outstretched hands.

"You almost converted yourself tonight, Bishop." He spoke harshly, a rumbling in his throat. "That was one of the best Abolitionist sermons I ever heard."

Involuntarily Alexander stiffened, and then held out his hand in sudden recognition, a broad smile on his face. It was John Brown, his wool-clip agent for seven years. They had not met since the last general meeting of the Woolgrowers' Association at Steubenville in 1847, but even in the dim light of the street lamp there was apparent the same erectness, the same stern ruggedness of feature, relieved now by a twisted grin. There was also the same burning glow in the wide-spaced deep blue eyes he had noticed before, heightened now by a piercing intensity. John Brown was a man of unbending convictions. He was an Abolitionist, but he was also a man of peace. He shook hands warmly, forgetting for a moment the waiting carriage.

"I'll accept that as a compliment, Friend Brown," he said. "But it was not an Abolitionist sermon. It was a sermon based on the twenty-third chapter of Matthew, a denunciation of hypocrites!"

"A fancy parlor name for slaveholders!" Brown laughed harshly. "But I won't preach you a sermon myself, Bishop. When I heard you were going to be here, I lay over, just to hear you. And to say good-by."

For a moment they faced each other; two tall, stern men, both filled with purpose and a sense of righteousness; yet somehow, Alexander realized, as far apart as the poles.

"You must come to see me again at Bethany," said Alexander. "These are violent times, and we are men of peace. There is much for us to do."

"In our own ways, Bishop," amended John Brown. "I live in Kansas now, in Osawatomie; just passing through Detroit with some materials we'll be needing soon. Someday you must come see me at Osawatomie. By underground railroad," he added grimly. "You'll be seeing things you never knew."

388

He moved as though to walk away, and Alexander spoke quickly in order to hold him, his eyes upon the man's face, a constriction in his throat at what he saw there.

"Mrs. Campbell and my daughter Decima are here," he began. "And our hosts, Brother and Mrs. Richard Hawley." He turned toward the carriage as though to present them.

John Brown bowed, a half-smile on his lined face, but made no effort to move nearer. He turned again to Alexander.

"There is violence ahead, too, sir. God is marshaling His forces, girding us for war. I'm ready to fight under His banner." He clasped Alexander's hand with a quick, hard, clenching grip, and then as suddenly released it, an impassiveness in his face now, a grim brooding lighted only by the hot blue eyes that seemed to burn like tortured things deep within their sockets. "Good-by, Bishop Campbell! I'll not forget you!"

He turned about as though there was no further need for words, and while Alexander watched, a helplessness in him, the tall, slightly stooped figure disappeared like a dark specter in the gloom of the street. For a moment Alexander listened to the lumbering steps, lost now in the street noises, and then climbed wearily into the carriage beside Selina.

"We'll cancel our visit to the meeting in Warren, Ohio," he said. "I must leave for Bethany tomorrow."

"We aren't due home for two weeks," Selina protested.

"We start for home tomorrow," Alexander said. "I am filled with foreboding."

Back in the hills of Bethany, the restful quiet and peace of the countryside made the encounter with his former wool agent seem unreal. But there persisted a presentiment of evil, dissolving only partially as the weeks flowed into months and the winter slipped into spring. God was still in His heaven and the world was in His keeping. Or was it?

It was late in May and Alexander was leaving the college after his morning lecture for the half-mile walk to the house when a student handed him a copy of the Richmond *Enquirer*. Black headlines were strung across the front page. John Brown and his four sons had murdered five unarmed pro-slavery men on the banks of the Pot-tawatomie River in Kansas. It was the trumpet sound for guerrilla warfare.

For a long time that afternoon Alexander sat in his sunlit study in troubled discussion with William Pendleton and Robert Richardson.

"I knew John Brown was a man of iron conviction from the time he first came here fourteen years ago on a sheep-buying trip," he told them. "But he was a man of peace then; he believed in persuasion instead of force. Something happened to him; I knew when we met last August he was not the same. There were demons in his face." He paused and stared up at the sky through the cupola. "He said he was passing through Detroit with materials he'd be needing; I won-der now if they weren't arms. Perhaps I might have said something; perhaps I might have done something—"

"I forbid you to entertain such notions, Bishop." Dr. Richardson used the professional tone he adopted only with his patients. "At the best the man is insane, and at the worst a deliberate cold-blooded murderer of unarmed, sleeping men. You can't hold yourself ac-countable in any way for this massacre."

"He called my sermon that night a good Abolitionist sermon," Al-exander went on as if Richardson had not spoken. "Perhaps he got some thought from it, some word that may have encouraged him." He got up and began pacing the floor of the small room. "If so, then I am as guilty as he! According to my own text, I am a 'whitened sepulcher, within full of dead men's bones and of all un-cleanness.'"

"Nonsense!" said William Pendleton. "You probably exercised a restraining influence over the man for years. I recall a discussion we had when he was here one night ten years ago organizing his protective wool association. He was an Abolitionist then but a non-resistant one, he called himself. He claimed he would reject the use of arms in any form, even if opposed by them. That could have been due to your influence. He admired you, and as long as he remained in contact with you, he held himself under control."

"He's a symbol now," Alexander said, "a bloody, insane symbol of the future." He sat down heavily, as though he had been thinking aloud. "I have known intimately two John Browns. Father Brown of Wellsburg after many years of a good life entered upon his eternal reward only last June. And John Brown of Osawatomie, claiming to be the instrument of our Heavenly Father, becomes a mass murderer a few months later. They symbolize the choice our nation faces. We must choose a gradual, peaceful Christian settlement of our problems, or violence and destruction and sudden death will be our lot."

It was the ninth day of December 1857. Alexander remained in his study until almost midnight, writing copy for the *Millennial Harbinger* by the new kerosene lamp. He had been on tour almost constantly since early summer, doing what he could to spread the Gospel of forbearance among the people, dividing his time between the North and the South. John Brown of Osawatomie was lionized by the Abolitionists and the extremists of the North as the avenging instrument of God, he had found, and was hated by the South as the personification of evil itself.

"A change of heart is essential to a change of character." He stared at the words for a moment and then continued: "And both are essential to admission into the Kingdom of God."

Abruptly he threw the paper into the trash box. How often had he expressed that view? How long would men quibble about the letter of the law, neglecting the spirit of it? Though as scrupulous as a Pharisee, he reflected, in tithing mint, anise, and cumin, and rigid to the letter in all observances, without morality, usually called righteousness, no man can be saved, no nation can be redeemed, no peace secured among men.

Selina was already asleep when he entered their bedroom. There were no creaking of floors, no night noises; the house was unusually quiet. He undressed, and lay for a long time, his eyes wide open, staring into the darkness. And then the darkness faded into nothingness, and he slept.

The sound of shouting voices awakened him. He sat bolt upright. The room was streaked with the light of darting flames that seared his eyeballs with a dreadful threat. He swung his feet to the floor and ran to the window, glancing involuntarily at the tall eight-day clock beside it. Three o'clock. He had been asleep since midnight. And even then this devil's plot had begun its work.

One glance at the west and he saw the hilltop sky a flaming, leaping arc. The room was growing lighter by the moment. It was not Steward's Inn, he could tell from the location of the center of the light. It was the college building itself; his lifework; the apex of his dreams. It must have been burning for hours, slowly, stealthily gathering power for one mighty, derisive, consuming surge of flame.

In a sudden frenzy he grabbed his trousers and pulled them over his flannel nightshirt, and stuck his bare feet into his boots while a pounding against the door became a hammering, and hoarse, excited voices called in increasing volume from the yard.

Selina had arisen and was standing by the bed, her long, braided graying hair falling unloosened about her face while she fumbled with the neckband of her nightgown, uncomprehending horror in her face.

He turned to her as he started out the door. "The college," he said simply, "is on fire!"

Chapter 33

UNTIL IT BECAME A SMOULDERING MASS OF RUIN, ALEXANDER STAYED by the burning college, suddenly a stooped, bundled figure of an old man, standing voiceless among his stricken hopes. The main building, already a mass of flame before the fire was discovered, was totally destroyed, taking with it the library and all the chemical apparatus and most of the physical equipment. Only Steward's Inn, a hundred yards away, remained. But no one had been injured, and as he watched the walls crumble into the furnace of what had been his chief personal pride, Alexander gave a prayer of thanksgiving that the young life about him had been kept safe. Throughout the deepest adversity, God was always good.

"The Lord is testing us," he said to William Pendleton as they made their way to Pendleton Heights for a few hours' rest toward morning. "The crucible of fire is burning out the dross." He straightened his shoulders as they reached the crest of the slope, an aged warrior aroused for one last tremendous effort, and turned for a final look at the glowing ashes and blackened ruin behind them. "Set up recitation rooms in Steward's Inn," he said. "Classes will continue as usual. And notify the trustees of a special meeting on Monday. We shall prepare to rebuild at once."

On December 14 the board of trustees met in emergency session in the new parlor of his home, and listened with rising hope as Alexander outlined his plans for rebuilding.

"I need not tell you that Bethany College will continue," he announced quietly, "although nothing but absolute necessity could induce me at this season and my time of life to undertake the labors I see ahead. If I did not feel that the College is doing the Lord's work, I would shrink from the task. Sometimes, in recent months, I have felt I should be relieved from further service, but I know now that I cannot hope to rest until I am called to my Father's house. Such as they may be, all my days must be given to the Lord."

He paused and looked at the faces about him, impassive faces for the most part, expressionless, reflecting the doubt he knew they felt in the wisdom of undertaking such a project in the disturbing atmosphere of the times and yet an unwillingness, a reluctance, to discourage him in the venture.

"The origin of the fire will probably never be determined," he went on. "A fund of not less than $50,000 will be required for replacement. Mr. Pendleton and I are prepared to start out at once to obtain it. We must not only rebuild but build for the future— better and larger and finer than before."

The trustees were apathetic but authorized the two men to solicit the funds, and in less than a week, with building plans already in process of preparation, they were ready to start. They arranged to go first to Washington City and confer with Judge Jeremiah Black, now attorney general in President Buchanan's cabinet, before going on to the East and the South.

But although he pushed himself as hard as ever, Alexander felt unwell, his old vibrancy and enthusiasm replaced by a dogged determination. In response to the news of their coming, Judge Black invited him to bring Selina and the girls also, the whole party to visit at the Black home; and Selina, studying her husband's lined face and stooped shoulders, agreed to accompany him.

"Virginia can go with us." She spoke briefly and to the point, as she busied herself in packing two large portmanteaus. "She has never seen Washington City and would be good company for us. Besides, she might meet some interesting young men there."

It was late in January before they reached Washington City, and as they rode through the tree-lined streets in Judge Black's carriage, fascinated by the low-hanging, bare branches of the locusts and elms and oaks gleaming with crystalled snow in the morning sun, Alexander reached for Selina's hand.

"Judge Black tells me that the President has invited us to call at the White House on Monday," he said. "Would you like that, Selina?"

Her angular face flushed with unexpected pleasure. She had brought her chocolate-colored taffeta with its closely fitting basque and full sleeves trimmed with buttons. And Virginia's new dress of blue cashmere was in the hamper.

"Well," she answered slowly, as if weighing the matter, a gleam of humor in her eyes, "I guess that would be all right. It wouldn't be exactly sinful, would it, to be the guest of the President?"

Two days later they drove up to the White House in the carriage with William Pendleton and Attorney General and Mrs. Black, and were ushered into the Red Parlor. They remained standing, Selina fidgeting with the pin at her throat, Virginia beside her father cool and poised, until the door opened at the far end of the room and the President's niece, Miss Harriet Lane, came toward them, a smiling, friendly woman, her hand extended in welcome. Behind her President Buchanan walked slowly, his chalklike face, his pale, red-rimmed eyes crinkling into a warm smile as he grasped Alexander's hand.

"Bishop Campbell, that sermon you preached yesterday in the Baptist Church was the finest exposition of Christian love I ever heard!" His voice was high and strained but there was no mistaking the feeling behind his words. "Several of my cabinet members mentioned it to me this morning. The Apostle Paul could have been speaking directly to our own times."

"The Apostle, like Christ, spoke for eternity," said Alexander. " 'Though I speak with the tongues of men and of angels, and have not love, I am become as sounding brass.' That is an eternal truth, Mr. President. The need for Christian love and understanding seems never greater than now."

They talked easily, seated in gilded straight-backed chairs in a tight little circle, the charm and attentiveness of Miss Lane and the affability of the President erasing the momentary stiffness, the conversation ranging from religion and literature to the fire at Bethany and the hardships of travel, with careful avoidance of any mention of the guerrilla warfare in Kansas or the mounting tension in the nation. It was a happy interlude, and when they arose to leave, a half-hour later, they felt they were parting from personal friends.

"If all your contacts are as successful as this one with the President, you should soon raise that $50,000," said Judge Black as they drove away. "A little more time and I think you might even have converted him to our primitive faith."

"It is the power of the truth that converts, not I," said Alexander. "Whatever his enemies say, Mr. Buchanan is doing his best to be a good president. But"—he shook his head—"his problems seem insoluble. If peace can be preserved, it will not be by tampering with the laws; it is too late for that. It will be because people want peace above all else. Only by changing the heart of the people can we change the mood of the nation now."

From Washington City Selina and Virginia returned to Bethany by the cars while Alexander and William Pendleton journeyed on to

Baltimore, New York, Philadelphia, and then turned their faces South. Although sympathetic audiences greeted them everywhere, and donations and pledges to the college were received at every speaking place, as the tour continued Alexander realized that it would take longer than he had anticipated to reach their goal. The emotional temper of the country was not attuned to plans for tomorrow; today was all-absorbing. But they continued doggedly, both men speaking once and often twice a day, Pendleton principally for the college and Alexander pleading for peace. "Not by might, nor by power, but by my spirit, saith the Lord of Hosts!" he cried again and again. They spoke before churches, societies, colleges, and mass meetings of citizens, wherever they could find an audience; in Alabama, Mississippi, Louisiana, and Kentucky—a task of increasing labor and waning strength that Alexander would not admit, even to himself, his days endlessly consumed by the demands upon him.

William Pendleton left him at Louisville to return to his teaching duties at Bethany, and Alexander boarded the steamer *Tempest* for Nashville alone.

"I have been working in my cabin on copy for the *Harbinger*," he wrote Selina two days later. "I have slept on board already two nights. The river is very full, overflowing its banks and filled with driftwood. The peach trees are expanding their blossoms and the early growth of shrubs are showing their buds. The glorious resurrection of spring is at hand to repair the dreary waste and ruin of winter. And so it will be with Bethany College."

The quill slipped from his fingers and dropped to the floor of the cabin, his accumulated weariness suddenly too heavy a burden. Although he always tried to write cheerfully, he was tired now, filled with a mounting wave of fatigue and a deep longing for the wooded hills of Bethany, the hepatica and dogwood and trillium bursting into bloom on the banks of the Buffalo; heartsick at the passion he found everywhere in the people. He stooped and picked up the pen and, placing it on the desk, capped the inkpot and stretched out fully clothed in his berth. It would be three days before the *Tempest* would reach Nashville; it was off schedule, stopping at every dock for hurrying passengers, taking on unaccustomed cargo that meant endless delays. He would finish the letter tomorrow. In a few minutes he was sound asleep.

From Nashville he went North, through Tennessee and back into Kentucky, and a month later returned to Louisville, travel-worn, his strength depleted. He had secured in gifts and pledges only about $30,000—far short of his goal. It was a sufficient sum, however, he argued with himself, to start rebuilding the college.

An electrical storm broke on the second night and, unable to sleep, he got up and stood at the window of his hotel room, watching the slashing rain beat against the trees and the cobblestones in the court-yard below. The flashes of lightning across the black, pouring clouds followed by the rolling thunder were elements of a storm that seemed to drain his energies and his spirits, leaving him with the feeling that his name was written in water; that his work for the unity of God's people would be washed away even as the work of the founders of the country for a united nation was being laid desolate. Were men never to live together in peace and harmony in either nations or churches? Were dreamers who worked for such a vision to be eternally mocked?

In the hotel lobby the next morning he bought a copy of the Louisville *Journal*, and after scanning the front-page news turned to the editorial page. His eye fell upon a column titled "Alexander Campbell." As if in prescient answer to his need for reassurance, the editor had written:

This venerable and distinguished man is now in our city on business connected with his college at Bethany, so recently visited, as our readers know, with a very disastrous calamity. . . . Alexander Campbell is unquestionably one of the most extraordinary men of our time. Putting wholly out of view his tenets, with which we of course have nothing to do, he claims, by virtue of his intrinsic qualities, as manifest in his achievements, a place among the very foremost spirits of the age. His energy, self-reliance, and self-fidelity, if we may use the expression, are of the stamp that belongs only to the world's first leaders in thought and action. His personal excellence is certainly without a stain or shadow. His intellect, it is scarcely too much to say, is among the clearest, richest, profoundest ever vouchsafed to man. No poet's soul is more crowded with imagery than his with the ripest forms of thought. Surely the life of a man thus excellent and gifted is a part of the common treasure of

397

society. In his essential character, he belongs to no sect or party, but to the world.

There was more to it, but Alexander laid the paper aside, a mist in his eyes. A few years ago, even a few months ago, he would have been filled with stout pride at such a tribute; yes, even with arrogance. But that seemed a long time ago. He was chastened now, a humility in him, a compassion which he knew had been absent before. The Lord had shown him many times that it was not enough to do justly and love mercy, but a man must also walk humbly with his God.

Back at home he plunged into plans for the new building. It would be Gothic in style, he determined, reflecting the influence of the great Glasgow University of his youth; built solidly of brick with a substructure of stone and roof of slate; the windows and doors faced with the finest and most enduring sandstone. And it would be as fireproof as human ingenuity could make it; strong and secure and beautiful, and set farther up on the brow of the rolling hill of the campus to stand for the ages.

With the general plans completed, work began on the actual construction. William Pendleton gave detailed supervision and Alexander made himself available at all times for general consultation. On the morning of May 31 the cornerstone was laid. Before a standing assembly of hundreds of friends who had traveled long distances to be present Alexander again dedicated the institution to the spiritual as well as the intellectual development of the youth of the land. The way had been long and toilsome, but Bethany College, the first college in the United States, and the first known to any history accessible to him, to be founded upon the Holy Bible as the basis of all true science and true learning, would survive.

Alexander was in his study completing selections of his public addresses for book publication on Monday afternoon, October 17, 1859, when the door was pushed open and William Pendleton stood in the entrance, his face sternly drawn.

"John Brown has started a slave insurrection!" he announced. "He seized Harper's Ferry last night!"

For a moment Alexander sat rigid, his mind grappling with the significance of the news. He placed the sheaf of papers in his hand face downward on the desk and motioned to the vacant chair opposite him.

For a moment the two men stared at each other across the small desk, a deepening horror in their hearts. And then Alexander spoke.

"It's fantastic! How could he have seized Harper's Ferry?"

"He led an armed band across the Potomac from Maryland, killed the baggagemaster, a free Negro named Shepherd Heyward, gained control of the federal arsenal, the armory, and the rifle factory, and is holding several prisoners in the engine house. He claims he'll free the slaves by force and they'll rise up and join him! It could be war!"

"There won't be any slave insurrection." Alexander tried to speak calmly, his voice low and unnaturally harsh. "The Government will act promptly, and the fracas will be over in a day or two. It won't mean war." Abruptly he arose from his high-backed Bible chair with its wide writing arm. "I think it's hot in here. Let's walk over to the college and look around. What would you think if we raised our goal for the new building to $75,000?"

But they did not discuss the college. Instead, they walked the half-mile almost silently, each busy with his own thoughts, filled with a numbing dread of the future.

The weeks passed—crawling, tortuous weeks, weeks that flowed into months with an almost unbearable tension. Because of prompt action by Colonel Robert E. Lee and his company of marines, John Brown was captured and tried for treason and murder. Prominent Abolitionists in the North hailed him as a martyr, a "Lord High Admiral of the Almighty," Wendell Phillips proclaimed him from his echoing pulpit in New England, but Alexander observed that most thoughtful persons of all sections considered him a fanatical murderer, and when he was found guilty by a jury of his peers, and hanged for his crimes on December 2, there seemed almost a national sigh of relief. Perhaps, Alexander pondered, there was yet time for cool heads and Christian hearts to take command.

In November 1860, Abraham Lincoln of Illinois was elected President of the divided country, and on December 20, while Alexander was speaking in Indiana, word came that South Carolina had seceded from the Federal Union and proclaimed itself a separate republic. Mississippi seceded on January 9, followed in rapid succession by Florida, Alabama, and Georgia. The nation had split asunder at last.

Alexander returned home, sick at heart. He had done what he could. And it had not been enough.

The first bound copies of his selected public addresses were awaiting him from Challen and Son of Philadelphia. He opened a copy and scanned the opening lines of the dedication: "To Selina, my dutiful and affectionate wife, who has greatly assisted me in my labors in the Gospel at home and abroad. . . ."

He had not told Selina of the dedication, and when he handed her a copy that night in the bedroom, to his surprise she was visibly moved.

"I've tried to be a good wife." She sat down heavily in the rocker before the hearth, holding the book against her breast. "Because I love you, Mr. Campbell. I've loved you since the first time I heard you preach in Wellsburg." She glanced at him almost shyly, and then laughed self-consciously. "My goodness me, that's forty years ago!" She opened the book and ran her finger over the printed lines of the dedication. "And all these years I've felt I was living in Margaret's shadow!"

The words were hardly more than a whisper but suddenly, as though on rare impulse, Alexander reached forward and took her hands in his.

"I love you, Selina. You are the wife of my mature years, sharing my tragedies and little triumphs. I couldn't have gone on without you."

A deep mistiness clouded her eyes, and her long, angular face under her tight knot of graying hair at the top of her head flushed crimson at the unexpected intimacy of the moment. And then she shook herself and her mouth tightened in a wry smile. "I don't intend for you ever to do without me, Mr. Campbell." She attempted to make her voice light. "That's the reason I keep fourteen years younger. You'll have no third wife if I can help it!"

400

He laughed and kissed her lightly on the cheek. "Such foolish talk for an old couple. Now look at the book, my dear, and tell me what you think of it."

While President Buchanan waited helplessly for the inauguration of Mr. Lincoln, the seceding states organized into the Confederate States of America, and on February 9, 1861, at Montgomery, Alabama, Jefferson Davis of Mississippi was elected their president.

"I recall how cordial Mr. Davis was to me when I preached in Congress, and his interest in Bethany," Alexander said to Pendleton as they walked toward the college a week later. "We talked briefly of his young nephew, William Stamps, the student who was killed here by a fall on the ice during the first winter of the college. Mr. Davis is an aloof, an austere, but a good and kindly man; he comes from a Baptist family in Mississippi who are warm supporters of the Restoration Movement."

"Mr. Lincoln is equally as close to our Movement." Pendleton nodded in recollection. "His family is also Baptist, but his father, Tom Lincoln, became a member of our group at Charleston, Illinois. They are good people."

"Yes, I know that," Alexander said. "Josephus Hewett, who organized our first church at Springfield, knows Mr. Lincoln very well; both he and Elder Ben Smith of Bloomington have preached before him. He appears deeply concerned about religion. Strange that two men so close to our Movement, such patriotic and religious-minded men as Jefferson Davis and Abraham Lincoln, should today face each other as hostile leaders of our divided nation. May God guide them!"

The nation seethed with growing dissension as Abraham Lincoln was inaugurated as President in March, and over Selina's protests, as well as those of Robert Richardson and William Pendleton, Alexander determined upon another tour.

"Peace is bound up with individual Christians," he said. "I see that now more clearly than ever. A righteous nation cannot be created by law. It can be brought about only as individual citizens become righteous. My job is to help do that!"

401

"But one voice among so many," Selina protested. "What would it amount to? Don't be foolish!"

Alexander stopped pacing the floor of the new parlor where the family had assembled following evening worship. "I've always been foolish," he said. "I've been a fool all my life, thinking I could accomplish the impossible." He went to the mantel and leaned his head on his hands. "Who knows? A few more seeds planted, a few more words on Christian love, a few more pleas for understanding and forbearance might swing the balance." He looked up. "The state of Virginia has not yet left the Union. If the Old Dominion can hold steady, perhaps the seceding states can be persuaded to return, and we would have peace! Yes, I must go!"

Selina insisted on accompanying him to guard his health, and long before the end of the first day's travel it seemed to her that everybody in the country was either rushing home or leaving it; the cars overcrowded and uncomfortable; a strained expectancy about most of the faces as though awaiting some dreaded happening which would throw their world into convulsions. Sober, anxious groups of men and women crowded the stations at every stop, clambering tensely aboard, jostling each other in the aisles, staring fretfully or in stiff-necked silence, and in occasional strained exuberance, through the soiled windowpanes as the train puffed its way slowly through the Allegheny Mountains and into the rolling foothills and valleys of the East.

For three days in early April Alexander spoke in Charlottesville, Virginia, the congregation packing the box-shaped Christian meetinghouse and standing about the open doors and windows for a breath of the spring air as they listened hungrily and yet with curious apathy to the ancient, comforting story of redemptive love.

The next morning at daybreak, Friday, April 12, the Confederate forces fired upon Fort Sumter in nearby Charleston Harbor. The war had begun.

It was midnight, Saturday, before they left on the cars for home.

For a long time after Selina was asleep, sitting bolt upright on the hard straw seat beside him, her head cushioned against her folded shawl, Alexander remained wide awake, staring through the darkened window. About them other people as harassed as he stirred uneasily in the close air, the sepulchral gloom of the jolting car heightened by the two kerosene lamps at either end of the aisle. These were his people, members of the family of his God, now rushing headlong into a war that would crush them and leave its scars for generations. He loved them all: his brethren scattered both North and South, Abolitionists and slaveowners; their beloved country soon to be a battleground for divided families, including his own. Yet all the trouble could have been avoided, all the problems solved if they had only heeded the power of love as revealed in the Gospel.

He had failed to make them see it.

He tried to pray, but the words would not come. He moved restlessly, the sense of defeat, of wasted effort growing upon him. He should have stood more firmly against slavery. His work at the Virginia Constitutional Convention, his efforts to promote Henry Clay's emancipation proposal, his years of preaching and writing, had not been enough. Perhaps he might even have influenced John Brown of Osawatomie to hold to Christian ways if he had talked to him more of God's love and less of the price of wool during the years of their association.

He had been too ambitious, too proud before the Lord of leadership of the movement to restore Christian unity; too vain of his intellect, his riches, of the family with which God had blessed him, and had so largely taken away. The Lord had loved him, and showered him with gifts and great opportunities; and had chastised him and tried to make him humble. But each time he had gone back into the old ways, believing that no one else could do the Lord's work as well as he, proud in his self-righteousness.

He was an old man now, separated by his own weaknesses from the presence of God.

As though they had been spoken aloud beside him, the words of Paul came to him, shattering his gloom with their eternal verities:

Nay, in all these things we are more than conquerors through Him that loved us. For I am persuaded that neither death nor life, nor angels nor principalities, nor powers, nor things present nor things to come, nor height nor depth, nor any other creature shall be able to separate us from the love of God which is in Christ Jesus our Lord.

Peacefully, a vindication and a triumph in him, he turned his face to the window. The first streaks of dawn were hurrying across the sky. It was the Lord's day. The sun was rising again.

An Afterword

ALEXANDER CAMPBELL WAS TO UNDERTAKE NO MORE TOURS; HIS ACTIVE
days as a great religious leader were ended, but there still remained
to him almost a half decade of years in his beloved Bethany, sur-
rounded by family and friends, and with the turmoil and the tragedies of that terrible war he had hoped so earnestly to prevent
seemingly remote from his peaceful hills and valleys.

Walter Scott, his warm friend and "most cordial and indefatigable
fellow worker," died at his home near Mayslick, Kentucky, on April
23, 1861, and of the four great leaders of the Restoration Movement,
Thomas Campbell, Alexander Campbell, Barton W. Stone, and
Walter Scott, Alexander alone was left. With the death of his sister,
Dorothea Bryant, at Indianapolis on December 12, 1861, at the age
of sixty-nine, there remained with Alexander only Jane McKeever
at Mount Pleasant and Dr. Archibald Campbell of Bethany and
Wellsburg of the family of Thomas Campbell who had so hopefully
set sail for America on the ill-fated *Hibernia* that first day of October 1808.

But he was spared the physical horrors of the war which flowed
about them, and the growing infirmities of age prevented him from
drinking to its depths its mental and spiritual anguish. His own position, and the official position of Bethany College, was Unionist,
although he was personally bound to the South by many ties, and it
would have warmed his heart could he have seen the future and have
known that alone of the evangelical religious brotherhoods his own

brethren would not divide over the issues of the war, but would remain steadfast as one body, and thus set an example in Christian unity which would in time yeast the Christian world.

His own family, like so many families of the border states, was divided in sympathy. His son, Alexander, Jr., served as an officer with the Confederacy while his nephew, Archibald, Jr., editor of the Wheeling *Intelligencer*, was a fiery Unionist and an early leader in the movement that made of West Virginia a separate state in 1863.

But there were many compensations, personal joys which came gracefully to jewel the fading sunset of a long and arduous life. The marriage of his youngest daughter, Decima, to J. Judson Barclay, the United States Consul at Cyprus on April 7, 1863, and their immediate departure for that distant isle, was followed in October by the marriage of Virginia to lawyer W. R. Thompson of Louisville, Kentucky, leaving at home only his son, William Pendleton, the youngest of his fourteen children. And earlier in the same month he delivered the annual address for the fifteenth and last time as the president of the American Christian Missionary Society at Cincinnati. In July 1864, accompanied by Selina, he paid a final visit to James Foster at his modest home near Glen Easton. The two old friends fell into each other's arms and wept for joy, and during the next day and night spent long hours in happy and never-to-be-repeated reminiscence. Late in the spring of 1865, after the surrender at Appomattox, again with his devoted Selina, he visited Virginia at Louisville and spoke twice at the Christian churches. And then he returned to his Bethany hills to leave no more.

Throughout the war the college, although much reduced in both students and faculty, missed no single day of its regular sessions, nor has it to this day—a living, growing tribute to its founder's wisdom. The *Millennial Harbinger* skipped no issues, and not until the spring of 1865 did Alexander Campbell relinquish the editorship to William Pendleton. He preached his last sermon in the Bethany College chapel in December 1865, an effort in which no trace was discernible of the defects in memory and occasional delusions as to places visited which momentarily plagued him during the last three years of his life. On February 11, 1866, he attended services at the Bethany Church and assisted in the ordination of two additional elders, presiding later at the Lord's Table, where he made a few appropriate remarks, and listened with close attention to a sermon by his long-time friend and associate, Robert Richardson.

From this time onward his weakness increased; a slow and settled fever consumed him, and as the Lord's day was drawing to a close on the fourth day of March 1866 he entered into his eternal rest. His earthly family, including his daughters Decima and Virginia, and some of his closest friends, were with him at the end; his funeral in God's Acre, preached by Dr. Robert Richardson, was attended by hundreds of the great and the near-great and the humble from many states. And among them, and not the least, was his former slave Charlie Poole, a free man now these thirty years, and his long-time pensioner.

On his modest monument in God's Acre at Bethany are carved these words:

IN MEMORIAM

ALEXANDER CAMPBELL

Born in County Antrim, Ireland, September 12, 1788
Died at Bethany, West Virginia, March 4, 1866
Founder of Bethany College
Defender of the Faith once delivered to the Saints

Acknowledgments

F<small>IFTEEN YEARS AGO I BEGAN TO GATHER SOURCE MATERIAL FOR THIS</small> book; three years ago I completed the final research and began the actual writing. From time to time I have been in every principal locality frequented by Alexander Campbell, and he was an incessant and enthusiastic traveler. Many people have helped me, both in this country and abroad.

Thanking individuals for assistance on any book is always risky. Somebody is nearly always left out. The risk becomes greater when that book is about the life of a religious leader whose spiritual descendants are today numbered in the millions, a considerable number of whom in one way or another have made some contribution to this work. Many people, particularly in the ministry, have furnished valuable data and suggestions, and persons not connected with the church have gone far out of their way to give information that otherwise would not have been available.

In attempting to resolve this dilemma I have decided not to thank publicly any of my friends in the ministry or other professional workers in the field of religion, with one or two exceptions, who have been so generous in their help and encouragement, but to take this means of expressing to them individually and collectively my gratitude and lasting appreciation.

There are, however, certain persons who should be particularly noted because of their unusual contributions in the research for the book. My grateful thanks, therefore, to Dr. Perry Epler Gresham, president of Bethany College in the succession of Campbell, who made available an inexhaustible store of Campbelliana during a summer's residence at that great and unique college; Miss Pearl Mahaffey, professor emeritus of the college who, with unmatched enthusiasm, assisted in the exploration of Campbell landmarks about the Bethany countryside; Earle R. Forrest of the *Observer and Reporter*, Washington, Pennsylvania, which newspaper published the early writings of Alexander Campbell, who is literally a walking encyclopedia of the early life and times of that section of the Campbell country; Boyd B. Stutler, Charleston, West Virginia, the first historian to explore and authenticate the relationship between John Brown, the future Abolitionist, and Alexander Campbell, the religious reformer; Dr. Allen W. Moger, professor of history, Washington and Lee University, authority on the correspondence of General Robert E. Lee; Dr. Louis A. Warren, director emeritus, The Lincoln National Life Foundation, Fort Wayne, Indiana, who furnished data on the relationship of Thomas Lincoln with the Restoration Movement; and to H. E. Matheny, Akron, Ohio, who made available for study his extensive collection of Selina Bakewell Campbell letters and other original Campbell documents.

During the course of this research I have been freely furnished with every facility and considerable family information by the Misses Jeanette and Alice Campbell of Los Angeles, daughters of William Pendleton Campbell; and by Elder Robert M. Campbell of Santa Monica, the devoted follower in the Christian Ministry of his illustrious grandsire, son of Alexander Campbell, Jr., with whom I have had many heartwarming contacts through the years, and who passed away as this book went to press.

Special acknowledgment should also be made to Elder James R. Jenkins, pastor of the Church of Christ, Glasgow, Scotland, and to Roscoe M. Pierson, librarian, College of the Bible, Lexington, Kentucky; Mrs. Edna W. Woolery, assistant libarian, Bethany College; Claude E. Spencer, curator, and James E. McKinney, director, Disciples of Christ Historical Society, Nashville, for their enthusiastic cooperation in the hunt for old documents and special information; and to Paul M. Shuford, attorney, for his faithful search of old court records in and near Richmond, Virginia.

Other institutions and societies which contributed their own special quota of historical data were the Historical Society of Pennsylvania, Philadelphia, Pennsylvania; Pennsylvania State Library, Harrisburg, Pennsylvania; Department of Records, City of Philadelphia; Pennsylvania Historical and Museum Commission, Harrisburg, Pennsylvania; Prothonotary of the Courts of Common Pleas, Philadelphia, Pennsylvania; Louisiana State Museum, New Orleans, Louisiana; Virginia Board of Medical Examiners, Roanoke, Virginia; Virginia State Law Library, Richmond, Virginia; Virginia State Library, Richmond, Virginia; Virginia Historical Society, Richmond, Virginia; the Mariners' Museum, Newport News, Virginia; the West Virginia State Medical Association, Charleston, West Virginia; West Virginia State Department of Archives and History, Charleston, West Virginia; the State Department of Archives and History, Jackson, Mississippi; the Ohio Historical Society, Columbus, Ohio; the Historical and Philosophical Society of Cincinnati, Cincinnati, Ohio; the University of Cincinnati, and the Cincinnati Public Library.

My special thanks, also, to Mr. C. R. Pagan, director, Messrs. Pinkerton & Co., Ltd., shipbuilders, Londonberry, North Ireland; the National Maritime Museum, Greenwich, London; the General Register and Record Office of Shipping and Seamen, Llandaff, Cardiff; Lloyd's Registry of Shipping, London, and the British Embassy, Washington, D.C., for information concerning the *Hibernia* and other Atlantic Ocean passenger ships traveled by Alexander Campbell.

Additional libraries, institutions, and colleges which also cheerfully furnished valuable data are the New York Public Library, the Yale University Library, the National Archives and Records, and the Library of Congress, Washington, D.C., which generously furnished a study and every possible assistance during a residence there in 1955. Grateful acknowledgment is made of the cooperation and assistance of Texas Christian University, Fort Worth, Texas; the Lexington Public Library, the College of the Bible, Transylvania University, and Kentucky University, at Lexington, Kentucky; the David Lipscomb College and Vanderbilt University, Nashville,

Tennessee; Phillips University, Enid, Oklahoma; Drake University, Des Moines, Iowa; Butler University, Indianapolis, Indiana; the Santa Monica Public Library, the Los Angeles Public Library, and the library of the George Pepperdine College at Los Angeles. Last but never the least must be mentioned in deep appreciation the valuable data supplied by the University of Glasgow, Glasgow, Scotland, relative to the student days of Alexander Campbell at that institution.

Among the rewarding contemporary publications consulted as source material were: *The Evangelist, The Christian Messenger, Lard's Quarterly, The Apostolic Times,* the Cincinnati *Daily Gazette,* Cincinnati *Advertiser,* Cincinnati *Chronicle,* the Washington *Globe,* the Richmond *Whig,* the Richmond *Enquirer,* the Philadelphia *Public Ledger,* the Philadelphia *Gazette,* and *The Western Review,* edited by Timothy Flint. Through the cooperation of Dr. Percy C. Powell of the Manuscript Division, Library of Congress, and other officials of that incomparable institution, I also had access to unpublished letter files of James A. Garfield, Henry Clay, Jeremiah Sullivan Black, John Brown of Osawatomie, and Jefferson Davis, all friends of Alexander Campbell, and to many other rare and pertinent documents.

No acknowledgment would be complete without, of course, mentioning the enormous debt owing to the writings of Alexander Campbell himself, especially his personal letters, too few of which survive scattered throughout the libraries of various colleges devoted to the Restoration Movement, the West Virginia Department of Archives and History, the Historical Society of the Disciples of Christ, and in the hands of private collectors. A special debt is acknowledged to the one-volume selected edition of Campbell's *Christian Baptist,* as edited by David S. Burnet in 1835, and the bound volumes of Campbell's *Millennial Harbinger* edited by him for thirty-five years prior to his death in 1866. Grateful acknowledgment must also be made to the *Memoirs of Alexander Campbell* by Dr. Robert Richardson, a two-volume primarily theological biography of Campbell published in 1869, which, though incomplete, will always remain important source material. *The Home Life and Rem-*

iniscences of Alexander Campbell by His Wife, by Mrs. Selina Bakewell Campbell, published in 1882, and *The Story of an Earnest Life*, by Mrs. Eliza Davis (1881), furnished glimpses into the family and personal life of the "Bishop of Bethany" which might otherwise have remained unknown.

And last, and in the final analysis possibly the most important of all, my enduring gratitude to my wife, Bess White Cochran, whose enthusiasm as a researcher, skill as an editor, persistence as a prodder, and endurance as a typist have resulted in a work that is almost a collaboration.